HIGH ROYDS HOSPITAL
MEDICAL LIBRARY

Psychiatry in Multicultural Britain

**Medical Library
The Mount
44 Hyde Terrace
Leeds
LS2 9LN
Tel: 0113 3055643**

Books should be returned by the last date shown above. Renewals may be made in person, by telephone or by writing/e-mail.
Fines are charged for overdue books

Edited by
DINESH BHUGRA
and RAY COCHRANE

Psychiatry in Multicultural Britain

GASKELL

Chapter 2 republished from and © *International Journal of Social Psychiatry*, 1996 (vol. 42, pp. 245–265).

Cover image: 'Three generations – grandmother, granddaughter, great granddaughter and grandson, London' © Anita Mckenzie/ mckenzie heritage picture archive

Gaskell is an imprint of the Royal College of Psychiatrists
17 Belgrave Square, London SW1X 8PG

British Library Cataloguing-in-Publication Data
A catalogue record for this book is available from the British Library.
ISBN 1-901242-45-5

Distributed in North America
by American Psychiatric Press, Inc.

The views presented in this book do not necessarily reflect those of the Royal College of Psychiatrists, and the publishers are not responsible for any error of omission or fact.

Gaskell is a registered trademark of the Royal College of Psychiatrists.

The Royal College of Psychiatrists is a registered charity (no. 228636).

Printed by Bell & Bain Limited, Glasgow, UK.

Contents

List of contributors   vii

Introduction   *Ray Cochrane and Dinesh Bhugra*   1

1   Psychiatry in a multi-ethnic context   *Dinesh Bhugra and Ray Cochrane*   6

2   Psychiatry's culture   *Roland Littlewood*   18

3   Epidemiology and social issues   *Kamaldeep Bhui*   49

4   Race, prejudice and ethnic identity   *Ray Cochrane*   75

5   Racial life events and psychiatric morbidity   *Dinesh Bhugra and Oyedeji Ayonrinde*   91

6   Acculturation, cultural identity and mental health   *Dinesh Bhugra*   112

7   Mental illness and ethnic minority groups   *Dinesh Bhugra and Ray Cochrane*   137

8   Psychiatry of old age and ethnic minority groups   *Ajit Shah*   151

9   Effective services? Understanding the care of the ethnic minority elderly   *Naina Patel and Naheed R. Mirza*   177

10   Child psychiatry   *Anula D. Nikapota*   191

11   Learning disabilities in multicultural Britain   *Zenobia Nadirshaw*   211

12 Substance misuse and ethnic minorities: issues for the UK
    Shamil Wanigaratne, Sujatha Unnithan and John Strang   243

13 Forensic psychiatry   *Rosemarie Cope*   264

14 Training and supervision in cross-cultural mental health
    services   *Kamaldeep Bhui and Dinesh Bhugra*   284

15 Needs assessment and service evaluation   *Dinesh Bhugra,*
    Sashi Sashidharan and Martin Commander   300

16 Primary prevention and ethnic minority mental health:
    a path for the future?   *Kwame McKenzie*   309

17 Services for ethnic minorities: conceptual issues
    Dinesh Bhugra   330

    Index   350

Contributors

Oyedeji Ayonrinde, The Maudsley Hospital, Denmark Hill, London SE5 8AZ

Dinesh Bhugra, Health Services Research Department, Institute of Psychiatry, De Crespigny Park, Denmark Hill, London SE5 8AF

Kamaldeep Bhui, Institute of Psychiatry, De Crespigny Park, Denmark Hill, London SE5 8AF

Ray Cochrane, School of Psychology, The University of Birmingham, Edgbaston, Birmingham B15 2TT

Martin Commander, North Birmingham Mental Health Trust, Academic Unit, 71 Fentham Road, Erdingham, Birmingham B23 6AL

Rosemarie Cope, Reaside Clinic, Birmingham Great Park, Bristol Road South, Rubery, Birmingham B45 9BE

Roland Littlewood, Departments of Anthropology and Psychiatry, University College London, Gower Street, London WC1E 6BT

Kwame McKenzie, Department of Psychiatry, Royal free Hospital, Pond Street, London NW3 2QG

Naheed R. Mirza, NeuroSearch, 93 Pederstrupvej, DK-2750 Ballerup, Denmark

Zenobia Nadirshaw, Parkside Health NHS Trust, 20 Kingsbridge Road, London W10 6PU

Anula D. Nikapota, Child and Adolescent Directorate, The Maudsley Hospital, Denmark Hill, London SE5 8AF

Naina Patel, Policy Research Institue on Ageing and Ethnicity (PRIAE), University of Bradford, Emm Lane, Bradford BD9 4JL

Sashi Sashidharan, North Birmingham Mental Health Trust, Academic Unit, 71 Fentham Road, Erdingham, Birmingham B23 6AL

Ajit Shah, John Connolly Wing, West London Healthcare NHS Trust, Uxbridge Road, Southall, Middlesex UB1 3EU

John Strang, Institute of Psychiatry, Addiction Science Building, De Crespigny Park, Denmark Hill, London SE5 8AF

Sujatha Unnithan, Institute of Psychiatry, De Crespigny Park, Denmark Hill, London SE5 8AF

Shamil Wanigaratne, Institute of Psychiatry, Addiction Science Building, De Crespigny Park, Denmark Hill, London SE5 8AF

Introduction

RAY COCHRANE and DINESH BHUGRA

Perhaps more than in any other area of medicine and health service-related research, psychiatry has to be understood in a broader socio-political context – nowhere is this more important than when considering issues relating to ethnicity and culture. Unlike many other medical specialities psychiatry has problems of definition, of meaning and of relationship with service users. By and large, the raw materials of psychiatry are peoples' behaviour (often received via secondhand accounts) and self-reports of emotional state and cognitive processes. There are very few objective, scientific tests that can be carried out to help with diagnosis or to monitor treatment effectiveness. Although a medical model is usually adopted there is no real distinction between the symptoms and the hypothesized underlying disease in many cases. Yet the process of diagnosis purports to go beyond a mere description of symptoms and attempts to identify a (hidden) disease entity which is producing these symptoms, but without any method of accessing the disease other than through the symptoms. This would make the diagnostic process problematic (and unreliable) at the best of times, but when cultural overlays are placed on the very material upon which diagnosis is based, then the problems are multiplied many times.

Psychiatry and the disciplines which support it, such as psychology, are basically Eurocentric, even when practised elsewhere in the world or by doctors from non-European cultural backgrounds. Ethnic minority patients in Britain, by definition, come from cultural backgrounds which differ from those of European origin. This gives rise to several potential problems. On a superficial, but non-trivial, level there may be language barriers between psychiatrist and patient. Even if this is overcome satisfactorily through professional translating services it is the case that many psychological problems are described by analogies or in local idiom (nervous breakdown, broken-hearted, low spirits etc.) which are culturally or linguistically specific. There are also well-documented cultural differences in the way psychological problems may be presented, for example, via somatic

1

symptoms, such as backache or thinness of semen, which may seem remote from the 'real' problem identified by clinicians trained on cases where 'psychological' presentation maybe commonplace

The problem goes even deeper than this, however. As pointed out in Chapter 1, the whole nosological system employed by psychiatry is ridden with a Eurocentric bias and almost forces practitioners to assume that the mental illnesses commonly found in European patients (schizophrenia, depression, neuroses etc.) are also to be found in non-European patients.

It should be noted that the dangers of cultural and Eurocentric bias are just as great in research on ethnicity and mental health as in the practice of psychiatry. There is a long history of research comparing European and non-European behaviour and mental processes which has often come to conclusions which now seem blatantly racist (Littlewood & Lipsedge, 1982), but which were accepted as valid at the time. Although crude racist conclusions are no longer apparent in transcultural psychiatry research, implicit or subtle racism still pervades the discipline. This kind of research still tends to be undertaken by White people and to focus on areas where non-Whites appear to have more problems. As shown in the chapters which follow, there are dozens of studies on the apparently high rate of schizophrenia in Britain's Black population, but only one study on the apparently low rate of alcohol-related problems in this population. It is also a common assumption that the behaviours (and problems) of the White population are normative and that deviation from the White pattern shown by another ethnic group in either direction reveals some cultural or racial pathology: higher rates of schizophrenia among Black than White people must be produced by genetic factors, cultural disintegration or abnormal family structures; lower treatment rates for depression among Pakistani women must be because they cannot express their psychological problems clearly to doctors or because their relatives keep them locked away from services for fear of bringing shame on the family.

Whereas in most areas of medicine, wealth, power and influence facilitate access to health care services and poorer and less powerful groups have more difficulties in accessing these valued services, the opposite is the case with psychiatry. Here the poor, the ill educated, the unemployed and the otherwise disadvantaged populate our mental hospitals. Psychiatry also has a unique privilege – the ability to forcibly detain and treat people against their will. The powers conferred on psychiatrists (and others) by the Mental Health Act 1983 exceed even those available to police officers or virtually anyone else in our society. Add the ethnic dimension to this and a very potent brew of racial suspicion and distrust is created. What are we, and more significantly the community concerned, to make of the fact young Black men are two or three times as likely to be brought to a mental hospital by the police or doctors and detained there compulsorily than are White men? The very same group are also more likely to be detained in prison.

The relevance of all this for this book lies in the way in which certain data on treated prevalence rates may be interpreted. If, for example, it was discovered that seven times as many Black people as White people were admitted to hospital for heart bypass operations, then it would be a reasonable conclusion that there was a greater level of cardiovascular morbidity in the Black population. The same relative risk of being admitted to a mental hospital for treatment for schizophrenia is often attributed to other, more sinister interpretations.

A final methodological point concerns the definition and composition of minority ethnic groups in Britain. The largest single foreign-born group in Britain consists of those people who have migrated from Ireland and who, together with their descendants, are over twice as numerous as any other minority group. Despite the fact that the distribution of psychopathology in the Irish in Britain is quite different from that of the native born (Cochrane, 1977; Cochrane & Bal, 1989) very few research projects include the Irish as a distinct ethnic group (see Cochrane & Stopes-Roe, 1979, for an exception). The absence of current data means that the Irish will not be considered specifically in this book either, but that we will concentrate on 'visible' minority ethnic groups.

With regard to the other commonly recognised ethnic minority groups in Britain (South Asian, African–Caribbean, Chinese etc.), there is a major element in the composition of these populations which confounds attempts to relate ethnicity to mental health and illness migration. A very substantial (but declining) proportion of ethnic minorities in Britain are first-generation immigrants. In any discussion of 'ethnicity' as a variable one has to be aware of the fact that many members (until recently a majority of adults) of these populations have characteristics and experiences which distinguish them from the White majority in addition to their ethnic origin. For example, it is clear that migrants are far from representative of the population from which they are drawn. At times it has been argued that they are either strongly predisposed to mental illness (Odegard, 1932) or they are exceptionally psychologically stable (Cochrane, 1983). Many first-generation immigrants from the 'New Commonwealth' to Britain have had to make a transition from a stable, traditional, rural, collective culture to a Western, urban, individualistic society in a state of flux (Furnham & Bochner, 1990). In addition, it is a common feature of economically motivated migration from the developing world to the developed world countries that the social class distribution of the first generation of migrants is skewed downwards, so the incomers are likely to be exposed to harsh working conditions, economic uncertainty, substandard and overcrowded housing and other forms of social deprivation. Depending upon context, these experiences will, themselves, have mental health implications which may mistakenly be attributed to ethnicity. These potential confounds will reduce, but not disappear entirely, as a greater and greater proportion of ethnic minority groups are born in this country.

One factor which all generations of non-White ethnic minorities in Britain have in common is exposure to racism. Racism, in so far as it is manifested in discrimination and economic disadvantage, may well have an effect on physical as well as mental health, as poverty and low socio-economic status are among the best predictors of risk for many forms of morbidity. But unlike physical conditions the other manifestation of racism, prejudice, will also impact upon psychological well-being (see Chapters 4 and 5). It will come as no surprise to discover that the experience of stereotyping and denial of humanity, jokes and other verbal disparagement, the easy assumption that skin colour is associated with a whole range of assumed problems from academic underachievement to serious criminal activity, as well as explicit social rejection, have very significant influences on self-esteem and mental health.

In this book we have attempted to bring together the best of contemporary research and scholarship – both pure and applied – that is relevant to understanding the patterns of mental health and illness found in minority ethnic communities in Britain at the dawn of a new millennium. While recognising that there are limitations to the extent and validity of the data available in many areas, we have asked contributors wherever possible to draw out practical implications of the research to date to help take forward the search for quality provision of mental health services in a multi-cultural environment.

Despite all the criticisms aimed at it, psychiatry is one of the few disciplines in medicine that has attempted (some might say 'been forced') to grapple with cultural factors. The aim of this book is to create an academic focus for mental health professionals to consider the complex interaction of culture, health, illness and medicine. While the book is aimed primarily at the psychiatrist in training, the interests of other mental health professionals have been borne in mind. We hope that all clinicians who work with ethnic minorities will find the book helpful in providing a theoretical background as well as in identifying important diagnostic, management and service development issues. With due modesty we hope that this book, together with the volume edited by Fernando (1995), can stimulate a debate about psychiatry in a multicultural environment similar to that provoked nearly 20 years ago by the classic works by Rack (1982) and Littlewood & Lipsedge (1982).

References

COCHRANE, R. (1977) Mental illness in immigrants to England and Wales: an analysis of mental hospital admissions, 1971. *Social Psychiatry*, **12**, 25–35.
—— (1983) *The Social Creation of Mental Illness*. London: Longmans.

—— & Stopes-Roe, M. (1979) Psychiatric disturbance in Ireland, England and in Irish emigrants to England: a comparative study. *Social and Economic Review*, **10**, 301–320.

—— & Bal, S. S. (1989) Mental hospital admission rates of immigrants to England: a comparison of 1971 and 1981. *Social Psychiatry and Psychiatric Epidemiology*, **24**, 2–12.

Fernando, S. (ed.) (1995) *Mental Health in a Multi-Ethnic Society*. London: Routledge.

Furnham, A. & Bochner, S. (1990) *Culture Shock*. London: Routledge.

Littlewood, R. & Lipsedge, M. (1982) *Aliens and Alienists: Ethnic Minorities and Psychiatry*. Harmondsworth: Penguin.

Odegard, O. (1932) Immigration and insanity: a study of mental disease among the Norwegian-born population in Minnesota. *Acta Psychiatrica Scandinavica*, **4**, 1–206.

Rack, P. (1982) *Race, Culture and Mental Disorder*. London: Tavistock.

1 Psychiatry in a multi-ethnic context

DINESH BHUGRA and RAY COCHRANE

Editors' introduction

The practice of psychiatry in a multicultural society has to take several key factors into account. Not all cultures will have experienced similar levels of distress, discrimination or alienation. Their experiences of arrival and settling down in a culture where they may well be in a minority will be different. They may have varying sets of reasons for migration and not all members of Black and other ethnic minority groups are going to be migrants. In this chapter the authors set the scene in the theoretical context of psychiatric practice in a multicultural society. After defining migration and classifying different types of migration the authors discuss various changes and experiences individuals are faced with in premigratory, migatory and post-migratory phases. The role of cultural identity, acculturation and sense of alienation from the host society are discussed. These roles are influenced by a multitude of factors such as personality, social support, networks, employment, etc. The differences between experiences of those who migrated and those who were born in the host society but belong to the same ethnic group must be understood and taken into account by clinicians.

Mental health of ethnic minorities in the UK remains an issue of paramount importance for several reasons. First, there is the concern that ethnic minorities have higher than expected psychiatric and psychological morbidity, for example, schizophrenia in African–Caribbeans and attempted suicide in Asian women. Second, there is some clinical and research evidence to suggest that Black and other ethnic minority individuals do not use general practitioners and statutory services to the same extent as White people, or the majority of the population, do. However, there remains a considerable amount of controversy on the methodology of ethnic health research and the generalisability of individual studies to minority groups at large (see Chapter 13). Yet it is possible to draw some general conclusions regarding the mental health needs of ethnic minorities in this country and the specific implications for service providers as well as purchasers.

It must be emphasised that psychiatry must be seen in a broader socio-political context, especially in the context of ethnicity and culture. There remain several ongoing issues dealing with some of these aspects, in particular problems of definition and operational criteria as well as the image of psychiatry and stigma attached to mental illness and help seeking. Owing to constraints of space, it is not our intention to present an exhaustive review of any of these issues: interested readers are referred to Sashidharan (1993).

History of migration

Migrants can be defined as individuals who change their place of residence for any purpose or for any period of time. Thus, technically 'visiting' students and businessmen will count as migrants. The group we are concerned with in this chapter are individuals who have made another country their home either permanently or semi-permanently. The difference between the place of leaving and place of arriving may simply be geographical. Migrants are not necessarily typical of the population they come from. Some may be rich, successful and enterprising, whereas others may well be unsuccessful, unsettled or deprived.

Significant migration to Britain has occurred since the 19th century. In the latter part of that century large numbers of Jews migrated from eastern Europe, including Russia. Another peak occurred around the time of the Second World War. The second significant group to migrate on a regular basis was the Irish. This group is a mixture of *Gastarbeiter* (guestworkers) as well as settlers and retains close contact with their families in Ireland. In discussion of ethnic minorities and their needs, this group tends to get overlooked (see Chapter 13). Post-war refugee influx also included Poles, Ukrainians, Lithuanians, Hungarians and others from eastern Europe. In the 1960s, West Indian people were encouraged to migrate to fill low-paid posts and because of a common language it was easy to recruit large numbers. Post-war migration from the Indian subcontinent also reached its peak just after the West Indian migration. Just before changes in the Immigration Law there was a mass exodus of Asian people from Uganda. Since the 1980s only relatively small numbers of refugees and primary migrants have been allowed to enter Britain.

Types of migration

Classification of migrants can serve several purposes. Legal categories of migration may well affect the individual's privileges and social and financial security. Migration can be classified according to geographical variables such as one country to another, urban–rural etc. The reasons for migration, such as political or economic, can also be used for classification. Individual occupations, such as diplomats or anthropologists, may be used as categories. Duration of relocation and willingness to relocate can be used along with socio-demographic factors like social class ('jet-setters') and education (students, academics); some relocations involve extensive linguistic, ecological, political, technological, social and family change, whereas others demand very little change (Westermeyer, 1989). Furthermore, geographical distance from the original place dictates the frequency of visits and contact and will determine levels and qualities of social support. All of these factors play some role in the psychological well-being of the individual.

Rack (1982) suggests that the term 'migrant worker' be reserved for those who are admitted for a limited period to take up particular employment and will be expected to leave the country immediately if they leave that employment. This is the pattern of *Gastarbeiter* mobile labour in Germany and other industrialised nations in Europe. Following the simple distinction (pull *v.* push, i.e. whether individuals are positively attracted to the new country or were simply escaping from the old), Rack (1982) advocates a distinction between *Gastarbeiters,* exiles and settlers. He cautions that such a distinction is not obsolete.

The *Gasterbeiter* is seen as a consequence of industrialisation and the movement is generally from the rural to urban areas. Commonly, a young man goes abroad alone to improve his social and economic position back home and hence to this end his preoccupation is with working hard at maybe more than one job and to live as cheaply as possible; may have no motivation to learn about the majority culture. His linguistic skills may be limited to the job situation and he may prefer to live with his fellow countrymen and is not disposed towards changing his habits except to avoid trouble. His emotional roots remain in his country of origin (Rack, 1982).

Settlers, conversely, migrate with a clear intention of settling down in the new country. They may, therefore, be young families or young couples whose ambitions may remain unfulfilled at home. The settlers' ambition is not to return home but to compete with new peers and establish themselves in as much security as possible in the new place. Thus, there may be a clearer indication and desire to assimilate. Such an individual, having taken the hard decision to migrate, will therefore want to prove that the decision was right. Initially there will be a streak of optimism which may prove short-lived if the new country turns out to be hostile, not welcoming or difficult to become assimilated in, and the individual, in spite of his or her high hopes and hard work, may feel rejected and may show paranoid projection.

The processes of acculturation and assimilation are vital in the individual's life. This process of acculturation occurs at two levels: first, as a group, and second, as an individual (see Chapter 6). Having taken the decision to migrate the settler may well make conscious efforts to accommodate himself or herself and may well over-identify, feeling embarrassed by compatriots who may not demonstrate the same degree of enthusiasm for the new country, and may achieve successful adaptation. Rack (1982) proposes that paranoid projection in such cases may simply be a result of the underlying personality trait where the individual looks for the causes of problems in the environment rather than within him- or herself. Such an individual becomes attached to the new country if successful and may well become nostalgic for the old country once transition has been achieved.

The settlers may well have to deal with very stringent legal and migration procedures and this is where their psychological stamina may be tested, especially if the move is to alien cultures and different language skills are required. Such a process is also likely to screen out individuals with mental illness and other vulnerabilities.

There remains a marked degree of ambiguity in the distinction between settlers and *Gastarbeiter*. It can be argued that the migration from the Indian subcontinent was largely *Gastarbeiter* and only when in the early 1970s there was a threat with impending changes in immigration rules did males sent for their families. Until then, individuals cherished a vision of returning home, hence had adopted an isolationist attitude to the British society – and held on to their own traditions.

African–Caribbean people, on the other hand, were recruited for the specific purpose of helping the mother country and were lured by the prospect of economic betterment; they behaved more like settlers and their expectations were those of a settler. It also meant that once they found that the British society was using them and there was no sense of welcome and acceptance, the feelings of being cheated, hard done by and abused appeared; and the sense of alienation developed.

The third group of migrants – refugees – varies from both these groups on a number of parameters as well as in motivation which affects their place in society and their attitudes to long-term integration. Like the previous two groups, refugees are heterogeneous and the reasons for migration are political. The initial reception at the resettlement centres and the bureaucratic nightmares along with problems of diet, interpretation and medical services and later needs of housing, education and employment can all contribute to a profound sense of alienation. The group of refugees can further be classified into those who have had some anticipatory notice and are prepared for it (especially if they have the money and social support in the new countries), and those who had no preparation and even less time to prepare before leaving. Thus, it is not surprising that the latter group was more prone to emotional and psychological problems.

The literature on vulnerability factors for psychological morbidity in refugees is a mixed bag of observations. Nguyen (1980) suggests nuclear families are more at risk, whereas Rahe *et al* (1978) suggest young women or single people as the most likely candidates. The problems may emerge either immediately on arrival or several years later. The range of problems reported is wide – Tyhurst (1951) called it 'social displacement syndrome', but paranoid behaviour, generalised hypochondriasis, anxiety and depression, disorientation and confusion, and desocialisation may all be seen. Long-term problems in this vulnerable group include symptoms of post-traumatic stress disorder, bereavement, prolonged mourning, loss, depression and anxiety, and they may well have outbursts of anger, rage and emotional overreactions to minor stimuli.

Changes associated with migration

The duration of relocation remains an important variable in ascertaining the period of readjustment as well as the likelihood of social maladaptation and psychiatric disorder. The processes of acculturation need to be mentioned for completion. Migrants are compared on the basis of cultural similarity and/or dissimilarity between the culture of origin and the culture of settlement.

Several additional factors play an important role in the settlement of the refugees. The first of these is language and communication. Communication involves more than language which is crucial in the day-to-day interactions (see below).

The second is social networks, which also play a very important role. In circumstances where individuals have fled alone the solitary migrant is at increased risk from a variety of mental health disorders. In the absence of an extended family or existing social network, easy access to the expatriate community and acceptance by them can work as a protective factor. Isolation within the family and an expatriate community can also lead to problems by prolonging, delaying or blocking adjustment to the new society and thereby fostering cultural isolation (Westermeyer, 1989).

The third crucial factor is employment. Not only may jobs be difficult to find, but not knowing the system and lack of recognition of the qualifications may also contribute to the stress. Even those continuing in the same vocation must adjust to new co-workers and unfamiliar working environments. Social roles and expectations may well change. New colleagues may not recognise the individual's previous credentials and achievements, thereby undermining the individual's confidence. Social and recreational activities may have to change and the individual may be asked to learn (or even be expected to have) new skills. Rites of passage, religious affiliations, legal systems and divided loyalties between the past and the present may contribute more stress.

Cultural identity, acculturation and alienation

Cultural identity is but one component of an individual's identity and this is likely to change under the influence of a majority culture. Acculturation on the other hand has been defined as:

> "culture change that is initiated by the conjunction of two or more autonomous cultural systems. Its dynamics can be seen as the selective adaptation of value systems, the processes of integration and differentiation, the generation of developmental sequences and the operation of role determinants and personality factors" (Social Sciences Research Council, 1954).

Alienation on the other hand can be defined as a sense of not belonging and not being welcomed either. Various components of alienation have been identified. These include feelings of powerlessness, normlessness (purposelessness and conflict of norms), social isolation, meaninglessness and self-estrangement. Of these normlessness and social isolation are traced back to Durkheim's concept of *anomie.* Durkheim had conceived it in the subjective sense with three characteristics: a painful uneasiness or anxiety, a feeling of separation from group standards, a feeling of pointlessness or that no certain goals exist. The social isolation where the individual feels alienated and sees him- or herself as anonymous but with additional lack of support contributes to poor self-esteem. (These factors are discussed in detail in Chapter 6.)

The psychosocial changes experienced by immigrants are subsumed under the terms assimilation and acculturation. Three stages in the migration process can be identified. The first stage is virtually pre-migratory where the individual is identifying the needs or dispositions that encourage them to move. The second stage is that physical transition – the physical process of migration from one place to another. The third stage refers to the absorption of the immigrant within the social and cultural framework of the new society. In this phase, the immigrant learns new roles and becomes interested in transforming the primary group and extending its spheres of influence as well as his own (see also Chapter 6).

Assimilation is a process of adjustment or accommodation which occurs following prolonged contact (Simons, 1900). Assimilation can be seen as a process of interpretation and fusion in which persons or groups acquire the memories, sentiments and attitudes of other persons or groups, and share theirs. Assimilation therefore provides a unidirectional process of explanation and the immigrant is said to be 'absorbed' into the host or majority culture. However, rarely will the latter not be affected at all by the immigrants, however small their numbers. Berry (1990) distinguishes between acculturation and psychological acculturation. Whereas the former involves a process resulting in population level changes that are due to contact with other cultures, the latter is at an individual level – the process by which the individual changes both by being influenced by contact with another culture and by being a participant in the general acculturative changes under way in their own culture.

Models of acculturation

These have been classified into linear models of change. Gordon (1964) proposed a seven-stage model which included assimilation in the spheres of cultural, structural (taking part in the host society on a primary group level), marital, identificational, attitude recaptional (encountering no prejudiced attitudes), behaviour receptional (encountering no discriminatory behaviour) and civic behaviour. Such an approach measures pre-migration characteristics and situational determinants in the receiving society that influence both objective and subjective categories in the individual's life.

A bi-dimensional model proposed an understanding of acculturation in which identification to the two cultures is assessed on two separate dimensions; change is measured on four different dimensions (integration, separation, assimilation and marginalisation) along each cultural dimension.

It is apparent that in a majority of cases the less dominant group will tend to shift towards the dominant group. On occasions, especially in younger generations, there may be a backlash and the individuals may well go back to being more cosseted and isolationist to protect their cultural roots. As culture and personality are intertwined, it makes sense that experiences with other cultures will determine the development of personality and therefore the point made by Rack (1982) about reaction formation to treatment by the dominant culture becomes relevant.

Generational difference

The mental health needs of children of immigrants (who may well be adults themselves) present special needs which must be identified. They should not be seen as clones of British adults. Several caveats need to be borne in mind. The assumptions that there remain major and increasingly irresolvable conflicts between children and their parents must be put aside. Asians are seen as traditional, and when the first generation is in turn conceptualised as authoritarian, 'culture conflict' is seen as the most important cause of psychological morbidity. Younger Asian people are set apart as a problem category and this approach ignores comparable conflicts across generations in other cultures (Ballard, 1979; also see Chapter 4 for a discussion of generational differences and prejudice).

There is considerable research evidence to suggest that the second generation of African–Caribbean migrants have increased rates of schizophrenia and the most plausible explanation put forward concerns various social factors – especially unemployment, poor housing and poor social integration (Bhugra *et al*, 1997). Although second-generation Asians have been shown to be more likely to have anxiety and depression (Beliappa, 1991) the evidence is still emerging. Childhood disorders have been shown to demonstrate ethnic differences where ratio of emotional to conduct disorders and psychotic and autistic disorders were disproportionately more common in the African–Caribbean samples (Goodman & Richards, 1995; also see Chapter 9).

Some of these differences can be attributed to genetic disorders although the evidence is weak, whereas others can be attributed to social factors. In all this the individual's identity will remain a very important factor. If an individual feels comfortable in either culture and is likely to be more settled and able to deal with questions and problems in both groups, he or she is more likely to have higher self-esteem and is able to cope better (see Chapter 4). On the other hand, if such an individual feels left out of his or her own culture and is unlikely to be accepted by the majority culture, a sense of alienation and rejection is likely to lead to poor self-esteem and poor social support, thereby generating feelings of hostility. Society must, therefore, accept notions of a 'rainbow coalition' rather than a 'melting pot'. The levels of psychological morbidity are likely to be different across generations. There is a clear need for ethnic monitoring and accurate data collection.

Diagnosis across cultures

By and large the basic foundation of diagnosis is the observation and assessment of people's behaviour along with self-reports of emotional state and cognitive processes. There are few objective scientific tests that can be conducted to reach an irrefutable diagnosis. Even then the role of culture can not be underestimated in the presentation and management. In psychiatric diagnosis, a medical model is traditionally employed. Yet the process of diagnosis goes beyond (or certainly purports to) a mere description of symptoms and attempts to identify and deal with a concealed illness identity which is producing these symptoms, but without specfic methods of accessing such a 'pathology'. This would make the diagnostic process problematical, as well as unreliable, especially when cultural overlays are placed on the very material upon which diagnosis is based, further worsening the problems.

Cultural relativism is one of the major controversial areas along the interface between psychiatry and anthropology and this relativism virtually precludes cross-cultural comparisons of syndroms or psychiatric epidemiology as the notions of cause and meanings of illness vary from one culture to another (Prince *et al,* 1998). It is vital that clinicians when attempting to understand human behaviour take into account both its variability and its consistency.

An additional difficulty lies in the historical development of the disciplines of psychiatry and psychology. Steeped in Eurocentric traditions, especially the mind–body dichotomy put forward by Descartes, these disciplines tend to look down upon cultures that do not follow this dichotomy as less developed or problematical. The dominance of such approaches in training and practice around the world has meant that even the doctors from non-European backgrounds and cultures use the same model. In Britain, most ethnic minority groups come from cultural backgrounds which are different, and particularly in the context of the colonial past this raises several serious problems. There may be language difficulties and within such communication non-verbal communication can be incredibly important. If clinicians are not aware of subtle differences in communication as well as conceptual and semantic differences, the alienation of the patients and their carers can but increase. A common use of local idioms of distress (e.g. *Vai-Badi* in the Punjabi population) makes understanding of their discomfort by European clinicians less likely. There are well-documented cultural differences in the way psychological problems may be presented, for example, somatic symptoms which may not only appear rare and distant from the clinician's ambit of experience but may also be construed as physical, leading to inappropriate investigations and ultimately misdiagnosing the problem as hypochondriasis.

Another area fraught with difficulties within the field of diagnosis needs to be highlighted here. The nosological system employed by psychiatry is Eurocentric and forces clinicians to assume that the mental illnesses commonly found in European patients (e.g. schizophrenia) are to be found in the same way and to the same extent in the non-European patients, taking a very universalist approach. The system does not easily allow for other disorders to be identified which do not conform to those recognised in the European patients. Although culture-bound syndromes are acknowledged, described and studied, barring a few honourable exceptions the emphasis remains on the rare, exotic and seen in the less developed or the 'natives' (Bhugra & Jacob, 1997). The relativist position in diagnosis as emphasised by the anthropologists is hardly seen in the busy clinical practices of primary and secondary health care professionals. These ethno-semantic and cultural issues go beyond the issue of diagnosis. The treatment is dictated by the individual's training, experience and knowledge. As Jayasuriya *et al* (1992) highlight:

> "psychiatric treatment practices such as psychotherapy and counselling are heavily laden with western beliefs and value systems stemming from the Judeo-Christian tradition, which places a premium on the philosophy of individualism, the right to self-determination and the desirability of independence and assertiveness. Systems of treatment based on these cultural tenets are hardly likely to be universally appropriate."

Psychiatry is also distinguished from most other medical specialties by the ethnic minority groups in that its practice is not seen as benign. Psychiatry and its practice have been interpreted as one way of legitimising the suppression of non-normative and subversive behaviour by applying labels of madness to activities which may threaten the status quo. In other areas of medicine, especially if universal access to health care systems is barred, the poor, uneducated and disadvantaged have difficulty gaining access, whereas in psychiatry it is the reverse. An ability to hold and treat people against their will them against their will is a key power mental health professionals, especially psychiatrists, have. Additional pressure to coerce people into asylums and being able to use the police to do so adds yet another potent factor to the distrust and racial suspicion Black and other ethnic minority groups may feel about the whole concept of psychiatry.

These factors must play a role in the way in which certain data on treated prevalence rates may be interpreted. The definition and composition of ethnic minority groups in clinical as well as research settings is problematical too. As mentioned earlier, the largest single foreign group in Britain is those who have migrated from Ireland and together with their descendants are over twice as numerous than other minority groups. Despite the observation that the distribution of psychopathology in the Irish is quite different from that of the native

British (Cochrane, 1977; Cochrane & Bal, 1989), with few exceptions (Cochrane & Stopes-Roe, 1979) this group has been ignored altogether.

As regards other ethnic minority groups in Britain (such as South Asian, African–Caribbean and Chinese) there is a major element in the composition of these populations which confounds any attempt to relate ethnicity to migration and mental illness. As already noted, in any discussion of 'ethnicity' as a variable one has to be aware that many members of these populations have experiences and characteristics which distinguish them from the White majority in addition to their ethnic origin. It is clear that migrants are far from representative of the populations they originate from. Many first-generation immigrants, especially those from the new Commonwealth, have had to make a transition from a stable, rural, collective culture to a Western, urban, industrialised and individualistic society (with a state of flux) (Furnham & Bochner, 1990). To complicate this scenario further, in such cases of migration the social class distribution of the first-generation migrants is skewed downwards, so the in-comers are much more likely to face harder working conditions, poorer and substandard and possibly over-crowded housing and economic uncertainty. Depending upon the context, these experiences will themselves have mental health implications but are likely to be misattributed to ethnicity. These may well reduce in the younger generations but are less likely to disappear altogether.

A key factor which tends to get forgotten about is exposure to racism. Manifested in discrimination and economic disadvantage, racism by its overt and covert impact may well have an effect on physical as well as mental health. Unemployment, poverty and low socio-economic status have all been shown to be good predictors of risk for many forms of morbidity. Prejudice in any field will contribute to poor psychological well-being and the experiences of stereotyping, denial of humanity and assumptions that skin colour is associated with a whole range of assumed problems from academic underachievement to serious criminal activity, as well as explicit social rejections, have very significant influences on self-esteem and mental health.

This chapter is within the conventional paradigm of pathways into care. Using the same model of different levels of care (from the general population through primary care into specialist settings or secondary care) means that variations in the pathways across various ethnic groups and various psychiatric conditions tend to get lost. We urge the reader to be cautious while interpreting these observations and the observations on the research findings.

The heterogeneity of migrant groups, their experiences with the majority culture and their models of perceived ill health are all important factors in help-seeking, as well as their world-view, and clinicians must be aware of these while interviewing and planning treatment.

References

BALLARD, C. (1979) Second generation Asians. In *Minority Families in Britain* (ed. V. Saifullah Khan). London: Tavistock.

BELIAPPA, J. (1991) *Idioms of Distress*. London: CIO.

BERRY, J. W. (1980) Acculturation as a variety of adaptation. In *Acculturation* (ed. A. M. Padilla). Boulder, CO: Westview.

—— (1990) Psychology of acculturation. In *Applied Cross-Cultural Psychology* (ed R. W. Brislin). Newbury Park, CA: Sage.

BHUGRA, D. & JACOB, K. (1997) Culture-bound syndromes. In *Troublesome Disguises* (eds D. Bhugra & A. Munro). Oxford: Blackwells.

BHUGRA, D., LEFF, J., MALLETT, R., *et al* (1997) Incidence and outcome of schizophrenia in Whites, African–Caribbeans and Asians in London. *Psychological Medicine*, **27**, 791–795.

COCHRANE, R. (1977) Mental illness in immigrants to England and Wales. *Social Psychiatry*, **12**, 25–30.

—— & STOPES-ROE, M. (1979) Psychiatric disturbance in Ireland. *Social and Economic Review*, **10**, 301–320.

—— & BAL, S. (1989) Mental hospital admission rates of immigrants to England. *Social Psychiatry and Psychiatric Epidemiology*, **24**, 2–12.

FURNHAM, A. & BOCHNER, S. (1990) *Culture Shock*. London: Routledge.

GOODMAN, R. & RICHARDS, H. (1995) Child and adolescent psychiatric presentations of second-generation Afro-Caribbeans in Britain. *British Journal of Psychiatry*, **167**, 362–369.

GORDON, M. (1964) *Assimilation in American Life*. New York: Oxford University Press.

JAYASURIYA, L., SANG, D. & FIELDING, A. (1992) *Ethnicity, Immigration and Mental Illness: A Critical Review of Australian Research*. Canberra: Australian Government Printing Source.

NGUYEN, S. A. N. (1980) *The Refugee Experience. A Conceptual Model of Social Disintegration*. Guelph, Canada: Homewood Sanatorium.

PRINCE, R., OKPAKU, S. & MERKEL, L. (1998) Transcultural psychiatry: a note on origins and definitions. In *Clinical Methods in Transcultural Psychiatry* (ed. S. Okpaku). Washington, DC: American Psychiatric Association Press.

RACK, P. (1982) *Race, Culture and Mental Disorder*. London: Tavistock.

RAHE R., LOONEY, J., WARD, H., *et al* (1978) Psychiatric consultations in a Vietnamese refugee camp. *American Journal of Psychiatry*, **135**, 185–190.

SOCIAL SCIENCES RESEARCH COUNCIL (1954) Acculturation: an exploratory formulation. *American Anthropologist*, **56**, 973–1002.

SASHIDHARAN, S. (1993) Afro-Caribbeans and schizophrenia: The ethnic vulnerability hypothesis re-examined. *International Review of Psychiatry*, **5**, 129–144.

SIMONS, S. E. (1900) Social assimilations. *American Journal of Sociology*, **6**, 790–822.

TYHURST, L. (1951) Displacement and migration. *American Journal of Psychiatry*, **107**, 561–568.

WESTERMEYER, J. (1989) *Psychiatric Care of Migrants: A Clinical Guide*. Washington, DC: American Psychiatric Association Press.

2 Psychiatry's culture*

ROLAND LITTLEWOOD

Editors' introduction

The role of culture in the psychopathology of individuals is well known. However, mental health professionals often tend to treat culture as an ambiguous concept belonging to the 'other' rather than to themselves. They may deprecate culture as something secondary to biological models within the biopsychosocial approaches to diagnosis and management of psychiatric disorders.In this chapter, Littlewood argues that contemporary understanding of culture derives from imperial medicine which had applied the accepted distinction between the biological form and the cultural content of psychopathology to local illnesses which could then be easily fitted into the Eurocentric nosology. He suggests that the later concepts of culture-bound pathology, such as psychoanalytic concepts, failed to provide an imperial nation with significant ideological justification. The conflict between the colonised and the coloniser also influenced the legal definitions of pathologies and their disposal. The conflict between the individual's perceptions of psychopathology and society's response has suggested that culture plays an important role in defining mental illness and help-seeking. The later concepts of 'culture-bound' syndromes were based on partly imperialist notions: different cultures being seen as at different stages of 'development'.

*Republished with permission from: *Int. J. Soc. Psychiatry* (1996), **42**, 245–265.

Core and periphery

In its attempt to become recognised as a purely naturalistic science, independent of the particular historical context and moral values in which it has developed, Western medicine has played down the social relationship between patient and doctor, and between the experience of suffering and the local understandings through which suffering occurs. Medicine seeks the laws and regularities of a physical world immune to changes in historical frames of reference or in human cognition. It objectifies human experience as if experience were constructed out of natural entities, and, ascribing to them the conditions of their clinical observation, it reifies our personal contingencies as biological necessity; as the French anthropologist Pierre Bourdieu (1977) has put it, "the observer transfers into the object the principles of his relation to the object", as indeed we do when, as patients or doctors, we talk of 'psychiatry' as some entity rather than as the actions of certain individuals in their particular ethical and political world.

If we want to understand patterns of psychological distress, not simply as biological changes which appear from beyond our awareness until they are diagnosed, but also as part of meaningful experience and action – as what we might term cultural patterns – we need to pay some attention to psychiatry's own culture: to the historical origins and politics of its nosologies, to its clinical engagement with its subjects, and indeed to its very understanding of 'culture'. When psychiatry developed as a clinical speciality in late 18th century Europe, physicians recognised that certain of the concerns which (by analogy with physical disease) they examined as sicknesses could appear more commonly in one country rather than in another. Psychiatry took up existing speculations on a nation's 'manners' and 'spirit': in his *Poétique* of 1561, the Italian humanist Julius Scaliger had identified the character of his compatriots as "cunctatores, irrisores, factiosi" (Fumaroli, 1996). Britain was described by its physicians as a country particularly liable to the *morbus anglicus* (despair and suicide) as a consequence of its climate (cold and wet), its diet (beef) and the pace of its commercial life (fast), all contributing to the vulnerabilities of the national character (melancholic) (Cheyne, 1734). Illnesses like melancholia, spleen and neurasthenia were recognised as the cost of accepting new public responsibilities by men of the emerging middle classes in the period of early industrialisation and extending political representation. Other sicknesses – hysteria and moral retardation – were rather a distressing inability to accept such responsibility, an outward manifestation of the weaker bodily or moral constitution of European workers, criminals and women or of African slaves and other colonised peoples, when they were threatened with the possibility of similar obligations (Brigham, 1832). Mental illnesses were taken as characteristic of life in one or other nation or social stratum, more immediately to be understood as the manifestation of occupation, age, gender, temperament, habit, bodily constitution and physical environment, as individuals variously conformed to or neglected their immediate obligations (Boudin, 1857), or more generally through some idiom which tried to put together those obligations and sentiments, social organisation and history, modes of sustenance and technical knowledge, individual character and family life, rituals and symbolisations which seemed to characterise a particular society – what has become known as its 'culture'.

Together with the Romantic idea of the nation as an entity which demonstrated shared inheritance, language and customs, 'culture' became accepted as a term to place together all those characteristics attributable to living in a particular society, through acquiring which, children, like plants in a nursery, were cultivated into maturity (Eagleton, 2000). Johann Herder proposed that national cultures resembled plants, each distinct and destined to grow in its own way. Whether human groups could be said to have a separate biological origin still remained uncertain, but 'culture' was generally placed in opposition to the existing term 'nature'; once the physical world created by divine action, nature now denoted those features of human life which were found in other living beings – physical form and function, growth and reproduction; or which more specifically were shared only with animals – including the passions, sexuality, violence and even such propensities as benevolence and sociality, all natural attributes which could be found in human societies in differing degrees (Collingwood, 1945; Thomas, 1983). Maurice and Jean Bloch (1980) have suggested that the term 'nature' carries a number of related meanings for contemporary Europeans: the archaic and the chronologically presocial; our internal bodily processes; the universal and inevitable order of the organic and inorganic; and (identified and imagined) primitive peoples.

By contrast, 'culture' argued for the moral and aesthetic moulding of natural growth, for a precarious binding of that which was more elemental and basic but which still sought expression in human life. Non-Europeans and European proletarians, women and children, inaccessible to culture or still to be cultivated, remained "in a state of nature" (Michaelis, 1814). Donna Harraway has argued recently (1989) that in the early industrial period Europeans took as nature "only the material of nature appropriated, preserved, enslaved, exalted or otherwise made flexible for disposal by culture in the logic of capitalist colonialism". Culture was not only an historical process in human time but, like nature, some thing which could be accumulated for use, and thus commodified. The more culture, the less significant was nature in a human society: and the converse. As in the earlier Christian schema, nature in herself was independent of willed intention, but she could be mastered by man's agency; the development of civilisation demonstrated that European men had gradually acquired dominion over nature, both as an industrial resource 'out there', as raw material or slaves, and also in their own bodies – as Francis Bacon put it, in a "truly masculine birth of time [in which men] would conquer and subdue Nature" (Easlea, 1980). If they had eventually learnt that they could not control the natural depredations of their bodies' diseases by an act of magical speech or sorcery or even by divine supplication (John XXI, 1550), they could often effect bodily healing through culture's technical power over nature.

The actual relationship between nature and culture, what we might now consider rather as modes of thought taken for concrete entities, was and remains problematic. Different professional disciplines developed to specialise in each – what from Germany became known as the natural and moral (human) sciences. The pervasive notion of a hierarchy within nature – initially ordered as the Creator's Great Chain of Being, later as an unfolding evolutionary struggle – placed together what we still distinguish as the biological and the moral into a unitary schema: certain races had particularly high rates of one sort of psychological illness or another through their position in the evolutionary chain and their ability (or failure) to dominate their nature. If melancholy was the fruit of European civilisation's gradual accumulation of culture and self-consciousness, then primitive mental illness – a lack of control over instinct and impulsivity – was demonstrated by tribal peoples (Madden, 1857). Yet one's 'psychic energy', a measure of health, reflected the number of (newly discovered) brain cells. If biological and cultural were variously elided in different ways, the common conclusion was that, 'culture' was primarily an attribute of Europeans, a function of their 'development'. Illnesses like 'Down's mongolism' or 'mass hysteria' warned Europeans of their possible degeneration to an earlier and more protean nature (*ibid.*; Morel, 1860).

Form and content

Clinical psychiatry developed as an academic discipline in the 19th century hospitals and clinics of Europe, where a new industrial order had confined those recognised as insane, and the majority of hospitalised patients still remain diagnosed as psychotic – as demonstrating diseases which, if pathological changes in the brain cannot readily be demonstrated, are at least presumed to be present (Schneider, 1959), and which reduce responsibility and thus legal accountability. The scientific ambitions of hospital medicine, and its identification of an illness which corresponded to what was popularly recognised as chronic insanity (which in the early 20th century came to be known as schizophrenia), tended to make the predominant understanding of mental illness the medical one (Gaskell, 1860). When the new 'nervous specialists' and 'alienists' were called to deal with patterns of distress or unusual behaviour among people who could not be obviously recognised as physically diseased or insane, they were faced with a practical issue of deciding if the patient was responsible for their symptoms and whether they were accountable when making a will or giving evidence in a court of law, or if they could be expected to take responsibility for criminal acts or for rearing their children. If a member of the upper or middle classes, some disease-like category such as hysteria or nervous prostration (neurasthenia) might be advanced which minimised the patient's responsibility for the condition itself but not for their other actions (Beard, 1881). Doctors in private practice realised that to challenge a patient's own ascription of illness too radically was to lose their client, as sardonically illustrated by Molière and Proust. When deciding accountability for criminal acts where the individual claimed to be ill, doctors might, or might not, hold the prisoner accountable; decisions had to be made as to whether the illness was 'real', caused by physical changes which were independent of the prisoner's awareness and whose actions were unintended, or feigned, as they might be among those awaiting trial or sentence. The simulation of insanity under such circumstances might itself be considered an illness, yet not one which should provide exculpation for past crimes (Ganser, 1897).

Not every person who was diagnosed as having a particular mental illness reported exactly the same experiences. To deal with variations in the symptoms between individuals, clinical psychiatry still makes a distinction between the essential pathogenic determinants of a mental disorder, those biological processes which are held to be necessary and sufficient to cause it, and the pathoplastic personal and cultural variations in the pattern (Birnbaum, 1923). These two are still distinguished in everyday clinical practice by the particularly 19th century German distinction between form and content[1]. To distinguish form from content was once a virtually ubiquitous practice in comparative studies in art history, ethnology, literary criticism and archaeology, indeed in the humanities in general; but in those areas it has been superseded by looser

---

[1] For example, Birnbaum (1923) and Schneider (1959), but on the way apparently reversing Kant's characterisation of form as subjective ordering, content as the physical material, a distinction that goes back to Aristotle's distinction between form and matter in his *Metaphysics*. Without examining the 19th century German philosophical and psychiatric arguments in detail it is unclear how this happened, but if we assume links between the two as Jaspers (1963) argues, I would suggest something like this: (a) Kant had argued against the British sensationalists in his *Critique of Pure Reason* that perception must involve our subjective ordering of the external natural world to produce the world as our mind can grasp

thematic, mimetic or emergent approaches, in part because of the inevitable uncertainty over deciding what was properly form and what content, together with the problem of justifying whether one or the other was somehow more fundamental, whether (ontologically) in a pattern's historical appearance or in its immediate causation, or (epistemologically) in its observed configuration and scholarly typology. It has been argued that the form/content dichotomy is facilitated by Indo-European subject–predicate syntax, or more specifically that it is characteristic of the scientific method whose advances have been fuelled by the analysis of apparent wholes through the underlying natural properties of their presumed parts, together with an empiricist theory of linguistic realism in which names simply label distinct entities such as diseases which are already present in the external world (Yap, 1974; Good & Good, 1982; Lewontin *et al*, 1984). To which we might add the modern imperative to concretise experience; so our experience of hotness, translated into temperature, becomes something like a natural entity which, like the idea of manic depression, could easily be rated as a linear scale (Littlewood, 1994).

---

it (that is, as 'phenomenon'), and that aspect of our phenomenal world which seems most evidently subjectively ordered (as opposed to that more evidently produced through immediate sensation of the world but which our minds still order) Kant termed 'form'; (b) German phenomenological studies of psychopathology then became restricted through immediate neuropsychiatric interests to the categorisation of the more unusual subjective orderings which were characteristic of the insane (rather than in the total lived subjectivity of any individual in the world); this 'form' became objectified nosologically as various discrete experiences – the 'phenomena' to be examined in psychiatric inquiry (presumably because hallucinations and delusions had no external reference in the consensual world); (c) by the late 19th century, neuropsychiatry begun to be divided up between the neurologists who emphasised observable anatomical structure and the psychiatrists who were stuck with insanity where there were no observable one-to-one correspondences between lesion and illness but only altered functioning and experience. (As a residual medical area, psychiatry remains happier talking of 'mental illness' than 'mental disease'.) The more evidently subjective process of generating radically new 'form' (for there was nothing out there which the insane mind ordered except in the case of illusions) became elided with its scientifically more promising (if, for the psychiatrists, only presumed) structuring – altered biology; while that remaining external sensory evidence which was consensually given and which the mind, insane or otherwise, ordered became clinically residual as simply shared 'content'. By contrast, the generally more radical French "science de l'homme", as described by Williams (1994), placed greater emphasis on the environmental and social causation of psychopathology, even if (through Broca's biologisation of culture) French psychiatry yielded not dissimilar racist theories by the end of the 19th century. It would not be inappropriate to see the French tradition as having contributed most evidently to theories of neurosis in the dominant Anglo-American psychiatry of the 1970–1990s, German medicine as providing the clinical schemata for psychosis. In all three, however, there is repeated oscillation between (and conflation of) what may be distinguished as the naturalistic and the personalistic (Littlewood, 1993*b*).

However this may be, the form/content dichotomy continues in psychiatry as a medical proxy for distinguishing the biological (which we can explain) from the cultural (which we can only seek to understand) (Jaspers, 1963). It has seemed most applicable when abnormal experiences and actions were associated with a recognised and presumably ubiquitous disease such as brain or thyroid tumour, anaemia, or with traumatic and vascular damage to the brain. The hallucinations which were experienced during the delirium of the brain-damaged 'alcoholic' were taken as directly reflecting the biological form which was expressed through an insignificant content which reflected their particular character and the standard preoccupations of their society. Thus, looking at persecutory ideas in the West Indies, one study in the 1960s argued that for the local Blacks, paranoid suspicions (the form) were directed against their relatives and neighbours (the content), following local ideas of sorcery in an egalitarian village community; while for the White Creoles, preoccupied with retaining control as a precarious elite, the phantom poisoners were identified among the surrounding Black population (Weinstein, 1962).

If nature was form and culture content, treatment was to be directed to the underlying biological cause, relatively easily, at least in theory, if it was identified by neuropsychiatrists as an object like a tumour or a bacterium. But to distinguish form from content was problematic in psychiatric illness where there were no evident biological changes, and thus where the distinction had to be made on the basis of the patient's symptoms as presented to the physician. Hallucinations and delusions contrary to shared everyday reality were nearly always regarded as primary and thus biological; their particular themes had even less bearing on the cause (and thus treatment) of the disease than the way patients might understand pain had any significance for ascertaining the origins of the pain. To take an example from the German psychiatrist Emil Kraepelin: that a patient said he was the Kaiser rather than Napoleon (that is, the content) was of little clinical value compared with the fact of a delusion of grandiose identification (the form). Now this left the shared social world fairly redundant in psychiatric illness as it was observed in the hospital, except inasmuch as a society might facilitate one or other physical cause – as patterns of drinking might encourage alcohol-induced dementia, or local conceptions of risk increase the likelihood of traumatic accidents, or in a less direct way through a society's transformation of the physical environment and thus of human biology through genetic selection (as with sickle cell anaemia). If cultural values could thus sometimes cause disease through transforming natural causes, they could not cause serious mental illness directly in the way that Christianity, Islam and popular understandings might still identify moral turpitude as the immediate cause of insanity (Littlewood, 1993*b*).

The form/content schema worked fairly smoothly in European mental hospitals, where the scope of what counted as clinical observation was limited by the institutional context, but by the beginning of this century psychiatry began to extend its practice to the peoples of the colonial empires. Many local patterns which suggested novel types of mental illness had been previously recorded by travellers, missionaries and colonial administrators, sometimes indeed as illnesses but often as examples of the criminal perversity of native life or just as picturesque if rather troublesome oddities. Most notable among these was *amok* (Oxley, 1849), a Malay word which has passed into the English language for indiscriminant and unmotivated violence against others. In one of the first discussions of the problems of comparing psychiatric illness across societies, Kraepelin (1904), after a trip to Java during which he collected accounts of *amok*s and also observed hospitalised patients, suggested that the characteristic symptoms of a particular mental illness – those which one could find everywhere in the world – were the essential pathogenic ones which directly reflected its physical cause. Yet, as he noted, "reliable comparison is of course only possible if we are able to draw clear distinctions between identifiable illnesses". This proved difficult given the variety of local patterns together with the intention, which Kraepelin enthusiastically shared, to fit them into the restricted number of categories already identified in European hospitals.

Eugen Bleuler, the Swiss psychiatrist who coined the term 'schizophrenia', argued that those symptoms by which we can distinguish this illness from other patterns directly reflect the underlying biological process (Bleuler, 1911). This coalesced with Kraepelin's idea that the characteristic features are the universal ones, to produce the still current model of psychiatric illness which may be described as something like a Russian doll: the essential biological determinants which specify an illness are surrounded by a confusing series of cultural and idiosyncratic envelopes which have to be picked away in diagnosis to reveal the real disease[2]. As Kraepelin's pupil Karl Birnbaum (1923) put it, these pathoplastic envelopes give "content, colouring and contour to individual illnesses whose basic form and character have already been biologically established". Wittgenstein (1958) critically likened the same

---

[2] Young (1995) has suggested that this model recalls 19th century 'positivism' in which the chemical determines the biological, the biological the social. The direction of diagnosis reverses that of natural causation. While it may appear as excessively concrete – and, when pressed, academic social psychiatrists agree that psychiatric illnesses are not natural entities but rather observed concurrences (Wing, 1978) – something very like this, I would argue, is the clinical psychiatrist's naive realism (to use our customary term for the epistemology of practising scientists).

sort of approach in the psychological sciences to our picking away the leaves of an artichoke in a hopeless attempt to uncover some real artichoke, on the assumption that (to use the anthropologist Clifford Geertz's (1986) sarcastic aphorism) "culture is icing, biology cake … difference is shallow, likeness deep". The medical observer was to focus on those symptoms which seem distinguishing and characteristic, and thus biologically determining: symptoms notably elusive in psychiatry, where anxiety, irritation, insomnia, anorexia, depression, self-doubt and suicidal preoccupations are common to virtually all identified illnesses, and which themselves shade into everyday experience. Such common features now then tend to be ignored in diagnostic practice, more by an act of faith in the Kraepelin–Birnbaum model than through an empirical consideration of all the available evidence. And even the statistical attempt to develop a nomenclature favoured by epidemiologists in the 1980s resulted in circular and quite varied arguments about categorisation and universality[3]. Psychiatric illnesses have not been

---

[3] Psychiatric diagnostic categories are ideally monothetic – that is that they have robust core symptoms which specify that diagnosis and no other. Yet it is perhaps only for schizophrenia that psychiatrists can agree on any defining symptoms which are not found in other illnesses: the 'first-rank' symptoms described by the younger Schneider. Yet these are found in only a half of patients with identified schizophrenia in Britain and are 'overridden' by evidence of organic brain disease (which then becomes the diagnosis). The form/content (pathogenic/pathoplastic) model in comparative psychiatry (like its associated 'category fallacy' (Kleinman, 1988) which presumes the European core symptoms everywhere) does seem to produce useful conclusions where there is evidence of invariant biological change which may be said to 'determine' behaviour and experience in a unique way such that they do not seem to occur without it. Examples would be delirium tremens and possibly Gilles de la Tourette's syndrome (although behaviours recalling Tourette's are found with other types of brain lesions and with severe anxiety, and with the experimentally induced hyperstartle response and such social institutions as latah which encourages hyperstartling). The World Health Organization's International Pilot Study of Schizophrenia (IPSS) produced evidence in the 1970s that a similar core schizophrenic pattern (following Schneider's criteria) can be identified in widely differing societies. What it did not show was the extent of the cultural contribution to the illness, supposedly one of the intentions of the study, as Kleinman (1988) has observed; emphasis on the core group, which was shown to have comparable rates across cultures, ignored the cases at the edges where there was a much greater difference in rates such as a three-fold difference between Denmark and India for a 'broad' category of schizophrenia similar to that actually used in British psychiatric practice. The core symptoms of schizophrenia thus appeared to be a manifestation of an underlying disease process; taking a wider category of schizophrenia suggests alternatively that schizophrenic symptoms might also be understood as a response to a variety of insults, whether neurological or social. Examining stable societies rather than groups of refugees or communities in the midst of civil upheavals will emphasise intra-personal biological differences in the aetiology of schizophrenia (analogous to the finding that, when studying affluent societies, genetic associations appear more salient in looking at differences in height, for we have already minimised one environmental source of variation – nutrition). Nevertheless, the similarity of core symptoms and rates found in the IPSS argues

shown to fit neatly bounded monothetic categories (which supposedly "carve nature at the joint" as Young (1995) rather nicely puts it), so multivariate analysis of a multitude of possible symptoms produces rather different schemata for classification, depending on the statistical procedure, on whether one includes or omits shared symptoms, and indeed on what is to count as a symptom[4].

The local understandings of illness which a society shared were ignored by colonial doctors, who, as in Europe, restricted themselves to examination of those admitted to prison or later to the psychiatric hospital (Fisher, 1985; McCulloch, 1994). When faced with patients from a society or minority group with which they are unfamiliar, British and American psychiatrists still complain of the culturally confusing factors which obscure the elusive disease process. With European patients in a predominantly European society they have fewer problems in finding universal categories because 'culture' is always there, tacit, to be implicitly omitted in what counted as the clinical assessment, for, being fairly uniform, it does not contribute to variability between patients. Indeed, any differences within the shared social context of Western patterns, say between women and men, have been ignored until recently in favour of biological or bio-psychological aetiologies to explain variation (and thence 'causation'). There could not seem to be anything immediately 'cultural' in those patterns identified particularly in the West – eating disorders, panic reactions, phobias, self-harm or shoplifting (Littlewood & Lipsedge, 1987). And thus these could be easily presumed to be worldwide patterns. Socially appropriate ways of experiencing and demonstrating distress, like everyday notions

---

that we are unlikely to be able to explain all instances of schizophrenia by a more cultural and political understanding as was assumed by anthropologists like Gregory Bateson and by the British anti-psychiatrists of the 1960s. Cultural considerations of the IPSS results have been limited to speculating on the prognosis of an illness whose origin is taken as primarily biological: vague generalisations about industrialisation (Cooper & Sartorius, 1977), or possible correlations with unemployment in capitalist economies (Warner, 1985), or differences in relatives' affective responses to a person with schizophrenia (Leff *et al*, 1987). While the latter suggests that the response which predicts a poor prognosis in Britain has a similar predictive value when 'translated' to India, this conclusion avoids the problem that one British measure, 'overinvolvement', tended to be generally rated less commonly in the Indian context (*ibid.*). Nor can we assume that social responses which make for a poor prognosis within a society are those which necessarily differentiate prognosis between societies.

[4] The so-called 'neo-Kraepelinian' (Young, 1995) diagnostic systems of the 1980s and 1990s such as DSM–III to DSM–IV, which are a reaction against the earlier classification's hypothetical psychodynamics, maintain a hierarchy of diagnostic significance: passivity experiences are still more important in specifying schizophrenia than depressive experiences.

of personhood and responsibility, have not been taken as causal, for what appeared as a constant could not determine a variable like illness. Ignoring the full range of symptoms across societies and their relationship to the patients' own beliefs and expectations (and to the therapeutic context) did not seem inappropriate for practice within apparently homogeneous societies, because there doctor–patient interactions and the process of diagnosis were already significant and taken-for-granted aspects of daily life. Diagnostic decisions were followed by generally accepted patterns of social response – by medication, hospital admission and on occasion suspension of civil rights.

Imperial psychiatry

It was when they took their diagnostic systems with them to their colonies at the beginning of the 20th century that psychiatrists first recognised some of these difficulties. Dysphoric moods and unusual actions were locally recognised in Africa and Asia, not necessarily as something recalling a physical illness but often as part of totally different patterns of social classification and order – as spirit possession or rituals of mourning, or in the course of initiation, sorcery or warfare. Those patterns that recalled the psychoses of the West seemed generally recognised as unwelcome but not always as akin to sickness (Rivers, 1924). Yet, when colonial doctors turned to writing reports and academic communications, local understandings of self and illness which might now seem to us as analogous to psychiatric theories were described, not as self-contained, meaningful and functional conceptions in themselves, but rather as inadequate approximations to Western scientific knowledge.

At times, however, the understandings of small-scale rural societies, like the more recognisably medical traditions of India and China, cut dramatically across European experience. The anthropologist Charles Seligman (1929) who had trained as a doctor reported that there seemed to have been nothing in New Guinea before European contact which could be said to resemble schizophrenia; as cases analogous to schizophrenia have been later identified by psychiatrists, he has been criticised for what is known as 'the Seligman error' – missing a universal illness, because local understandings and social response did not allow it to appear objectivised through social extrusion as in a Western hospital, but rather incorporated it into some shared institution where it lay unremarked by the medical observer. Similarly, Amerindian and circum-polar patterns of healing, religious inspiration and leadership, in which election to the shamanic role might be signalled by a sudden illness, accident or other troubling experience, were said to mask underlying schizophrenia (Devereux, 1956).

Patterns like *amok* or *piblokto* ('arctic hysteria') were initially taken as rather odd, generally simpler, variants of the psychiatric disorders described in Europe. Mental illness in Java, said Kraepelin (1904), showed "broadly the same clinical picture as we see in our country ... The overall similarity far outweighed the deviant features". Individuals locally regarded as *amok*s were thus really demonstrating epilepsy or perhaps catatonic schizophrenia (*ibid.*). But what were to be taken as these 'deviant features', and what was being compared with what? Presumably the form of the illness, the basis for categorisation of the pattern as some clinical entity. If one looked, for instance, at a Malay patient who had an unjustified belief that she was persecuted by her neighbours, then her delusion was the form, and the neighbours provided the content, but the persecution seemed variously one or the other. That she was deluded is important for arguing that she is mentally ill; the neighbours are of no diagnostic significance, but that her delusions were persecutory could be or not, depending on the selected illness. The assumptions made by Kraepelin in his studies in Java remain the dominant paradigms in comparative psychiatry: how similar do patterns have to be before we can say that we are talking about the same pattern? How do we distinguish those features which appear to be generally the same from those.which vary? What are our units of categorisation going to be when deciding sameness and difference, normality and pathology? Does something like 'depression' occur everywhere? Or perhaps just a less specific experience such as 'distress'?

Psychiatric textbooks have generally argued that locally recognised patterns like *amok* are "not new diagnostic entities: they are in fact similar to those already known in the West" (Kiev, 1972). This equivalence has often been extraordinarily optimistic. To take one pattern which attracted comment because of its exotic salience, *windigo*, the 'cannibal-compulsion' syndrome of the North American Ojibwa and Inuit, was locally described as an individual becoming possessed by a cannibalistic vampire and who then attacked other people in an attempt to devour them. *Windigo* was identified by psychiatrists confidently but quite variously with patterns as disparate as depression, schizophrenia, hysteria and anxiety. Similarly, *amok* was explained not only as the local manifestation of either epilepsy or schizophrenia, but as malaria, syphilis, cannabis psychosis, sunstroke, mania, hysteria, depression, disinhibited aggression and anxiety. *Latah*s, women of the Malay Peninsula who uttered obscene remarks when startled, and who parodied the speech and actions of others apparently without intent (O'Brien 1883), were identified as demonstrating a "psychosis [or] hysteria, arctic hysteria, reactive psychosis, startle reaction, fright neurosis, hysterical psychosis [or] hypnoid state" (Kiev, 1972). Identifying symptoms rather than the local context meant that *amok* and *latah* have generally been regarded not as autonomous cultural institutions, but simply as erroneous Malay explanations which shaped one single universal disease, although the psychiatric observers disagreed radically as to which disease this might be. The extent to which such patterns could be fitted into a universal schema depended on how far the medical observer was prepared to stretch a known psychiatric category, and thus on the preferred theoretical model. By the 1970s, Weston La Barre and Georges Devereux, psychoanalysts who were much less attached to purely biomedical arguments, had gone further in including as instances of schizophrenia a wide variety of local institutions – possession states, shamanism, prophecy, millennial religions and indeed, for La Barre, social change in general. They argued not just that schizophrenia might typically appear in these social institutions but that the institutions exemplified schizophrenic experiences (Littlewood, 1993*b*): everyday culture in non-Western societies could be understood, as it were, as insanity spread out thin.

If psychiatrists of the colonial period remained puzzled about the cultural encrustations they saw adhering to the essential symptoms, they could be struck by the opposite: "barrenness of the clinical picture ... In more primitive culture schizophrenia is 'a poor imitation of European forms' " (Yap, 1951). Culturally obscured, or simply a primitive form, in neither case did culture determine anything, but rather, acted as a sort of indeterminant soup which passively filled in or distorted the biological matrix. Yet 'culture' itself could be a proxy for biological 'race'. Categorisations of illness, professional or popular, are adjacent to other social classifications – to those of character, ethnicity, gender, the natural world and historical experience – on which they draw and which they plagiarise. The distinction, and indeed opposition, between form and content had depended on a fairly clear distinction between universal biology and the variant culture which constrained it, yet, by the end of the 19th century descriptive psychiatry was increasingly influenced by social Darwinism's idea of racial biology in which, while humans were agreed to have a common origin, neurological, psychological, social and moral variations were all considered as reflections of each other at a particular level on the linear scale of 'development'. Young (1995) has proposed the term 'the normalisation of pathology' for the Victorian topology (associated particularly with the neurologist Jackson (1884) and thence found in Rivers and Freud) that the central nervous system, like the colonial order, was organised in a series of levels of control in which the 'higher' could generally override the 'lower' (Jackson's analogy was a rider and a horse). Hysteria was recognised as dysfunctional at the 'lower' level, and Kraepelin (1904) explained the unusual symptomatology of mental illness among the Javanese as reflecting their "lower stage of intellectual development". Variations (in what doctors called the 'presentation' of illness in different societies) have been attributed until recently not just to particular historical and political experiences, as we might have expected from the 'pathoplastic' model, but to the existence of a fairly uniform primitive mentality (more nature than culture) which was shared with European children and with the 'degenerate', 'regressed' and 'retarded' adult European, and which manifest symptoms characteristic of a loss of higher control: 'hyperidic states', 'catastrophic reactions', 'malignant anxiety', 'simple responses available to psychologically disorganised individuals' and 'primitive reactions corresponding to outbursts of psychopathic persons in developed countries' (Kiev, 1972). Not altogether unrelated physiological explanations attributed *piblokto* ('arctic hysteria') and *kayak angst* to the undeveloped mind reflecting on "the stillness and the sense of impending doom that are so characteristic of the Arctic climate" (*ibid.*).

Depression

This topological psychology of linear development, put together with the assumption that symptoms observed in Europe were somehow more real and less obfuscated by cultural values, led to the common argument that depression did not yet occur in non-Europeans for its essential Western characteristic of self-blame (a consequence of mature selfhood) was not observed (Carothers, 1953). The absence of depression was sometimes directly attributed to a less evolved brain where the 'primitive layers' predominated (Vint, 1932), an idea which could have had (but didn't) implications for the Colonial Office when it considered the possibility of independence for colonial Africa, as J.C. Carothers (1954) recommended. Guilty self-accusations of the type found in clinical depression in the West had in fact been identified in colonial Africa in the 1930s, not by doctors in the colonial hospitals but by an anthropologist looking at witchcraft and the distribution of shrines (Field, 1960). Reactions which recall Western depression are now frequently described in small-scale non-industrialised communities, but the issue depends not only on the frequency with which people with less socially disturbing problems come to the hospital to be treated and thus studied, or on medical failure to empathise with another's experience, or on a rather cursory epidemiology based on colonial hospital statistics, but on what one means by 'depression'. Is it something like the misery which we might identify in various situations of loss or bereavement, or the pattern of rather physical experiences such as loss of interest, waking up early, and poor appetite, which are recognised as clinical depression (and which appear likely to be universal), or else some more specific expressed sentiment of Judaeo-Christian guilt and a wish to die? Greater psychiatric familiarity with the experience of personal distress in the former colonies has suggested that 'depression' may be simply a variant of widespread patterns of what we might term dysphoric mood, which in depression is represented through a particularly Western moral psychology which assumes an autonomous self as the invariant locus of experience, memory and agency. When looking across societies, a more common experience of everyday distress than 'depression' (which figures a phenomenological sinking downwards of the once active self into an inertia for which we remain responsible (Littlewood, 1994)), may be one of depletion and the loss of something essential which has been taken out of the self – a pattern well glossed in various Latin American idioms of 'soul loss' (Shweder, 1985).

Culture-bound syndromes

In the 1950s, following revulsion at German academic psychiatry's 'eugenics' under the Nazis and its development into ethnic exter-mination[5], the social and medical sciences gradually discarded the ideas of biological evolution and psychological development as explanations for differences of experience and action between contemporary societies. All societies were recognised as having 'a culture' in similar ways, and biological differences between groups as a whole, that between men and women still excepted, could not explain their different types of mental illness. The recognition that many non-Western illnesses could no longer be subsumed as primitive forms of universal categories led comparative psychiatry (or as it now came to be called, cultural psychiatry) to propose a new sort of illness altogether whose study did not entail the biological form/cultural content dichotomy. Patterns like *amok* and *latah*, which had recalled the idea of psychological illness in Europe but still remained unclassifiable, came to be known as 'culture-bound syndromes' (Yap, 1951, 1974). They were usually episodic and dramatic reactions, limited to a particular society where they were locally identified as distinct patterns of action very different from those of everyday life and which, we might now note, had been of colonial concern because they were bizarre, outrageous or frankly troublesome. Less dramatic patterns of distress – personal withdrawal from shared activities, troubling thoughts, chronic pain, bereavement, despondency

---

[5] Reasons of space preclude consideration of psychiatric anti-Semitism which has been recently examined by Lifton, Gilman, Degkwitz, Efron, Gay and McGrath.

– which did not come to the attention of the colonial administration or the local police were ignored until the development of medical anthropology in the 1980s.

A large number of such 'culture-bound' illnesses have now been catalogued (Simons & Hughes, 1985) as distinctive and consistent patterns, transmitted to each generation in a continuing cultural tradition, and which are taken as closely related to a society's distinctive understanding of self and its prescribed norms[6]. However high the incidence of reactions like grief or terror might be in war-torn communities, they were not regarded as culture-specific unless they continued in some consistently recognisable form in successive generations as part of an enduring identity. What exactly was it that was 'bound' in culture-bound syndromes? Had 'culture' now achieved the master status of 'biology' in the international nosology? There is a continuing debate as to what the category refers: usually restricted to a pattern found only in the society in question and which symbolises and represents fundamental local concerns, on occasion it has been applied to apparently universal and biologically understood illnesses which are shaped, distinguished and treated in a local content (on the changing applications of the term see Ritenbaugh, 1982; Littlewood & Lipsedge, 1987; Lee, 1996; Littlewood, 1996). One might include *kifafa, malkadi* and *moth madness*, locally recognised patterns in Tanzania, Trinidad and among the Navaho which closely recall the medical description of epilepsy (Neutra *et al*, 1977; Littlewood, 1993*b*). A locally recognised reaction in New Guinea, *kuru*, was once regarded as a culture-bound syndrome akin to hysteria, but no longer, given the likely role of a slow virus identified in its aetiology (which has made it even more exotic through recognition that it could be transmitted through cannibalism). Patterns like *kuru* or the restricted abilities of senescence, or such apparently motivated patterns as homicide and rape, the deliria of malnutrition or alcohol intoxication, or the use of other psychoactive substances have certainly been regarded as characteristic of a particular society but are seldom described as 'culture-bound' because they appear potentially available in any society or else do not immediately recall European 'mental illness'. Yet, if these patterns persisted – like the alcohol misuse, anomic depression and suicide consequent on the relocation of Native Americans onto reservations – they were taken as manifestations of 'American Indian culture', ignoring the political relationship between coloniser and native, and thus the context of the

---

[6] By the 1990s, they were acknowledged in the American Psychiatric Association's fourth Diagnostic and Statistical Manual (on whose novel cultural deliberations see Littlewood, 1992).

psychiatric observation. 'New illnesses' identified by more sophisticated epidemiological techniques in urban populations or through the expansion of psychiatric observation to a wider population have been termed 'culture-change' or 'acculturation illnesses' exemplified by the *brain-fag syndrome* identified in West African students (Prince, 1960; Littlewood, 1984, 1995).

Conflict and resistance

If these local patterns were distinguished as 'culture-bound' by the European psychiatrist only in that they occurred in (other) cultures, how then did a culture lead to illness? Did 'culture' mean simply shared conceptualisations, so that the psychiatrist could identify local concerns and sentiments either in the type of person who was vulnerable or else in the actual symptoms which represented the culture in a way that recalled 17th and 18th century ideas of a national character? Or could 'culture' be located in social and biological stressors which occurred in a particular society but were not necessarily recognised in it? Anyway, how could such illness be clearly distinguished from the other cultural patterns in which it was embedded? A later question, reserved for the 1980s, was whether to extend the category to illnesses such as eating disorders which were apparently only to be found in European societies (Littlewood & Lipsedge, 1987; Lee, 1996).

In part, the continuing problem of 'culture', for psychiatrists lay in its double-edged connotations. 'Culture' was still a valued commodity, that constraint on nature which distinguished human from animal, educated European from primitive (and which often referred to 'high culture' alone) (Williams, 1958). Yet, for Western psychiatrists establishing their discipline as a medical speciality, 'culture' remained secondary to scientific biological reality. As frank biological racism became disreputable after the Second World War, and the unifying idiom of 'development' separated out into the distinct fields of child psychology, economics and technology, the psychological differences between European and non-European could again be perceived only in rather uncertain 'cultural' terms, as a medical proxy for the other's 'difference' (or even for the lingering idea of 'race'), which still emersed the individual in some undifferentiated other, now less their biological level than their way of life. As medicine had little idea of how to deal with 'culture', it drew on other disciplines, particularly psychoanalysis and social anthropology, which claimed to be able to relate the interests of medicine to the inter-subjective social world in a more empirical and humanistic way than had evolutionary medicine. The new cultural psychiatrists generally held appointments in Western university departments, away from the poorly funded and intellectually marginal concerns of colonial psychiatry, which still remained close to popular Western ideas of race (Carothers, 1954). Psychoanalysts and anthropologists interested in providing a 'cultural psychiatry' of local patterns in 'British Africa' based on intensive fieldwork in local communities were seldom interested in examining hospital statistics, unlike the epidemiologists associated with the World Health Organization who until recently have preferred to stick with the presumed biomedical universals, and thus with the form/content idioms of hospital psychiatry.

Particularly in the USA, where a strong inclination towards psycho-analysis was apparent in medicine and the social sciences from the 1930s, psychiatrists emphasised the similarity of local illnesses to the 'modal personality' which an individual developed in their culture. The affected person was now suffering less from something recalling a medical disease with a bit of culture tacked on, so much as demonstrating in an exaggerated form those psychological conflicts established in the course of childhood socialisation. So *windigo* (the Ojibwa cannibal compulsion psychosis) was interpreted as a local preoccupation with food in a hostile environment, fuelled by residues of infantile resentment at the mother for the early weaning necessitated by the scarcity of food. After an indulgent childhood, the young boy was precipitated into early adulthood by brutal tests of self-reliance and encouraged to fast to attain ultra human powers. Dependence on his parents was replaced by a precarious dependence on spirits which encouraged solitary self-reliance in hunting. The mother, feared and hated for her violent rejection of her son, returned to possess him in the form of the *windigo* (Parker, 1960).

Psychoanalytically orientated anthropologists proposed in this sort of way that any culture was a dynamic compromise between conflicting interests: ecological and physiological, between self and others, between parents and children, men and women. Symptoms, dreams, religious symbols and social institutions could all be taken as aspects of the same conflicts refracted through an individual's psychological functioning (Seligman, 1928). Was the European observer now to take the locally identified illness as the expression of such conflicts in unconscious motivations: as a society's symptoms? Or, given the incorporation of personal conflicts into local institutions, was the 'illness' to be considered as a type of collective psychological adjustment, indeed as a sort of healing? Psychoanalysis agreed with psychiatry that one could distinguish problem, causation and treatment (Seligman, 1928), but differed as to how to go about it. Devereux, perhaps the most sophisticated psychoanalytical anthropologist, eventually proposed that institutions like shamanism (which had often been taken as employing altered states of consciousness to facilitate something akin to Western psychotherapy (Janet, 1926)) were themselves the expression of psychological disturbances in what he called the 'ethnic unconscious': disturbances which could then be enhanced by a society to produce 'ethnic psychoses', as he called these pathological institutions (Devereux, 1970). Criticising the historian Edwin Ackernecht (1943) who had argued for a clear distinction between cultural meaning and medical terminology, Devereux (1956) argued that the local healing of unconscious social conflicts simply exacerbated them:

> "there exist societies so enmeshed in a vicious circle that everything they do to save themselves only causes them to sink deeper into the quicksand".

The British biological psychiatrist William Sargant, an ex-Methodist who had taken to arguing that religious ecstasy and spirit possession were a type of brainwashing, emphasised the cathartic function of culture-specific patterns which allowed the individual, when in a state of dissociated consciousness, to express otherwise socially forbidden inclinations in a non-threatening and relatively sanctioned manner – as if they were halfway between an 'illness' and its 'treatment' (Sargant, 1973). Like Devereux, he still regarded it as all distinctly unhealthy. Alternatively, Weston La Barre, Ari Kiev and Thomas Scheff took the cathartic expression of hidden desires as a resolution rather than an exacerbation of cultural conflicts – as something closer to healing.

This all got rather circular and, like hospital psychiatry, ignored local conceptions of healing in favour of Western assumptions of normality and illness. Paralleling the earlier assumption that non-Western pathologies were masked or incomplete forms, non-Western healing was now taken as an elementary version of psychoanalytical therapy but one which employed 'suggestion' rather than 'insight' (Frank, 1961; Kiev, 1964). What remained constant in all of this was the conviction, however muted, that Western categories were still the appropriate way to frame the question, and that these provided universal criteria by which one could agree that certain local patterns were justifiably termed dysfunctional or maladaptive (Doi, 1971). On rare occasions analysts carried out formal psychoanalysis with their African and Amerindian informants (Sachs, 1937; Devereux, 1951; to some extent Laubscher, 1937), even if they presumed Freudian ideals of psychological maturity to be universally valid. Few of the classic culture-bound syndromes were not at some time explained as the projection of unconscious fantasies and thwarted incestuous wishes, as the consequences of traumatic weaning, or simply as the overwhelming existential anxiety of tribal societies which followed from their unsophisticated psychology (Roheim, 1950; Devereux, 1956).

Eliding the conventional distinction between pathology as an individual phenomenon and treatment as a social response, the cost to the psychoanalysts was, as Ackernecht had warned, "the wholesale pathologisation of cultures". Equivalence between modal personality, characteristic personal illness and social structure led to an interpretation of small-scale communities as paranoid, obsessive or whatever – even if the implication of these terms was evidently less 'strong' than the clinical usage from which they derived (eg. Benedict, 1935; Lambo, 1955). During and after the Second World War, American psychoanalysts were funded to study the 'cultural pathologies' of enemy nations (Benedict, 1946). Psychoanalysis still subscribed to those positivist ideals of the late nineteenth century which had sought a moral understanding of human society in science rather than in religion; like the French neurologists under whom he had studied, Freud had explained the medieval persecution of Europe's witches on the grounds that they had really been suffering from mental illness, and psychoanalysts like Devereux took with them the assumption that spirit possession was a variant of hysteria when they turned to look at non-European cultures. The universality of the Oedipus complex even in matrilineal (mother-descended) societies which did not recognise a male role in procreation was a matter of particular interest (following Malinowski, 1927); not unlike the hospital psychiatrist Kraepelin, the psychoanalysts took a European pattern for which theories had been elaborated as the basic form which other societies then manifested as masked or incomplete (Jones, 1924). And they tended to the evolutionary idioms of late 19th century psychiatry, if in a less biologised way, still arguing developmental parallels between archaic ancestor, contemporary primitive, child and neurotic, all as early, arrested or regressed levels characterised by an infantile psychology in which 'psychic omnipotence' and 'magical thinking' trailed behind the advancing line of mature rationality. Nor, with rare exceptions (Sachs, 1937), was colonial power of much psychoanalytical interest, whether regarded as the rather unusual site for their observations, or occasional comments on the perils of imitating primitives for the Whites apart (Jung, 1930), as itself pathogenic (Mannoni, 1950; Fanon, 1952; Loudon, 1959).

More recently, local illnesses have been regarded by psychiatrists influenced by anthropology less as diseases or unconscious conflicts than as particularly salient everyday sensibilities and values or exaggerated idioms of distress (Kleinman, 1988): as with the Hindu *suchi-bar* ('purity mania') and the related ascetic syndrome, or the Taiwanese *shen kuei* and Japanese *taijin kyofusho* ('interpersonal phobia'). If these had been termed pathological or maladaptive by Western psychiatry, it was because normative institutions – Brahmanical obligations to avoid certain foods and preserve bodily purity, or Japanese expectations of self-restraint and the avoidance of inappropriate familiarity – were taken too enthusiastically by certain individuals, resulting in anxieties or interpersonal problems which could be recognised as disproportionate both in the local context and by psychiatric observers. Or alternatively, recalling the psychoanalytical view, the patterns represent in the individual a conflict or contradiction between the local institutions themselves: it has been argued that the continuing antagonism between the values of sexuality and asceticism in India generates the 'purity syndromes' (Malhotra & Wig, 1975). Or else, as Sargant had argued, personal conflicts are expressed in limited contravention of role-specific norms in fairly standardised situations, and that it is these contraventions which had been identified, correctly or otherwise, as pathologies. It has been suggested that all cultures have such loopholes which are themselves "socially reinforced and have the same structural characteristics as other behavioural norms in the system"; and that at least in the case of *latah* and *amok*, we should employ a less medical term than 'syndrome': perhaps something like 'stylised expressive traditional behaviours' for those deviant patterns which are fairly standardised and limited in time, but which, while they certainly contravene everyday behaviour, are somehow culturally condoned to allow the expression of apparently repressed but not uncommon sentiments (Carr, 1978). This does push the psychiatrist's normative question back even further, but if deviance (or pathology) is sometimes locally condoned or even encouraged, what is the frame by which one should term it deviant? The lingering Western presumption of pathology, or some local 'don't do this but if you must, do it this way'? As with the earlier colonial psychiatry, the idea of 'a culture' has, however, remained one which is fairly homogenous, with values and social order accepted in the same way by all members: a model which followed the idea of a tightly bounded society once sought by colonial officers and anthropologists, and which ignored any unequal distribution of knowledge and power, of local contestation or global change (Littlewood, 1984, 1995).

Limits of cultural psychiatry

Hospital psychiatrists and those inclined to psychoanalysis both argued for unitary theories of the phenomena once observed by missionaries, army doctors and colonial administrators, even if they disagreed as to what any such unity comprised: universally recognisable disease entity, exaggeration of norm, cultural conflict, social change, sanctioned rejection of the norm or even therapeutic response. Social anthropologists have objected that their error was to use a medical grid which inevitably objectified social action as disease entity. Rather, one should start by simply describing a society in its own terms, for societies are not traditional residues of some forgotten past which is passing away, but always constitute themselves anew in their chosen memories and actions. If the term 'culture-bound syndrome' is to retain value only as a concept of local sickness, whether or not psychiatry recognises it as akin to Western disease, what then is to count as a 'concept of sickness'? Social scientists are hardly immune from comparing one society with another to obtain regularities and general patterns, and in order to do that they too define apparently analogous domains in each – whether those of social structure, kinship, religion or sickness. These domains inevitably derive from Western terminology. Another society then simply comes to be read as an aggregate of such areas of comparison which have a structured and causal relationship to each other (Littlewood, 1991). The comparative problem is hardly unique to medicine. As the British anthropologist Edward Evans- Pritchard is said to have observed, "if social anthropology is anything, it is a comparative discipline – and that is impossible". It is not that psychiatry's inevitable grid, pathology, is necessarily inappropriate for comparing what looks to the European like 'suffering' or 'madness' in different societies, but pathology is just one possible grid and one which carries with it particular assumptions about normality and abnormality which explicitly ignore consideration of power and of the context of observation, and of what is observed and how 'observation' itself might shape it.

The evolutionary schema did offer one mode of comparison by placing societies (or illnesses) as states of transformation along a historical spectrum driven by certain processes. Few social anthropologists, some sociobiologists, Freudians and Marxists perhaps excepted, would now subscribe to the idea of a unilinear human development through which local institutions and mentalities are to be understood as determined by underlying processes, whether those of evolutionary selection or of the relations of production. While it is still argued that the insights offered by psychoanalysts may provide a useful perspective when trying to understand psychological experience in non-European societies (Doi, 1971; Kakar, 1978), others have argued that Freud's followers have little to contribute to the critical or social sciences for they offer a moralised version of commonsense Western assumptions about the inevitability of European rationality with entrepreneurial autonomy as 'health' or 'adaptation' (Littlewood, 1993*a*). On the whole, with the exception of a few psychoanalytically oriented anthropologists such as Melford Spiro and Gananath Obeyesekere, the ethnographic monographs written by anthropologists now place little emphasis on the early childhood experiences which the psychoanalysts had argued was significant in generating culture. They take particular patterns of childrearing as the manifestation rather than the cause of social knowledge[7]. The assumption that non-Europeans thought is less rational has been superseded by recognition that all societies employ both deductive and inductive logic, both concrete and abstract reasoning, but that they do so within limits which are determined by their own social interests. Societies differ psychologically not in their capabilities, but in their modes of thought, through cognitions and categorisations of space and time, gender and the natural world, their understandings of causality and invidia, and which are encoded in their systems of representation, particularly language. What was once regarded as primitive (magical) thinking on the origins of sickness or misfortune appears now as a focus on the moral 'why' rather than the technical 'how', for societies differ in the focus of their immediate interests and practised knowledge, indeed, in terms of the everyday understanding of sickness.

Western medicine is less efficacious in relieving distress through its emphasis on the proximate mechanisms of misfortune, leaving the individual with chronic or serious illness little help in answering 'why me?' (Kleinman, 1988). In the case of severe mental illness we might note that psychiatry remains unable to offer its patients any understanding, technical or moral, in terms of everyday knowledge (or, indeed, of biology).

To recognise some other's pattern as especially 'cultural' is to assume a privileged perspective concerning it, whether colonial hubris or academic analysis (as Pascal had put it, we have truth but they have customs). By the mid-1980s culture-specific illnesses had become recognised by critics a psychiatry's 'twilight zone' (Hughes, 1985), "what other people have, not us" (Hahn, 1985). Medical interest in isolated and disembodied exotic patterns was seen to have directed attention from more immediate questions of economic development, poverty, exploitation or nutrition, besides providing yet another justification of the otherness of non-Europeans, and one which ignored the role of Western medicine once in facilitating imperial expansion and now in the global marketing of untested pharmaceutical drugs.

---

[7] A partial reaction may be found however in the anthropological work of Rodney Needham, Scott Atran, Pascal Boyer, Mark Johnson and C.D. Laughlin who have argued against a purely conventional understanding of shared adult cognitions. The extent to which 'culture' and 'nature' may be said to represent not actually existing entities but rather reified modes of thought (Littlewood, 1993*b*) is beyond the scope of a brief historical survey; yet we might wonder if the fashionable demedicalisation of disease as a biological reality in favour of a cultural understanding is not perhaps a final post-modern privileging of Western 'culture' over 'nature'.

How directly relevant had psychiatry been to imperialism? Both evidently developed in the same period. They shared certain modes of reasoning: we might note, for instance, affinities between the scientific objectification of illness experience as disease and the objectification of people as chattel slaves or a colonial manpower, or the topological parallels between the nervous system and the colonial order. Both argued for an absence of 'higher' functions or sense of personal responsibility among patients and non-Europeans. The extent, however, to which any elaborated set of ideas which might be termed 'imperial psychiatry' provided a rationale for colonialism in British Africa or India is debateable: in a recent review I have argued that the evidence is meagre (Littlewood, 1993*a*; *cf.* McCulloch, 1994). With remarkably few exceptions (Laubscher, 1937; Tooth, 1950; Carothers, 1953), the small number of colonial psychiatrists barely participated in the debates I have outlined above. Segregated facilities, of course (Lugard, 1923; Ernst, 1991); prejudice and neglect, undoubtedly; but hardly practicable ideologies for racial or cultural inferiority[8]. (Indeed, we might

---

[8] The anthropologist Evans-Pritchard, for example, was commissioned to examine the role of prophets in inciting anti-British resistance among the Nuer of the Sudan; in his text we can note that on a couple of occasions he refers to some of them as 'psychotic' but this is nowhere developed as any sort of racial or medical theory (Evans-Pritchard, 1940). While colonialism took for granted a difference between 'higher' and 'lower' levels of civilisation, this was not linked to any neurological topology beyond the isolated speculations of Vint, Carothers and Tooth. By contrast, in the USA, psychiatry was deployed extensively during the 19th and 20th centuries to justify what we may term the internal colonisation of Amerindians and African–Americans (Haller, 1970). Maurice Lipsedge and I (1982) have argued that this was not simply because of the greater influence of medicine in the USA. In the early stages of imperial expansion, domination is explicitly economic or military, and any necessary justification rests simply on evident technical or administrative superiority, sometimes manifest destiny, security of trade or the historical requirements of civilisation; only when dominated peoples 'inside the walls' threaten to achieve some sort of equality do apologies appear couched as a discourse on primitive pathology or biological inferiority. To an extent we may argue that Europe prepared to abandon her settlements well before equality threatened (except for the significant instances of Kenya, Algeria and the French Caribbean (see Vint, 1932; Fanon, 1952; Carothers, 1954)), and before colonial administrations had established much beyond a basic mental hospital for the native criminally insane. (Space prevents consideration of the special case of South Africa (Littlewood, 1993*a*)). In North America, arguments in favour of the emancipation of slaves had appeared by the time of Independence only to be countered by medical justifications for continued servitude which invoked such novel diseases as drapetomania (the impulse to escape) (Brigham, 1832) or even, as argued by Benjamin Rush (1799), that African ancestry was itself an attenuated disease, justifications which became even more necessary for White supremacy after Emancipation. Among Native Americans, for whom collective political action was impossible after they were dispersed on reservations at the 'boundary' of the European state, 20th century administrators and medical officers developed increasingly psychological, and thence psychopathological, explanations to explain their high rates of suicide, alcohol dependency and general failure to participate in national life: the internalisation of the frontier as Andreas Heinz has put it.

more plausibly argue the case of contemporary psychiatric practice in Britain.) One possible exception was the common medical assumption in the 1940s that too rapid social change (that is access to schools and wage labour) were causing an increase in African psychiatric illness (Tooth, 1950; Carothers, 1953), but this increase was often explained by others as a better access to hospital services. Whether this argument was taken seriously in London I am doubtful; it could of course be turned on its head by arguing that it was colonisation, not 'change', that was pathogenic (Mannoni, 1950). While the few colonial psychiatrists were quite tangential to the making of Colonial Office policy (and were themselves rather 'marginal' individuals within both British and colonial society (McCulloch, 1994)), in the francophone colonies and in Haiti, local Black psychiatrists developed radical critiques of European domination to argue for a distinct 'African identity' as against that of the settlers, and one which was couched in terms of 'ethnopsychiatry' (Mars, 1946; Fanon, 1952)[9]. Ethnographers like W.H.R. Rivers (1924) and Bronislaw Malinowski (1927), aspects of whose work developed into what was to become medical anthropology, while they relied on missionary evidence and Colonial Office support, did not significantly influence British policy in Africa or elsewhere (Goody, 1995). If diseases in the colonies were of any political interest to the metropolis, the concern was not madness but the acute infections which threatened to deprive the imperial administration of its labour force (Lyons 1992), or else the psychological health of the colonists themselves (Price, 1913; Culpin, 1953; Littlewood, 1985; Barrell, 1991; Ernst, 1991).

Contemporary anthropologists have proposed that all illnesses may be said to be 'culture-bound' in that our adaptation to illness experience is always socially prescribed, while human behaviour can never be taken in independence from human action. The classic 'cultural syndromes' still remain as titillating relief in the margins of British psychiatric textbooks in the 1990s. Often the hearsay repetition of previous descriptions, travellers' tales and missionary anxieties, frequently in their most bizarre form, they distort local significance and context in providing a voyeuristic image of the other. The *windigo* cannibal-compulsion has now been recognised as psychiatric folklore, a 'near mythical syndrome' with perhaps three reported instances and one which

---

[9] Why the English/French difference? Perhaps because French colonialism favoured a model of cultural and biological assimilation, the English arguing for segregation (Taguieff, 1988; Osborne, 1994). French psychiatry was (and is) a much more 'intellectual' profession than its British counterpart, and medical students from Martinique or Senegal when studying in Paris were more likely to be exposed to political and philosophical debate than they would have been in a British medical school (cf. the anthropologists Kenyatta and Busia.)

has never been observed by Europeans (Neutra *et al*, 1977). Similar doubts have been cast on the evidence for *voodoo death* ('pointing the bone') in which awareness that one had been ensorcered apparently precipitated sudden death through "a fatal spirit of despondency" (Mauss, 1926; Eastwell, 1982). Psychiatrists concerned with establishing basic mental health services in post-colonial Africa and Asia have deplored the endless collecting of novel syndromes

> "by a host of short-term visitors [producing] a wealth of data about some strange ritual of an obscure tribe, analysed with style and erudition, but without comment on general trends particularly as they relate to the more mundane aspects of clinical psychiatry" (German, 1972; but compare De Jong, 1987).

For those concerned with establishing basic medical services and providing humane treatment in situations of poverty and exploitation, debates on the cultural specificity of suffering may appear otiose.

'Culture-bound syndromes' represent salient instances of a particular community's dilemmas as extreme, if sometimes contentious, representations of human distress in its distinctive milieu. To essentialise such social dramas as medical diseases in independence of everyday meanings or other experiences of distress, or in independence of the political context of our observation, is to render them exotic curiosities. To ignore them altogether is to render human adversity bland and familiar, to affirm that the European's experience alone is true, and thus to naturalise the patterns of Western psychiatric illnesses, to affirm them as transcending our intentions, as necessary and immutable.

Acknowledgement

An earlier draft of this chapter was published in the *International Journal of Social Psychiatry*, and I am grateful to the editors and to Inga-Britt Krause both for criticisms and permission to republish. Sushrut Jadhav kindly commented on an earlier draft.

References

ACKERNECHT, E. (1943) Psychopathology, primitive medicine and primitive culture. *Bulletin of the History of Medicine*, **14**, 30–68.
BARRELL, J. (1991) *The Infection of Thomas De Quincey: A Psychopathology of Imperialism*. New Haven, CT: Yale University Press.
BEARD, G. M. (1881) *American Nervousness: Its Causes and Consequences*. New York: Putnam.

44   *Littlewood*

BENEDICT, R. (1935) *Patterns of Culture.* London: Routledge and Kegan Paul.
— (1946) *The Chrysanthemum and the Sword: Patterns of Japanese Culture.* Boston: Houghton Mifflin.
BIRNBAUM, K. (1923) *Der Aufbau der Psychosen.* Translated as 'The Making of a Psychosis' in *Themes and Variation in European Psychiatry* (eds S. R. Hirsch & M. Shepherd (1974)). Bristol: Wright.
BLEULER, E. (1911) *Dementia Praecox.* New York: International Universities Press.
BLOCH, M. & BLOCH, J. (1980) Women and the dialectics of nature. In *Nature, Culture, Gender* (eds C. MacCormack & M. Strathern). Cambridge: Cambridge University Press.
BOUDIN, J. (1857) Traité de Géographie et de Statistiques Médicales et des Maladies Endémiques. Paris: Baillière.
BOURDIEU, P. (1977) *Outline of a Theory of Practice.* Cambridge: Cambridge University Press.
BRIGHAM, A. (1832) *Remarks on the Influence of Mental Cultivation Upon Health.* Hartford, NY: Huntingdon.
BROWN, T. M. (1985) Descartes, dualism and psychosomatic medicine. In *The Anatomy of Madness I* (eds W. F. Bynum, R. Porter & M. Shepherd). London: Tavistock.
CAROTHERS, J. C. (1953) *The African Mind in Health and Disease.* Geneva: World Health Organization.
— (1954) *The Psychology of Mau Mau.* Nairobi: Government Printers.
CARR, J. E. (1978) Ethno-behaviourism and the culture-bound syndromes: the case of amok. *Culture, Medicine and Psychiatry,* **2,** 269–293.
CHEYNE, G. (1734) *The English Malady.* Cited in V. Skultans (1979) *English Madness: Ideas on Insanity, 1580–1890.* London: Routledge & Kegan Paul.
COLLINGWOOD, R. G. (1945) *The Idea of Nature.* Oxford: Clarendon Press.
COOPER, J. E. & SARTORIUS, N. (1977) Cultural and temporal variation in schizophrenia: a speculation on the importance of industrialisation. *British Journal of Psychiatry,* **130,** 50–55.
CULPIN, M. (1953) Neurosthenia in the tropics. *The Practitioner,* **85,** 146–154.
DE JONG, J. T. V. M. (1987) *A Descent Into African Psychiatry.* Amsterdam: Royal Tropical Institute.
DEVEREUX, G. (1951) *Reality and Dream: Psychotherapy of a Plains Indian.* New York: International Universities Press.
— (1956) The normal and abnormal: the key problem in psychiatric anthropology. Translated in G. Devereux (1970) *Essais d'Ethnopsychiatrie Generale.* Paris: Gallimard.
— (1970) *Essais d'Ethnopsychiatrie Generale.* Paris: Gallimard.
DOI, T. (1971) *Amae no Kozo* (trans. *The Anatomy of Dependence).* Tokyo: Kodansha.
EAGLETON, T. (2000) *The Idea of Culture.* Oxford: Blackwell.
EASLEA, B. (1980) *Witch Hunting, Magic and the New Philosophy: An Introduction to the Debates of the Scientific Revolution.* Sussex: Harvester.
EASTWELL, H. D. (1982) Voodoo death and the mechanism for the despatch of the dying in East Arnhem. *American Anthropologist,* **84,** 5–18.
ERNST, W. (1991) *Mad Tales from the Raj: The European Insane in British India.* London: Routledge.
EVANS-PRITCHARD, E. E. (1940) *The Nuer.* Oxford: Oxford University Press.
FANON, F. (1952) *Peau Noir, Masques Noirs.* Paris: Seuil.
FIELD, M. J. (1960) *Search for Security: An Ethno-Psychiatric Study of Rural Ghana.* London: Faber & Faber.
FISHER, L. E. (1985) *Colonial Madness: Mental Health in the Barbadian Social Order.* New Brunswick, NJ: Rutgers University Press.
FRANK, J. D. (1961) *Persuasion and Healing: A Comparative Study of Psychotherapy.* New York: Schocken.

FUMAROLI, M. (1996) A Scottish Voltaire: John Barclay and the character of nations. *Times Literary Supplement*, January 19, 16–17.

GANSER, S. J. M. (1897) A peculiar hysterical state. Translated in *Themes and Variations in European Psychiatry* (eds S. R. Hirsch & M. Shepherd (1974)). Bristol: Wright.

GASKELL, S. (1860) On the wont of better provisions for the labouring and middle classes when attacked or threatened with insanity. *Journal of Mental Science*, **6**, 321–327.

GEERTZ, C. (1986) Anti-anti-relativism. *American Anthropologist*, **86**, 263–278.

GERMAN, A. A. (1972) Aspects of clinical psychiatry in sub-Saharan Africa. *British Journal of Psychiatry*, **121**, 461–479.

GILMAN, S. L. (1985) *Difference and Pathology: Stereotypes of Sexuality, Race and Madness*. Ithaca, NY: Cornell University Press.

GOOD, B. J. & GOOD, M-J. D. (1982) Towards a meaning-centred analysis of popular illness categories. In *Cultural Conceptions of Mental Health and Therapy* (eds A. Marselia & G. M. White). Dordrecht: D. Reidel.

GOODY, J. (1995) *The Expansive Moment: Anthropology in Britain and Africa 1918–1970*. Cambridge: Cambridge University Press.

GREENLESS, T. D. (1895) Insanity among the natives of South Africa. *Journal of Mental Science*, **41**, 697–708.

HAHN, R. A. (1985) Culture-bound syndromes unbound. *Social Science and Medicine*, **21**, 165–180.

HALLER, J.S. (1970) The physician versus the Negro: medical and anthropological concepts of race in the nineteenth century. *Bulletin of the History of Medicine*, **44**, 154–167.

HARRAWAY, D. (1989) *Primate Visions: Gender, Race and Nature in the World of Modern Science*. New York: Routledge.

HUGHES, C. C. (1985) Culture-bound or construct-bound? In *The Culture-Bound Syndromes: Folk Illnesses of Psychiatric and Anthronoloaical Interest* (eds R. C. Simons & C. C. Hughes). Dordrecht: D. Reidel.

JACKSON, J. H. (1884) *Croonian Lectures on the Evolution and Dissolution of the Nervous System*. Cambridge: Cambridge University Press.

JANET, P. (trans.)(1926) *Psychological Healing*. London: Allen & Unwin.

JASPERS, K. (1963) *General Psychopathology* (7th edn). Manchester: Manchester University Press.

JOHN XXI, POPE (1550) Folk remedies against madness. In *Three Hundred Years of Psychiatry 1535–1860* (eds R. Hunter & I. MacAlpine). London: Oxford University Press.

JONES, E. (1924) Mother-right and the sexual ignorance of savages. In *Psycho-Myths, Psycho-History: Essays in Applied Psychoanalysis* (ed. E. Jones). New York: Stonehill.

JUNG, C. G. (1930) Your Negroid and Indian behaviour. *Forum*, **83**, 193–199.

KAKAR, S. (1978) *The Inner World: A Psychoanalytical Study of Childhood and Society in India*. Delhi: Oxford University Press.

KIEV, A. (1964) The study of folk psychiatry. In *Magic, Faith and Healing: Studies in Primitive Psychiatry Today* (ed. A. Kiev). New York: Free Press
––– (1972) *Transcultural Psychiatry*. Penguin: Harmondsworth.

KLEINMAN, A. (1988) *Rethinking Psychiatry: From Cultural Category to Personal Experience*. New York: Free Press.

KRAEPELIN, E. (1904) *Vergleichende Psychiatrie*. Translated as 'Comparative psychiatry' in *Themes and Variation in European Psychiatry* (eds S. R. Hirsch & M.Shepherd (1974)). Bristol: Wright.

LA BARRE, W. (1970) *The Ghost Dance: Origins of Religion*. London: Allen & Unwin.

LAMBO, T. A. (1955) The role of cultural factors in paranoid psychoses among the Yoruba tribe. *Journal of Mental Science*, **101**, 239–266.

LAUBSCHER, B. J. F. (1937) *Sex, Custom and Pathology: A Study of South African Pagan Natives*. London: Routledge.

46   Littlewood

LEE, S. (1996) Reconsidering the status of anorexia nervosa as a Western culture-bound syndrome. *Social Science and Medicine*, **42**, 21–34.

LEFF, J. *et al* (1987) Influence of relatives' expressed emotion on the course of schizophrenia in Chandigarh. *British Journal of Psychiatry*, **151**, 166–173.

LEWONTIN, R. C., ROSE, S. & KAMIN, L. J. (1984) *Not In Our Genes: Biology, Ideology and Human Nature.* New York: Pantheon.

LITTLEWOOD, R. (1984) La migration des syndromes liés à la culture. *Psychopathology Africaine*, **20**, 5–16.

—— (1985) Jungle madness: Some observations on expatriate psychopathology. *International Journal of Social Psychiatry*, **31**, 194–197.

—— (1991) Against pathology: The new psychiatry and its critics. *British Journal of Psychiatry*, **159**, 696–702.

—— (1992) DSM–IV and culture: Is the classification intentionally valid? *Psychiatric Bulletin*, **16**, 257–261.

—— (1993*a*) Ideology, camouflage or contingency?: Racism in British psychiatry. *Transcultural Psychiatric Research Review*, **30**, 243–290.

—— (1993*b*) *Pathology and Identity: The Work of Mother Earth in Trinidad.* Cambridge: Cambridge University Press.

—— (1993*c*) Culture-bound syndromes: Cultural comments. In *Working Papers for the DSM–IV Cultural Committee* (eds J. E. Mezzich, A. Kleinman & H. Fabrega). New York: American Psychiatric Press.

—— (1994) Verticality as the idiom for mood and disorder: A note on an eighteenth-century representation. *British Medical Anthropology Review*, **2**, 44–48.

—— (1995) Psychopathology and personal agency: Modernity, culture change and eating disorders in South Asian societies. *British Journal of Medical Psychology*, **68**, 45–63.

—— (1996) Ethnopsychiatry. In *Encyclopaedic Dictionary of Social and Cultural Anthropology* (eds A. Barnard & J. Spencer). London: Routledge.

—— & Lipsedge, M. (1982) *Aliens and Alienists: Ethnic Minorities and Psychiatry.* Harmondsworth: Penguin.

—— & —— (1987) The Butterfly and the Serpent. *Culture, Medicine and Psychiatry*, **11**, 289–335.

LOUDON, J. (1959) Psychogenic disorder and social conflict among the Zulu. In *Culture and Mental Health* (ed. M. K. Opler). New York: Macmillan.

LUGARD, F. D. (1929) *The Dual Mandate in British Tropical Africa.* Edinburgh: Blackwood.

LYONS, M. (1992) *The Colonial Disease: A Social History of Sleeping Sickness in Northern Zaire 1900–1940.* Cambridge: Cambridge University Press.

MCCULLOCH, J. (1994) *Colonial Psychiatry and the African Mind.* Cambridge: Cambridge University Press.

MADDEN, R. R. (1857) *Phantasmata or Illusions and Fanaticisms of Protean Forms Productive of Great Evils.* London: Newby.

MALHOTRA, H. K. & WIG, T. (1975) Dhat syndrome: A culture-bound sex neurosis. *Archives of Sexual Behaviour*, **4**, 519–528.

MALINOWSKI, B. (1927) *Sex and Regression in Savage Society.* London: Routledge.

MANGAN, J. A. (ed.) (1993) *The Imperial Curriculum: Racial Images and Education in the Colonial Experience.* London: Routledge.

MANNONI, O. (1950) *Psychologie de la Colonisation.* Paris: Seuil.

MARS, L. (1946) *La Lutte Contra La Folie.* Port-au-Prince: Imprimerie de l'Etat.

MAUSS, M. (1926) A definition of the collective suggestion of the idea of death. Translated in *Sociology and Psychology: Essays* (M. Mauss (1979)). London: Routledge & Kegan Paul.

MICHAELIS, J. D. (1814) *Commentaries on the Law of Moses* (trans.). London: Rivington.

MOREL, B. A. (1860) *Traité Des Maladies Mentales*. Paris: Masson.

NEUTRA, R., LEVY, J. E. & PARKER, D. (1977) Cultural expectations versus reality in Navaho seizure patterns and sick roles. *Culture, Medicine and Psychiatry*, 1, 255–275.

O'BRIEN, H. A. (1883) Latah. *Journal of the Royal Asiatic Society (Straits Branch)*, 11, 143–153.

OSBORNE, M. A. (1994) *Nature, the Exotic and the Science of French Colonialism*. Indianapolis, IN: Indiana University Press.

OXLEY, T. (1849) Malay amoks. *Journal of the Indian Archipelago and Eastern Asia*, 3, 532–533.

PARKER, S. (1960) The windigo psychosis. *American Anthropologist*, 62, 602–655.

PRICE, G. B. (1913) Discussion on the causes of invaliding from the tropics. *British Medical Journal*, ii, 1290–1297.

PRINCE, R. (1960) The 'brain fag' syndrome in Nigerian students. *Journal of Mental Science*, 106, 559–570.

RICHARDSON, A. & HOFKOSH, S. (eds) (1996) *Romanticism, Race and Imperial Culture*. Indianapolis, IN: Indiana University Press.

RITENBAUGH, C. (1982) Obesity as a culture-bound syndrome. *Culture, Medicine and Psychiatry*, 6, 347–364.

RIVERS, W. H. R. (1924) *Magic, Medicine and Religion*. London: Kegan Paul and Trench & Trubner.

ROHEIM, G. (1950) *Psychoanalysis and Anthropology: Culture, Personality and the Unconscious*. New York: International Universities Press.

RUSH, B. (1799) Observations intended to favour a supposition that the black colour (as it is called) of the Negroes is derived from the Leprosy. *Transactions of the American Philosophical Society*, 4, 289–297.

SACHS, W. (1937) *Black Hamlet*. London: Bles.

SARGANT, W. (1973) *The Mind Possessed: from Ecstasy to Exorcism*. London: Heinemann.

SCHNEIDER, K. (1959) *Clinical Psychopathogy* (5th edn, trans. M. W. Hamilton). New York: Grune and Stratton.

SELIGMAN, C. G. (1928) The unconscious in relation to anthropology. *British Journal of Psychology*, 18, 373–387.

—— (1929) Sex, temperament, conflict and psychosis in a Stone Age population. *British Journal of Medical Psychology*, 9, 187–228.

SHWEDER, R. A. (1985) Menstrual pollution, soul loss and the comparative study of emotions. In *Culture and Depression* (eds A. Kleinman & B. Good). Berkeley, CA: California University Press.

SIMONS, R. C. (1985) Nature and nurture: Belief and behaviour in the culture-bound syndromes. In *The Culture-Bound Syndromes: Folk Illnesses of Psychiatric and Anthronoloaical Interest* (eds R. C. Simons & C. C. Hughes). Dordrecht: D. Reidel.

—— & HUGHES, C. C. (eds) (1985) *The Culture-Bound Syndromes: Folk Illnesses of Psychiatric and Anthronoloaical Interest*. Dordrecht: D. Reidel.

TAGUIEFF, P. A. (1988) *La Force du Prejugé: Essais sur le Racism et ses Doubles*. Paris: La Decouverte.

THOMAS, K. (1983) *Man and the Natural World: Changing Attitudes in Britain 1500–1800*. London: Allen Lane.

TOOTH, G. (1950) *Studies in Mental Illness on the Gold Coast*. Colonial Research Publication No.6. London: HMSO.

VINT, F. W. (1932) A preliminary note on the cell content of the prefrontal cortex of the East African native. *East African Medical Journal*, 9, 30–55

WARNER, R. (1985) *Recovery from Schizophrenia: Psychiatry and Political Economy*. New York: Routledge and Kegan Paul.

WEINSTEIN, E. (1962) *Cultural Aspects of Delusion*. New York: Free Press.

WILLIAMS, E. A. (1994) *The Physical and the Moral: Anthropology, Physiology and Philosophical Medicine in France 1750–1850.* Cambridge: Cambridge University Press.

WILLIAMS, R. (1958) *Culture and Society, 1780–1950.* London: Chatto and Windus.

WING, J. K. (1978) *Reasoning About Madness.* Oxford: Oxford University Press.

WITTGENSTEIN, L. (1958) *Philosophical Investigations.* Oxford: Blackwell.

YAP, P. M. (1951) Mental diseases peculiar to certain cultures. *Journal of Mental Science*, **97**, 313–337.

—— (1974) *Comparative Psychiatry: A Theoretical Framework.* Toronto: Toronto University Press.

YOUNG, A. (1995) *The Harmony of Illusions: Inventing Post-Traumatic Stress Disorder.* Princeton, NJ: Princeton University Press.

3 Epidemiology and social issues

KAMALDEEP BHUI

Editors' introduction

This chapter examines research as a useful way to improve health care for ethnic minority communities. The introduction focuses on questions of 'what is valid research?' and how it is different from 'valuable' research, that is valuable to the subjects of study. The nature of epidemiology and its suitability as a paradigm in culturally effective mental health service research are discussed. Other social research paradigms are introduced as an alternative approach. Bhui highlights the definitions of race, ethnicity, culture and 'class of the person' as a way of selecting the correct research variable. Socio-anthropological and epidemiological de-constructions of 'ethnicity' illustrate the limitations of applying ethnic categories in mental health research. The relationship of ethnic to cultural variables emphasises the difficulties of conducting cultural research in place of ethnic research. The focus then moves on to determinants of health and ill health, that is risk factors in cross-cultural research. Bhui uses religion as an example of such a risk factor and demonstrates how a reductionist approach to religion leads to a complex interpretation of findings. He then goes on to life events, a different form of risk factor, in a cross-cultural context. The focus then shifts to specific classical sources of bias in epidemiology: selection bias, information bias and observer bias. Measuring psychiatric disorder across cultures is a complex subject of debate; there is often disagreement about the most appropriate criterion measure and 'valid measures'. This approach is contrasted with the 'relativistic' socio-anthropological perspective of using ethnographic methods modified for epidemiological surveys. Examples of such approaches are presented.

The ethnic minority population in the UK has increased rapidly since the Second World War and to an even greater extent since the 1950s. Minority ethnic people represented 1% of the population in 1961; this had grown to 5.5% of the population at the time of the last census in 1991 (Peach, 1996). As minority groups with a diversity of languages, customs and health beliefs become more prominent in British society, and as the second and third generations legitimately see themselves as British citizens in terms of their sense of belonging as well as their nationality, inequalities of health care across ethnic groups are less tolerated.

Much of the literature linking ethnicity to health is based on two assumptions: that the health status of minorities is poorer than indigenous groups and that minority groups underutilise health services (Gillam, 1990). These assumptions seem to stem from social class-related inequalities being extrapolated; there is an over-representation of minority groups amongst the unemployed and poor. Such extrapolations do not accommodate unique sets of circumstances experienced by minorities: racism, refugee status, linguistic isolation, break up of families and bereavement experiences.

Valid research or valuable research findings

Research into race, ethnicity and health has a long history. Bhopal (1997) recently examined whether race, ethnicity and health research is actually racist or good science. Racist motivations as well as racist consequences of research pepper the research record of academic institutions. There are examples of mental health research on both sides of the Atlantic which are exemplary in their racist intentions and application. For example, such research has been used to limit immigration (Bolt, 1971), to explain poor performance of Black people in the educational system (Brah, 1996) and to explain the wish of slaves to run away from their masters' plantations (Ahmad, 1993). Such research is understood by invoking explanations such as 'poorly planned', culturally insensitive, ethnocentric in its planning and interpretation. The consequence is that little change has been witnessed in the day-to-day quality of services received by minority groups. In some instances research was used to support race-based policy which disadvantaged Black and other ethnic minority people (Stepan, 1982; Fernando, 1988; Brah, 1996;). The temptation is to suspiciously disregard all research as inherently racist, because research can perpetuate the disempowerment familiar to minority groups. Despite high-quality research which clearly captures these inequalities (Thornicroft *et al*, 1999), the powerlessness continues to be articulated by a lack of information, a lack of a voice to influence purchasers and providers, a lack of confidence in an institutional system of care and planning that historically has disadvantaged minorities, and finally a lack of hope that change-effecting procedures are available and accessible to the public. As soon as there is a potential to misuse power then Black and other ethnic minority groups' historical experience of oppression is activated to oppose and expose the oppressive force. A persistent sense of deprivation in health, housing, employment and what I shall call 'civilised oppression' manifests itself in outrage each time a further piece of research is attempted; yet research remains essential to understand and remedy inequality. At best the outcome of research is a greater awareness of the limitations of existing services and skills, but at worst a series of stereotypes are reinforced or the research findings are never translated into effective remedial action. Health service research (HSR) is heralded as a solution to implementation and evaluation of policy, planning and research as well as the assessment of population or individual treatment methods. As such, HSR is clearly a discipline which can link effective service development with research.

Mental health services and the epidemiology of race, culture and ethnicity

Epidemiology as a branch of medicine is well placed to make critical contributions to the new era of health service and health care evaluation. Epidemiology informs health policy and planning and helps generate an understanding of the laws governing health and disease. Therefore, epidemiology, as a way of gathering information and by its use of powerful methodologies to tease out subtle effects between risk factors and states of health, carries a significant responsibility. The application of epidemiology to the study of the relationship between race, ethnicity and culture and states of health and disease receives much attention (Balarajan *et al*, 1991; Balarajan & Raleigh, 1992; Balarajan, 1996; Bhopal, 1997). Mental health clinicians are also trying to use epidemiology as a tool to improve health among ethnic minorities (Cochrane & Sashidharan, 1996).

The scientific basis of psychiatry is now firmly established and reflected in the increasingly collaborative research initiatives to discover better ways of caring for the mentally ill. However, mental health research into Black and other ethnic minority issues has received a very serious attack from the public and professionals (Wilson, 1993; NHS Task Force, 1994; Sashidharan, 1994; Mental Health Foundation, 1995).

Choosing the right research paradigm

The whole process of researching race and ethnicity as risk factors, and carrying forward recommendations to improve health care, has been 'derailed' by scepticism about the validity of biomedically determined research methodologies (Kleinman, 1987; Krause, 1989; Bhui, 1997). Mental health researchers in an attempt to produce better scientific research unexpectedly encounter other academic disciplines which also have a contribution to the assessment of better ways of caring for the mentally ill. Mental illness itself can be understood from a diversity of theoretical and experiential perspectives, and so attempts to improve on existing mental health research and service provision should also take full account of the many windows to the mind. The social sciences in particular have added much to our understanding of the mind and have a central humanising effect on strictly quantitative research-based theoretical and pragmatic innovations. Other chapters in this volume focus on anthropology, which has had such a powerful, critical role on the 'opposition benches' of debate. This chapter attends to epidemiology as a discipline which contributes to mental health research where race, ethnicity and culture are central to hypotheses. I examine the epidemiological approach in a critical light using my own fieldwork to illustrate problems inherent in applying research methodologies across cultures. Thus, the notions of ethnicity, race and culture will be discussed as classes of the 'person' and as markers of adverse or favourable outcomes. I will examine the research challenge posed by studies of culture, ethnicity and mental ill health. Some of the key findings in national and international studies will be briefly presented to illustrate and anticipate how the interpretation of data from such studies can lead to erroneous conclusions if the cultural dimension is examined from only the epidemiological perspective and with a eurocentric interpretative frame of reference. The role of life events and ways of studying their impact across cultures is in its infancy. I will look at some of the key difficulties of life event research applied across cultures.

Race, ethnicity, culture and classes of the person: choosing the research variable

Epidemiology is defined as the study of the distribution and determinants of health-related states and events in specified populations and the application of this study to the control of health problems (Last, 1995). Last continues in elaborating on this definition: 'study' includes observational, analytic, hypothesis testing, surveillance and experiments. Distribution refers to analysis by time, place and 'classes of person'. Descriptive epidemiology is that branch of the discipline which examines distributions of disease to basic characteristics such as age, gender, race, social class, geographical location. These few definitions already create many contradictions of classification. Classes of person is a sufficiently general term that the investigator is left to define what classes of person they are studying. Indeed the chosen classes of person were initially racial categories; the political implications of using race-based categories, the realisation that the genes responsible for phenotypic racial variations were only a very small proportion of the total genetic material, the recognition that genetic variation between races was less than that within races and the recognition that environmental factors were also instrumental in the pathogenesis, perpetuation, and alleviation of many psychiatric disorders all gave way to the use of ethnic categories. These were used bluntly and often were inappropriately interpreted such that biological or genetic factors were never mentioned overtly, but nonetheless were generated as potential explanations for the findings of difference.

Although much race research uses ethnic categories, the flaws of this approach have only been examined more recently (Smaje, 1995; McKenzie & Crowcroft, 1996). Ethnic categories were used in the census for the first time in 1991; the problems of designation necessitated the construction of algorithms which remain imperfect. Although this represents an attempt to move away from racialised research where notions of racial inferiority might insidiously emerge, the semantic halo carried by ethnic categories retains a strong racial component. When people examine ethnic variations they are, therefore, implicitly examining racial variations and explanations under the guise of a more culturally valid variable. The meta-message of ethnic research often includes a racial message as well as an intended cultural message. After all, ethnic categories are extremely poor scientific markers of cultural and behavioural lifestyle patterns. They are not stable over time and different ethnic categories may be designated by the researcher and the individual themselves (Senior & Bhopal, 1994). The exact definition of a specific ethnic group varies across continents. Thus American researchers use terms such as African–American while in the UK terms such as Black British are deployed. How does an African–American differ from a Black British person? One might conclude that they differ in their immediate country, environmental social history and culture, and among other things the accent and way of viewing the world that their children acquire. Such cultural factors are often overlooked for the more race-centred notions such that Black groups are considered to be more similar regardless of their location on the globe. 'Asians' in the USA refers to people from all over the Asian continent, whereas in Britain the term was used to describe those who according to the British perspective were conspicuously representative of Asia, that is Indian and Pakistani immigrants. Black groups were often all lumped into a single Black category as if individuals from say Kenya were similar to those from the Caribbean. Indians, Pakistanis, Bangladeshis and Sri Lankans all would fall under the rubric Asian. Racial similarity is unmistakable, but this generates the illusion that these peoples are so similar that they can be treated identically. Much early research in Britain even used categories of 'New Commonwealth and Pakistan' as a class of person. This is clearly a meaningless term in terms of race and culture; it only represents 'otherness' to White British culture and sustains colonial categories as if they were meaningful concepts with predictive power when applied to mental ill health, help-seeking and utilisation of services. This dilemma presented by classes of person is not restricted to non-White populations, but it seems that most debates about comparative pathologies are centred on non-White populations. Thus, there have been comparatively few studies on Irish immigrants who comprise a substantial proportion of the British population. Is it appropriate to locate people from Scotland, Northern Ireland and London in the same cultural framework? Certainly there are many similarities but the differences are often neglected. A 24-year-old White woman that I interviewed about her identity had great difficulty classifying herself. Her parents were from Southern Ireland but she was born in London. At times she felt as if she did belong to London and had some pride in this sense of belonging; at other times she very much felt Irish and wanted not to be identified as British or as White UK. She could not designate herself in accord with any specific category.

Constructions of ethnicity

The inherent inadequacies of these ethnic categories is surprising given the recognition that an ethnic group is supposed to be:

> "a social group characterised by distinctive social and cultural tradition, maintained within the group from generation to generation, a common history and origin, and a sense of identification with the group. Members of the group have distinctive features in their way of life, shared experiences, and often a common genetic heritage" (Last, 1995).

Thus, ethnicity has been used as a dummy variable, as a crude proxy for complex combinations of social, economic and cultural circumstances (Benzeval *et al*, 1995). Ethnicity appeared to have value as a marker of deprivation (Jarman, 1983) as if somehow deprivation was a property of ethnic minorities and where there were ethnic minorities then deprivation was somehow inevitable. Ethnic categories are ascriptively mobilised by members of society to mediate and represent the dominant tensions to do with identity and belonging and deprivation and injustice (Gupta, 1995). Thus, they are inevitably fluid and accommodate the required configuration which is of value to those deploying the category. Researchers using ethnicity data must be clear as to what ethnicity in their study actually means:

> "What is central to ethnicity construction is not some objective criterion of cultural distinctiveness from another. Ethnicity is a 'process' whereby one group constructs its distinctiveness from another. Processes of boundary construction vary over time and are subject to economic, political and social pressures; bonds of ethnicity may shift in meaning, be strengthened, weakened or dissolved and they will have varied salience at different points in an individual's and group's biography" (Brah, 1996).

Other more stable characteristics such as place of birth, first language and religion are also of value as cultural markers, but none by themselves can predict an individual's sense of belonging and/or indeed the sum total of health-promoting or adverse lifestyle and behaviour.

The definition of ethnicity must be made explicit and it must be of direct relevance to the hypotheses under study. It may be that ethnic origin is not an appropriate class of person if the hypothesis is about culture, religion and language rather than race. Some of my fieldwork has been focused on Punjabis, that is people who are of Asian origin (Indian subcontinent origin in British schema: see Brah, 1996) and have the region of Punjab as the source of their customs, language and identity. Of course, British-born second-generation Punjabis may not speak Punjabi – but they do identify with 'Punjabiness' through their experience of, and internalisation of, religion, kinship, song, dance, food, festivals, dress, taboo, folk stories and history. However, the category of Punjabi, although a subcategory of Asian is distinct from being Indian. Punjab spans the Indian and Pakistan border. So Punjabis either side of the border have similar cultures in some respects, but there are also differences. Pakistani Punjabis are Muslim, whereas those from India are mainly Sikh. This is a historical inheritance. Both Pakistani and Indian Punjabis speak Punjabi, but their respective languages are written with different scripts (Urdu and Gurmukhi).

Hence, there is never an easy descriptor which captures a group's culture presuming it to be homogenous; as long as the class of person used is suited to the hypothesis under study then the purpose of the study will be served, but this does reduce the usefulness of comparative data.

How does ethnicity relate to culture?

Ethnic groups may approximate sufficiently to culture if the sample from which the ethnic group is drawn contains an already self-selected cultural group. For example, studying Asians in the East End of London around Commerical Road would yield samples of mainly Bangladeshi Muslim peoples. Asian samples drawn from Southall would yield mainly Punjabi Sikh and Hindu people. One could not easily compare the findings from each of these studies without attending to the cultural differences; yet that is precisely what has been done in much mental health research on ethnic minorities. Hence data that indicate differences of prevalence between say Asian and other ethnic groups are not easily interpreted. Indeed, any preventive policy or activity which emerges from data which does not take account of subtle cultural variations is likely to be flawed. Any data need to be meaningfully interpreted and translated into culturally syntonic policy and intervention. This relies on a better culturally grounded understanding of lifestyle, health beliefs and behaviour. This is the first example of many that illustrate how applying a purely epidemiological approach to other cultures without sufficient cultural knowledge leads to erroneous inferences and limited conclusions. Any recommendations intended to improve the health care of Asians would be defeated by abutting against overlooked barriers with culturally specific and circumscribed origins. Such barriers to changing lifestyle are often perceived by health professionals to be a nuisance, but are in fact so resistant to change that they have, in the context of immigration and survival, become a part of the cultural identity of the group. Advice to alter lifestyle may be experienced as an attack on culture- and identity-sustaining behaviours. In the pilot phase of epidemiological surveys and other forms of research activity involving cultures there must be significant attention to these hurdles in research designs, hypotheses, and 'class of person' categories. Some ways of doing this have already been explored in Chapter 2 and will not be discussed in detail here. The link between ethnicity and ethnic identity and notions of self are also explored in other chapters. It is clear that if ethnic origin is to be used as a key variable in research as a class of person, its validity as a measure of culture, identity, religion and race must be fully ascertained and relies on the context in which the sample will be recruited.

Determinants of health and ill health

Determinants are the physical, biological, social, cultural and behavioural factors that influence health (Last, 1995). There is a separation between classes of person and cultural or behavioural determinants. It is the distinction between classifications of classes of person and the operationalisation of culture and behaviour that has been overlooked by researchers. 'Determinants' refers to variables which might explain research findings and may or may not have an aetiological significance. Bhopal (1997) laments at the repeated demonstration of associations between a variety of potential determinants; he is critical of what he called 'black box epidemiology' whereby aetiological mechanisms are never established. There are repeated demonstrations of associations with little attention to how potential aetiological mechanisms could be further explored such that preventive action could be taken. In order to generate sound data on which primary, secondary and tertiary interventions may succeed, one needs confidence in the scientific method. In the context of multicultural work I now wish to turn to a more basic flaw in existing methodologies: the reliability and validity of measuring determinants of health; these are more commonly called exposures or risk factors.

Risk factors can be broadly understood as risk markers, risk determinants and modifiable risk factors.

> "Risk factors are aspects of the person's behaviour or lifestyle, an environmental exposure or an inborn or inherited characteristic which on the basis of epidemiological evidence is known to be associated with health-related conditions considered important to prevent. The term is also used loosely to refer to (a) an attribute or exposure that is associated with an increased probability of a specified outcome such as the occurrence of disease; this is a risk marker; (b) an attribute or marker that increases the probability of occurrence of the disease or other health-related outcome; this is a determinant; (c) a determinant that may be modified by intervention to reduce the probability of occurrence of disease or other specified outcome; this is a modifiable risk factor" (Last, 1995).

The selection of risk factors that emerge from a diversity of methodologies should be based on some hypothesis that the risk factor of interest is a marker or determinant. I have discussed how ethnicity is often used as a proxy for the apparent measurement of something that is racial and cultural and presumed to be reliable and valid. I have also outlined how this is not always the case. The same difficulty arises with the definition and measurement of risk factors which are determinants of ill health.

Religion as a risk factor

I will use religion as an example of a cultural and behavioural proxy which might be a risk factor for states of ill health. If it were so, then one would need to open the black box and identify the aetiological determinants (which could be specific foods or behaviours for example). The problems of definition and measurement could be extended to other such proxy measures; for example, social class (Benzeval *et al*, 1995). Psychometrics as applied to religion are in their infancy (Crossley, 1995), and although some researchers have developed and used questionnaires and instruments to examine specific hypotheses about religious belonging and mental health (Bergin, 1983; Koenig, 1992), I do not intend to review the literature pertaining to the findings of these studies. The notion that religious belonging can be compartmentalised into discrete risk factors which will contain all the 'active' ingredients which could explain a therapeutic or adverse effect is highly problematic. Larson *et al* (1992) advocate a multidimensional measure of religiousness to take account of meaning, ceremony, ritual, social support and relationship with a deity. Each of these dimensions can then be separately examined for a statistical association with psychiatric diagnosis. Yet by packaging such a complex phenomenon into discrete measures one risks omitting important aspects of the original religious experience which are not reflected in the risk factors identified. What is clear is that a single categorical measure of religious belonging such as Christian, Muslim or Hindu is too simplistic as there are likely to be behaviours or ways of thinking which are common to all of these different religious groups.

Response bias and misclassifications

Extending epidemiological principles to the measurement of how religiosity affects emotional states seem useful yet is highly problematic. The presence or absence of a belief in God is readily ascertained, but even an apparently simple question such as 'do you believe in God?' can be answered in accord with the individual's immediate perception of what the questioner is wanting to examine. An answer of 'No', for example, may yield a research categorisation of 'not religious', yet that individual may involve themselves in many weekly activities which originated in religious doctrine and therefore fulfil a religious function. Religious knowledge or metaphor is, for example, universally accessible as decor, art and music; such experience also penetrates our developmental experiences and comes to represent the common sense lay knowledge of how the world works and how to live in it successfully (Geertz, 1979).

Religious thought and imagery can pervade societal rules even where individuals will describe themselves as irreligious (Wilson, 1992). School curricula, for example, include annual festivals (Christmas, Easter) which are celebrated by Christian and non-Christians as well as the non-religious. Each individual's religiosity is a personal experience which may not be consciously articulated; enquiry may yield an individual's perception of what is a socially desirable and morally sanctioned response. The actual risk factor may be an internal state or experience which is not subject to direct scrutiny. The question remains: can such responses usefully act as proxy risk factors for more stable yet elusive attributes of religiousness? If the answer is yes, then these proxy responses could still be used as indirect measures of 'true' degrees of religiousness, assuming that in reporting their experience all individuals similarly distort their true experience (religious and irreligious); if there is distortion it may be sufficiently powerful in magnitude or direction of bias to mask and dominate any subtle true effects of religious activity on mental well-being.

At one extreme two religious systems of thought that could not be compared as the risk factors pertinent to each would not be shared factors but unique to each. If Cultures A and B share a particular religious attribute both in its existence and in the invested meaning then a further problem arises. Where would we find the cut-off points or categorical distinction to distinguish disease from religion? These distinctions would have to be coincidental with local grounded distinctions in religious behaviour or belief. Thus, going to church daily might be considered as religious as going to theosque daily. Would praying five times a day be more religious than praying once a day for both Christians and Muslims? If God exists should we be able measure units of Godliness? Should we not be able to at least measure the impact of God? Common sense notions convey that validity is not a function of statistics but of social and experiential realities. This is especially important where the subject of research is beyond a direct sensory scrutiny. Even medical practice has components of interventions which are beyond precise definition. Furthermore, in my own work it is clear that asking Punjabis how often they pray leads to a variety of responses which are partially determined by their religious group and what they know they 'should be doing' and partly by their level of education, social class and familiarity with other sources of relieving distress. Muslim women do not go to a place of worship – so if attendance was a measure of religiosity, it would not be useful in discriminating between those who were religious from those who were not. One is then left with an example of how measurement across cultures is not easily achieved if one's intention is to compare data across cultures. If these flawed or misclassified variables were used it would lead, at best, to a loss of power, assuming the misclassifications were random; at worst an erroneous result would emerge if the conceptual validity of the questions was poor. The indigenous concepts of religion (or any risk factor to be used) must, therefore, be fully explored. A pilot study should include not only a 'test' of the instruments in their translated form (see below), but also a more ethnographic approach to really grasp some of the conceptual inequivalence which would influence the validity of the risk factors being sought.

Life events in multicultural epidemiology

In different ethnic, cultural and racial groups risk factors are often treated as having the same impact on the disease state, whereas the class of person variable is the one considered to be responsible for any apparent differences found between ethnic and racial groups. In some instances this might be a valid assumption. For example, it could be assumed that poverty for a Black Caribbean man living in London has a similar impact as on a White English man living in London. This of course could be a flawed assumption. The origins of poverty could be similar, but as soon as they are in any way grounded in racial, ethnic or cultural difference, then the impact of poverty has to be understood in the light of these narratives. The impact of higher rates of unemployment in Black groups may more adversely affect mental health if more members of a family are unemployed and there is little hope for future employment; data indicating much higher rates of unemployment among Black people supports the view that potential buffers to distress are therefore compromised. Similarly racial (inter-racial) attacks might be considered to have the same impact on Black men as would be expected if the victims were White men. This does not necessarily follow. A racial attack on a Black man in Britain takes place where the majority society is White. The Black man may suffer a series of minor insults as everyday experience. This means that the overall 'exposure' to racial events is higher. The White man as a victim of racial abuse may be just as immediately traumatised. But would the consequences of such an occurrence be similar? Attacks would be less frequent, unexpected and the White man would have more psychosocial buffers, living on average in better housing and with a greater likelihood of the assailant being remembered if they were Black (Burney & Pearson, 1995). These are complex phenomenon. Just because we do not understand the sequence and there has been little work done on the differential impact of life events across cultures does not mean that such factors are not operative. Unfortunately, such potentially more illuminating scrutiny of determinants rarely takes place; risk factors are often assumed to be similarly handled by different classes of person and to have a similar impact on the probability of a psychiatric disorder. Thus, invoking the Brown & Harris (1978) model, protective and vulnerability factors may well differ across racial and cultural groups (Hussain *et al*, 1997). There is a marked lack of attention to less familiar culturally determined protective and vulnerability factors. Appraisals of coping behaviour using culturally determined help-givers and culturally sanctioned internal states of mind are also lacking. Belliapa (1991) for example demonstrates how prayer acts as a common form of coping for isolated Bangladeshi women in the East End of London. Of course the types of life event to which ethnic minorities in the UK are exposed also differ; for example, many refugees will have had experiences of traumatic migration, torture, separation, grief, isolation and persecution. Selecting appropriate measures of these events will involve developing new instruments which are suited to capture the experience of adversity of this group of people in its full cultural context; grafting the isolated experience onto methodologies and concepts of health and disease originating in other cultures risks losing information and generating flawed conclusions.

Selection bias and the dynamics of recruitment

All epidemiological surveys pose unique problems of study design and data collection. The problems of design are usually addressed at the planning stage in consultation with a diversity of professional colleagues each with their unique contribution in terms of academic and theoretical expertise as well as experience of fieldwork. However, both in the planning stages and once the data collection is under way, a number of potentially serious problems can arise. I will not be discussing the issues of selection bias generally, but will limit myself to issues to do with studies among ethnic minority communities. I will illustrate some of the hurdles with examples from my own fieldwork as well as recent local and national studies.

A common problem in many studies examining the impact of ethnicity is the actual numbers of people recruited from any one ethnic group. The large Office of Population Censuses and Surveys (1995) study of national psychiatric morbidity had insufficient power to make any consistent conclusions about the role of ethnicity. This is inevitable if random samples of the population are taken, as ethnic minorities represent 5.5% of the national population; any conclusions that are drawn are limited as the individuals comprising the ethnic minorities in the sample were drawn from across the UK. Such a low representation of all ethnic groups makes any meaningful comparison impossible, especially if in accord with the discussion about the validity of ethnic groups as a proxy for culture and lifestyle, specific ethnic, cultural and geographical attributes were to be investigated for either their health promoting effects or their adverse effects on health. That is not to say that useful information can never be learnt from studies with small numbers of a particular ethnic or cultural group, but the precision of the estimates of effect is likely to be poorer and hence the overall confidence with which ethnic group differences can be accepted as real findings rather than chance findings is reduced. In addition the sample and hence the findings might not be representative of the population they were intended to represent.

The fourth national morbidity survey carried out by the Policy Studies Institute has attempted to improve on this by focusing specifically on certain ethnic groups. It is a national survey comprising over 5000 ethnic minority respondents that is fully representative of Caribbean, Indian, Pakistani and Bangladeshi groups, and also has a comparison group of almost 3000 White respondents (Nazroo, 1997). Ethnic, language and gender matching of researcher and subject have been used in this survey to maximise response; however, individuals may prefer someone from a different ethnic group if they are concerned about their own community knowing about their health status. Yet if the research interview cannot be conducted in a linguistically competent manner, then the interviewee is likely to become confused and lose faith in the value of the work to him or her or the community. Cooperation will be lost and this is especially problematic if the interview is lengthy. Ethnic, gender and language matching is surely beneficial, but there are instances in which interviewees prefer someone from outside their culture; or indeed despite English being second language, they prefer to speak in English. Bilingual researchers are to be preferred, as the language competence of the interviewee is not known before the research interview and involving a second or third interviewer with the right language skills is likely to lead to more people withdrawing from the study. Certainly this has been my experience among English and Punjabi patients. Whenever we altered the interviewer to be a better match linguistically, and this did not always mean a racial, ethnic or gender match, the quality of the information was improved but people had to readjust to the second interviewer; if a second-stage interview were to be done, then the unknown second interviewer was also more readily refused consent to complete the interview as no rapport (or trust) had been established. For optimal outcomes in terms of completing research interviews and minimising non-completers, multilingual competency was more important; this meant not only a working knowledge of the languages, but familiarity with dialect and the rules of social behaviour.

Recruitment of the chosen 'class of person' becomes a major part of the planning as ethnic minority groups are under-represented in any official statistics except those involving custodial care or imprisonment. The 1991 census is known to have under-enumerated young men and especially young Black men. This presents several problems.

First, estimates of the base population are flawed and estimates of rates of disorders which use this denominator are likely to be overestimated. This is one reason often advanced to explain the apparently higher rates of conspicuous psychosis among minority groups; however, this alone cannot explain the findings but could bias them, making the excess risk of schizophrenia among African and Caribbean people appear even greater than it actually is.

Second, if one wishes to locate the targeted cultural or ethnic group one would not have reliable local demographic data on which to base chosen study sites and sources of sample. Lloyd (1993) showed that African and Caribbean people were under-represented among general practice attenders identified to have a psychiatric disorder, although ethnic minorities do attend their general practice as often, if not more often, than the White population for physical disorders (Gillam *et al*, 1989). The study base population must be carefully selected to include the target 'classes of person' in sufficient numbers to enable the hypotheses to be tested with sufficient power. Random samples of general practice surgery attenders, or hospital attenders or in-patients could be used, but there needs to be some selection of the general practice surgeries, hospitals or in-patient units such that the target population is a significant proportion of the attenders. The danger is that in the process of selecting a particular surgery or hospital, one is inadvertently selecting a biased sample that is not truly representative of the intended study population. This is especially a problem of case–control studies where one chooses study sites on the basis of ethnicity to maximise samples sizes and the efficiency of data collection. It is possible that if one is aware of how the selected sample might differ from the population from which the sample was drawn then some allowance could be made for this in the analysis; but more often than not one might be biasing the sample without being aware which sample characteristics are represented in the sample in a biased manner.

Choosing control groups can also introduce bias in the study design. For example, let us say one uses control patients who are recruited from the same geographical region (or general practice, etc.), in which it is known that that minority groups live in more deprived and adverse conditions than non-White groups. The control group may not be truly representative of the total population from which it is drawn. Census data can be used to identify regions in which particular ethnic groups reside, but data regarding the location of specific cultural or religious groups is not so easily available. Preliminary enquiries should be made of general practitioners (GPs), social services, voluntary organisations and any other significant local organisations which may be able to give such information. Local residents will also have views about the specific places where certain groups live. Local knowledge can be rich in terms of discovering cultural subgroups.

Throughout this process there is a research-driven urgency to recruit enough people from the chosen 'class of person' to meet the study objectives. Care is required. 'Selection bias' is an error that is due to systematic differences in characteristics between those who are selected and those who are not. Selection bias can invalidate generalisations and conclusions about the study findings. One source of selection bias is refusal to participate or attrition of recruited subjects. Those who are easily recruited might be quite different from refusers. If the refusers form a significant part of those approached then those subjects who participate and provide data will be different from the original population that was to be recruited. Educational level, social class, familiarity with surveys, work commitments and shortage of time, feeling physically unwell and unable to complete an interview all influence participation. For example, those in employment are known to be healthier and if they have insufficient time to complete an interview, then completers will be generally less healthy than the general population. In multicultural and ethnic minority populations there are specific concerns about ensuring that all those who could be potentially included are included and not excluded because of linguistic, cultural, geographical, social class or ethnic differences and factors associated with these characteristics.

Some examples of problems in research: Punjabis in general practice

In my own work many Punjabis had a variable level of literacy in English and Punjabi. Often they were reluctant to admit to illiteracy and would even pretend to read questionnaires. It was evident that self-report questionnaires could not be used unless the questions were read out and the questionnaire completed by the researcher. I found interviewees keen to satisfy, please and to keep on good terms with their GPs despite my reassurance that the research findings would not influence their future care. They were keen to secure as much help as possible in their battle to obtain the social benefits to which they were entitled; some were suspicious of the intentions of the survey despite several explanations at regular intervals throughout the interview. Many wanted to ensure that it would not jeopardise existing or future benefits. Some would not sign the consent forms, saying they would answer questions but signing forms, even if they understood their contents, was not acceptable as that would commit them to 'something' in a world in which they were not confident that information was truly confidential. Many suspected that, despite my best intentions, in a computerised world somehow the information would get back to government and they might see some disadvantage in the future when I would be long gone. Some people, especially the elderly, welcomed social contact and wanted to chat, but not to do the survey; so they would suggest the researcher fill in the forms with whatever was appropriate, trusting the researcher to be a better judge of what was required by officialdom. After all, the researcher they saw as educated and more familiar with forms.

Many patients projected familial roles onto the person of the researcher. They would by very polite and friendly, expressing affection and consciously stating that to them the researcher was like a son or daughter. However, this imposed a restriction on the researcher in that they were then expected to behave like a son or daughter; not to question their word; indeed, if the patient did not want to answer in the manner required they would not, and if questioned with more tenacity they would feel offended. Subjects also expected the researcher to give them lifts home and to act on their behalf in court or to do other favours. I shirked my responsibilities when asked to help find marriage partners! Not to help with these tasks was considered disrespectful or offensive; the research interview could therefore end in a number of non-research activities in order to maximise cooperation, whereas the English subjects generally understood surveys and the purpose to which they would be put. English subjects were, therefore, more trusting of the reseacher's intentions. A further subgroup of patients could make no sense of the psychosocial questions, feeling that they were irrelevant and stupid and of no value to them. They wanted immediate improvements in health – not lengthy surveys following which nothing changes. They would then refuse to answer or, while answering the questions, become silent and just not say anything. This arose either because they were reluctant to answer direct questions which seemed to them irrelevant, painful or offensive; they would then suggest it was of no value to the researcher as they could not provide the necessary responses. They would point out that it was not helpful to the researcher to continue and the interview would be abruptly ended. On some occasions husbands would not allow wives to participate. Similarly, in view of social taboos of contact between men and women, women would be more reluctant to encourage subsequent contact by a home visit or telephone call if the interview had not been completed. Those not participating may well be either excessively morbid or less morbid or differ in other respects from those who completed the interviews; not taking this into account could bias the findings.

Information bias and observer bias

If English is a second language, only those fluent in English are usually recruited. The quality of the data gathered is questionable if the standard of English among participants was so variable that they responded to poorly understood questions in the manner in which they imagined the interviewer wanted them to answer. The interviewer, on the other hand, might have assumed full understanding of the question and trusted that the instructions about the study and information about its purpose had been understood. Those with English as a second language might interpret questions in a subtly different way than would a native English speaker. Even if accurate literal translations of material are made available, the semantic halo, the onomatopoeic impact, the context of common usage and the associated slang meanings of a single sentence or word would inevitably differ between two languages. Flaherty *et al* (1988) described a methodology for adapting instruments. Five dimensions of cross-cultural equivalence were sought: content, semantic, technical, criterion and construct. Translation and back-translation has become an accepted approach but more consideration is needed to determine whether the newly translated instrument actually taps equivalent phenomenon in both cultures (Flaherty & Hoskinson, 1989).

Furthermore, the hidden reasons for patients not participating may still be operative amongst responders and influence their answers; responses from the target groups would be subject to different social cues, social sanctions and roles, leading to different handling in comparison to the control group. Where judgements about the presence or absence of specific experiences is made by the observer, these also will be subject to the influence of stereotypes and deductive inference especially if there are linguistic differences. Much effort in the piloting stages must be devoted to ensuring procedural equivalence in the study design and execution. The response bias induced by unfamiliar methods of data collection, such as pencil-and-paper tests, face-to-face interviews, telephone interviews and interviews at home or with other family members, should also be considered. Clearly it is difficult for the interviewer to be blind to ethnicity and in some instances the subject's religious affiliation is readily deduced. Bias is minimised if the study procedures are as structured as possible with clear operationalised criteria whenever the researcher's judgement is required. Independent raters could be used to rate diagnosis or to transcribe and rate data blind to the ethnic, racial, cultural and religious origin of the subject. Using taped interviews is one way of examining inter-rater reliability, but this may add a further hurdle, as my experience has been that many individuals, irrespective of their cultural origin, do not like to be taped.

Measuring psychiatric disorder across cultures

The measurement of psychiatric disorder has been subject to intense critical scrutiny in recent years. It is of great importance for any type of study design; case–control studies require a strict operationalised definition of a 'case' such that cases and controls can then be included. Cohort studies need a clearly defined outcome. The problem in psychiatry is that the presence or absence of psychiatric disorder is not an all or nothing phenomenon; patients with common anxiety and depressive states have been regarded as having symptoms on a continuum (Goldberg & Huxley, 1980). Defining cases then becomes a judgement and only of importance if caseness is actually predictive of altered treatment response or outcome or aetiology.

The debate in cross-cultural psychiatry has always had a socio-political edge to it, as the findings of an excess incidence of schizophrenia among African–Caribbeans (Harrison *et al* 1988; Wessley *et al*, 1991; King *et al* 1994) were startling when first described. These findings were ascribed to genetic causes, misdiagnosis and racism within psychiatry, and more recently as a true effect but with social origins (Fernando, 1988; Bhugra *et al*, 1997). The debate became more heated, more theoretical and cross-disciplined with the publication of influential papers by Arthur Kleinman (1987) and Roland Littlewood (1990); these authors persuasively argued for a radical rethink of the nosological construction of psychiatric disorders from a bio-medical perspective. The essence of these critiques was that the existing manner in which psychiatric diagnosis is made, and the measurement of psychiatric disorder across cultures using the same instruments which have only been validated in one culture, is a flawed methodology and would always yield biased findings. The way forward was mapped out as a process of discovering new nosologies: indigenous concepts of mental distress and culturally coherent groups identifying for themselves what is a illness, sickness and in need of therapeutic attention. Leff (1990) argued that this was like "throwing the baby out with the bathwater". If psychiatry were to be reinvented for each cultural group, then much of the decades of research findings would be regarded as flawed; a better approach was to examine the limitations of existing methodologies and of existing research data and then ensure that future research were improved in its cultural validity. Meaningful findings could be built upon. Thus, the scene was set for a number of creative approaches.

At one extreme one finds that epidemiological surveys using existing research instruments are easily mounted. For example, the International Pilot Study of Schizophrenia (IPSS) has been much quoted and examined from a diversity of interpretative approaches (World Health Organization, 1973). The Present State Examination and its associated computerised programme were used in the IPSS. Disorders which met strict criteria for schizophrenia were identified in a variety of countries. There was diagnostic variability between American and British psychiatrists. American psychiatrists diagnosed schizophrenia more often and mania and depression less often. This was confirmed as a diagnostic practice in a separate study (Cooper *et al*, 1972). In Moscow, psychiatrists had a broad concept of schizophrenia. In addition there was four-fold variability in the broad diagnosis of schizophrenia between centres, but insufficient power to demonstrate difference in narrowly defined schizophrenia. These findings were very much accepted and highlighted as indicating that narrowly defined schizophrenia had a similar incidence across the globe.

There were, however, less attended to aspects of the findings which indicated that schizophrenia had a better prognosis in developing countries than in the UK. The IPSS has been subject to much critical scrutiny for using the PSE across cultural groups (Kleinman, 1987; Fernando, 1988); the main arguments have been that by using this instrument one is looking for the accepted diagnosis of a narrowly defined condition, and hence one is likely to find only what one looks for. There may be other symptoms and diagnostic entities which make local sense and are described as illness locally; these would not be identified by the PSE or other diagnostic systems (Fabrega, 1992).For example, first-rank symptoms in other ethnic groups can occur in other states of distress and might be heavily weighted to infer a schizophrenia diagnosis, but they vary between ethnic and cultural groups in any case (Chandrasena, 1987). That is the culture-specific relativist argument, that one cannot compare cultures using the same one-culture terms of reference; it was used to invalidate the universal approach that this thing called schizophrenia exists all over the world. The findings of a different prognosis also makes for interesting hypotheses that there may be other environmental factors which influence prognosis and hence potentially the 'natural history' of the disorder (McKenzie & Crowcroft, 1996); a genetic and strictly biomedical model does not then make sense as it should be universally applicable (Bhugra *et al*, 1997). With these thoughts in mind several recent research centres have generated solutions.

Ethnography and epidemiology

Ethnographic fieldwork using 'participant observation', key informant interviews and focus groups have all been advocated as a means to identify 'culture-centred narratives' of states of emotional distress. Indeed, the case for non-quantitative health research where cultural difference is explored is powerfully gaining momentum as a valid approach where truly culture-sensitive information is sought in the form of 'meanings' rather than numbers (Kelleher & Hillier, 1996). Focus groups are one way of acquiring data rich in description, concepts and idiom. These do not inform the public health agenda directly about amount of morbidity but can (a) inform the construction of culturally sensitive instruments which take into account unique concepts of health, illness and idioms of distress, and (b) inform any preventive strategy to be truly culturally sensitive in that policies and preventive strategies are not doomed to failure because they directly or indirectly conflict with culture-based directives and rules of living. Existing instruments can be adapted with new items or completely new instruments constructed and validated against existing ones (Patel & Todd, 1996). This appears to be happening for common mental disorders such as anxiety and depressive states but less so for psychosis where existing instruments are still largely deployed.

There are instruments emerging which attempt to combine epidemiological rigour and structure with the flexibility of adapting to local narratives of mental disorder. The Explanatory Model Interview Catalogue (EMIC) has been developed to elicit illness perceptions, beliefs and practices in different cultural settings and seeks to obtain an 'insiders' view of illness (Weiss *et al*, 1992). The methodology attains both generalisability and validity by combining an invariant interview format composed of consistent categories of inquiry and standard general questions including locally specific queries that can vary between different studies. In the UK Lloyd *et al* (1996) have constructed a similar semi-structured questionnaire which elicits health concepts and help-seeking behaviour. It is used to categorise intact verbatim responses. It ensures that qualitative data is available as intact excerpts of responses to non-directive questions about health and help-seeking, while at the same time enabling these excerpts to be categorised such that quantitative analysis using each subject's responses is also possible. The assumption is that the preordained categories really do reflect meaningful concepts within the study population's culture. Here a purely qualitative study using ethnographic principles would help to validate the categories.

It is clear that epidemiologists need to learn more of qualitative data analysis, its use with quantitative data and the limitations of each approach. Such an approach also affords a more sophisticated examination of the distribution of health beliefs in the study populations. The influence of health beliefs on help seeking, levels of morbidity, patterns of self-treatment and patterns of interaction with health services all become accessible to scrutiny. This is especially important in psychiatry where diagnosis is a label given to a complex of social, psychological and biological changes of function. The label is intended to convey the necessary treatment type and response. If the essential building block of diagnosis, that is the experience of illness, differs between cultural groups such that distinct cultural groups deal with disease and illness processes in different ways, then diagnosis itself becomes less meaningful. It is assumed to be meaningful because little work has been done to examine how features other than diagnosis differ between cultural groups. For example, McKenzie & Crowcroft (1996) reported that African–Caribbeans may have a better prognosis schizophrenia than do White British patients. Do we conclude that their illness state is still the same disease process as is schizophrenia? It had been argued that societal responses to the mentally ill do determine their prognosis. This was the explanation often advanced for the better prognosis of schizophrenia in the developing world. Hence to define a distinct psychiatric disorder as an outcome can only be done if it is understood to be a valid nosological concept within the culture under study. On the whole this is more reliably the case with psychosis where changes of behaviour and communication seem to alert relatives and friends of the sufferer of their illness state in all cultures. The subjective experience across cultures remains a mystery and if it is the subjective experience which determines outcome then an objective diagnostic label is meaningless as a marker of prognosis and treatment.

Broadly diagnosed schizophrenia might include conditions which are more responsive to changes of environment, explaining the variability of incidence across cultures and continents. Where depressive and anxious reactions are concerned, they seem to be more culturally determined. Hence whenever psychiatric diagnosis is used across cultures and whenever instruments intended to measure the degree of distress are used consideration must be given to an evaluation of the culturally enriched and experience-near view of the disorder; firstly one must see if it exists in the society or class of person as a distinct meaningful entity, whether there are other aspects of behaviour or thought associated with it from the culture of origin of the subject. Where there are similarities one should ensure that they are carefully defined alongside dissimilarities. Hence states of distress should not be assumed to be the same because that is the most economical and readily adopted conclusion; careful redefinition of the disorder is necessary and the limitations of assumptions of universality should always be considered. For example, depression may not involve the same emphasis on guilt or sense of worthlessness in other cultures. In response to 'do you feel inferior to others as if you are second rate' many of the Punjabis I have interviewed are puzzled. They see this state of being as something to be aspired to as part of respect for elders, peers and betters in the context of interpersonal humility. A Euro-American psychiatric interpretation would immediately locate this in a depressive diagnostic framework.

Conclusions

The subject matter of psychiatry is not as easily handled clinically or in a research context as are more specific medical and surgical conditions. It is a speciality of subjective experience and conversation, and the interaction of these with biology and the environment. All these affect the total psychosocial well-being of the individual. As illness experience and mental disorders are so intertwined in psychiatry the process of measuring aspects of internal experience as if they were objective measurable entities with a physical or even a psychical reality is hazardous. In order to overcome this limitation of quantitative research and clinical activity based on quantitative data, one really needs to develop a new methodology which ensures the complexity and necessary flexibility of approach are not overlooked for more tried and trusted Eurocentric methodologies. This has been partially successful and required considerable adaptation and cooperation between previously unconnected disciplines; indeed, these disciplines, such as sociology, anthropology, epidemiology and statistical science to name but a few, are only unconnected in the organisational sense rather than having little overlap in terms of their subject matter. The danger of not pursuing the subject of epidemiology in cross-cultural settings in its full complexity is that the findings of studies will not be readily translated into preventive programmes and nor will they effectively inform planners of health services. If changes of approach are not examined cross-cultural epidemiology will continue to be an inexact application of Eurocentric methodologies.

References

AHMAD, W. I. U. (1993) *Race and Health in Contemporary Britain.* London: Open University Press.
BALARAJAN, R. (1996) Health trends ethnicity and variations in the nation's health. *Health Trends,* **27,** 114–119.
—— & RALEIGH, V. S. (1992) The ethnic populations of England and Wales: the 1991 census. *Health Trends,* **24,** 113–115.
——, RALEIGH, V. & YUEN, P. (1991) Hospital care among ethnic minorities in Britain. *Health Trends,* **23,** 237–239.
BELLIAPA, J (1991) *Illness of Distress? Alternative Models of Mental Health.* Confederation of Indian Organisations: London.
BENZEVAL, M., JUDGE, K. & SMAJE, C. (1995) Beyond class, race and ethnicity: deprivation and health in Britain. *Health Services Research,* **30,** 163–177.
BERGIN, A. E. (1983) Religiosity and mental health: a critical re-evaluation and meta-analysis. *Professional Psychology Research and Practice,* **14,** 170–184.
BHOPAL, R. (1997) Is research into ethnicity and health racist, unsound or important science? *British Medical Journal,* **314,** 1751–1756.
BHUGRA, D., LEFF, J., MALLETT, R., *et al* (1997) Incidence and outcome of schizophrenia in Afro-Caribbeans and Asians in London. *Psychological Medicine,* **27,** 791–798.
BHUI, K. (1997) London's ethnic minorities and the provision of mental health services. In *London's Mental Health* (eds S. Johnson, *et al*). London: King's Fund Institute.
BOLT, C. (1971) *Victorian Attitudes to Race.* London: Routledge and Keegan Paul.
BRAH, A. (1996) *Cartographies of Diaspora. Contesting Identities.* Routledge: London.
BROWN, G. & HARRIS, T. (1978) *Social Origins of Depression.* London: Tavistock.
BURNEY, E. & PEARSON, G. (1995) Mentally disordered offenders: finding a focus for diversion. *Howard Journal,* **34,** 291–313.
CHANDRASENA, R. (1987) Schneider's first-rank symptoms – an international and interethnic comparative study. *Acta Psychiatrica Scandinavica,* **76,** 574–578.
COCHRANE, R. & SASHIDHARAN, S. P. (1996) Mental health and ethnic minorities: a review of the literature and service implications. In *Ethnicity and Health: Reviews of Literature and Guidance for Purchasers in the Areas of Cardiovascular Disease, Mental Health and Haemoglobinopathies.* CRD Report 5. NHS Centre for Reviews and Dissemination Social Policy Research Unit, University of York.
COOPER, J., KENDALL, R. E., GURLAND, B. J., *et al* (1972) *Psychiatric Diagnosis in New York and London.* Maudsley Monograph 20. London: Oxford University Press.
CROSSLEY, D. (1995) Religious experience within mental illness. Opening the door on research. *British Journal of Psychiatry,* **166,** 284–286.
FABREGA, H. (1992) Culture, social structure, and quandaries of psychiatric diagnosis: a Vietnamese case study. *Psychiatry,* **55,** 230–249.

FERNANDO, S. (1988) *Race and Culture in Psychiatry*. Worcester: Billing & Sons Ltd.

FLAHERTY, J. A., GAVIRA, F. M., PATHAK, D., *et al* (1988) Developing instruments for cross cultural psychiatric research. *Journal of Nervous and Mental Disorder*, **176**, 257–263.

—— & Hoskinson, K. M. (1989) Cross-cultural research on schizophrenia and depression. *Current Opinions in Psychiatry*, **2**, 35–40.

GEERTZ, C. (1979) Suz: the Bazaar economy of Sefron. In *Meaning and Order in Moroccan Society* (eds C. Geertz., *et al*). Cambridge University Press.

GILLAM, S. (1990) Ethnicity and the use of health services *Postgraduate Medical Journal*, **66**, 989–993.

——, JARMAN, B., WHITE, P., *et al* (1989) Ethnic differences in consultant rates in urban general practice. *British Medical Journal*, **299**, 953–958.

GOLDBERG, D. & HUXLEY, P. (1980) *Mental Illness in the Community*. London: Tavistock.

GUPTA, D. (1995) *The Context of Ethnicity. Sikh Identity in a Comparative Perspective*. Delhi: Oxford University Press.

HARRISON, G., OWENS, D., HOLTEN, A., *et al* (1988) A prospective study of severe mental disorder in Afro-Caribbean people. *Psychological Medicine*, **18**, 643–657.

HUSSAIN, N., CREED, F. & TOMENSON, B. (1997) Adverse social circumstances and depression in people of Pakistani origin in the UK. *British Journal of Psychiatry*, **171**, 434–438.

JARMAN, B. (1983) Identification of underpriviledged areas. *British Medical Journal*, **286**, 1705–1709.

KELLEHER, D. & HILLIER, S. (1996) *Researching Cultural Differences in Health*. Routledge: London.

KING, M., COKER, E., LEAVEY, G., *et al* (1994) Incidence of psychotic illness in London: comparison of ethnic groups. *British Medical Journal*, **309**, 1115–1119.

KLEINMAN, A. (1987) Anthropology and psychiatry. *British Journal of Psychiatry*, **151**, 447–454.

KOENIG, H., COHEN, H., BLAZER, D., *et al* (1992). Religious coping and depression among the elderly, hospitalized medical ill men. *American Journal of Psychiatry*, **149**, 1693–1700.

KRAUSE, I. B. (1989) Sinking heart: a Punjabi communication of distress. *Social Science and Medicine*, **29**, 563–575.

LARSON, D. B., SHERRILL, K. A., LYONS, J. S., *et al* (1992) Associations between dimensions of religious commitment and mental health reported in the *American Journal of Psychiatry* and *Archives of General Psychiatry*: 1978–1989. *American Journal of Psychiatry*, **149**, 557–559.

LAST, J. M. (1995) *A Dictionary of Epidemiology* (3rd edn). Oxford: Oxford University Press.

LEFF, J. (1990) The 'new cross-cultural psychiatry': a case of the baby and the bathwater. *British Journal of Psychiatry*, **156**, 305–307.

LITTLEWOOD, R. (1990) From categories to contexts: a decade of the 'new cross-cultural psychiatry'. *British Journal of Psychiatry*, **156**, 308–327.

LLOYD, K. (1993) Depression and anxiety among Afro-Caribbean general practice attenders in Britain. *International Journal of Social Psychiatry*, **39**, 1–9.

——, Jacob, K. S. & Patel, V. (1996) *The Development of the Short Explanatory Model Interview and its Use Among Primary Care Attenders*. London: Institute of Psychiatry.

MCKENZIE, K. & Crowcroft, N. S. (1996) Describing race, ethnicity and culture in medical research. *British Medical Journal*, **312**, 1054.

——, VAN OS, J., FAHY, T., *et al* (1996) Psychosis with good prognosis in Afro-Caribbean people now living in the United Kingdom. *British Medical Journal*, **311**, 1325–1328.

MENTAL HEALTH FOUNDATION (1995) '*Towards a Strategy*'. *Proceedings of a Seminar on Race and Mental Health*. London: Mental Health Foundation.

NAZROO, J. (1997) *Ethnicity and Mental Health*. London: Policy Studies Institute.

NHS TASK FORCE (1994) *Black Mental Health: A Dialogue for Change*. London: NHS Management Executive, Mental Health Task Force.

OFFICE OF POPULATION CENSUSES AND SURVEYS (1995) *The Prevalence of Psychiatric Morbidity Amongst Adults aged 16–64 Living in Private Households in Great Britain*. Surveys of Psychiatric Morbidity in Great Britain. Report No. 1. London: HMSO.

74 *Bhui*

PATEL, V. & TODD, C. (1996) The validity of the Shona Version of the Self-Report Questionnaire and the development of the SRQ–8. *International Journal of Methods in Psychiatric Research*, **6**, 153–160.

PEACH, C. (1996) Introduction to: Ethnicity in the 1991 Census. Vol 2: *The Ethnic Minority Populations of Great Britain.* (ed. C. Peach). London: HMSO.

SASHIDHARAN, S. (1994) The need for community-based alternatives to institutional psychiatry. *SHARE Newsletter*, **7**, 3.

SENIOR, P. & BHOPAL, R. S. (1994) Ethnicity as a variable in epidemiological research. *British Medical Journal*, **309**, 327–329.

SMAJE, C. (1995) *Race, Ethnicity and Health.* London: King's Fund Institute.

STEPAN, N. (1982) *The Idea of Race in Science.* London. MacMillan Press.

THORNICROFT, G., DAVIES, S. & LEESE, M. (1999) Health service research and forensic psychiatry: a black and white case. *International Review of Psychiatry*, **11**, 250–257.

WEISS, M., DOONAGAJI, S., SIDDHARTHA, D., *et al* (1992) The Explanatory Model Interview Catalogue. (EMIC): contribution to cross-cultural research methods from a study of leprosy and mental health. *British Journal of Psychiatry*, **160**, 819–830.

WESSLEY, S., *et al* (1991) Schizophrenia and Afro-Caribbeans: a case-control study. *British Journal of Psychiatry*, 159, 795–801.

WILSON, B. (1992) *Religion from a Sociological Perspective.* Oxford: Oxford University Press.

WILSON, M. (1993) *Britain's Black Communities.* London: NHS Management Executive. Mental Health Task Force & King's Fund Centre.

WORLD HEALTH ORGANIZATION (1973) *Report of the International Pilot Study of Schizophrenia.* Geneva: World Health Organization.

4 Race, prejudice and ethnic identity

RAY COCHRANE

Editors' introduction

In this chapter Cochrane proposes to consider racial prejudice in Britain at the end of the twentieth century – its nature, its forms and its impact on prejudice against groups – particularly in the context of psychiatric services. This will involve a consideration of how prejudice affects the way people develop their own identities, the way they interact with people from different racial backgrounds and the way in which services are perceived and utilised. He also reviews the evidence relating to the way in which services which have been developed largely for a White majority society may, inadvertently, be perpetuating racial stereotypes and disadvantages even though the large majority of the staff in these services would vehemently deny any racist motivation or intention.

Racism

There are three linked concepts which it is important to distinguish in discussing the psychological basis of race relations in contemporary society. 'Racism' is a particular kind of discrimination and refers to behaviour that stems from a belief that people can be differentiated mainly, or entirely, on the basis of their ancestral lineage. In addition, racism leads to the assumption that people are to be treated differently because some groups are considered inferior, and some groups superior, to others. 'Prejudice', on the other hand, is a negative attitude towards ethnic or minority groups held in the absence of evidence for these attitudes, or in the face of contradictory evidence. While prejudice produces a tendency to respond to people in terms of their race or ethnic status rather than as individuals, it does not necessarily produce overt behavioural effects. 'Race thinking' underlies both racism and prejudice. It is an assumption that race is an objective fact which can be used to explain differences between individuals and groups, rather than that race is an artificial, socially constructed label which can be used in many different ways. Race thinking does not necessarily imply biological differences between groups and does not necessarily imply notions of inferiority and superiority, but race thinking often leads to these conclusions.

One final definition is important as it refers to a concept which lies at the heart of how people think, behave and define themselves and how they perceive and react to other people – 'culture'. Marsella & Kameoka (1989) define culture as

> "shared learned behaviour that is transmitted from one generation to another for purposes of human adjustment, adaptation and growth. Culture has both external and internal referents. External referents include artifacts, roles and institutions. Internal referents include attitudes, values, beliefs, expectations, epistemologies and consciousness".

Cultural heritage, therefore, determines the way in which people experience reality, understand their social world, define what is moral and immoral, explain various phenomena (including madness), and shape their sense of self (perhaps as an individual, perhaps as part of a collective).

Although culture in this sense is inherited, it is not inborn but is learned afresh by each generation during the normal process of socialisation. In a 'multicultural' society such as Britain it must be recognised that a middle-class, White woman whose family ancestry can be traced back to the Norman conquest will not experience the world, have the same attitudes and values, or have the same way of relating to others as, say, a foundry worker from Bangladesh. Recognising these differences is of neutral value. However, there has been, and is, an enormous temptation to construe them in terms of superior/inferior, better/worse, right/wrong, normal/deviant. Where this response influences our attitudes it becomes prejudice, where it influences our behaviour it becomes racism.

This chapter will deal mainly with the concept of prejudice, but will also consider racism as a result of prejudice. Racial prejudice in one form or another is very common. The exact extent of prejudice is uncertain and the level that is detected in various studies depends largely on the definition of prejudice that is used. What is important about the findings that prejudice is very common, however, is that any explanation for it must recognise that it is a statistically 'normal' psychological phenomena and not an aberration limited to a minority of unstable or disturbed people (Cochrane, 1991). Although theoretically prejudice can be manifested by any group or individual in society, most of the psychological research, and most of the political significance that surrounds racial prejudice, refers to that kind of prejudice held by the more powerful groups towards the less powerful groups in our society. Thus, in contemporary Britain we are concerned with the prejudice of White towards Black people.

Prejudice finds many forms of expression. The most extreme manifestations, such as attempts at genocide, political and legal systems which systematically discriminate against some groups in favour of others (such as was found in South Africa until the mid-1990s), and physical assault or damage to property based on racial motives would be universally regarded as indicators of prejudice. So, probably, would incidents of open discrimination even where this is illegal, and the suggestion made by some extreme right-wing political parties that certain people should be 'repatriated', or deported, without their consent purely because of the ethnic group to which they belong. These manifestations of prejudice have largely disappeared from the mainstream of life in many (but not all) areas in Britain and will have only an indirect effect on the interaction between patients and psychiatric services.

Then there is a middle band of behaviour and style of interaction which many objective observers would consider to result from prejudice but which the person exhibiting these behaviours might well deny stem from prejudice. An example of this is 'disguised discrimination' where making decisions based on so called 'objective criteria' lead to the consequence that some racial or ethnic groups are disadvantaged compared with others. In employment, for example, situations often arise where the choice between candidates for a job, or for promotion, is influenced by factors which are not directly relevant to that job promotion. Thus, an employer would not say 'we are not going to employ you because you are Black' but might say 'I am sorry that we cannot offer you the post because your English is not good enough' or more likely would say 'I'm sorry this post has already been filled' when this is not the case. A recent survey by the Manpower Services Commission of Job Centres in London showed that, on average, a White worker had to apply for eight jobs before he/she was offered one. A Black worker had to apply for 13 jobs before one was allocated, and an Asian worker had to apply for 16 jobs before he or she was taken on. There is more than a suspicion that racism in this form does still operate within the health service and affects, for example, promotion prospects in both clinical and managerial spheres.

Another insidious manifestation of prejudice which those who engage in often deny is a result of prejudice is 'adjectival racism'. This is the attachment of a racial or ethnic identifying adjective to a person or group where this confirms a stereotype in terms of the behaviour being described. Certain sections of the popular media are past-masters at playing this game and many of the stereotype-confirming incidents are absorbed into popular lore. Examples are referring to a 'Jewish business' or 'Black muggers'. Then there are the stories which resurface from time to time about homeless families being placed in expensive hotels while more permanent accommodation is found and where the family is identified as 'Asian' when this is totally irrelevant to the real point of the story.

An even more covert (and likely to be denied) form of prejudice is the making of racial jokes within one's own group and not directed at individuals of other groups. Thus, the telling of West Indian stories or Irish stories in gatherings in a public house when no people from those groups are present is often regarded as harmless fun. Justification is often sought by reference to professional comedians who peddle such jokes about their own ethnic group. Clearly, the jokes are only funny because they are based on stereotypes and they confirm the prejudiced view that some groups are more stupid, more venial or more victimised than others.

Then there is a form of prejudice which is often described as tolerance or merely reporting objective 'facts' with no apparent question of opinion. In 1982, for example, the Metropolitan Police first released certain types of crime statistics broken down by suspected ethnic origin of the perpetrator. This could only be 'suspected ethnic origin', because only a very small minority of perpetrators were actually apprehended by the police. Not all types of crime were broken down by ethnic group; indeed, it was only those categories of crimes where the police and public held stereotypes of ethnic involvement that were released in this way. Thus, for example, street robberies, commonly known as 'muggings', were broken down by the ethnic origin of attacker, but burglaries and car thefts were not. The day after the police released these data the *Daily Mail* (11 March 1982) carried the following piece:

> "Britain faces the chilling spectre of an increase in the type of crime which plagues the ghettos of America. This was the blunt message from Scotland Yard yesterday as the extent of Black involvement in violent crime was revealed for the first time".

These two sentences cleverly imply that crimes committed by Black people were on the increase – when there was absolutely no evidence of this – and that these data had been available for some while but were only 'revealed' yesterday because of their serious nature. Neither the police nor the *Daily Mail* reported that Black people in London are very much over-represented among the victims of violent crimes.

A further example is the way in which the various Immigration Acts introduced by governments of both political parties from the 1960s onwards have been justified. Defending the 1971 Act, Reginald Maudling, the then Home Secretary, said that the main reason for restricting the number of non-White immigrants into Britain was to produce 'peace and harmony'. He went on, "we must give reassurance to the people who were already here before immigration, that this will be the end and there will be no further large scale immigration". This comes very close to saying that it is immigration which causes racial resentment and the solution is to prevent non-White people from entering Britain so that the psychological tranquillity of the White indigenous population can be protected.

Over the past two decades the more blatant expressions of prejudice have reduced among the more educated and liberal sections of White society and many public institutions (including the NHS) have taken public and overt stands against racism. In many sectors, racial discrimination, racial abuse and even racist jokes in the workplace are disciplinary offences and, even more importantly, are likely to lead to disapproval and ostracism by colleagues. It is tempting for those of us who work in such environments to start to believe that prejudice and racism are declining forces in our society. However, there are several very strong indications that this is an over-optimistic assumption. First, the statistics of racial disadvantage in health, education, politics, the economy, the legal system, etc. are stark. To take but a few examples: unemployment rates among Black minorities in Britain are two to three times higher than for the White population; Asians are 50 times, and African–Caribbeans 36 times, more likely than Whites to be subject to racially motivated attacks; 6% of the White population live in overcrowded conditions compared to 43% of the Bangladeshi population; although less than 5% of the population of Britain is from ethnic minority groups, 16% of the prison population comes from ethnic minority groups – in 1991 there were no Black or Asian High Court Judges and only two of 450 Circuit Court Judges were not White. The list of such comparisons could go on and on.

Even as blatant racism has reduced, another form of racism has taken its place – the so-called 'new racism'. The new racism does not rest upon beliefs in biological differences between races or even assertions of superiority and inferiority but on an assumption that cultural differences produce incompatibilities which, while regrettable, have to be recognised. The newer forms of prejudice avoid skin colour as a marker, and antipathy towards out groups is symbolically or indirectly expressed. Indeed, many White people may say, and on one level believe, that they are not racist and may even endorse sentiments that are very progressive. They may at the same time, and also genuinely, have beliefs and engage in behaviours which can be construed as racist. So, for example, they may send their children to private schools ('for a better education, not to avoid mixing with Black children you understand'). They may be concerned about immigration because of the pressure it puts on housing, jobs and other services or because further immigration threatens to upset race relations. They may be strongly opposed to positive discrimination, or 'affirmative' action as it is known in the USA, because they believe that all discrimination is bad, even that which is in favour of groups who have suffered disadvantage in the past.

The modern form of racism is not accompanied by expression of negative sentiments about other groups but the absence of positive sentiments and a fear of, and aversion to, certain cultural differences, which may be taken as symbols of racism. In the 1970s there was uproar because Sikh motorcyclists and Sikh bus drivers were excused wearing the otherwise mandatory headware even though this did nothing directly to threaten the safety or comfort of White people who were forced to wear crash helmets or peaked caps. In the 1990s some school governing bodies got worked up over the issue of whether Muslim girls should be allowed to wear trousers to school when White girls were not.

Perhaps the most memorable example of the new racism was Margaret Thatcher's famous statement on immigration prior to the 1979 general election which struck a cord with so many White Britons:

> "People are really either afraid that this country might be rather swamped by people with a different cultural background. The British character has done so much for democracy, for law, and done so much throughout the world, that if there is any fear that it might be swamped, people are going to react and be rather hostile to those coming in".

Mrs Thatcher, an avowed anti-racist, was not directly expressing racist sentiments in this passage, nor did she ever mention colour. In a symbolic way, however, her statement is clearly racist. She expressed an 'understanding' for those who might appear to be racist by being in favour of restricting immigration. She also explicitly contrasted the 'British character' which had done so much for democracy, law, etc. (conveniently overlooking the British characters' penchant for imperialism and oppression) with the characters of those who might swamp it, which presumably have nothing of similar benefit to offer.

New or symbolic racism is most marked by an emotional defence of 'traditional values', an inability to tolerate cultural differences, and a belief that 'birds of a feather flock together'. Traditional values include hard work and independence of the state and a belief that as Britain is a fair and just meritocracy, minorities should 'work their way up' and not receive special help or protection. There may also be a belief that an employer dare not discipline an idle or incompetent worker if that person is Black because of over-intrusive race equality legislation. Intolerance of cultural differences is evidenced by beliefs that if immigrants want to live here, then they should adopt the 'British' way of doing things and abandon traditional dress and customs. The belief that people from different ethnic/cultural backgrounds prefer to keep a certain separateness is also widespread. In *Race through the 90s* (Commission for Racial Equality, 1993) the example is given of the defence of maintaining an all White working mans' club in the Handsworth district of Birmingham where 60% of the local population is Black; "surely you're entitled to your own little island whatever your colour or creed? In Handsworth we're the minority. Why should we bow to the majority?" In all these ways ostensibly non-prejudiced statements and actions betray underlying racist attitudes.

Ethnic identity

Clearly no one is born with an intact sense of self and who they are. Indeed, very young children are not self-reflective and so have no subjective identity in the adult sense. Quickly, though, children do acquire an understanding of who they are and where their place is in the social environment. They gain a sense of self, an ability to imagine alternative selves and alternative realities, and the ability to see things from other peoples' perspectives. In other words children develop a self-concept and are able to distinguish the self from the non-self. This transition from a non-self-conscious into a self-conscious being is what distinguishes humans from all other species and from all machines yet developed. Self-consciousness brings many positive advantages – the ability to separate a real and constant inner life from superficial sets of outward behaviours (i.e. what we really are is contained inside, how we behave is determined by the social environment – we have several public selves, but only one true self); the ability to rehearse what may happen in the future and reinterpret events of the past; the ability to be self-motivated, to plan and achieve a predefined goal. There are also negative aspects of self-awareness – for example, the ability to deliberately deceive others and to be unhappy and dissatisfied.

Two related developmental factors are crucial to the development of a self-concept: the acquisition of language and social interaction with other people. Imagine a hypothetical child locked for ever inside a machine that automatically catered for all its physical needs. Without any human contact would this person develop self-awareness, a concept of self and self-esteem? Could this being imagine an alternative existence, could they be happy or unhappy? Without interaction with other people the developing human being would never become a person in any meaningful sense. I will not dwell on the role of language in self-awareness as, although it is central to the development of self in the vast majority of people with normal sensory facilities, it may not be absolutely essential in the same way as is social intercourse.

We develop a knowledge of ourselves though interpreting our interactions with others, trying to understand what their actions mean and what they really think about us. This is a difficult task and almost as difficult to explain because of the numerous feedback loops involved. The very young child typically receives more or less unconditional positive regard from its parents as well as comfort and nurturance. But very early he or she will encounter other people (an older sibling, for example) who may not be quite so consistently affectionate. Soon the child will encounter other children with whom they may come into conflict and who may exhibit very negative feelings towards them, even temporary hatred and violence. The parents' doting may become tempered by the needs of other children and their own needs. Some constraints will be put on the child's behaviour and parents may restrict, punish or make signs of affection contingent on the display of approved behaviour. All through these experiences the child will be developing a self-concept by absorbing the responses of others towards him or her and looking for meaning in those responses.

Children who meet unconditional approval in all circumstances will develop a very positive self-image (or high self-esteem), so much so that they may be regarded by others later in life as smug and self-satisfied, conceited even. However, by this time the responses of others towards them will be filtered through the interpretations placed upon them by the recipient and these will, in turn be influenced by self-image. So the smug, self-satisfied self will interpret rejection and disapproval as a sign of jealousy or lack of intelligence on the others' part, rather than understand his or her own social shortcomings.

After an initial and possibly brief period of infant security another child might find itself constantly regarded as something of a disappointment to its parents, criticised as a failure and constantly put down. The schema for understanding and interpreting the behaviour and comments of others developed by this child will be quite different. Here a rejection or critical comment will be taken as just one more piece of evidence of their lack of worth and confirm the low opinion they have of themselves.

Of course, most people steer a middle course and appreciate that they will encounter some positive and some negative social interactions and be able to deal with both. However, we all learn not to take things at face value and that what other people do and say needs interpretation. People do not always mean it when they say 'nice to see you' or even 'I love you'. Nor do they always mean it when they say 'I will never talk to you again' or 'I hate you'. How we interpret these utterances is filtered through our memories of previous encounters with the other and our view of other people in general and of ourselves. I offer two examples. Some psychology undergraduates experience difficulties with the statistics modules in their course. When told they have failed a statistics exam some students respond by blaming themselves for being stupid or idle. Others respond quite differently – the exam was unfair, the teaching was poor and they did not come to university to study statistics anyway. Second, a colleague tells how she criticises her daughter for her appearance and behaviour in a way that she would never do with her son. This is because the daughter has a secure sense of her own worth and identity and can accept criticism as part of a mother's role, while the son is extremely worried about how he looks and how his behaviour is seen by others, and would be devastated by criticism from his mother.

As children come to develop their own identities there are certain dimensions which get included early and others come later. For almost everyone our name is the first part of our self concept that is acquired. This is quickly followed by gender identity and then relational identities (son, brother, sister, etc.). Later other elements are acquired in relation to sport, friendships, academic performance, social partnerships, career, interests and enthusiasms. The 'Who Are You' test simply asks people to list 10 self-descriptors. These 10 words or phrases almost always include gender, relationships, occupation, personality variables and interests.

Where does ethnicity fit into the picture? Probably for a White person in an overwhelmingly White European society ethnicity is unimportant and would not figure prominently in the list of self-descriptors. For people from an ethnic minority, however, ethnicity would be more frequently mentioned. Hutnik (1991) found that 60% of Black adolescents, compared to only 26% of White adolescents, included race in their self-descriptive categories. As children, Black people in the UK will have learned that they differ in significant ways from the wider cultural norm of Whiteness partly from their own observation, partly under instruction from parents, but mainly from interaction with other people. Ethnic identity has two dimensions – that derived from with an affiliation to an ethnic group, and that derived from an awareness that other people regard you as belonging to that group and respond to you accordingly.

Of course ethnic identity is only one component of identity for members of minority groups – gender, age, relationships will also be important. The salience of the ethnic dimension in identity will vary from individual to individual and depend upon their learning history and the prevailing intergroup climate.

There may be little correspondence between the ethnic identity which the person adopts for themselves and that which other people ascribe to them. For example, a person may perceive themselves to be 'British' while most White people consider them to be 'Black'. Not only will the centrality of ethnicity in self-concept vary from one to another, but so will the meaning attached to it. Britishness may be important to many people – some people may be proud to be British, others may be ashamed.

As already indicated, it is rare, and certainly not the situation in 21st-century Britain, for all ethnic groups to have the same status, security and privileges. A dominant view of the majority is that Britain is basically a White European country with a Christian cultural heritage, and that others who have come to live here are alien in some regard and that they should either return to from whence they came or rapidly abandon their culture of origin and become acculturated to a 'British' way of life. This is the message that pervades the whole of formal and informal social structures in Britain. It can lead to problems of identity formation and doubts about ethnic dignity (Hutnik, 1991).

This challenge to the integrity of ethnic minority identity exists at all levels – God is White, the Queen is White, the Prime Minister is White, most people in positions of power and influence are White, TV and newspapers are white dominated and prone to using ethnic stereotypes. The odds are that a child's school teacher will be White. But so will be the majority of people with whom the ethnic minority child interacts on a daily basis. Gilborn (1997) reports a study of a mixed-race girls school which showed that the most common form of inter-ethnic interaction in the playground consisted of White girls shouting "You dirty Paki" or "Fuck off, Paki" at Asian girls. Many Black and Asian children in Britain experience almost routine racial harassment outside the family home. For example, one Asian girl quoted by Gilborn said that every day on her way home from college with other Asian girls she was met with chants of "Come and fuck us, Paki whores" from White boys. The girl later said, "I don't think any White person can possibly know what it is like". It would be surprising indeed if this constant racial (and sexual) abuse did not have an impact on self-identity and self-esteem. Of course, for many individuals the effect is somewhat mitigated by the support of friends and family which will give the victims legitimate alternative explanations for the experience other than that they are valueless.

The impact of racism on identity is obviously going to be greatest in the period when identity is developing but racial abuse experienced in adulthood will have a substantial psychological impact on people whose identity has already been undermined by childhood experiences of racism. A piece of racial hatemail pushed through the letter box of a Black mother read "Yuir going to learn a good lesson soon black bitch. Go back to Africa, slag. You black bastard, if I can't get you I will get your kids" (*The Independent,* 13 February 1990). Receiving this kind of threat would be frightening enough for any mother, but imagine the impact on someone who may actually have experienced racial violence, perhaps being one of only a handful of Black people on a large housing estate, and who felt they could not turn to the (White) police for protection.

Ethnic identity and mental health

There has been a substantial amount of research and theorising on the impact of racism on self-esteem, self-identity and psychological well-being – much of it from the USA. We will examine just one strand of this research here.

The work of Clark & Clark (1947) is very well known and has had an enormous impact on the way in which ethnic identity is perceived even by those who know nothing of the original research. The Clarks asked 3–7-year-old Black American children to choose between two dolls – one black, the other white. Most of the children chose the black doll when asked to choose the one most like them (but 33% chose the white doll) but they chose the white doll when asked for the 'nice doll', 'the doll that you like to play with' and 'the nice colour doll'. The Black children mainly chose the black doll when asked to indicate the 'bad doll'. One may think that this research is interesting but out-of-date and of little relevance today, having been carried out in the 1940s, pre-civil liberties, Black pride and other significant developments which have had an impact on ethnic identity. However, in Britain in the 1980s, Davey (1983) found results very similar to those found by Clark & Clark 40 years earlier in the USA. This time using life-sized photos almost all of the 7–10-year-old Black, Asian and White schoolchildren chose the appropriate ethnic stimulus when asked to choose the 'one that looks most like you'. Eighty-six per cent of White children chose the White stimulus when asked 'which one would you most like to be'. Less than half of the Black and Asian children chose their own race stimulus in response to this question with substantial proportions preferring the white stimulus. The largest proportion (though not a majority) of respondents from all three ethnic groups chose the white picture when asked for which child was 'clever' and 'worked hard'.

These and many other studies like them (see Brand *et al*, 1974; Tyson, 1985 for reviews) fed into a hypothesis of ethnic minority self-rejection, or even self-hatred, and consequent low self-esteem and psychological damage. This hypothesis was first formulated by Lewin (1948) on the theme of self-hatred among Jews. The argument was that because a particular ethnic minority group has inferior status to the majority ethnic group and is exposed from birth to prejudice and discrimination some members of the minority group internalise majority (White) values and stereotypes. They come to believe that their own ethnic group *is* inferior and develop a preference for the white group. Kenneth Clark (1965) wrote:

> "Since every human being depends on his cumulative experiences with others for clues as to how he should view and value himself, children who are consistently rejected understandably begin to question and doubt whether they, their family and their group really deserve no more respect from the larger society than they receive. There doubts become the seeds of a pernicious self- and group- hatred, the Negro's [sic] complex and debilitating prejudice against himself".

From this body of evidence an assumption was made that ethnic minority children would grow up with lower levels of self-esteem and would therefore be more vulnerable to psychological pressures as adults.

Some authors have gone further and suggested even more far-reaching consequences of growing up in a society where ethnic minority identity is stigmatised and denigrated and where prejudice and discrimination restrict opportunities for success in school and the workplace. Comer (1995), writing of African Americans, described a state of:

> "perpetual adolescence: irresponsibility; a lack of discipline; uneven, unpredictable, sometimes contradictory behaviour and the inability to take hold, follow through and achieve in the mainstream social world ... the negative overall identity leading to feelings of inferiority, inadequacy or being evil or bad, and sometimes to psychological illness, particularly depression".

However, researchers who have directly measured self-esteem levels in majority and minority ethnic groups have found very small differences on average. Even Black children who chose a white doll in preference to a black doll have self-esteem levels equivalent to their White counterparts. Of course, there will be some non-White adolescents with lowered self-esteem resulting directly from their experiences of prejudice and discrimination, but most do not have low self-esteem. It seems that even where people internalise the ethnic majority's negative stereotype of their own ethnic group, they do not necessarily apply these negative stereotypes to themselves as individuals. As an Englishman, I may fully accept the French view that, in general, the English are boring, conservative, snobbish and with low standards of personal hygiene. However, I am exciting, innovative, open-minded and very clean! In fact, this phenomenon of a distinction between own group self-rejection and personal self-esteem is probably not uncommon. So long as identification with the ethnic group is not of overwhelming importance a person may happily live with both.

Of course, some authors (e.g. Thomas, 1971; Cross, 1991) regard the acceptance of a distinction between one's ethnic group and one's self-identity as, in itself, pathological. Various types or stages of Black identity are described starting with 'Negromachy' (Thomas, 1971) where there is complete acceptance of White values and stereotypes and dependence on Whites for approval and for self-definition. This produces a confusion over self-worth and a desire to be other than what one actually is. Although possibly outwardly calm and well functioning, such a person is characterised by repressed rage and self-loathing (Carter, 1995). They are, by extension, very vulnerable to mental health problems. Only when certain events are encountered which shatter the persons illusions about their identity security (e.g. rejection by a fiancé's family because of skin colour) may the person come to recognise the pain, suffering and deprivation they have tolerated for so long. However, the person remains especially vulnerable because of identity confusion, disorientation and marginality – a feeling of not belonging to either the Black or White world. According to Helms & Piper (1994) the healthy way to resolve these conflicts is for the person to search for, and find, a new totally Black identity. This often involves a phase of obsessive involvement in Black culture, constant reaffirmation of Black identity, Black pride and a hostile rejection of everything White and especially Black people who are 'White on the inside'. Finally, the person matures into an acceptance of the strengths and weaknesses of Black culture and Black people and integrates Black racial identity with their own personality which has many roots other than racial experiences. The person is proud of being Black and secure in their identity, so that they take a balanced view of race relations and will have White as well as Black friends. It has to be said that, instinctively appealing as this typology is, there is precious little empirical evidence for it.

Racism and mental health services

There are many ways in which racism and race thinking can have an impact on the way in which ethnic minority groups experience mental health services. We have already seen how racism may directly and indirectly affect the personal resources available to minority group individuals. Someone with fewer personal resources, lower ego strength and a less secure identity will be less well equipped to cope with the stresses and strains that every one is likely to encounter at some time in their lives (Cochrane, 1983). There might be more vulnerable people in prejudiced-against groups than in the dominant ethnic majority. Indirectly too, prejudice and discrimination may affect a person's risk of developing mental health problems. Poverty, unemployment, poor housing, and restricted economic opportunities are all established aetiological agents for some forms of mental health problems. These are the same variables which are the product of racial disadvantage. Hence, to the direct effects of prejudice (as a life stressor and as a possible inhibitor of secure identity formation) must be added the secondary consequences. Perhaps rather than being additive the two types of effects are multiplicative.

Mental health services themselves are not immune from the values, attitudes, beliefs and stereotypes that pervade the rest of society. Both at the institutional and at the individual level it is certain that racism exists within mental health services. Hence, again we may distinguish between the overt and covert racism that might be found in mental health services. Table 4.1 contains examples at both the individual and institutional level.

Ridley (1995) reviewed nearly 100 studies published between 1950 and 1989 that had found racism (intentional or unintentional) in American mental health services. On the basis of his review, he concluded that racism is to be found in all aspects of mental health services. Over the last decade there have been a stream of similar studies in Britain (see Cochrane & Sashidharan, 1996 for a review). Adding to the review of American research what has been discovered in the UK there is firm research evidence that racism has an impact on the following dimensions of mental health service delivery.

Pathways to care

Ethnic minority service users have more aversive pathways to care – the police are more likely to be involved and the Mental Health Act used.

Diagnosis

Ethnic minority group service users are more likely to be misdiagnosed and more likely to receive a more severe diagnosis.

TABLE 4.1
Types of racism in mental health services (adapted from Ridley, 1995)

Type	Individual racism	Institutional racism
Overt	A mental health professional actively harasses a service user because of ethnicity	Management refuses to take seriously complaints of racial discrimination by ethnic minority service users
Covert	A consultant spends less time with ethnic minority service users than with White service users because of a belief that they are less amenable to psychological therapies	Mental health services provide food, settings and services which are less congenial to some ethnic minority users, deterring them from accessing the service
Unintentional	A nurse, under the illusion of colour blindness nevertheless perceives Black service users as more dangerous than White service users and responds towards them accordingly	A psychology department routinely uses psychometric tests standardised on White populations without consideration of the cultural bias this may introduce when interpreting the results

Staff assignment

Ethnic minority service users tend to see more junior members of staff and para-professionals rather than professionals.

Treatment

Ethnic minority service users tend to receive low-cost, less preferred treatments with minimal contact, high dosages of psycho-tropic medication and custodial care rather than psychological therapies.

Utilisation

Some ethnic minority groups are overrepresented in mental health facilities.

Conflict with services

Uncooperative and aggressive behaviour are more likely to be exhibited by ethnic minority group patients. This in turn means that they are more likely to be moved to locked wards, intensive treatment and secure units than are White patients.

Adherence

Ethnic minority patients are less likely to comply with treatment regimens both while in hospital and after discharge.

Satisfaction

Ethnic minority patients report lower levels of satisfaction with most aspects of their care than do White patients.

References

BRAND, E. S., RUIZ, R. A. & PADILLA, A. M. (1974) Ethnic identification and preference: a review. *Psychological Bulletin*, **81**, 860–890.

CARTER, R. T. (1995) *The Influence of Race and Racial Identity in Psychotherapy.* New York: John Wiley & Sons.

CLARK, K. B. (1965) *Dark Ghetto.* New York: Harper & Row.

—— & CLARK, M. P. (1947). Emotional factors in racial identification and preference in Negro pre-school children. *Journal of Negro Education*, **19**, 341–350.

COCHRANE, R. (1983) *The Social Creation of Mental Illness.* London: Longman.

—— (1991) Racial prejudice. In *Psychology and Social Issues* (eds R. Cochrane & D. Carroll). London: Taylor & Francis.

—— & SASHIDHARAN, S. P. (1996) Mental health and ethnic minorities: review of the literature and implications for services. In *Ethnicity and Health* (eds W. Ahmad, T. Sheldon, & O. Stuart) CRD Report No 5. York: NHS Centre for Reviews and Dissemination.

COMER, J. P. (1995) Racism and African American development. In *Mental Health, Racism, and Sexism* (eds C. V. Willie, P. P. Rieker, B. M. Kramer, *et al*). London: Taylor & Francis.

COMMISSION FOR RACIAL EQUALITY (1993) *Race Through the 90s.* London: Commission for Racial Equality.

CROSS, W. E. (1991) *Shades of Black: Diversity in African-American Identity.* Philadelphia, PA: Temple University Press.

DAVEY, A. (1983) *Learning to be Prejudiced: Growing Up in Multi-Ethnic Britain.* London: Edward Arnold.

GILBORN, D. (1997). Ethnicity and educational performance in the United Kingdom: racism, ethnicity and variability in performance. *Anthropology and Education Quarterly*, **28**, 375–393.

HELMS, J. E. & PIPER, R. E. (1994) Implications of racial identity theory for vocational psychology. *Journal of Vocational Behaviour*, **44**, 124–138.

HUTNIK, N. (1991) *Ethnic Minority Identity: A Social Psychological Perspective.* Oxford: Clarendon Press.

LEWIN, K. (1948) *Resolving Social Conflicts.* New York: Harper Brothers.

MARSELLA, A. J. & KAMEOKA, V. A. (1989) Ethnocultural issues in the assessment of psychopathology. In *Measuring Mental Illness* (ed. S. Wexler). Washington, DC: American Psychiatric Association.

RIDLEY, C. R. (1995) *Overcoming Unintentional Racism in Counselling and Therapy: A Practitioners Guide to Intentional Intervention.* Thousand Oaks, CA: Sage.

THOMAS, C. (1971) *Boys No More.* Beverly Hill, CA: Glencoe Press.

TYSON, G. A. (1985) *Children's Racial Attitudes: A Review.* Pretoria: Human Sciences Research Council.

5 Racial life events and psychiatric morbidity

DINESH BHUGRA and OYEDEJI AYONRINDE

Editors' introduction

In Chapter 4, Cochrane pointed out the role of racism and racial prejudice in diagnosis, treatment planning and delivery, and satisfaction with services. In this chapter, Bhugra and Ayonrinde take the impact of racism on clinical diagnosis further. They argue that the levels of racial life events and perceived and real racism influence individuals' self-esteem. They draw comparisons between Britain and the USA and propose that some types of life events may be racial and will influence the rates of common mental disorders in Black and other ethnic minority groups. In addition to clearly identified racial life events, chronic difficulties related to perceived and real racism may act as vulnerability factors in the genesis of a number of psychiatric disorders. Mental health professionals must be aware of these factors and be sensitive in identifying them.

The relationship between social factors and psychiatric morbidity has been widely researched. There is an increasingly robust body of evidence highlighting the role of chronic stress and difficulty in the aetiology of common mental disorders across all ethnic groups.

The universality of the relationship between life events and psychiatric morbidity has also been demonstrated in different cultures. However, there is a paucity of research on the experience and nature of stressful life events by individuals of minority cultures or ethnic background within the larger population, and the impact on their psychological well-being. Most research in this field has focused on psychological aspects of migration and the adjustment process, and little emphasis has been placed on the psychological impact of racial experiences.

The following key questions need to be addressed: (a) Are ethnic minority individuals exposed to stressful experiences specific or related to their ethnic identity? (b) Do these stressors qualify as life events? (c) Are the life events of a nature or severity to cause psychiatric morbidity? (d) If so, what type or types of psychiatric morbidity? (e) How do these stressors act as aetiological factors? Do they act alone or in conjunction with other vulnerability factors?

This chapter reviews the literature on race, ethnicity and stressful life events. It will also examine the association between racial life events and psychological morbidity.

Life events

The relationship between stress, life events and psychiatric morbidity has been widely studied over the past three decades (Holmes & Rahe, 1967; Brown & Harris, 1978; Brown, 1998). Social stress models share the assumptions that exposure to stress is associated with psychological distress and that protective resources available to certain individuals modify the severity of these impacts. It is now recognised that adverse life events can influence the adaptive potential and mental health of human beings (Rutter, 1985) thereby contributing substantially to psychiatric morbidity. The strongest and most consistent associations have been found in the aetiology of depression (Brown & Harris, 1978; Paykel, 1994), although associations have been suggested with the onset of psychotic illness (Brown & Harris, 1978). The relationship between adverse life events and common mental disorders has also been researched in non-Western cultures such as Kenya, Dubai and Nigeria (Vadher & Ndetei, 1981; Gureje, 1986; Bebbington *et al*, 1998) with their findings supporting the earlier evidence of social contributions to aetiology of illness despite cultural differences. Other researchers (Owens & McGuffin, 1997; Brown, 1998) have discussed the genetics and familial nature of life events, suggesting that those who are more prone to depression are more likely to perceive events as threatening, or even have a tendency to expose themselves to adversity.

In their analysis of life events, Finlay-Jones & Brown (1981) found that 'loss' events were particularly important for the onset of depression, and 'danger' for anxiety disorders. 'Loss' was broadly defined to include not only loss of a person, but loss of a role, loss of resources and loss of a cherished idea about oneself or someone else, while 'danger' was defined as the threat of possible loss in the future. It is also important to delineate day-to-day hardship from difficulties and life events as defined by Brown & Harris (1978). They defined a difficulty as a problem that has gone on for at least four weeks, and a life event as a problem resulting from a life event within one year.

Although the severity of chronic difficulties and life events consists of subjective, objective and contextual components, its relationship to psychiatric morbidity was demonstrated. In a sample of general practice attenders, 38% of those who were depressed had experienced severe life events. However, those who had major difficulties (lasting at least two years) and severe events comprised 62% of those people with depression. Major difficulties are highly associated (15%) with depression and have cognitive consequences as they are on one's mind most of the time (Brown & Harris, 1978). Other social factors such as social class are felt to buffer the exposure and effect of provoking agents, hence reducing difficulties. The significance of experiences of hopelessness, entrapment, humiliation and defeat in the aetiology of depression has also been discussed (Brown, 1998). Depressogenic situations, namely direct attacks on a person's self-esteem and forcing them into a subordinate position, undermining a person's sense of rank, attractiveness and value, and blocked escape have also been emphasised by Gilbert (1989) to play crucial aetiological roles. It is arguable that the above situations may not be uncommon to members of 'minority' groups.

Race, racism and stress

Although people with diverse histories, cultures, beliefs and languages have migrated and settled in other parts of the world since the beginning of recorded time, it has not eroded the role of ethnic difference. In Britain, the arrival and assimilation of immigrant groups has been varied, for example the Huguenots in the 17th century and later the Irish and the Jews. Yet it was not until well after the Second World War that substantial numbers of people came to the UK from South Asia, Africa and the Caribbean to meet labour shortages (Commission for Racial Equality, 1999a). More recently, arrivals in Britain have included refugees and asylum-seekers from areas of political strife or war such as Vietnam, Somalia, Turkey, the Middle East and the former Yugoslavia. The mobility of persons within the European Union nations has also contributed to increased ethnic diversity within member states.

Collectively, non-indigenous (often with emphasis on non-White) groups are described as 'ethnic minority populations'. These groups may be differentiated by race, ethnicity and nationality (see Herman, 1996; Bhugra & Bhui, 1999 for problems with definitions).

In the 1991 census, 5.5% (3 015 050) of Britain's population was classified as ethnic minority (Commission for Racial Equality, 1999*a*). Approximately half of this ethnic minority population is South Asian (India, Pakistan, Bangladeshi descent) and 30% Black. Increasing numbers of ethnic minorities are second-generation immigrants with nearly half of Britain's non-White population having been born in the UK. There are marked variations in the regional distribution of ethnic minorities, with greater concentrations being found in the large urban areas, reflecting where the first settlers arrived. For instance, 20% of London's population (45% of Britain's non-White population) are ethnic minorities. Also about one-quarter of school pupils in London have a first language other than English, a diversity of 275 languages (Commission for Racial Equality, 1999*a*).

This highlights the hazards associated with generalising across ethnic minority groups with their different histories, cultures, and languages. Furthermore, while adjustment and assimilation issues may be paramount to the new immigrant, second- and third-generation migrants may continue to grapple with socio-economic disadvantage and incomplete assimilation.

Discrimination, prejudice and racism have been cited as potential barriers encountered frequently in the adjustment and assimilation process (see Chapter 4). Over recent years racial discrimination has been reported in both private and public (e.g. NHS, schools, armed forces) establishments. While overt racial harassment, threats and violence continue to receive wide public and media attention, more subtle racial experiences are frequently ignored or may not be brought to attention. Several reports suggest that actual incidents of racism may be more widespread in society than initially thought (MacPherson, 1999). Although these reports describe varying degrees of racial distress, there has been little quantitative and qualitative scientific assessment of the process and its impact.

Epidemiology of race-related crime, racial attacks and harassment

As noted in Chapter 4, accurate figures on the incidence and prevalence of racially motivated crime (victimisation, attacks, harassment) are difficult to obtain. Several explanations given for the paucity or difficulty obtaining these data are: (a) victims may have not seen the perpetrator; (b) victims may not suspect a racial motive; (c) victims may wrongly assume a racial motive; (d) insufficient evidence relating to the incident; (e) victims' fear of further victimisation.

In the UK, the key sources of recorded information on racial incidents are the British Crime Survey (BCS) and police records of racial incidents. The BCS estimates crime levels and trends in persons aged 16 years or over in England and Wales. This includes offences such as vandalism, burglary, other thefts, wounding, robbery and common assault. Threats of crime are also included in the survey. The police, on the other hand, are required to keep records of any incident in which it appears to the reporting or investigating officer that an element of racial motivation was involved or in which an allegation of racial motivation has been made. Police records cover criminal racial incidents with no age limits.

It is important to stress, however, that neither the BCS nor police records document non-criminal expressions of racial prejudice and hostility which is believed to account for the majority of racial harassment experienced by people in the UK.

In 1996, the BCS estimated that over 2% (382 000) of all criminal offences reported in their survey were considered by victims to be motivated by racism (see Fig. 5.1). Sixty-nine per cent of racially motivated threats were also associated with the use of racist language by perpetrators. A greater proportion of race-related offences were reported in non-inner city (24%) than inner city (16%) areas (Fitzgerald & Hale, 1996). This may be because of the protective

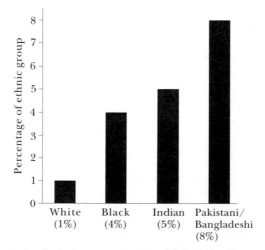

Fig. 5.1. Percentage of ethnic groups in UK who believe offences against them are racially motivated (Commission for Racial Equality, 1999b)

effect provided by greater concentrations of ethnic minorities in inner city areas. Between 1989 and 1996, the number of race-related incidents reported to the police increased nearly three-fold. In 1997/98 the police recorded 13 878 racial incidents, a 6% increase over the preceding year. It is worthy of note that increased reporting may not mean an increase in actual incidents and reporting may be affected by other variables.

In the USA, race-related crimes are recorded as a category of 'hate crimes'. The US Congress defines hate crime as "a crime in which the defendant intentionally selects a victim, or property … because of the actual or perceived race, color, national origin, ethnicity, gender, disability or sexual orientation of any person". In 1997, the Federal Bureau of Investigation (FBI) recorded 4710 racially motivated criminal incidents. Six of every 10 victims of hate crime were attacked because of their race, with bias against Blacks accounting for 39% of the total (US Department of Justice, 1997). The overall lower rates in the US than the UK suggest possible trans-atlantic differences in the threshold for reporting of racial incidents between organisations and countries.

The above statistics further demonstrate the wide differences in the reporting and documentation of racial crime in countries with different racial identities, historical backgrounds and geographical spread. In the documentation of incidents, differences are likely to emerge in the severity and nature of what is considered a racial crime in different countries and in the proportion of victims from the different ethnic groups. For instance, while African–Caribbeans in the UK are nine times more likely to report racial incidents than Whites (Commission for Racial Equality, 1999*b*), recorded incidents against Black people in the USA are over three times the rates recorded against the White population. Further comparison shows that in the UK, 15% of Asian crime victims thought offences against them were motivated by racism as compared with 1% of White victims. In the USA, however, recorded incidents against White members of the population were three times more common than those against Asians. The above figures demonstrate geographical and ethnic differences in race-related crime.

It must be emphasised that the above figures should be interpreted with caution as not all incidents are reported. The BCS estimates that only between 15 and 45% of racially motivated incidents are actually reported by ethnic minority persons in the UK. However, Chahal & Julienne (1999) observe that between 43 and 62% of incidents go unreported in the UK. Explanations for these different rates in reporting include: incident not recognised as racial by victim and/or police, actual increase in incidents, increased readiness of

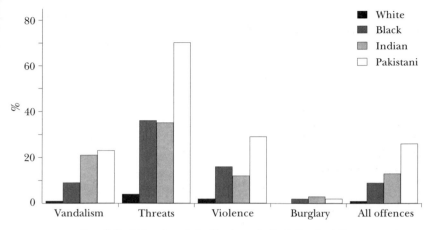

Fig. 5.2. Type of racial offence and ethnicity of victim

some ethnic groups to report or increased readiness of the police to record an incident as racial. Other possible explanations are the suspicion and mistrust of agencies and the immigration status of the victim. For instance, illegal immigrants may be reluctant to take any action that would draw the attention of law enforcement agencies to them.

Types of racial harassment and violence vary as does their impact (see Fig. 5.2). In 1996/97, 38% of recorded racial incidents in Britain involved verbal harassment, and 20% criminal damage to property. Assaults made up 21% of incidents, and 2% were serious crimes against the person, while eight racially motivated homicides were identified in 1997/98 (Fitzgerald & Hale, 1996).

While the above data give a useful insight into the scale of recorded racial offences, they fail to reflect the impact of day-to-day insults, pestering, phone threats, graffiti or noxious substances passed through letter boxes experienced by ethnic minority and certain non-ethnic minority individuals, for instance those in inter-racial relationships. Neither are the data a sensitive measure of covert or even unconscious racism, discriminatory practice or prejudice in various works of life. The above statistics are also unable to provide a quantitative or qualitative measure of institutional racism.

Institutional racism

The Macpherson Report (1999) defines institutional racism as:

> "The collective failure of an organisation to provide an appropriate and professional service to people because of their colour, culture

or ethnic origin. It can be seen or detected in processes, attitudes and behaviour which amount to discrimination through unwitting prejudice, ignorance, thoughtlessness and racist stereotyping which disadvantage minority ethnic people".

Subjective experiences of racism or perceived racism may be difficult to validate particularly since the expression of difference in a multicultural society may have alternative meanings other than the overtly racial (Ayonrinde, 1999).

Research by Chahal & Julienne (1999) provides an in-depth resource on qualitative and subjective experiences of racism. In their study, subjects described the routine nature of racial experiences in their lives. As regards disclosure of these experiences to others, several pathways (see Fig. 5.3) were identified depending on the presence of social support, frequency and severity of incidents. While children often reported incidents to their parents, adult experiences were mainly shared with close confidants such as family and friends. In some situations, however, racial incidents were not disclosed by victims to others. This failed disclosure was found to be associated with feelings of shame, inadequacy, hopelessness or mistrust.

Influencing the decision to disclose information to an agency was an increase in incidents, injury, threat to life, or serious damage to property. A number of respondents detailed further distress when their racial perception of events was questioned by agencies. Over a quarter had experienced incidents for between 18 months to two years before complaints were made. A favoured point of disclosure was the local general practitioner (GP), the main reasons being: (a) to request letters to housing or social services departments to explain the deleterious effects of experiences on the family; (b) for treatment of ensuing difficulties, for example, insomnia, depression or injuries; and (c) as a confidant to share emotional difficulties – thus emphasising the importance of primary care in dealing with the sequelae of racial life events. Behavioural responses to attacks among victims include moving home, changing school, leaving work, staying indoors, avoiding certain neighbourhoods and limiting night travel (Chahal & Julienne, 1999). The erection of high fences, surveillance cameras, and in the USA the purchase of guns (Barnes & Ephross, 1994) have also been described as responses to racial life events.

Racial life events, chronic difficulties and stress mechanisms

Although it has been demonstrated that life stresses are associated with increased psychiatric morbidity in different countries and

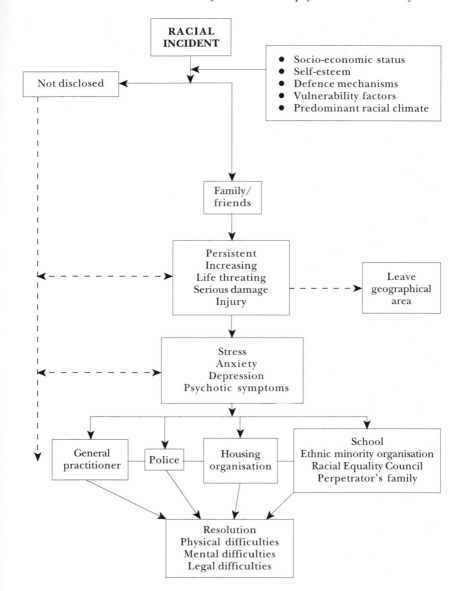

Fig. 5.3. Pathways to disclosure of racial incidents

cultures, researchers have mainly focused on subjects from the majority ethnic populations. What are the types of life stresses that members of ethnic minority groups experience? Does culture form the contexts in which stressful life events derive meaning? Are racial life events quantitatively or qualitatively different from any other form of socially induced stress?

There are few known studies of the life events that precede mental illness among ethnic minority populations. Williams (1996) observed that stress researchers had not incorporated experiences of racial discrimination in standard stress inventories. For instance, in their study of women in Camberwell, Brown & Harris (1978) excluded West Indian women and any women who had not lived in the UK for at least 15 years, so as to reduce problems of different cultural influences. It is, therefore, striking that this landmark study not only excluded a significant proportion of the population, but did not measure serious life events which may play an important role in the aetiology of psychological morbidity in ethnic minority populations. In a more recent multinational analysis, however, Brown (1998) noted that culture may help to create depressogenic events.

Racial life events can be defined as problems resulting as a direct result of racial events; racial difficulties may be defined as a race-related problem that has gone on for at least four weeks.

If race or membership of a ethnic minority group is a source of stress or chronic difficulty, what are the stress mechanisms? It is argued that discrimination and racial experiences function to keep ethnic minority groups chronically exposed to other stresses as well, such as a lifetime of poor incomes, poor jobs and poor housing (Broman, 1996). Smith (1985) also discussed this question applying the Dohrenwend & Dohrenwend (1979) model of factors contributing to general levels of stress. These factors are defined as stressor stimuli (e.g. prejudice, hostility and discrimination), external mediating forces (social support), and internal mediating forces (cognitive factors) that influence individuals' perception of life events.

Proffering several theoretical perspectives about why minority status can be stressful, Smith (1985) applied the 'out-group–in-group' model, emphasising the 'out-group' status experienced by ethnic minority populations. Out-group status for Blacks and other minorities may result in social isolation, social marginalisation, and status inconsistency, thereby creating within individuals a heightened sense of stress. The incomplete assimilation of persons who have partially relinquished their former culture and yet have not been fully accepted in the new culture has been found to be stressful. Bhugra *et al* (1999) and Brown (1998) further described the relationship between hopelessness about restoring a core identity and psychopathology (also see Chapter 6). Status inconsistency is said to occur when an individual has two or more distinct and incompatible social statuses, for example, the contamination of an individuals' social status by status associated with the individual's ethnicity. These role and status contradictions may be lead to adjustment difficulties or psychopathology (Smith, 1985).

As non-White individuals may be seen as representatives of their group their actions also take on an added symbolic meaning, hence their behaviour is viewed as predictive of what other members of their ethnic group would do. Overall, Smith (1985) recognised factors such as high visibility, over-observation (heightened self-awareness), lack of anonymity, polarisation, role entrapment and status levelling as common causes of stress and chronic difficulties experienced by ethnic minority individuals.

In their 13-year study Jackson *et al* (1996) identified that perceived racism and reports of maltreatment because of race affected not only mental but also physical health. It was observed that the cumulative exposure to racism and racial discrimination resulted in poorer mental than physical health.

Racial discrimination is, however, not randomly distributed in society as several socio-demographic factors predict variation in exposure; for example, the finding that persons with financial difficulties, as well as those who perceive their neighbourhoods to be unsafe or deficient in basic amenities, are more likely to be distressed by racial discrimination. The middle-class affluent African Americans did not show an effect of racial discrimination (Broman, 1996), suggesting that social status may be more important than ethnicity in the perception of racial distress.

Defences used to tackle race-related stressors may differ from one individual to another. For instance some may apply denial and self-degradation, others may embrace vigilance and resistance, while others may accept status quo. However, whatever pathway is taken, health outcomes are likely to be significantly and differentially affected (Jackson *et al*,1996).

Instruments and measures of perceived racism and racial life events

The term 'racism' has been used in many ways (Bhugra & Bhui, 1999). It may be defined as a negative attribution made by people of one social group towards people of a different social group because of putative biological characteristics. As has been shown in the previous chapter, racism is a multidimensional phenomenon with dimensions related to types of racism and the context of racial events. Few instruments have been developed to measure perceptions of racism or racial life events experienced by victims of racism. The majority of existing racism measures have been designed to assess variables such as exposure to racist incidents, beliefs and attitudes.

Some of these include:

(a) Climate for Racism Scale (Barbarin & Gilbert, 1981) – a measure of institutional racism by assessing individual and organisational attributes.

(b) Personal Discrimination and Racial Climate Scales (Allan-Clairborne & Taylor, 1981) – measures individual experiences of discrimination and racism in the organisational or institutional context.

(c) Difference Indicators Scale (Fiman, 1981) – a quantitative index of institutional racism.

(d) Cultural Mistrust Inventory (Terrell & Terrell, 1981) – an attitudinal measure of cultural mistrust and racism among African Americans.

(e) Racial Reactions Scale (Thompson *et al*, 1990) – designed to assess reactions related to race in African American students.

(f) Racial Life Events Scale (RALES) (Bhugra *et al*, 1994) – a multidimensional measure of racial life events and chronic difficulties in ethnic minority and immigrant populations.

(g) Perceptions of Racism Scale (Green, 1995) – an affective, behavioural and cognitive measure of perceived racism in African American women.

(h) Perceived Racism Scale (McNeilly *et al*, 1996) – a multi-dimensional (contextual, attitudinal, behavioural and cultural) measure of racism in African Americans.

Many of these instruments were designed for the study of specific ethnic groups sometimes in specific contexts. For example, the Perceptions of Racism Scale was designed to measure affective, behavioural and cognitive categories of perceived racism by child-bearing African American women. Meanwhile the Perceived Racism Scale was constructed to assess exposure to individual, institutional, overt, covert, attitudinal, behavioural and cultural manifestations of racism in several domains. However, this scale was also designed for use among African American subjects.

The RALES is a semi-structured interview schedule designed to assess race-related life events and chronic difficulties in immigrant and ethnic minority populations. The RALES is a multidimensional instrument comprising subscales on pre-immigration, accommodation, employment, education, racial incidents (type and consequences), attitudes and beliefs regarding discrimination. Unlike several other instruments, the RALES was designed for use across ethnic groups in the UK. Some items also address pre- and post-immigration experiences. It has been applied in the study of race-related life events among Asian subjects in the UK (Bhugra *et al*, 1994) and piloted on Black (African and African Caribbean) individuals by the author. Alongside demographic characteristics it assesses individuals' perceived experiences of racial discrimination or threat in daily social functioning.

It has been found to be of relative ease to administer. It also serves as a useful clinical tool in the assessment of chronic racial difficulties among ethnic minority persons by clinicians previously unfamiliar with race-related stressors and uses descriptive methods.

Potential difficulties with the measurement of race-related stress or life events might be bias created by the subject's perception of the researcher's ethnicity and the social desirability of their responses (Hawthorne and halo effects), an association observed by Jackson *et al* (1996). Researcher bias may also occur due to the misunderstanding or misinterpretation of idioms of distress. Common to retrospective studies is the questionable accuracy of recall over time and need for corroborative evidence if available.

Highly publicised incidents (e.g. the Stephen Lawrence murder inquiry in the UK, and the O. J. Simpson trial in the USA) can also impact the overall racial climate, hence generating heightened sensitivity about ethnic difference. It may be that the predominant racial climate influences (directly or indirectly) the perception of racial events.

Chahal and Julienne (1999) argue that quantitative measures "drown out the voices of the victimised", hence neglecting experiences, feelings and the impact of racial life events on the individual. Their qualitative study of ethnic minority groups through focus groups followed by in-depth interviews highlights the limitations of checklists or oversimplification in researching these complex issues.

Racism and health

The relationship between racism, general health and emotional well-being is a complex one (see Fig. 5.4). Racial discrimination may create and sustain a social status that results in differential housing, education and employment. Chronic racial difficulties and low socio-economic functioning may also be associated with increased risk of disease, such as cardiovascular disorders and alcohol-related problems. Furthermore, discriminatory experiences, mistrust and social marginalisation may reduce access to available health resources

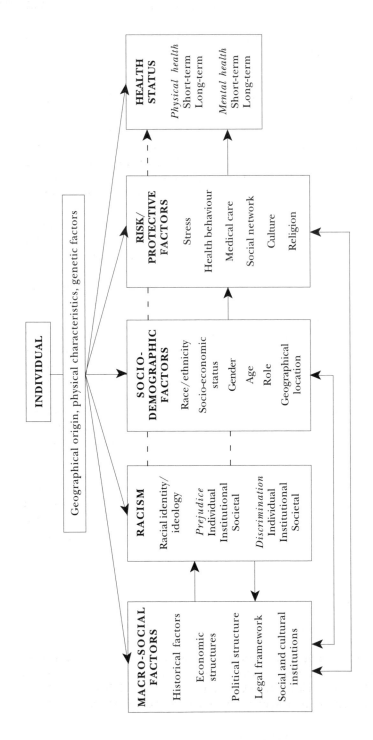

Fig 5.4. Relationship between race/ethnicity and health (adapted from Williams, 1996)

(Herman, 1996; Jackson *et al*, 1996; Williams, 1996; Williams-Morris, 1996; Northridge & Shepard, 1997; Muntaner, 1999).

Racism and psychological and psychiatric morbidity

Although several authors have described the theoretical and hypothetical relationship between experiences of racism and psychological morbidity (Fernando,1984; Smith, 1985) there is a dearth of empirical studies. Jackson *et al* (1996) demonstrated that cumulative perceptions of racism and racial discrimination result in poorer mental than physical health. Several models and theories have also been put forward to explain pathways in the aetiology of disorders. In their seminal epidemiological study, Parker & Kleiner (1966) observed a significant relationship between stress of thwarted aspirations and symptoms of distress among African Americans. They observed that "downwardly mobile low socio-economic Blacks with high goal-striving showed the lowest self-esteem and consequently, the highest rate of psychological distress".

However, it is recognised that stress alone does not lead to psychological morbidity and that other factors, known as mediating factors, explain the variability in health outcome. One of the most widely quoted mediating factor models is Rotter's (1966) locus of control. Applying this model, Neighbors *et al* (1996) described two fundamental positions: taking personal responsibility for ones' situation (self-blame/ internal control), and holding racism and discrimination responsible for unfairly holding Blacks or Asians down (system blame/external control). It has been argued that a system–blame perspective is ego-protective because it allows the ethnic minority individual to avoid the painful psychological effects of self-blame (Smith, 1985). The role of racial identity as a mediating factor is less clear, however, as Thompson (1996) found no effect while Jones *et al* (1996) observed that strong racial identity reduced responsivity to racist events.

Psychiatric disorders

Depression

By far the most widely documented association between racial life events and mental illness has been that of the onset of depression (Burke, 1984; Fernando, 1984; Smith, 1985; Jackson *et al*, 1996; Jones *et al*, 1996; Neighbors *et al*, 1996; see

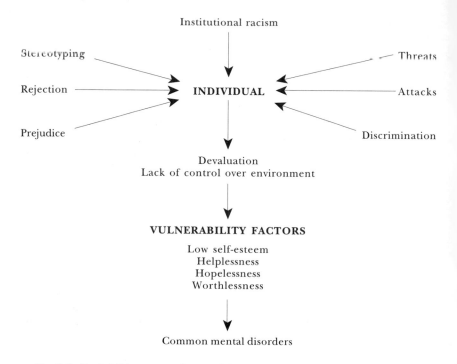

Fig 5.5. Racial life events, chronic difficulties and common mental disorders

Fig. 5.5). Several aetiological models have already been put forward with the most common pathway identifying racial stress as both a vulnerability factor and stressful life event in the lives of many ethnic minority individuals. Several studies have found higher community prevalence rates of depression in minority groups than in the dominant population (Lloyd, 1998; Nazroo, 1998; Shaw *et al*, 1999), with suggested explanations being, exposure to different social or environmental loss events such as poverty, unemployment and racism. Depression in ethnic minority groups was also less likely to be recognised or receive treatment. Goldberg & Hodes (1992) have also proposed that high rates of overdosing (attacks on the self) among their sample of young Asian women was possibly a reflection of racial attacks they had experienced. Researching psychological disturbance and racism, Burke (1984) described grief-like reactions, despair, anger, rejection and exclusion among African–Caribbean people with depression. Although depression has received the most detailed theoretical and clinical attention, it is crucial that future studies apply standardised diagnostic tools when screening for depression.

Anxiety states

Social models of stress describe a relationship between threatening events and the onset of anxiety symptoms. Racial discrimination was found by researchers (Pernice & Brook, 1996) in New Zealand to be the crucial factor associated with high levels of anxiety among non-White immigrants. They also found high levels among those who spent a lot of leisure time with their own ethnic group. It was felt that the severely anxious individuals may seek others from their ethnic group more often than the well adjusted. Anxiety symptoms following racial threat have also been described by Thompson (1996) and by Jones *et al* (1996).

Post-traumatic stress disorder

Crucial to a diagnosis of post-traumatic stress disorder (PTSD) is that an individual "has been exposed, witnessed or been confronted with an event(s) that involved actual or threatened death, serious injury or a threat to the physical integrity of the individual or others" (DSM–IV; American Psychiatric Association, 1994). The relationship between PTSD, violent crime and victimisation is well established (Brewin *et al*, 1999). As already discussed, some racial stressors meet the stress criterion for PTSD. PTSD following experiences of racial discrimination and violence has been documented (Barnes & Ephross, 1994; Loo, 1994; Kim-Goh *et al*, 1995; Dassori & Silva, 1998). Loo (1994) describes PTSD following race-related verbal and physical assaults, racial stigmatisation and the cumulative effect of racism as a trauma in an Asian group. PTSD reactions characterised by hypervigilance, withdrawal, reduced concentration, intrusive images, avoidance and sleep disturbance were described by Thompson (1996). Similarly, Goldberg & Hodes (1992) have also described difficulty concentrating, frustration, hypervigilance, denial, withdrawal and avoidance behaviour with increased psychiatric morbidity following racial incidents. Autonomic arousal (another feature of PTSD) in the form of increased heart rate and raised blood pressure following experiences of racism has also been reported (Armstead *et al*, 1989).

Psychosis

Several explanations have been put forward for the excess of ethnic minority persons diagnosed and treated for psychotic illnesses. Anecdotal reports of racism as a cause of illness by psychotic patients are unclear about causality and effect of racial stress. Brantley (1983)

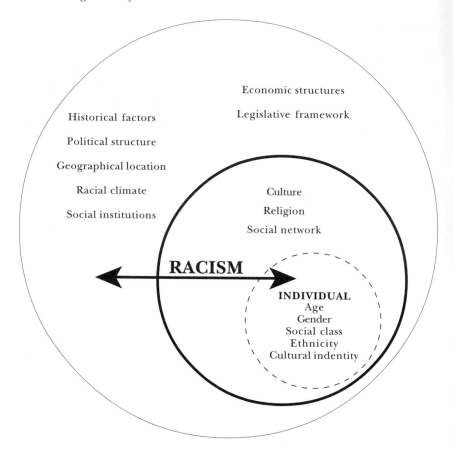

Fig. 5.6. Impact of racial life events: a multi-contextual model. ——— *extrinsic factors;* ▬▬ *intrinsic factors;* – – – *individual factors*

emphasises this complexity, stating "the effects of racism can be devastating to psychiatric patients who have been made vulnerable by already weakened coping mechanisms, for they must use their fragile defensive structure to protect themselves from a real external assault on their sense of self".

Societal racism has been suggested as a possible cause of increased risk of schizophrenia (Littlewood & Lipsedge, 1988) in Black populations in the UK. Institutional racism, life events and chronic stress may also be associated with an increased risk of developing psychosis (Perera *et al*, 1991). However, in the absence of empirical studies, the evidence remains inconclusive.

Conclusion

The relationship between race, racism and mental illness is complex. This review of the literature emphasises a need for further quantitative and qualitative research into the psychological impact of race-related stressors. The emerging evidence suggests racial life events are associated with emotional, psychological and psychiatric morbidity. Unfortunately, many of these studies do not apply standardised diagnostic tools in their measures of psychological morbidity or subjective distress. Neither have racial experiences been systematically assessed. The strongest link between racial life events and psychiatric morbidity is an association with the onset of depression. However, disagreement among mental health and social science professionals regarding the response of ethnic minority groups to racial discrimination has yet failed to provide a universally acceptable consensus.

References

ALLAN-CLAIRBORNE, J. G. & TAYLOR, J. (1981) *The Racialistic Incidents Inventory: Measuring Awareness of Racialism. Institutional Racism and Community Competence.* Washington, DC: US Government Printing Office.

AMERICAN PSYCHIATRIC ASSOCIATION (1994) *Diagnostic and Statistical Manual of Mental Disorders* (4th edn) (DSM–IV). Washington, DC: APA.

ARMSTEAD, C. A., LAWLER, K. A., GORDON, G., et al (1989) Relationship of racial stressors to blood pressure responses and anger expression in black college students. *Health Psychology,* **8**, 541–556.

AYONRINDE, O. (1999) Black, White or shades of grey: the challenges of ethnic difference (or similarity) in the therapeutic process. *International Review of Psychiatry,* **11**, 191–196.

BARBARIN, O. A. & GILBERT, R. (1981) *Institutional Racism Scale: Assessing Self and Organizational Attributes. Institutional Racism and Community Competence.* Washington, DC: US Government Printing Office.

BARNES, A. & EPHROSS, P. H. (1994) The impact of hate violence on victims: emotional and behavioral responses to attacks. *Social Work,* **39**, 247–251.

BEBBINGTON, P., HAMDI, E. & GHUBASH, R. (1998) The Dubai Community Psychiatric Survey IV. Life events, chronic difficulties and psychiatric morbidity. *Social Psychiatry and Psychiatric Epidemiology,* **33**, 501–509.

BHUGRA, D. & BHUI, K. (1999) Racism in psychiatry: paradigm lost–paradigm regained. *International Review of Psychiatry,* **11**, 236–243.

——, Mallett, R. & Leff, J. (1994) *Racial Life Events (RALES), Rating Scale.* London: MRC Social Research & Community Psychiatry Unit.

——, BHUI, K., MALLETT, R., et al (1999) Cultural identity and its measurement: a questionnaire for Asians. *International Review of Psychiatry,* **11**, 244–249.

BRANTLEY, T. (1983) Racism and its impact on psychotherapy. *American Journal of Psychiatry,* **140**, 1605–1608.

BREWIN, C. R., et al (1999) Acute stress disorder and posttraumatic stress disorder in victims of violent crime. *American Journal of Psychiatry,* **156**, 360–366.

BROMAN, C. L. (1996) The health consequences of racial discrimination: a study of African Americans. *Ethnicity and Disease,* **6,** 148–153.

BROWN, G. W. (1998) Genetic and population perspectives on life events and depression. *Social Psychiatry and Psychiatric Epidemiology,* **33,** 363–372.

—— & HARRIS, T. (1998) *Social Origins of Depression. A Study of Psychiatric Disorders in Women.* London: Tavistock.

BURKE, A. W. (1984) Racism and psychological disturbances among West Indians in Britain. *International Journal of Social Psychiatry,* **30,** 50–68.

CHAHAL, K. & JULIENNE, L. (1999) *We Can't All Be White!* York: York Publishing Services.

COMMISSION FOR RACIAL EQUALITY (1999*a*) *Ethnic Minorities in Britain.* London: CRE.

—— (1999*b*) *Racial Attacks and Harassment.* London: CRE.

DASSORI, A. M. & SILVA, J. A. (1998) PTSD and ethnic violence. *Psychiatric Services,* **49,** 108.

DOHRENWEND, B. S. & DOHRENWEND, B. P. (1979) Class and race as status-related sources of stress. In *Social Stress.* (eds S. Levine & B. Scotch). Chicago, IL: Aldine.

FERNANDO, S. (1984) Racism as a cause of depression. *International Journal of Social Psychiatry,* **30,** 41–49.

FIMAN, B. G. (1981) The difference indicator: quantitative index of institutional racism. In *Institutional Racism and Community Competence.* Washington, DC: Department of Health and Human Services.

FINLAY-JONES, R. & BROWN, G. W. (1981) Types of stressful life event and the onset of anxiety and depressive disorders. *Psychological Medicine,* **11,** 803–815.

FITZGERALD, M. & HALE, C. (1996) *Ethnic Minorities, Victimisation and Racial Harassment.* Home Office Research Findings No. 39. London: Home Office.

GILBERT, P. (1989) *Human Nature and Suffering.* Hove: Lawrence Erlbaum.

GOLDBERG, D. & HODES, M. (1992) The poison of racism and the self-poisoning of adolescents. *Journal of Family Therapy,* **14,** 51–67.

GREEN, N. L. (1995) Development of the perceptions of racism scale. *Image, the Journal of Nursing Scholarship,* **27,** 141–146.

GUREJE, O. (1986) Social factors and depression in Nigerian women. *Acta Psychiatrica Scandinavica,* **74,** 392–395.

HERMAN, A. A. (1996) Toward a conceptualization of race in epidemiologic research. *Ethnicity and Disease,* **6,** 7–20.

HOLMES, T. H. & RAHE, R. H. (1967) The Social Readjustment Rating Scale. *Journal of Psychosomatic Research,* **11,** 213–218.

JACKSON, J. S., BROWN, T. N., WILLIAMS, D. R., *et al* (1996) Racism and the physical and mental health status of African Americans: a thirteen-year national panel study. *Ethnicity and Disease,* **6,** 132–147.

JONES, D. R., HARRELL, J. P., MORRISS-PRATHER, C. E., *et al* (1996) Affective and physiological responses to racism: the roles of Afrocentrism and mode of presentation. *Ethnicity and Disease,* **6,** 109–122.

KIM-GOH, M., SUH, C., *et al* (1995) Psychological impact of the Los-Angeles riots on Korean–American victims: implications for treatment. *American Journal of Orthopsychiatry,* **65,** 138–146.

LEFF, J., BHUGRA, D. & MALLETT, R. (1994) *RALES: Racial Life Events Schedule.* Social Psychiatry Section Document. London: Medical Research Council.

LITTLEWOOD, R. & LIPSEDGE, M. (1988) Psychiatric illness among British Afro-Caribbeans. *British Medical Journal,* **296,** 950–951.

LLOYD, K. (1998) Ethnicity, social inequality and mental illness. *British Medical Journal,* **316,** 1763.

LOO, C. M. (1994) Race-related PTSD: the Asian American Vietnam veteran. *Journal of Traumatic Stress,* **7,** 637–656.

MACPHERSON, W. (1999) *The Stephen Lawrence Inquiry. Report of an Inquiry by Sir William Macpherson of Cluny.* London: The Stationery Office.

McNeilly, M. D., Anderson, N. B., Armstead, C. A., *et al* (1996) The perceived racism scale: a multidimensional assessment of the experience of white racism among African Americans. *Ethnicity and Disease*, **6**, 154–166.

Muntaner, C. (1999) Social mechanisms, race and social epidemiology. *American Journal of Epidemiology*, **150**, 121–126.

Nazroo, J. Y. (1998) Rethinking the relationship between ethnicity and mental health: the British Fourth National Survey of Ethnic Minorities. *Social Psychiatry and Psychiatric Epidemiology*, **33**, 145–148.

Neighbors, H. W., Jackson, J. S., Broman, C., *et al* (1996) Racism and mental health of African Americans: the role of self and system blame. *Ethnicity and Disease*, **6**, 167–175.

Northridge, M. E. & Shepard, P. M. (1997) Environmental racism and public health. *American Journal of Public Health*, **87**, 730–732.

Owens, M. J. & McGuffin, P. (1997) Genetics and psychiatry. *British Journal of Psychiatry*, **171**, 201–202.

Parker, S. & Kleiner, R. (1966) *Mental Illness in the Urban Negro Community*. New York: Free Press.

Paykel, E. S., (1994) Life events, social support and depression. *Acta Psychiatrica Scandinavica Supplementum*, **377**, 50–58.

Perera, R., Owens, D. G. & Johnstone, E. C. (1991) Ethnic aspects. A comparison of three matched groups. *British Journal of Psychiatry*, **159** (suppl. 13), 40–42.

Pernice, R. & Brook, J. (1996) Refugees' and immigrants' mental health: association of demographic and post immigration factors. *Journal of Social Psychology*, **136**, 511–519.

Rotter, J. B. (1966) Generalized expectancies of internal versus external control of reinforcement. *Psychological Monographs*, **80**, 1–28.

Rutter, M. (1985) Resilience in the face of adversity: protective factors and resistance to psychiatric disorder. *British Journal of Psychiatry*, **147**, 598–611.

Shaw, C. M., Creed, F., *et al* (1999) Prevalence of anxiety and depressive illness and help seeking behaviour in African Caribbeans and white Europeans: two phase general population survey. *British Medical Journal*, **318**, 302–306.

Smith, E. M. J. (1985) Ethnic minorities: life stress, social support, and mental health issues. *Counseling Psychologist*, **4**, 537–579.

Terrell, F. & Terrell, S. (1981) An inventory to measure cultural mistrust among blacks. *Western Journal of Black Studies*, **5**, 180–185.

Thompson, C. E., Neville, H., Weathers, P. L., *et al* (1990) Cultural mistrust and racism reaction among African–American students. *Journal of College Student Development*, **31**, 162–168.

Thompson, V. L. S. (1996) Perceived experiences of racism as stressful life events. *Community Mental Health Journal*, **32**, 223–233.

US Department of Justice & Federal Bureau of Investigation: Criminal Justice Information Services Division (1997) *Hate Crime Statistics 1997*. Uniform Crime Reports. Washington, DC: US Government Printing Office.

Vadher, A. & Ndetei, D. (1981) Life events and depression in a Kenyan setting. *British Journal of Psychiatry*, **139**, 134–137.

Williams, D. R. (1996) Racism and health: a research agenda. *Ethnicity and Disease*, **6**, 1–6.

Williams-Morris, R. S. (1996) Racism and children's health: issues in development. *Ethnicity and Disease*, **6**, 69–82.

6 Acculturation, cultural identity and mental health

DINESH BHUGRA

Editors' introduction

As discussed earlier in Chapter 1, the role of acculturation and cultural identity needs to be understood in context of clinical diagnosis and management of mental illness. In this chapter Bhugra delineates detailed components of cultural identity as well as acculturation. The latter process can lead to assimilation at one end and deculturation and alienation at the other. Biculturalism may be seen as a more manageable response. However, the individual and group responses to the process of acculturation is affected by an individual's personality profile, absence or presence of social support and support networks, and the host society's response. Concepts of the self are useful in understanding the process of acculturation. Bhugra argues that different components of cultural identity and behaviours related to cultural identity will vary and can be measured. However, such measurements have to take into account not only the individual's self, but also interactions with their own cultural group and with the majority cultural group. The concept of the self has often been neglected but appears to be crucial in the psychological well-being of the individuals.

Culture plays a very important role in the emotional and personal development of any individual. Individuals learn their culture thereby allowing them to experiment with interpretations and meanings of action which can then be adopted and become part of their social and personal repertoire. Sapir (1932) commented that the true locus of culture was in the interactions of specific individuals in the world of meanings which each one of these individuals may unconsciously abstract for themselves. Devereux (1945/1978) concluded "were anthropologists to draw up a complete list of all known types of cultural behaviour, this list would overlap, point by point, with a similarly complete list of impulses, wishes, fantasies etc., obtained by psychoanalysts in clinical settings". There are both covert and overt levels (or aspects) of culture (Linton, 1945) – the latter are socially determined patterns of behaviour utilised by everyone in relation to the important aspects of life from birth to death, that is, the society's design for living (Kluckhohn, 1944), whereas the former, that is, covert aspects, are the common knowledge, psychological states, attitudes and values underlying the design (Linton, 1945). These two levels can be equated with aspects of the self which occur in outer and inner layers, thereby drawing parallels between the individual and culture.

As individual and society are linked, anthropology and psychology need to be linked. Acculturation occurs both at an individual and at a group level. In this chapter, the aim is to highlight the differences between these two levels of acculturation, especially because they work at different levels within the same individual, and their impact on individual's mental health and functioning. It is essential that, in attempting to understand human behaviour, psychology embraces anthropology, largely because anthropology has the strength and skills to understand culture and communities and psychology's focus on the individual can allow the working of the two together.

Process of acculturation

In an earlier area of anthropology, when it was assumed that societies differed according to their degrees of advancement on a universal scale of progress, culture was held to be synonymous with the process of civilisation (Ingold, 1994). In this section, we shall look at the processes of acculturation, especially the beginning of such a process and the results of such encounters.

Cultures encounter other cultures in a variety of ways. Immigration for social, economic or political reasons will have a different impact on individuals and cultures compared to, say, students or sojourners. Adaptation is a useful concept in the study of acculturation and can be of three varieties: adjustment, reaction and withdrawal (Berry, 1976). These are similar to the psychological models of moving towards, moving against and moving away from a stimulus (Berry, 1980). The relationship of the dominant group with the non-dominant group is crucial in this process as is the purpose of the interaction. The reaction of the group has to be seen in the context of the individuals as well as the prevailing social, economic and political climates. In the process of acculturation and assimilation various outcomes – at individual and group levels – are possible.

Acculturation requires the contact of at least two autonomous cultural groups – there must be change in one or both groups which results from this contact. Although, theoretically, changes can and do occur in both groups, in reality one group often dominates the other and may contribute more to this process than the other and this process may undergo several stages before the two cultural groups come into a stable system.

Definitions of acculturation

Acculturation is defined as the "phenomena which result when groups of individuals having different cultures come into continuous first-hand contact, with subsequent changes in the original culture patterns of either or both groups"(Redfield *et al*, 1936).

Berry (1990) suggests that this process of acculturation has to be seen at two levels – individual and group. Groves (1967) suggests using the term 'psychological acculturation' for the changes the individual experiences following close contact with other cultures. Obviously the whole group does not undergoe change at the same pace or to the same degree. Processes of acculturation, cultural changes and psychological acculturation need to be studied in order to identify their impact on individuals as well as culture as a whole, but often are studied as end-points and in a rigid way not allowing for fluidity in these processes.

Four varieties of acculturation have been identified – assimilation, integration, rejection and deculturation (Berry, 1980). In the process of assimilation, individuals relinquish cultural identity and move into the larger society. Assimilation may be defined as the gradual process whereby cultural differences (and rivalries) disappear (Cuber, 1955). Gordon (1964) argues that assimilation and acculturation refer to the same process – the terms are used by sociologists and anthropologists respectively. However, it would appear that acculturation is a broader concept as outlined by Berry (1980). Gordon (1964) goes on to differentiate between structural, identificational and behavioural assimilation. Berry's (1980) perspective has the advantage of using clearer demarcations linked to the degree of contact between two cultural groups and the main purpose of such contact. Integration is defined as the process where the group retains its cultural identity and at the same time moves to join the dominant society. Rejection is the process whereby the group withdraws from the larger society. When rejection is imposed by the dominant group it becomes a kind of segregation leading to mutual distrust and affecting the political economy of the state. Deculturation, argues Berry, is more difficult to define because it is characterised by feelings of alienation, loss of identity and acculturative stress.

It could lead to ethnocide if imposed by the larger group. The interactions between the group's cultural identity and the individual's and the group's relationship with the dominant group all play a role which affects the success or failure of such a process. The argument thus far suggests that the group's response to acculturation is often not uniform, fluid or smooth.

At an individual level, six different areas of psychological functioning in acculturation have been conceptualised; these include language, cognitive style, personality, identity, attitudes and acculturative stress. Of these, language is probably the easiest to identify and measure. However, what is often ignored in the processes of assessment of acculturation is the core of the self. Intermediate options of bilingualism as compared with total language shift at one end of the spectrum, and the maintenance or reinstatement of the traditional language and emphasising its purity at the other, can also form a part of assimilation as far as language is concerned. Berry (1976) argues that with acculturation the cognitive styles of the less dominant group tend to shift towards those of the dominant group. He places the emphasis on formal education and especially the experience of technical learning. However, the concepts of identity, self and self-esteem are closely interlinked and it is not easy to tease them out much less measure them in a practical manner. All such measurements have thus far taken place in isolation – self concept versus self-esteem versus self-identity. The choice of development of traditional or acculturated identity makes it obvious for the individuals that their interaction with the dominant group is also affected by their heritage.

Earlier anthropologists (e.g. Kardiner, 1945; Linton, 1945) proposed that as culture and personality are interrelated and early experiences determine thought processes, it is possible that different societies develop different personality types and, due to socialisation processes and pressures, individuals may develop in a similar way and yet have individual reactions to stress and circumstances. A further impact is dictated by the child-rearing methods and care which are culturally determined and patterned and are, therefore, likely to be similar. Their argument was that early experiences with broadly similar patterns will produce broadly similar individuals who will have similar personality types – basic varieties varying across societies. A major difficulty with this approach is the underlying assumption that these personality types remain static and solid and that no amount of change in the society or the culture is likely to bring about any change in the personality types. It would thus appear that anthropology may well have shied away from the measurements of the acculturative processes for various reasons.

Since the personality theories were influenced heavily by psycho-analysis, some of these factors are discussed in further detail when we look at the development of the self in psychoanalytic and cognitive contexts. Segall *et al* (1990) argue that even though psychoanalytic theory is hard to fault because the society's developed cultural norms encourage the individuals to behave in a certain manner and these norms are then internalised by the individuals, their measurement is problematic because researchers have often ignored individual differences within societies and the societies are seen as homogenous.

Concepts of the personality and self

The definition of self and subjectivity have become important and the varying concepts across cultures have led to a reviewing of the role of the self, perceptions of the self as well as identity (see Morris, 1991, 1994 for an overview). The developmental models of self vary according to personality theories three important models are discussed.

Psychoanalytic theories

Psychoanalytic theory based largely on the works of Freud and post-Freudians retains considerable influence in the individual anthropology field and the theory is often difficult to summarise and is subject to diverse and conflicting interpretations (Morris, 1991). The new-born child is seen as a seething mass of impulses or instinctual desires without guiding or directing consciousness and this was called 'id' because of its impersonal nature. However, as the child must come to terms with external reality a part of this primeval conglomeration becomes differentiated as the ego or self – the prime function of which is to test reality in order that the organism's reactions should be in terms of what is possible. At a later stage of development, out of the need to face society's moral prohibitions, the superego or the conscience emerges. The individual's character structure was thus a result of a three-way struggle between the external world, the id and the superego (Brown, 1961). There are three possible ways of obtaining this: by sublimated expression of pre-genital libidinal drives, a reaction formation against such drives and a residue of pre-genital drives. Freud's biological approach tended in the course of time to become more sociologically oriented (see Freud, 1922). The processes of growth through different phases in childhood and adulthood affect the self, but details of these and processes of ego defence mechanisms and libido theory are beyond the scope of this review. It must be stated, however, that Freud's concepts emerged from Europe and their blind application across other cultures remains a somewhat dubious venture.

Cognitive-development theories

The development of the personality as outlined by cognitive developmental theorists suggests that all children go through various stages of growth which are characterised by certain features and yet are affected by intelligence, cultural background and socio-economic factors. Acquiring sex roles and gender-typing, moral reasoning and subsequent development into personality traits continue throughout most of childhood and adolescence. When a development phase is affected by degrees of cognitive differentiation and incorporating social mores, demands and values contribute to individual growth (Zigler & Phillips, 1960; Zigler & Child, 1969). Factors related to how others respond to the individual in everyday social–psychological interactions have been found to be especially influential (Glick & Zigler, 1985).

The individual's self-image and self-identity are likely to be affected by three layers of interactions. At the earliest level exists the ideal self-image which is characterised by global organisation, but is unable to provide any motivation or direction for change. At the intermediate level there is a differentiation between real and ideal self-images, but that integration adds to the individual's cognitive schemata. At the highest level of integration, the ideal self-image incorporates personal as well as social values. Thus, the integration of ideal and real self-images can not only provide motivation for change, but also enable conceptualisation of appropriate directions and sub-goals, thereby facilitating adaptation (see Glick & Zigler, 1985). It is this adaptation which plays a crucial role in development of self-identity, which will include racial, ethnic or cultural identity. A degree of cognitive complexity is required for an integration of various images of the self and the central importance of this integration is facilitating adult development and adaptation (Erikson, 1968). One source of theoretical direction for understanding of the self and its development has been Mead's (1934) symbolic interactionist approach. Mead posits the self as a phenomenal object distinct from all other objects in its reflective character. For Mead, self-reflection is a social construction and these stages are typified by a social activity that embodies a distinct form of self-reflection. Leahy & Shirk (1985) go on to argue that Mead's theory has several empirical implications for the development of the self. Thus, the self becomes an object of experience by taking the role of the other towards the self. This otherness therefore becomes a critical part in the development of the individual. Thus, the greater the discrepancy between the self and the other, the more likely it is that the identity of the self and self-images (ideal and real) will be affected.

This role-taking ability continues to develop throughout the individual's growth period and allows a series of levels of perspective taking – egocentric, subjective, self-reflective, mutual and conventional systems role taking (Selman, 1980). Each level therefore represents a different level of understanding of how individuals perceive themselves and others, and at each level decentring of the self plays a part in encouraging the individual to focus on these two perspectives in a sequential manner. Even though Mead described a socialised self, this smacks of optimistic functionalism which carries the child from a point of individual isolation to a developmental milestone of sharing the views of others about the self (Leahy, 1983). The cognitive-developmental model suggests that these individual milestones are crucial and have to be reached before subsequent development can occur.

Social learning theory

Social learning approaches in contrast to psychoanalytic approaches emphasise the role of environmental factors in shaping individual personality. For social learning theorists, behaviour emerges as a result of continuous interaction between personal and environmental variables. It is a linked system where the individuals and their environments affect each other. Such an approach is linked with reward and punishment cycles. According to this approach, individual differences in behaviour result in a large part from differences in the kinds of learning experiences a person encounters in the process of growing up. Individuals may acquire many responses without direct reinforcements through vicarious or observational learning.

The individual's repertoire of learned behaviour may be extensive and the particular action chosen in a specific situation depends upon the expected outcome (Atkinson *et al*, 1990). The reinforcements can be direct, vicarious or self-administered. A distinction needs to be made here between personality as a trait on the one hand and as a concept resulting from the processes of acculturation (which are behaviours in themselves) on the other. Human beings have history and that makes them virtually unique and allows learning through methods of transmitting information (i.e. history) across cultures and through the innate capacity to recognise certain varieties of categorical distinctions (Premack & Premack, 1994). This model of development places greater emphasis on social interaction. There is no doubt that social interaction does play some role in the development of the self, but this model does not deal well with individual differences, as noted earlier in this section.

The self in an individual context

The phenomenological approaches of Rogers and Maslow overlap and as Atkinson *et al* (1990) go on to argue, individuals themselves tend to be intuitive scientists and such an approach does not dispute that biological and environmental variables can determine behaviour but does emphasise the individual's own role in defining and creating a destiny which allows him or her to reach peak experiences. Philosophical positions also have political implications. Unlike the behavioural approach, this method provides an outlet for achievement and fulfilling one's potential to its maximum.

The concept of personality as outlined above remains a Western concept and Western ideal of individualism and does not necessarily correspond to the reality of how the Western individual lives in Western culture, far less how any other individual lives in any other culture. Hsu (1985) emphasises that the term personality needs to be ignored and replaced by notions of interpersonal relationships. His concept of self is vital to my hypothesis of acculturation, hence it is necessary to expand on this. The psychological concept of personality can be challenged on the basis that the superego acquired through the process of social interaction is the bridge between personality and culture. The delineation of such a relationship and that between the individuals and their world also need to measure intensity of affective involvement.

Elements of self

Hsu (1985) develops a more precise formulation of how people live as social and cultural beings. He defines the elements of human existence on the basis of ignoring wild swings from one extreme to another and avoiding the common failing of confounding the psychology of the individual (including individual psychopathology) with the socio-cultural orientation of the group (including its overall economic and political patterns and trends) and developed his precise formulation which is represented in seven irregular concentric layers (see Fig. 6.1).

The inner two Layers 7 and 6 are the 'unconscious' and the 'pre-conscious' according to psychoanalytic concepts mentioned earlier. They contain respectively repressed and semi-repressed psychic materials.

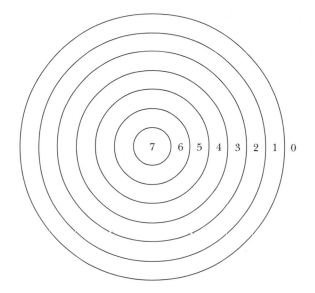

Fig. 1. Man, culture and society (Hsu, 1985):
7 unconscious; 6 pre-conscious; 5 unexpressible conscious; 4 expressible
conscious; 3 intimate society and culture; 2 operative society and culture;
1 wider society and culture; 0 outer world

Layer 5 is termed 'unexpressible conscious' because its contents
are generally kept to the individual. These contents are usually not
communicated to others because the individual may be scared to
do so; material may be too private and therefore others may not be
able to understand it; the individual may feel something but is
unable to verbalise it; or the individual is ashamed to do so.

Layer 4 is 'expressible conscious' because it contains ideas,
materials and feelings which the individual is able to communicate to
others and gets reciprocal feelings and feedback. Some of these ideas
or feelings are very personal, for example, hate, greed, love, whereas
others can be seen at a more global or national level, thereby
contributing to the stereotypes of national characters, for example,
expressions of patriotism. The communicability of such materials is of
course sometimes restricted to those with the same personal, socio-
economic or cultural background.

Layer 3 is that part of the external world with which each
individual has strong feelings of attachment, which often appear
irrational to members of other cultures. It contains others with
whom the individual shares intimacy – is able to share joys and fears
without fear of rejection. Mutual receptivity, emotional support and

verbal communication are all components of this relationship. Hsu (1985) argues that this layer contains what Talcott Parsons calls his "significant alter" but suggests that this layer also contains cultural usages such as caste pollution fears among high-caste Hindus. Any changes in this layer can be quite traumatic to the individual and are therefore likely to be resisted.

Layer 2 is characterised by role relationships. Here the individual finds humans and ideas that might be useful at several levels. The cultural rules at this level are those with which the individual deals without strong or even emotional attachments. Traffic rules, courtesy customs and patterns of greeting are some of the actions that fall within this category and roles are performed by individuals in association with these artefacts. In the normal course of events, the individual is likely to resist changes in Layer 2.

Layer 1 consists of human beings, cultural rules, knowledge and artefacts which are present in the larger society but which may or may not have any connection with the individual. In the normal course of events, the individual has no role or affective relationship with these at all.

In Layer 0 are people, customs and artefacts belonging to other societies with which most members of a society have no contact and, furthermore, of which they may have no idea or only erroneous ideas.

The awareness of these layers is important because understanding the measurements of acculturation focuses on external layers and ignores the others completely, which makes the measurement incomplete and of limited value and any relationship with mental disorders problematic.

Self in social contexts

It is apparent that the self 'changes' according to various external stimuli and yet psychologists continue to assume that it is a static characteristic and should be measured as such. Self-knowledge refers to the desire for accurate and certain evidence of one's traits and abilities and the need for such an experience is highlighted in the need for consistency (of the self). Such a process is required for reducing uncertainty and for the ability to predict and control the environment.

Self-enhancement, on the other hand, refers to the desire for positive feedback about the self and it is rooted in the more basic tendency to seek pleasure and to avoid pain. The pursuit of self-knowledge, self-enhancement and self-improvement can all account for a wide variety of social behaviours and all these motives are in turn rewarded by others around us which then go on to confirm their values in our minds. The link between the self and social behaviour focuses on strategies that an individual develops in order to satisfy these motives in particular social contexts.

The role of self-esteem and other self-preservation strategies are beyond the scope of this review. Suffice it to say that both of these processes are part and parcel of self-enhancement, which improves affect, and such strategies then confirm self-images. The collective identification strategies, on the other hand, deal with the individual's relationship with the collective. Self-categorisation is a concept within this broader category which comes closest to ethnic identity as well as describing the processes of self-identification in a cultural context. The effects of shifting the focus from the personal to the social identity is also likely to affect subsequent behaviour. Such a shift in focus (often described as depersonalisation) leads individuals to behave as group members, producing increased evidence for group behaviour such as stereotyping, cooperation, competition, conformity as well as polarisation (Oakes & Turner, 1990).

Social identity and self-categorisation theorists have frequently proposed views of personal and social identities in which they are defined not by the immediate social context but by the stable enduring characteristics of the individuals (Cheek, 1989). In Cheek's formulation, personal identity refers to one's self-knowledge and self-evaluation whereas social identity includes the characteristics of the self and it is important to be clear what is being measured under these circumstances. When Markus & Kitayama (1991) set out to demonstrate these differences and American respondents were approached they showed asymmetries in self – other similarity judgements in favour of self (i.e. self was judged as less similar to other than other to self) whereas Indian students showed the opposite asymmetry. Cousins (1989) reported that when asked to describe "Who am I?", Japanese students provided examples of specific behaviours whereas American students presented psychological attributes. However, with a contextualised prompt such as "Who am I with friends?", the American students referred to performance and wishes whereas the Japanese presented with psychological attributes.

These observations confirm two things. First, that the individual's perception of the self is very much linked with the context in which the question is being asked. Second, that these perceptions can be formally psychological (based on the Western psychological models) and yet fluid. The independent and inter-dependent self-construals can thus be measured through cognitive schema at some level, but the behavioural and motivational causative factors are easier to measure.

Measurement of acculturation

Problems in measurement

In their attempts to measure acculturation, researchers have ignored a number of methodological problems. For the purposes of quantitative measurement several different psychological and psychometric measurement methods have been developed. Quantitative models of acculturation are very closely linked with the operationalisation of concepts and how these models provide for an analysis of the relationship between acculturation and behaviour. There is little doubt that different dimensions of acculturation are related to different dimensions of behaviour, personality and cognition. A major problem in the process of measuring acculturation even before the process commences is related to deciding on the cross-cultural equivalence of measurement which in turn is influenced by the causal ordering of acculturation as an antecedent of behaviour.

Quantitative models of acculturation suggest that quantitative variables can be discreet or continuous and their levels of measurement can be nominal, ordinal or interval. Acculturation cannot, and should not, be seen as a unidimensional concept. Olmedo (1985) suggests that for the purposes of operational taxonomy of acculturation research, variables ought to be classified as independent versus dependent, qualitative versus quantitative, and unidimensional versus multidimensional. Most of the existing acculturation scales have used either the nominal level (e.g. ethnic group membership) or the ordinal level (e.g. generation). Therefore, the resulting scales have, in general, corresponded to a range of unordered or ordered qualitative variables.

Although acculturative stress has been identified as a major component of, and is clearly linked with, behaviours and experiences which are mildly pathological and disruptive both at the individual and the group levels, acculturative stress is clearly related to overall societal variables. Stress among migrants is said to be lower in multi-cultural societies when groups are able to maintain supportive cultural traditions. In unicultural societies, where there remains a single dominant culture with a clear set of national attitudes and values which all immigrants must either adjust to or oppose, there is greater potential for conflict and higher rates of stress. It is a mistake to ignore the nature of the dominant society and the type of culture it holds dear. Mere presence of various ethnic or cultural groups will not make a society multicultural.

Types of acculturation

Contact with another culture and the resulting change may well be difficult. It may turn out to be reactive and confidential, and a variety of relationships may occur. Culture on either side is not a homogenous mass which will produce a homogenous mass of change. The contact in the process of acculturation may well be physical or symbolic. This may occur through trade, invasion, enslavement and educational missionaries, and in our era also via telecommunications. It is arguable whether any acculturation can occur without any direct contact. Contact may lead to conflict, which may lead to adaptation – a process that enables a group to either reduce the conflict or, in a worst-case scenario, stabilise it. The degree, duration and quality of contact are all very important parameters. Least conflict may result from either accidental or non-purposive contact. It may be short lived, but if bilateral beneficial trade occurs, leading on to mutual satisfaction, the process of acculturation/adaptation may be much quicker. The degree of adaptation is usually reliant on the purpose for which two cultural groups, one dominant and one non-dominant, come together. A maximum amount of conflict will occur if there is an attempt to deliberately take over a society through invasion or through holding its skills and beliefs to ransom by education or evangelisation over a prolonged period of time.

As we have noted earlier, there are two levels of acculturation – group and individual. Poole (1994) highlights the differences between personhood (which consists of powers of cognitive, emotional, motivational and behavioural abilities) and selfhood (a set of orientations towards the culturally constituted behavioural environment). Consequently, quantitative measurements can be quite problematic.

The ideal measurement of acculturation will operate at both these levels and at all three stages of the process (i.e. contact, conflict and adaptation). It is essential to measure groups' experiences of contact and conflict along with the individuals' exposure and conflicts. Virtually all measuring inventions in psychology aim to get the individual's perspective (e.g. Maveras & Bebbington, 1990; Stopes-Roe & Cochrane, 1990; Ghubash *et al*, 1994; Cheung, 1995). All these questionnaires focus on the individual and convert their experiences into quantitative data which has limited value. In addition to these, two further questions need to be addressed but have often been ignored.

  (a) Is the cultural identity of the individual of value to the individual so that he or she is motivated to retain it?

(b) Are positive relations with the dominant group sought? If they are, is one or both of the following processes beginning to emerge: (i) relinquishing cultural identity leading to assimilation, and (ii) retaining cultural identity leading to integration?

Both these consequences are assumed to be healthy and any other outcome is seen as pathological. However, in certain situations it is possible that the rejection of one's own cultural values and cultural identity may exclude the individual from his or her own culture in which case psychological distress or Berry's (1980) term of acculturative stress may well apply.

Components of cultural identity

In contrast to the process of acculturation, we aim to focus on the structure of cultural identity which may well have been reached by the individual, and although not all six components have the equivalent value, they may well need to be studied and understood prior to embarking on any measurement.

Religion

The cornerstone of any identity, especially since childhood, is the religion of the individual along with the rituals that go with it. As an adult, the individual may choose not to follow a particular religion or not believe in God, but a part of the identity relates to religious feelings. It is of course possible that some of these feelings remain at Layers 1 and 2 of Hsu's (1985) model of self discussed earlier. In addition, an important aspect of the individual's religion may well come to the attention of researchers either at a very superficial level where only the religious domination is considered and the level of commitment to religion, religious rituals and active participation in religious gatherings and setting is ignored. The qualitative interpretation of such a control aspect will allow the researcher to achieve two things. First, there will be access to the core sub-conscious processes, allowing a truer measurement of the self; second, it will allow a degree of uderstanding of the processes of belonging to a particular religious group. Anticipated by the researcher, the additional knowledge of the individual's self allows the researcher to put the changes of assimilation into their true context. Such a development remains difficult to measure using pure quantitative techniques. Fowler (1981) describes six stages of faith – another concept often ignored in measuring the process of cultural identity. The conceptual subtleties of such a theory suggest that measurement in the religious–cultural contexts may yield some clues to the individual society.

Rites of passage

Various rites of passage and their following by an individual allows a degree of belonging and the development of a cultural identity. Most cultures have rites for boys and girls as they reach puberty. Adhering to these rites of passage allow individuals to belong to their own cultural group. This affirmation of their status, along with acceptance by other members, allows the individual to grow in a confident style. For example, among the Indian diaspora, arranged marriage plays a very important role and even though people in India do not necessarily follow the ritual, it is still an important tool for being accepted as a traditional individual. However, the question remains how does one measure the process of arranged marriage and the individual's belief in it? Similarly, if within one's own culture one is not following the rituals as prescribed by the religion, is it possible that the cultural group will accept the said individual wholeheartedly? Often, acculturation questionnaires will focus on this aspect, completely ignoring the fluidity of the concept and thereby labelling an individual modern or traditional without understanding the context.

Language

Language use is fundamental to the creation and expression of social identity and difference, and the translation of cultures relies on translation of languages as mentioned above. Sometimes, language is not an issue at all, whereas at other times it is the most obvious and apparent aspect of cultural identity change. Again, acculturation questionnaires often contain only simple questions about whether the individual speaks or understands the spoken language or reads or writes the specific language. Most bilingual individuals are able to clearly identify a period of switch between the two languages and the switch in thinking in the dominant language. Gordon (1964) proposes 'Anglo-conformity' as a broad umbrella term to cover a variety of viewpoints about assimilation and immigration to the USA. Gordon (1964) argues that "it is quite likely that 'Anglo-conformity' in its more moderate forms has been, however explicit its formulation, the most prevalent ideology of assimilation in America throughout the nation's history". Linguistic varieties, or ways of speaking, may be conscious or unconscious markers of personal and social identity, and language usage expresses and creates social differences as demonstrated by regional accents. The abandonment of one language for another may be an economic phenomenon or a political statement and yet it identifies individuals as well as their interactions. The analysis of such a 'discourse' is essential in anthropology but often ignored in psychology and psychiatry.

The impact of the assimilation process on non-dominant groups suggests that initially, because of either reasons of language or social network, groups tend to 'stick together', living in areas which may have large concentrations of the same ethnic group. It is only when individuals have become economically stable and linguistically viable that they may choose to leave these strongholds to make their own independent way. These may be urban or rural settings though they are most likely to be inner city areas because here the accommodation is cheap and affordable and also members of the dominant culture may not wish to live in these areas. With this flocking together groups have strengthened themselves socially, economically and occasionally politically. The memories of aspirations of native lands, recreational patterns, languages and networks, of personal friendships and families have contributed to these processes. Thus just measuring speaking, writing or reading of a language may ignore very many other aspects which may explain the processes of acculturation.

Food

In some cultures, for example, Indian (upper-caste Hindu house-holds especially), the purity of food remains an important aspect of functioning and maintaining an aura of exclusivity. Most cultures foster some food taboos, especially if they have been determined by religion, thereby permitting easy measurement of our attitudes to food, food preparation and places for shopping for foods. However, such measures ignore the rapid changes in the availability and obtaining of exotic foods and preparations at short notice, and the abundance of fast-food restaurants, which allow people much greater freedom in changing their food habits. Once again, these acts will fall in the outer layers of the Hsu model and although easy to measure the symbolism of food in various cultures is not addressed at all in acculturation questionnaires.

Leisure

The central issue here is whether a particular individual is able to modify his or her leisure activities according to acculturative processes.

Although easier to measure because the researcher can ask questions about the type of music an individual listens to, the kind of books and magazines the individual likes to read and in which language, as well as the kind of sports activities he or she takes part in or is interested in following, e.g. whether it is American Football or Kabaddi, there are two problems in assessing such activities. First, whether the individual is actually able to participate in these activities given the stresses of dealing with the dominant culture, and second, and perhaps more important, whether the culture itself encourages leisure activities or even allows them. Obviously the cultural and psychological characteristics of the two populations will affect the outcome of the acculturation process. The reaction of the larger group will thus provide a better degree of insight into the functioning of individuals in such a set-up.

Social and cultural qualities

Social and cultural attitudes are often one of the last factors to undergo any change in response to the acculturation process. As a result of direct contact and influence the changes may occur in the medium to long term. With contact, further influence from the dominant culture will play a very significant role in the development of attitudes and values and will perhaps allow the individuals to change at a pace which is tolerable and also acceptable to other members of the cultural group.

A parallel change will occur in psychological variables (as a result of the impact of both their own changing group and the dominant group) and these psychological changes may go on for a considerable length of time. As noted earlier, the course of change resulting from the process of acculturation is very variable and depends upon a number of characteristics in both the dominant and non-dominant groups. Not every individual will experience change at the same level or with the same speed, but this is one area where the individual cognitive variables are perhaps more easily measured when compared to other components. Although these areas of functioning of the individual self allow relatively easy quantitative measurement, it is essential that some detailed ethnographic information is collected, especially on the formation of self-identity as part of acculturation and socialisation, and that such qualitative measurement deals with understanding these processes both before and after cultural change.

Cognitive shifts occurring as a consequence of acculturation mean that these shifts are often the very goal of acculturation, as is the case of religious or educational missions.

Performance on cognitive tests may become better and Berry *et al* (1992) go on to emphasise that, if the point is to demonstrate that over time or over generations beliefs, abilities or even general intelligence (as defined and measured by the dominant society) change in the acculturating group in the direction of the norms in the larger society, then the task is rather easy.

The changes due to acculturation may well change acculturation attitudes and changes in contact participation, thereby making possible the measurements of the state or even the trait but possibly not the process. It is worth emphasising here that the process of acculturation although perceived as, and often reported as, linear is no such thing. It is immensely complex and in addition to the conflict and reaction other resistive strategies may well occur.

Acculturation and mental health

There is no doubt that deculturation as a process of settling down in a new and alien culture will produce psychological distress and that this distress will then go on to affect the individual's personal and social functioning. Such an event is likely to lead to development of mental illnesses such as adjustment reactions, eating disorders, affective illness, paranoid reactions and common mental disorders. Not every individual moving to a new culture will respond in the same way. These reactions will depend upon the individual's personality traits, previous experiences, self-esteem, previous functioning, current accessible social support etc. In planning delivery of services for refugees or migrants the individual factors and broad social factors as well as interaction between the two need to be taken into account. The following examples will illustrate some of the clinical conditions where acculturation may well prove to be a key factor in response to adversity. It must be emphasised that often factors related to migration (and the resultant stress) are not dissimilar to the factors related to acculturation (and the resultant stress).

Common mental disorders

The rates of common mental disorders in migrant communities vary across settings but have generally been suggested to be higher than in the general population. Landrine & Klonoff (1996) studied acculturation, social class, skin colour and education along with life events and racist events and suggested that in their African American sample acculturation accounted for 13.7% of the variance in symptoms above and beyond the variance accounted for by class, genetic stressors, skin colour and racism. Even when they re-evaluated their data, acculturation appeared to be a stronger and more important factor than racism. They propose that predictors of symptoms for African Americans vary with level of acculturation, and stressors may have different impacts on acculturated versus traditional African Americans, and that coping styles and mediators may well also be different (also see Chapters 4 and 5)

Another key factor is the generational difference. It is possible that first- and second-generation migrants will have differing patterns of acculturation. With increasing age acculturated and bicultural people experience a sense of loss regarding the extent to which they have departed from the practice values and traditions of the culture they came from, leading to a nostalgic attitude towards the old country (Landrine & Klonoff, 1996).

They may then turn their children into more traditional individuals or the second-generation may become more traditional, searching for their own roots. The younger generation may not identify the racism, prejudice or discrimination or may not be aware of it, and yet their response to rejection, unemployment etc. may be stronger and they may experience stronger levels of distress. If the younger generation is able to find a sense of belonging by identifying with a reference group, this group may provide certain protective factors. Successful adaptation will depend upon a number of factors, such as personality, self-esteem, realistic appraisal of the majority culture and social support.

Bearing in mind the methodological problems in identifying affect and emotion, what emerges is that there are cultural variations in the phenomenology of these experiences and these are not to do with underdiagnosis as previously assumed. Jenkins *et al* (1990) suggest that key elements in understanding this variation involve definitions of selfhood, indigenous categories of emotion and emphasis as particular aspects of the emotional life patterning of relationships among emotions, precipitating social situations and physiological accounts of bodily experiences of emotions.

The loss of status leading to poor self-esteem and poor social support may provide a clue to the aetiology of common mental disorders in migrants. However, the rates of common mental disorders in migrants vary dramatically, which may reflect different sites and methods of data collection. However, some of the incidence studies have targeted acculturation as a factor. Cochrane & Stopes-Roe (1981) conducted a community survey on people of Indian, Pakistani and White British origin in Birmingham and found that the former two groups had lower rates of emotional disorder compared with the latter group. On the other hand when Greek

Cypriots were compared with native White British the latter had rates similar to Greeks in Athens, but lower than Greek Cypriots in London (Maveras & Bebbington, 1988). The latter authors linked these high rates with lower levels of acculturation.

Lloyd (1992) reported that among general practice attendees men of African–Caribbean origin consulted more than their White counterparts and the groups least likely to be diagnosed as having non-psychotic disorders were women of Asian and African–Caribbean origin. In this sample, the perceived causation of their emotional distress by the patients (which can be construed as a proxy for acculturation) was attributable to a number of factors of which gender and socio-economic status are but two. Thus, social factors play a role in the causation and maintenance of psychological distress.

On the other hand some acculturative behaviours like language, listening to music and entertainment in the African–Caribbean group will not be dissimilar to those among Whites. This suggests that other migrants like Indians, Pakistanis, Bangladeshis, Cypriots and other Europeans who do not have English as their primary language may face more difficulties in settling down and the prediction would be that they will suffer from higher levels of common mental disorders.

Another related factor to acculturation is social class. A jet-setting pop star or businessman will not have same levels of acculturative stress. Furthermore, with lower social class there may be additional physical problems like infection and poor nutritional status which may isolate the individual even further, especially in mixing with the majority community and learning to deal with the majority culture. Beliappa (1991) reported that mental distress was higher among 25–36- and 16–55-year-old Asians and difficulties in preserving culture were seen as the most important factor in the genesis of this distress.

There is some suggestion that there is an adverse correlation between immigrants' rates of psychiatric admission and the relative size of the immigrant group (Mintz & Schwartz, 1964; Wechsler & Pugh, 1967; Murphy, 1977), although this has not been confirmed in Australia and the UK (Krupinski, 1975; Cochrane & Bal, 1988). There is clear evidence to suggest that migration and resettlement set in motion a phase-related mental health risk (Westermeyer *et al*, 1984; Rumbaut, 1985; Beiser, 1987). Beiser (1996) argues that refugees are likely to experience higher rates of distress within the first year of their arrival. Others have argued that there is a 12–18-month period of risk (Rumbaut, 1985). Not surprisingly, young, poorly educated, unemployed males who may not speak the host country's language are at particular risk for developing distress during the early years of resettlement (Krupinski *et al*, 1973; Beiser,

1983; Beiser *et al*, 1993). Unemployment can serve as a powerful mediator in development of emotional distress. Employment as a protector and provider of security, social support and self-esteem also allows individuals to fulfil family obligations, thereby reducing stress.

Nostalgia for the past is said to be one of the risk factors for developing depression in refugees (see Beiser, 1996). Loss of face, shame and guilt at surviving with persistent marginalisation may suggest that there are also other factors at play in adjustment reactions. Acculturation processes will get at loss of face and social support but additional measurements as generational differences in acculturation may provide an indication for identifying aetiological factors.

Culture shock can be defined as a feeling of disorientation both socially and environmentally leading the individual to a sense of bewilderment when previously known norms, values, words and expressions mean little in the new environment. Oberg (1960) after coining this term noted that psychological symptoms accompanying it range from anxiety, depression and obsessional symptoms to paranoid suspicious bewilderment. Kino (1951) argued that paranoid symptoms may reflect reaction to the majority culture. Rack (1982) argues that these paranoid reactions are not dissimilar to the reactions reported by individuals who may be suffering from one or more sensory deprivations. For example those who develop deafness may become more sensitive to other people's whispers and an increasing sense of isolation in themselves.

Furthemore, poor social functioning will contribute to a sense of isolation and alienation. Although it has been argued that a sense of isolation will lead to social withdrawal, this sense may be related to premorbid personality. The selective migration hypothesis cannot be applied universally to explain high rates of psychiatric disorders across all immigrant groups. Social isolation and social role changes will create insecurity and increase with social stress in an alien culture. Host reactions also play a role in development of individual migrants responses. There is no doubt that individuals belonging to an out-group are treated less favourably than those belonging to the in-group (Bochner, 1982). Stereotypes and racist assumptions thus play a key role in social isolation, financial under rewarding and social under functioning, thus setting a vicious circle of poor functioning and increasing isolation.

These illustrations suggest that a lot of work still needs to be done, not only in defining the acculturative processes, but also in their measurement and in the way they impinge on an individual's functioning. Any resulting conflicts within the individual, individual and family, individuals and their community and individuals and the majority culture need to be studied to tease out aetiological and mediating factors the in developing of psychopathology.

Bhugra *et al* (1999) demonstrated that using the Asian Cultural Identity Schedule among individuals of different ages who had committed deliberate self-harm and their carers, measures of acculturation highlight generational and cultural differences. The key factors which were found to be significant in differentiating traditional attitudes from modern attitudes were religion, religious rituals, languages spoken, views on arranged marriage, decision-making in the household and social contacts maintained within the same ethnic group. The individual self is measured by language and leisure activities, the familial self is measured by decision-making in the household and attitudes towards parents, and the social self is measured by degree of contact with other relatives, employment settings and attitudes and responsibility towards others in the community.

Conclusions

The concept of self is crucial to the psychological well-being of individuals. The process of acculturation not only affects the external layers of personality and functioning in behavioural terms but such processes are also likely to affect the inner core of the self, which most researchers in the field of acculturation appear to have ignored. The measurement of this core can be made possible by using qualitative methods of gaining information.

Such an endeavour is crucially important because it allows a clearer understanding of the processes as well as the structure of acculturation. Such an understanding allows us to foresee the direction and processes of change and by using this information the multicultural society can allow its members to belong and to grow at a pace that is suitable for them. An implication for measuring in this way is that there are a number of different 'selves' at different levels and their true psychological integration may well provide the much needed feeling of security and better psychological functioning. The process of change when related to these self-concepts will enable the individual to not only have stable relationships and bonds and cognitive challenges, but also roles which allow them to feel comfortable with both cultural groups. The existing approaches to measuring acculturation rely on a view of culture as a largely seamless and shared significant experience, and consider cultures to be pragmatically organised events of patterned interactions.

It would appear from this review that such approaches are insufficient unless and until additional qualitative measures are added to enable understanding of the cultural constitution of such phenomena.

There appears to be an urgent need for placing the self back at the core of the process of acculturation and cultural identity and changing concepts in response to external causative factors and longtitudinal contact will allow the researcher to link the individual self with 'the other' representing the dominant society. Anthropology with its skills in understanding cultures and the active processes can help psychology in its limited approaches to quantitative measures of the self.

References

ATKINSON, R., SMITH, R., BEM, P. J., *et al* (1990) *Introduction to Psychology*. New York: Harcourt Brace Jovanovich.

BEISER, M. (1983) Influences of time, ethnicity and attachment on depression in southeast Asian refugees. *American Journal of Psychiatry*, **145**, 46–51.

—— (1987) Changing time perspective and mental health amongst southeast Asian refugees. *Culture, Medicine and Psychiatry*, **11**, 437–464.

——, TURNER, R. & GANESAN, S. (1993) Unemployment, under employment and depressive affect among southeast Asian refugees. *Psychological Medicine*, **23**, 731–743.

—— (1996) Adjustment disorder in DSM–IV: cultural considerations. In *Culture and Psychiatric Diagnosis: a DSM–IV Perspective* (eds J. E. Mezzich, A. Kleinman, H. Fabrega, *et al*). Washington, DC: American Psychiatric Association Press.

BELIAPPA, J. (1991) *Illness or Distress?* London: Confederation of Indian Organisations.

BERRY, J. W. (1976) *Human Ecology and Cognitive Style*. New York: Sage.

—— (1980) Acculturation as varieties of adaption. In *Acculturation* (ed. A. M. Padilla), pp. 9–26. Boulder, CO: Westview.

—— (1990) Psychology of acculturation. In *Applied Cross-Cultural Psychology* (ed. R. W. Brislin), pp. 232–253. Newbury Park, CA: Sage.

——, Poortinga, Y. H., Segall, M. H., *et al* (1992) *Cross-Cultural Psychology*. New York: Cambridge University Press.

BHUGRA, D., BHUI, K., DESAI, M., *et al* (1999) Asian Cultural Identity Schedule. *International Journal of Methods in Psychiatric Research*, **8**, 212–218.

BOCHNER, S. (1982) The social psychology of cross-cultural relations. In *Cultures in Contact* (ed. S. Bochner), Oxford: Pergamon.

BROWN, J. A. C. (1961) *Freud and the Port-Freudians*. Harmondsworth: Penguin.

CHEEK, J. M. (1989) Identity orientation and self-interpretation. In *Personality Psychology: Recent Trends and Emerging Directions* (eds D. Buss & N. Cantor). New York: Springer-Verlag.

CHEUNG, P. (1995) Acculturation and psychiatric morbidity among Cambodian refugees in New Zealand. *International Journal of Social Psychiatry*, **41**, 108–119.

COCHRANE, R. & STOPES-ROE, M. (1977) Psychological and social adjustment of Asian immigrants to Britain. *Social Psychiatry*, **12**, 195–206.

—— & —— (1981) Psychological symptom levels in Indian immigrants to Britain. *Psychological Medicine*, **11**, 319–327.

—— & BAL, S. (1988) Ethnic density is unrelated to incidence of schizophrenia. *British Journal of Psychiatry*, **153**, 363–366.

COUSINS, S. D. (1989) Culture and self-perception in Japan and the United States. *Journal of Personality and Social Psychology*, **56**, 124–131.

CUBER, J. (1955) *Sociology, a Synopsis of Principles.* New York: Appleton-Century-Croft.

DEVEREUX, G. (1945) The logical foundations of culture and personality studies. *Transactions of New York Academy of Sciences,* **2,** 110–130.

ERIKSON, E. H. (1968) *Identity; Youth and Crisis.* New York: W. W. Norton.

FOWLER, J. W. (1981) *Stages of Faith: Psychology of Human Development and the Quest for Meaning.* San Fransicso, CA: Harper & Row.

FREUD, S. (1922) *The Ego and the Id.* London: Hogarth Press.

GHUBASH, R., HAMDI, E. & BEBBINGTON, P. (1994) The Dubai Community Psychiatric Survey: acculturation and the prevalence of psychiatric disorder. *Psychological Medicine,* **24,** 121–131.

GLICK, M. & ZIGLER, E. (1985) Self-image – a cognitive development approach. In *The Development of the Self* (ed. R. Leahy), pp. 1–53. New York: Academic Press.

GORDON, M. M. (1964) *Assimilation in American Life.* New York: Oxford University Press.

GROVES, T. D. (1967) Psychological acculturation in a tri-ethnic community. *Southwestern Journal of Anthropology,* **23,** 337–350.

HSU, F. L. K. (1985) The self in a cross-cultural perspective. In *The Self in a Cross-Cultural Perspective* (eds A. Marsella, F. K. Hsu & F. De Vos), pp. 24–55. Tavistock: New York.

INGOLD, T. (1994) Introduction to culture. In *Companion Encyclopaedia of Anthropology* (ed. T. Ingold). London: Routledge.

JENKINS, J., KLEINMAN, A. & GOOD, B. (1990) Cross-cultural studies of depression. In *Advances in Mood Disorders* (eds J. Becker & A. Kleinman). Hillside, NJ: Erlbaum.

KARDINER, A. (1945) *The Psychological Features of Society.* New York: Columbia University Press.

KINO, F. (1951) Aliens' paranoid reactions. *Journal of Mental Science,* **97,** 589–594.

KLUCKHOHN, C. (1944) *Mirror for Man.* New York: McGraw-Hill.

KRUPINSKI, J. (1975) Psychological maladaption in ethnic concentrations in Victoria. In *Cultures in Collision* (ed. I. Pilowsky), pp. 49–58. Adelaide: National Association of Mental Health.

——, STOLLER, A. & WALLACE, L. (1973) Psychiatric disorders in eastern European refugees now in Australia. *Social Science and Medicine,* **7,** 31–45.

LANDRINE, H. & KLONOFF, E. A. (1996) *African–American Acculturation.* Thousand Oaks, CA: Sage.

LEAHY, R. (1983) Development of self and the problems of social cognition. In *Review of Personality and Social Psychology* (eds L. Wheeler & P. Shaver). Beverly Hills, CA: Sage.

—— (1985): The development of the self: conclusion. In *The Development of the Self* (ed. R. Leahy), pp. 295–304. New York: Academic.

—— & SHIRK, S. (1985) Social cognition and the development of the self. In *The Development of the Self* (ed. R. Leahy), pp. 123–150. New York: Academic.

LINTON, R. (1945) *The Cultural Background of Personality.* New York: Appleton-Century-Croft.

LLOYD, K. (1992) Ethnicity, primary care and non-psychotic disorders. *International Review of Psychiatry,* **4,** 257–265.

MARKUS, H. & KITAYAMA, S. (1991) Culture and the self: implications for cognitive emotion and motivation. *Psychological Medicine,* **98,** 224–253.

MAVERAS, V. & BEBBINGTON, P. (1988) Greeks, British Greek Cypriots and Londoners: a comparison of morbidity. *Psychological Medicine,* **18,** 433–442.

—— & —— (1990) Acculturation and psychiatric disorder. *Psychological Medicine,* **20,** 941–952.

MEAD, M. (1934) *Minds, Self and Society.* Chicago, IL: University of Chicago.

MINTZ, N. & SCHWARTZ, D. (1964) Urban ecology and psychosis. *International Journal of Social Psychiatry,* **10,** 101–118.

MORRIS, B. (1991) *Western Concepts of the Individual.* Oxford: Berg.

—— (1994) *Anthropology of the Self.* London: Pluto Press.

MURPHY, H. B. (1977) Migration, culture and mental illness. *Psychological Medicine,* **7,** 677–684.

OAKES, P. & TURNER, J. (1990) Is limited information processing capacity the cause of social stereotyping? In *The European Review of Social Psychology* (eds W. Stroebe & M. Hewstone), pp. 111–135. New York: Wiley.

OBERG, K. (1960) Cultuie shock. *Practical Anthropology*, **7**, 177–182.

OLMEDO, E. L. (1985) Quantitative models of acculturation. In *Acculturation* (ed. A. Padilla). Boulder, CO: Westview Press.

POOLE, F. J. P. (1994) Socialisation, enculturation and the development of personal identity. In *Companion Encyclopaedia of Anthropology* (ed. T. lngold), pp. 831–840. London: Routledge.

PREMACK, D. & PREMACK, A. J. (1994) Why animals have neither culture nor history. In *Companion Encyclopaedia of Anthropology* (ed. T. Ingold), pp. 350–365. London: Routledge.

RACK, P. (1982) *Race, Culture and Mental Disorder.* London: Tavistock.

REDFIELD, R., LINTON, R. & HERSKOVITS, M. J. (1936) Memorandum on the study of acculturation. *American Anthroplogist*, **38**, 149–152.

RUMBAUT, R. (1985) *Mental Health and the Refugee Experience. Southeast Asian Mental Health: Treatment, Prevention Services and Research.* DDHS Publications ADM–1399. (eds M. T. Owan *et al*), Rockville, MD: NIMH.

SAPIR, E. (1932) Cultural anthropology and sociology. *Journal of Abnormal and Social Psychology*, **27**, 229–242.

SEGALL, M. H., DASEN, P. R., BERRY, J. W., *et al* (1990) *Human Behaviour in Global Perspective.* New York: Pergamon Press.

SELMAN, R. (1980) *The Growth of Interpersonal Understanding.* New York: Academic Press.

STOPES-ROE, M. & COCHRANE, R. (1990) *Citizens of this Country.* Clevedon: Multilingual Matters.

WECHSLER, H. & PUGH, T. (1967) Fit of individual and community characteristics and rates of psychiatric hospitalization. *American Journal of Sociology*, **73**, 331–338.

WESTERMEYER, J., NEIDER, J. & VANG, T. F. (1984) Acculturisation and mental health: a study of Hmong refugees at 1.5 and 3.5 years postmigration. *Social Science and Medicine*, **18**, 87–93.

ZIGLER, E. & CHILD, I. (1969) Socialization. In *The Handbook of Social Psychology* (eds G. Lindsey & E. Aronson). Reading, MA: Addison-Wesley.

—— & PHILLIPS, L. (1960) Social effectiveness and symptomatic behaviours. *Journal of Abnormal and Social Psychology*, **61**, 231–238.

7 Mental illness and ethnic minority groups

DINESH BHUGRA and RAY COCHRANE

> **Editors' introduction**
>
> *Psychiatric illnesses are mostly multi-factorial in their genesis. Social, biological and psychological factors play an important role in how psychiatric illnesses come about and ideally their management too should take all these factors into account. In this chapter, we propose to highlight some psychiatric conditions as well as the difficulties in researching these conditions and planning health delivery. The development of psychiatric services is described in Chapter 17.*

Cultures differ not by their cognitive facilities but in the focus of their interests (Littlewood, 1990). To the individual's basic biological patterns are added characteristic personality factors which strengthen or weaken his or her ability to cope and to withstand stresses. Such adaptive responses are also affected and modified by responses of the culture and society, for it is the culture that determines both the nature and the perception of stress, as well as the kinds of responses that have been developed for coping with it by members of the particular culture. While specific stresses may be more characteristic of one culture than another, it is the non-specific aspect of stress or the conflicts within the culture that may precipitate psychiatric disorder in a vulnerable individual (Kiev, 1972).

Illness patterns and service usage

The suggestion that some groups have high rates of one condition or another and that it is these rates which determine service usage is simplistic. There remain several methodological problems that need to be addressed.

Until recently most of the information available on general samples of ethnic minority groups were drawn from hospital admission data. Such an approach has both advantages and disadvantages. A major advantage is that they are available on a national scale and are non-reactive, that is, are not likely to be influenced by the research itself. A key disadvantage is that for ethnic minority groups these data are often inadequate and incomplete. There are four serious flaws in statistics related to ethnicity.

(a) Only data based on country of birth, not ethnicity, has been available. When a majority of individuals from ethnic minorities were born abroad this may not have been a major problem, but with increasing numbers born in the UK such data become increasingly confounded.

(b) Record keeping in the NHS has been very uncertain and unreliable. In 1981, for example, nearly one-third of mental hospital in-patient admission returns failed to provide information on country of birth even though this had been asked for explicitly. No such statistics are available for out-patients or other forms of psychiatric care. Ethnic monitoring has only recently been introduced systematically into NHS data collection.

(c) Although in theory clinicians are encouraged to fill in these returns using ICD–10 categories, the standardisation of such diagnoses and data is far from satisfactory. Recorded diagnoses may show regional and local variations, and the interpretation of data over time becomes even more difficult as diagnostic criteria and fashions change.

(d) Although there is a considerable amount of research evidence on the factors apart from severity of illness leading to admission, such as age, gender, marital status and social class, there is very limited research on the interaction of these factors with ethnicity and admission rates. If in-patient admissions represent the tip of the iceberg of total psychiatric morbidity in the community, it is not at all clear whether the tip represents a constant fraction of the total across all ethnic groups – indeed, existing evidence leans towards the suggestion that it is not constant.

Bearing in mind these caveats, the most comprehensive surveys conducted for the years 1971 and 1981 (Cochrane, 1977; Cochrane & Bal, 1989) calculated rates for various diagnostic categories and admissions. The findings across specialties are discussed elsewhere. The most obvious and important patterns for adult and community use evident from the 1981 data are:

(a) There was an excess of diagnosed schizophrenia in people born in the Caribbean. Males had nearly five times the rates of native English-born and females nearly four times. The younger Caribbean-born (<35 years) were admitted to psychiatric hospitals with a diagnosis of schizophrenia six times more commonly when compared with native-born males of the same age. This remains a crucial finding.

(b) For all diagnostic categories (excluding schizophrenia) the admission rates of the Caribbean-born were substantially lower than those of the native-born, especially when neuroses, personality disorders and alcohol misuse were considered.

(c) For migrants from the South Asian countries (Indian subcontinent and Hong Kong) overall admission rates were substantially lower (more so in the case of Hong Kong) when compared with those for people born in England. While rates of admission for schizophrenia in these groups were roughly comparable to the native-born rates, for less severe disorders they were substantially lower when compared with the native-born rates. A major exception was the rate of alcohol-related admissions among Indian-born men, which was twice that of the native-born and had increased substantially over the previous decade.

(d) For women born in the Indian subcontinent, the ratio of readmissions to first admission was below that of the nativborn. In the case of the Pakistani-born women there were 1.2 readmissions for every first admission compared with 2.8:1 for native-born women.

The use of admission data highlights some of the aspects of help-seeking. When rates of admission in one graph are low it may be due to the fact that the rates of underlying illness are genuinely low, or it may be that admission and help-seeking are so difficult and stigmatising for people in the graph that they suffer in silence. There have been proposals that specially culturally sensitive services would produce a better take-up rate, and although there is no clear documentary evidence, such an argument appears persuasive.

Further evidence on each of these observations drawn from other studies using data of the same sort as well as community or primary care based studies are used to delineate some of the problems.

Schizophrenia and African–Caribbeans

Several studies have shown high prevalence and incidence rates of schizophrenia in African–Caribbeans. Virtually all show an excess of diagnosed schizophrenia in Britain's African–Caribbean population – the excess ranging from 2 to 14 times that of the White rate depending on methodology. There has been a long-running and yet inconclusive debate about the accuracy of these figures (Sashidharan, 1993) and on the possible causes of excess (Cochrane & Bal, 1987). At least one other study has reported an excess of schizophrenia in Caribbeans in Holland (Selten & Sijben, 1994). It has not been possible to entirely explain away the excess of diagnosed schizophrenia in this group in the UK as a result of:

(a)   an artefact produced by inaccuracies in either the numerator or the denominator used in calculating these rates;

(b)   high rates of schizophrenia in the Caribbean;

(c)   social class and other demographic characteristics which distinguish the Black and White populations of England and which are known to be related to the risk of schizophrenia – a notable exception is a study by Bhugra *et al* (1997*a*) which suggests that unemployment in the African–Caribbeans is a notable cause of their excessive rate of schizophrenia.

(d)   selective migration of those predisposed to schizophrenia.

Two additional hypotheses which have often been put forward as key explanations, misdiagnosis and racism, need to be discussed at some length here.

The racism ingrained and widespread in society will have serious psychological consequences for those who are targets of this prejudice and the discrimination it breeds (see Chapter 4). However, it is difficult to sustain this by itself as an entirely credible explanation in the face of evidence that suggests that perception of such experiences rather than the actual experience itself may have an important role to play in the genesis of stress. It must be asked that if racism were the complete answer, why do South Asians, who are equally at risk of racism, not show similar high rates of serious psychological morbidity? Furthermore, the treated prevalence of other psychiatric conditions which may be more closely susceptible to racism-induced high rates (such as depression, neuroses etc.) is no higher, indeed often lower, in Black people than in White people. Yet this is complicated by the fact that Asian people may well not see depression as a medical illness and may find alternative explanations for the aetiology and treatment of such conditions (see Bhugra *et al*, 1997*b*). Another factor that must be taken into account is that if racism by itself was a cause, African Americans, who have been exposed to even more pervasive racism, do not show the same enormous differential in rates of schizophrenia when compared with White Americans.

The concept of misdiagnosis of schizophrenia has been taken up very strongly by various Black groups. The research evidence for this observation remains very weak. Several studies have reported that misdiagnosis is no more common with Black patients than it is with White patients (Harrison *et al*, 1988; Harvey *et al*, 1990), although others disagree (Mukherjee *et al*, 1983). Leff (1997) argues that the misdiagnosis hypothesis remains a difficult one to prove. The argument that individuals are suffering from psychosis, rather than which psychosis, needs to be taken on board both in management and in planning of service delivery. Misdiagnosis is much more likely to be a problem when a broad or heavily defined category of schizophrenia is applied.

Some basic conclusions can be reached from the overview of research on this topic:

(a) There is an elevated rate of schizophrenia in Britain's African–Caribbean population when compared with the White population. This elevation varies between 2 and 14 times.

(b) A similar picture has emerged from The Netherlands, where rates of schizophrenia among migrants from the Antilles have been shown to be high.

(c) The rate is, if anything, higher among the younger generation (McGovern & Cope, 1987*b*; Harrison *et al*, 1988, 1989; Thomas *et al*, 1993). This is in marked contrast with the usual pattern of the distribution of disease found in migrant populations, where the incomers' rates, whether initially higher or lower than those of the host population, approach those of the host population in the second and subsequent generations.

(d) Until recently, it was clear that African–Caribbean patients with a diagnosis of schizophrenia were more likely to be detained compulsorily for treatment and to have had a non-standard pathway into care. This is beginning to change. Whether this reflects changing patterns of admission for those with severe mental illness or a changed, more enlightened view of clinicians is difficult to say at the present time.

(e) There is some research evidence to suggest that the high rate of diagnosed schizophrenia may be unique to a cohort of African–Caribbean men born in the 1950s or 1960s either in the Caribbean or in the UK (Glover, 1989). Possibly the excess vulnerability in this cohort is linked to the mothers' exposure to influenza while pregnant in a population not previously immunised to the influenza virus. While research evidence of this observation remains somewhat weak it would, if correct, have important implications for how services would need to respond to the phenomenon both in terms of the cost-effectiveness of adapting services to what may be a transitory phenomenon and in terms of prevention of schizophrenia.

(f) As well as increased risk of schizophrenia there is growing evidence of a poorer course and outcome of the disorder in African–Caribbean people when compared with White people (Birchwood *et al*, 1992; McGovern *et al*, 1994; Bhugra *et al*, 1997*a*). After a first episode, African–Caribbeans are more likely to be readmitted, spend longer periods in hospital, have more residual symptoms and have poorer social outcomes than White patients. African–Caribbean patients remain more likely to drop out of contact with services, especially in inner city populations (Bhugra *et al*, 1997*a*). Reduced adherence to medication and disinclination to accept close supervision by mental health professionals may be other factors indicating their previous experiences with psychiatric services.

Lower rates of in-patient admissions of ethnic minority groups:

If admissions for schizophrenia are set aside, given the association between ethnicity and indices of deprivation (poor housing, unemployment, social class distribution) known to be associated with increased risk of psychological and psychiatric morbidity like anxiety and depression, it is surprising that the rates of admission for these conditions among ethnic minority populations are not higher. Three possible explanations exist:

(a) ethnic minority groups genuinely have lower rates of non-psychotic conditions;
(b) ethnic minority groups have the same rates when compared with Whites but seek alternative forms of care;
(c) ethnic minority groups have the same rates as those among Whites but do not access care to the same degree either because the services are unresponsive to their needs or because they are prevented from receiving services.

The second hypothesis remains an attractive one. Certainly for the South Asian group, newspapers and magazines are full of services advertised by hakims, futurologists, palmists, sex specialists etc. It may also be that by attributing attractiveness to such options, clinicians in statutory services may feel that they no longer have responsibility for these groups. The third hypothesis also deserves to be studied in detail and is discussed later in this chapter.

A major exception to this paucity of data for non-psychotic conditions is the study by Cochrane & Howell (1995), which looked at alcohol problems among African–Caribbean males in the West Midlands. Noting the low reported prevalence of alcohol-related disease revealed by in-patient and other treatment data, they set out to screen for alcohol problems in a random sample of Black men. The data showed conclusively that Black males were less likely to exceed safe drinking limits, less likely to get drunk, less likely to have social or personal problems related to alcohol and scored lower on the Alcohol Problems Scale when compared with a random sample of White men. At least for this particular diagnosis the relative in-patient rates of Blacks and Whites seem to be an accurate reflection of morbidity in the respective groups.

Low treated prevalence rates of South Asian populations

This has been a consistently observed finding in the literature, especially when one studies the in-patient data. Except for alcohol-related problems, there has not been any psychiatric condition which has consistently shown higher rates of admissions for the South Asian groups.

In schizophrenia, rates of first admission for South Asian populations in Britain are comparable to those for the White population when appropriate adjustments for demographic differences had been made (Cochrane & Bal, 1987; Bhugra *et al*, 1997*a*). King *et al* (1994) reported a much higher rate of psychoses in Asians but their rates were calculated from a sample size of only seven patients. These differences may be attributed to the population density of the different groups from which the data were collected. Asian patients are reported to have a better course and outcome pattern following first admission. Birchwood *et al* (1992), in a retrospective case-note study in Birmingham, showed that South Asian patients had fewer readmissions, fewer residual symptoms and better social adjustment than did White patients two years after their first admission for schizophrenia. Gupta (1991), employing a similar design, showed that Asian patients had fewer readmissions, spent less time as in-patients and were more likely to be rated as 'well' or 'much improved' than were White patients two years after an admission with a functional psychosis. He went on to report that Asian patients were also nearly twice as likely to lose touch with their general practitioner (GP) – but this was 5–20 years after the index admissions (Gupta, 1992). It is possible that Asians may lose touch because they are dissatisfied with the services. On the other hand, it is also possible that they may have been feeling well and decided not to maintain contact. Bhugra *et al* (1997*a*) reported much better rates of good outcome on a one-year follow-up of schizophrenia. However, the Asian sample was generally older and had more females in it when compared with other studies.

Common mental disorders

The rates of non-psychotic disorders among Asian groups have not been studied to the same degree as psychosis. Cochrane & Stopes-Roe (1981) in a community sample of the Indian-born population found a lower incidence of self-reported minor psychological illness which is consistent with lower rates of admission from non-psychotic disorders. An Office of Population Censuses and Surveys study (Meltzer *et al*, 1995) reported that, compared with White women, Asian, oriental and African–Caribbean women were more likely to have depression, especially the Asian and oriental groups, which were three times more likely to worry about their physical health. Asian and oriental men were less likely than their White counterparts to have symptoms of fatigue and compulsions as well as irritability. Among African–Caribbean men the prevalence of depressive ideas and worry about physical health were more than twice as likely as among White men. However, the numbers on which these conclusions are based are relatively small and they should be interpreted with caution.

Jacob *et al* (1997) reported that 37% of Asian females attending a general practice surgery had minor psychological morbidity on the General Health Questionnaire (GHQ–12) and Clinical Interview Schedule (Goldberg & Williams, 1988). Yet the GPs, who came from the same cultural background, detected only 17% of the morbidity. The low treated prevalence rates manifested by the Hong Kong and Chinese population in the UK (less than 50% of the White rate) are congruent with the findings of local community surveys of the incidence rates of psychological morbidity among the Chinese (Furnham & Li, 1993), which also showed very low rates in this community.

For other population groups from the Indian subcontinent even fewer data are available. Cochrane observed equal levels of morbidity in the random samples of the Pakistani-born and White populations of England but a treated prevalence rate of less than half the White rate for non-psychotic disorders (Cochrane, 1977). This may be seen as clear *prima facie* evidence for under-utilisation of mental health facilities by the Pakistani and Bangladeshi population. Lower acculturation and higher deprivation may influence their under-utilisation of services. As noted above, it is possible that underlying psychological morbidity is being missed both by the primary and secondary care providers. It is possible, although unlikely, that these groups are using alternative sources of care exclusively. Based on a small sample of Asians, Beliappa (1991) was able to illustrate that most Asian people turned to their own resources when having to cope with difficulties and only 3% would consider seeking help from statutory services. In this sample, nearly 17% did not respond to this particular question, hence the observations have to be understood in this particular context. Females were more likely to use socio-religious settings and prayers as coping strategies then compared with males. Stress was believed to be a major cause of ill health, and marriage, finances, children and health concerns were put forward as major stressors.

Attention has already been drawn to the universally low rates of readmission among Pakistani women compared with White women. It would be convenient to believe that this was because they had no further need for in-patient services, but there appears to be no evidence for this. It is possible that these patients want to go back to the home country largely because of the stigma associated with mental illness.

Alcohol

Looking at alcohol-related disorders in the Asian community a different pattern emerges. Indian-born men have more than twice the treated prevalence rates of alcohol-related disorders than White men, and alcohol-related admission accounted for 25% of all mental hospital admissions in this group in 1981. There is no evidence to suggest that this pattern has changed. A community survey of drinking patterns in the West Midlands suggests that Sikh and White groups consumed alcohol approximately to the same extent, whereas Hindus drank less, and Muslims hardly drank at all (Cochrane & Bal, 1990).

It is quite likely that high rates of in-patient treatment in the Sikh groups may reflect a lack of access to voluntary-sector alcohol services. It is also possible that this is seen by them as a medical condition rather than a psychological one and medicalizing the problem may make it less stigmatising. Another possible explanation is that there is evidence from the Indian subcontinent suggesting that South Asians are more likely to suffer liver damage at lower levels of alcohol consumption because of previous exposure to hepatitis. These factors will not apply to the same degree in the second generation.

Deliberate self-harm in Asian women

Another condition which appears to be much more common in Asian females is deliberate self-harm. The rates of attempted and completed suicide are much higher in this group. First identified by Marmot *et al* (1984), subsequent studies have confirmed these trends (Soni Raleigh *et al*, 1990; Soni-Raleigh & Balarajan, 1992). High rates of suicide are marked in younger female Asian age groups, whereas in Asian men and African–Caribbean men the rates are lower than the national average. Merrill & Owens (1986) suggested that these high rates may be linked to culture conflict. It must be emphasised that these high rates are not only confined to the UK but are found around the world in the Indian diaspora. Glover *et al* (1989) analysed the attendance of women after self-poisoning in a casualty department in east London and reported that Asians were over-represented when compared with the White population. Among the Irish the rates of self-harm and suicide are increased, which Leavy (1999) posits to be related to the ease of migration coupled with dislocation, feeling stranded and poor religious adherence. He argues that although migration and settlement are stressful for most ethnic minority groups, cultural methods of coping suggest a different and more negative outcome for Irish migrants. This association between ethnicity and suicidal behaviour is not mediated through an increased propensity to severe mental illness and attempted suicide is less likely to be related to untreated mental illness, which raises doubts about the application or usefulness of currently adaptable strategies for suicide prevention. The younger age profile, and the most common method of suicide by burning, suggest that some other factors are at play. Bhugra *et al* (1999*a,b*) demonstrated that the rates of deliberate self-harm in Asian women were much higher compared with White women and these were attributable to cultural and social factors.

From this necessarily brief overview it would appear that the rates of some psychiatric conditions are higher than expected in the South Asian community and are much lower than expected in others. The underlying social, psychological and psychodynamic factors need to be studied in some depth prior to setting preventive strategies in place.

Eating disorders and minority groups

Often described as the culture-bound syndromes of the West in anorexia and bulimia as well as obesity, rates of eating disorders have been reported to be significantly associated with processes of acculturation and cultural identity. Nasser (1997) suggests that eating disorders are symbolic of notions of thinness cherished and promoted by cultures. In an earlier study (Nasser, 1986), she had reported that female Arab students in London universities showed more levels of morbid concern over weight as measured on a questionnaire compared with Arab students in Cairo University and these were linked to Western norms. Mumford & Whitehouse (1988) had found that rates of bulimia were much higher than expected in second-generation Asian teenagers compared with their White counterparts. These authors explained these rates on the basis of high traditionalism scores. There is no doubt that family factors influence eating disorders, and family factors are themselves affected by migratory and acculturative stresses.

Primary care and ethnic minorities

For a long time African–Caribbean patients came into contact with secondary care through alternative pathways rather than via their GPs. There appears to be no substantial ethnic variation in registration with GPs (Johnson *et al*, 1983), although there remain a number of differences in overall consultation rates, with men and women of Pakistani origin and men of African–Caribbean origin consulting GPs more often than other groups (Balarajan *et al*, 1989; Gillam *et al*, 1989). However, looking at the diagnoses made by the GPs it would appear that White women are most likely to be diagnosed as having a psychological disorder when compared with African–Caribbean or Asian women, who are least likely to be identified as having significant psychological problems (Gillam *et al*, 1989). It is unclear whether this reflects GPs' inability to identify hidden morbidity. As noted above, it seems that in at least one study nearly one-third of Asian women had psychological morbidity and yet the GP identified fewer than one-fifth of these cases. Jacob (personal communication, K. S. Jacob, 1999) demonstrated that educating patients to use key words significantly increased the GPs' pick-up rates.

There is every likelihood that the presentation of such morbidity in the second-generation would be similar to that found in the White population. The apparent excess of somatisation symptoms in the Asian population (Bal & Cochrane, 1990) is not exclusive and it is not uncommon among White patients (Helman, 1990). It has been argued that ethnic minorities use alternative health practitioners more readily than GPs (Bhopal, 1986; Ineichen, 1990) but there is little empirical evidence to support such an assertion.

Before we leave this field it is worth stating that most of the studies in this area have been confined to first-generation migrants and the data on British-born ethnic minority individuals and their access to primary care are only now beginning to emerge. There is no reason to assume that the discrepancies suffered by first-generation migrants in the rates of various illnesses and pathways will persist in their offspring.

General population

The few studies conducted with community samples suggest that for both African–Caribbeans and South Asians, rates of psychiatric morbidity are lower than in the indigenous population (Cochrane & Stopes-Roe, 1981; Bebbington *et al*, 1991) – a surprising observation given the strong association between social and material adversity and prevalence rates for psychological distress in the population at large. Examining the impact of unemployment on British Asians it was reported that the unemployed group had lower rates of psychological well-being and self-esteem compared with those in employment (Shams, 1993; Shams & Jackson, 1994). Most of the research evidence would confirm that ethnic minority groups experience considerably greater levels of social and material adversity – hence it is surprising that these studies report lower than expected psychological morbidity. It may be that the inadequacy of case-finding methods is contributing to the low rates. This is partly upheld by the work of Beliappa (1991) and Krause (1989) who, by using not conventional case definitions but culturally appropriate definitions of mental distress, found high levels of mental distress consistent with high levels of adversity. Nazroo (1997), on the other hand, found that Caribbeans had higher rates of depression but were less likely to receive treatment for it. Among the Caribbean group those in households without a full-time worker had the highest rate of psychosis; those in households with an employed manual worker appeared to have lower rates than those in households with a non-manual worker; most of the differences between the Caribbean and White group could be accounted for by the high rates in these latter Caribbean households. Regarding neurosis across Caribbean, Indian/African Asian and White people, Nazroo (1997) showed a clear relationship in that non-manual households had the best health and those in households without a full-time worker had the worst, although there were no differences between the manual and non-manual categories for the Caribbean group and depression. These links were not proven for Bangaldeshi and Pakistani groups. Gupta (1999) suggests that despite methodological flaws this study shows a major advance in methodology. It is unfortunate that the quality of the data related to mental health is so patchy in this country, especially when related to ethnicity. The research at primary care level must focus on pathways into care and makes it likely that the period and various points of help-seeking between the onset of symptoms and eventual care within the statutory services needs to be studied. Given the poor recognition of psychological morbidity in all ethnic minority groups in primary care and the overall under-representation of such patients within counselling and psychotherapy different types of services must be made available (see Chapter 17).

References

BAL, S. S. & COCHRANE, R. (1990) Why do more Asians at primary care present psychological problems physically? *Health Psychology Papers*, **2**, 59–67.

BALARAJAN, R., YUEN, P. & SONI RALEIGH V. (1989) Ethnic differences in general practitioner consultations. *British Medical Journal*, **299**, 958–968.

BEBBINGTON, P. E., HURRY, J. & TENNANT, C. (1991) The Camberwell community survey – a summary of results. *Social Psychiatry and Psychiatric Epidemiology*, **26**, 195–201.

BELIAPPA, J. (1991) *Illness or Distress?* London: Confederation of Indian Organisations.

BHOPAL, R. (1986) Asians' knowledge and behaviour on preventive health issues; smoking, alcohol, heart disease, pregnancy, rickets, malaria prophylaxis and surmia. *Community Medicine*, **8**, 315–321.

BHUGRA, D., LEFF, J., MALLET, R., *et al* (1997*a*) Incidence and outcome of schizophrenia in whites, African–Caribbeans and Asians in London. *Psychological Medicine*, **27**, 791–798.

—, BALDWIN, D. & DESAI, M. (1997*b*) Focus groups: implications for primary care and cross-cultural psychiatry. *Primary Care Psychiatry*, **3**, 45–50.

—, DESAI, M. & BALDWIN, D. (1999*a*) Attempted suicide in West London. I. Rates across ethnic communities. *Psychological Medicine*, **29**, 1125–1130.

—, BALDWIN, D., DESAI, M., *et al* (1999*b*) Attempted suicide in West London. II. Intergroup comparisons. *Psychological Medicine*, 29, 1131–1139.

BIRCHWOOD, M., COCHRANE, R., McMILLAN, F., *et al* (1992) The influence of ethnicity and family structure on relapse in first episode schizophrenia: a comparison of Asian, Caribbean and white patients. *British Journal of Psychiatry*, **161**, 783–790.

COCHRANE, R. (1977) Mental illness in immigrants to England and Wales: an analysis of mental hospital admissions. *Social Psychiatry*, **12**, 25–35.

— & Bal, S. S. (1987) Migration and schizophrenia: an examination of five hypotheses. *Social Psychiatry*, **22**, 181–191.

— & — (1989) Mental hospital admission rates of immigrants to England: a comparison of 1971 and 1981. *Social Psychiatry and Psychiatric Epidemiology*, **24**, 2–12.

— & — (1990) Patterns of alcohol consumption by Sikh, Hindu and Muslim men in the West Midlands. *British Journal of Addiction*, **85**, 759–769.

— & HOWELL, M. (1995) Drinking patterns of black and white men in the West Midlands. *Social Psychiatry and Psychiatric Epidemiology*, **30**, 139–146.

— & STOPES-ROE, M. (1981) Psychological symptom levels in Indian immigrants to England – a comparison with native English. *Psychological Medicine*, **11**, 319–332.

FURNHAM, A. & LI, Y. (1993) The psychological adjustment of the Chinese community in Britain – a study of two generations: *British Journal of Psychiatry*, **162**, 109–113.

GILLAM, S., JARMAN, B. & WHITE, P. L. (1989) Ethnic differences in consultation rates in urban general practice: *British Medical Journal*, **229**, 953–957.

GLOVER, G. (1989) The pattern of psychiatric admissions of Caribbean-born immigrants in London. *Social Psychiatry and Psychiatric Epidemiology*, **24**, 49–56.

—, Marks, F. & Mowers, M. (1989) Parasuicide in young Asian women. *British Journal of Psychiatry*, **154**, 271–272.

GOLDBERG, D. & WILLIAMS, P. (1988) *A User's Guide to the General Health Questionnaire.* Windsor, Berkshire: NFER–Nelson.

GUPTA, S. (1991) Psychosis in migrants from the Indian subcontinent and English-born controls – a preliminary study on the use of psychiatric services. *British Journal of Psychiatry*, **159**, 222–225.

— (1992) Psychosis in Asian immigrants from the Indian subcontinent: preliminary findings from a follow-up study. *Social Psychiatry and Psychiatric Epidemiology*, **27**, 242–244.

— (1999) The fourth National survey of ethnic minorities. In *Ethnicity: An Agenda for Mental Health.* (eds D. Bhugra & V. Bahl), pp. 245–254. London: Gaskell.

HARRISON, G., OWENS, D., HOLTON, A., *et al* (1988): A prospective study of severe mental disorder in Afro-Caribbean patients. *Psychological Medicine*, **18**, 643–658.

—, HOLTON, A., NEILSON, D., *et al* (1989) Severe mental disorder in Afro-Caribbean patients: some social, demographic and service factors. *Psychological Medicine*, **19**, 683–696.

HARVEY, I., WILLIAMS, M., McGUFFIN, P., *et al* (1990) The functional psychoses in Afro-Caribbeans. *British Journal of Psychiatry*, **157**, 515–522.

HELMAN, C. G. (1990) *Culture, Health and Illness.* Bristol: Wright.

INEICHEN, B. (1990) The mental health of Asians in Britain: little disease or underreporting? *British Medical Journal*, **300**, 1669–1670.

JOHNSON, M., CROSS, M. & CASLEW, S. (1983) Inner-city residents, ethnic minorities and primary health care. *Postgraduate Medical Journal*, **59**, 664–667.

KIEV, A. (1972) *Transcultural Psychiatry*. New York: Free Press.

KING, M., COKER, E., LEAVY, G., *et al* (1994): Incidence of psychotic illness in London: comparison of ethnic groups. *British Medical Journal*, **309**, 1115–1119.

KRAUSE, I. (1989) Sinking heart: a Punjabi communication of distress. *Social Science and Medicine*, **29**, 565–575.

LEAVY, G. (1999) Suicide and Irish migrants in Britain. *International Review of Psychiatry*, **11**, 168–172.

LEFF, J. P. (1997) Epidemiological factors in research with ethnic minorities: In *Ethnicity: An Agenda for Mental Health* (eds D. Bhugra & V. Bahl), pp. 40–47. London: Gaskell.

LITTLEWOOD, R. (1990) From categories to context. *British Journal of Psychiatry*, **156**, 696–702.

MARMOT, J., ADELSTEIN, A. & BULUSU, L. (1984) *Immigrant mortality in England and Wales 1970–1978: causes of death by country of birth*. Studies in Medical and Population Subjects (47). London: University College.

McGOVERN, D. & COPE, R. (1987*a*) The compulsory detention of males of different ethnic groups, with special reference to offender patients. *British Journal of Psychiatry*, **150**, 505–512.

—— & —— (1987*b*): First psychiatric admission rates of first and second generation Afro-Caribbeans. *Social Psychiatry*, **22**, 139–149.

—— & ——, HEMMINGS, P., *et al* (1994) A long-term follow up of young Afro-Caribbean British and white British with a first admission diagnosis of schizophrenia. *Social Psychiatry and Psychiatric Epidemiology*, **29**, 8–19.

MELTZER, H., GILL, B., PETTIGREW, M., *et al* (1995) *The Prevalence of Psychiatric Morbidity Among Adults Living in Private Households*. London: The Stationery Office.

MERRILL, J. & OWENS, J. (1986) Ethnic differences in self-poisoning – a comparison of Asian and white groups. *British Journal of Psychiatry*, **148**, 708–712.

MUKHERJEE, S., SHUKLA, S., WOODLE, J., *et al* (1983) Misdiagnosis of schizophrenia in bipolar patients: a multiethnic comparison. *American Journal of Psychiatry*, **140**, 1571–1574.

MUMFORD, D. & WHITEHOUSE, A. (1988) Increased prevalence of bulimia nervosa among Asian schoolgirls. *British Medical Journal*, **297**, 718.

NASSER, M. (1986) Comparative study of the prevalence of abnormal eating attitudes among Arab female students at both London and Cairo universities. *Psychological Medicine*, **16**, 621–625.

—— (1997) *Culture and Weight Consciousness*. London: Routledge.

NAZROO, J. (1997) *Ethnicity and Mental Health*. London: Policy Studies Institute.

SASHIDHARAN, S. (1993) Afro-Caribbeans and schizophrenia: the ethnic vulnerability hypothesis re-examined. *International Review of Psychiatry*, **5**, 129–144.

SELTEN, J.-P. & SIJBEN, N. (1994) First admission rates for schizophrenia in immigrants to the Netherlands. The Dutch National Register. *Social Psychiatry and Psychiatric Epidemiology*, **29**, 71–77.

SHAMS, M. (1993) Social support and psychological well-being among unemployed British Asian men. *Social Behaviour and Personality*, **21**, 175–186.

—— & JACKSON, P. R. (1994) The impact of unemployment on the psychological well-being of British Asians. *Psychological Medicine*, **24**, 347–355.

SONI RALEIGH, V. & BALARAJAN, R. (1992) Suicide and self-burning among Indians and West Indians in England and Wales. *British Journal of Psychiatry*, **161**, 365–368.

——, BULUSU, L. & BALARAJAN, R. (1990) Suicide among immigrants from the Indian subcontinent. *British Journal of Psychiatry*, **156**, 46–50.

THOMAS, C., STONE, K., OSBORNE, M. N., *et al* (1993) Psychiatric morbidity and compulsory admission among UK-born Europeans, Afro-Carribeans and Asians in central Manchester. *British Journal of Psychiatry*, **163**, 91–99.

8 Psychiatry of old age and ethnic minority groups

AJIT SHAH

Editors' introduction

The vast majority of Black and other ethnic minority groups arrived in the UK in the 1960s and 1970s, when they were relatively young. As they age the number of elderly people in these groups increases. Their mental health care needs were not adequately addressed until recently. With an increased emphasis on family and carers, service planners have taken for granted that families will look after the ethnic minority elderly. There have been few studies on establishing the prevalence of organic and communal mental disorders. Chapters 8 and 9 consider this from different, and yet overlapping, viewpoints.

Shah argues that although basic data are needed to identify the numbers of vulnerable individuals, it is of paramount importance that diagnostic criteria take into account cultural perceptions of ageing and age-related diseases. The multiple jeopardy of being old, alien and having both physical and mental illnesses means that service developments must be multifaceted, and the education and training of health care professionals are vital. Initial assessment is likely to prove crucial in engagement and adherence – using different models of health care delivery Shah emphasises the multiplicity of needs and delivery.

Chapters 8 and 9 should be read in tandem, because Patel and Mirza provide a theoretical backdrop to Shah's clinical and pragmatic overview of developing psychiatric services for ethnic minority elders. Although there are overlaps these have been left in so that the readers can make their own decisions.

Psychogeriatrics is an important discipline of psychiatry (Brodaty, 1991; Jolley & Arie, 1992). In the UK it has achieved speciality status and other countries like Australia are not far behind (Shah, 1997a). Specialist psychogeriatric services are increasingly being developed, even in developing countries (Ogunlesi, 1989). However, such services for ethnic minority groups are poorly developed.

Need for data

Data on the following facets are required for planning and developing psychogeriatric services for ethnic minority groups: definition of ethnic minority elderly; demography; epidemiology; and the availability and utilisation of services.

Definition of ethnic minority elderly

The composite definition of ethnic minority elderly requires separate definitions of ethnic minority and the elderly.

Ethnic minority groups are difficult to define (Lloyd, 1992). The Race Relations Act 1976 distinguished people by race and ethnic origin; race refers to physical differences and ethnic to cultural differences. It is possible to be racially different but culturally similar. Thus, ethnic minority individuals should be defined as those with a cultural heritage distinct from the majority population (Manthorpe & Hettiarachy, 1993). This definition may be appropriate in the UK, where the indigenous White population forms the majority. However, the definition poses difficulties in countries like Australia, where the indigenous population forms a minority. Nevertheless, this remains a useful working definition.

Most contemporary psychogeriatric services utilise an age cut-off of 65 years to allow clear planning and demarcation of resources (Arie, 1970; Pitt, 1974; Lennon & Jolley, 1991). The age cut-off of 55 years has been used in some studies of ethnic elders (Barker, 1984; McCallum, 1990), perhaps to acquire adequate sample size. Which age cut-off should be applied for ethnic elders? The same age cut-off as for contemporary ethnocentric psychogeriatric services should be applied, to avoid confusion and fragmentation of service delivery.

Using the above definitions individuals of Indian subcontinent, African–Caribbean, Chinese, Irish, Jewish, South-African and East European origin can be described as ethnic elders. Closer political and economic union with Europe may lead to an influx of elders from Britain's neighbours. Thus, ethnic elders comprise a heterogeneous group with unique individual and collective experiences (Barker, 1984; Manthorpe & Hettiarachy, 1993). Therefore, different ethnic groups should not be amalgamated and consideration should be given to individual subgroups. Some service providers have not acknowledged this heterogenity (Age Concern & Help the Aged Housing Trust, 1984; Bowling, 1990).

Most ethnic elders are first-generation migrants, with less than 10% of the elderly of Indian subcontinent or Asian origin and 10% to 30% of the elderly classified as Black Caribbean, Black African and Black other being born in the UK (Office of Population Censuses and Surveys (OPCS), 1993). However, with time and an ageing population many more second-generation ethnic minority individuals will reach old age.

Demography

Estimates of the size, the age distribution and the projected trends for the ethnic minority elderly population are required. Almost 6% of those over 65 years were born outside the UK (OPCS, 1993). However, the elderly form only 3% of all ethnic minority individuals compared to 17% of the White population (OPCS, 1993). An increased life-expectancy and a falling birth rate in developed countries is increasing the proportion of the elderly, particularly those over 80 years (OPCS, 1987; Jorm & Henderson, 1993). The proportion of ethnic elders has increased from 1% in 1981 to 3% in 1991 (OPCS, 1983, 1993). In Australia, the number of individuals aged over 60 from non-English speaking countries will increase from 13% in 1986 to 25% in 2001 (Commonwealth Department of Health, Housing and Community Service, 1991). Moreover, as ethnic elders are generally younger than their indigenous counterparts, the corresponding increase in those over 80 years has not yet emerged.

The conventional pattern of the gender ratio in favour of women during old age does not apply to all ethnic groups (Manthorpe & Hettiarachy, 1993). Currently, in the UK, there are more Indian men of retirement age than women (Bhalia & Blakemore, 1981; Barker, 1984; Boneham, 1989). The marital status of ethnic elders is similar to the White population and follows an inverted U-shaped curve (OPCS, 1993).

African–Caribbean elders have similar household patterns to White elders, with many living alone (Bhalia & Blakemore, 1981; Barker, 1984; McCallum, 1990). Elderly individuals from Asian, Chinese and Vietnamese background typically live with several family members in the same household (Bhalia & Blakemore, 1981; Barker, 1984; Atkin *et al*, 1989; McCallum, 1990). However, it is worth noting as many as a quarter of Asians do not live in extended family settings. It is often erroneously assumed that the extended family provides adequate care (Age Concern & Help the

Aged Housing Trust, 1984; Boneham, 1989; Manthorpe & Hettiarachy, 1993; Redelinghuys & Shah, 1997).

There are several reasons for members of the extended family being unable to provide adequate care despite living together. Younger family members may lead culturally different lifestyles. Furthermore, they may have been in the UK for much longer (Barker, 1984) and their elder relatives may have migrated contrary to their wishes (Silveira & Ebrahim, 1995). Younger family members may work long hours and be very busy (Barker, 1984). Family tension (Boneham, 1989; Silveira & Ebrahim, 1995) and financial burden may also make it difficult for the extended family to provide care.

The effect of transcultural factors upon suicide rates illustrates this point elegantly. Among Arabs (Daradekh, 1989), Indians (Bhatia *et al*, 1987), Indian immigrants in Britain (Raleigh *et al*, 1990) and non-White Americans (Seiden, 1981) suicide rates decline with age. This is in contrast to the increase in suicide rates with age among the indigenous population (Surtees & Duffy, 1989). Traditionally, the elderly in these societies are respected, held in high esteem and live in a closely knit extended family. This persists in India, (Bhatia *et al*, 1987; Raleigh *et al*, 1990), the Middle East and among non-White Americans, offering protection towards suicide. However, suicide rates have increased in elderly Japanese and Hong Kong women who have lost their traditional role in the family (Shimuzu, 1990). Physical proximity (living under the same roof) of the extended family is not important, but emotional proximity is the main factor (Shah & Ganesvaran, 1994). An assumption is often made that geographical proximity also provides emotional proximity, but this may not always be the case.

Epidemiology

Epidemiological aspects which are important in planning psychogeriatric services for ethnic elders include prevalence of mental illness, severity of the mental illness, disability due to the illness, natural history of the illness and available social support.

Prevalence figures and current and projected demographic figures can be used to estimate the absolute number of elderly with a given mental illness at present and in the future. There are several good prevalence studies of indigenous elders (Cooper, 1991; Shah, 1992*a*) and studies of ethnic elders are emerging (Ebrahim *et al*, 1991; Silveira & Ebrahim, 1995; Abas *et al*, 1996; Richards *et al*, 1996; Bhatnagar & Frank, 1997; Lindesay *et al*, 1997*a*; McCrakken *et al*, 1997). There are also national and cross-national studies examining prevalence of dementia in ethnic groups such as African Americans and their comparison with White Americans and Nigerians (Osuntokun *et al*, 1992; Hendrie *et al*, 1995). Translated versions of the Geriatric Mental State Examination have been used to examine the prevalence of depression and dementia among older Asians, Chinese, Somalis, African–Caribbeans and British Black people in Liverpool (Blakemore & Boneham, 1994; McCrakken *et al*, 1997) and Indian subcontinent elders in Bradford (Bhatnagar & Frank, 1997). A culture-specific screening test for emotional distress, including depression and anxiety, for older Caribbean people in the UK has been developed (Abas, 1996; Abas *et al*, 1996). A Gujarati version of the Mini Mental State Examination (MMSE) (Folstein *et al*, 1975) has been developed in Leicester (Lindesay *et al*, 1997*a*). Both the MMSE and Mental Test Score (Qureshi & Hodkinson, 1974) are being further developed for use among several Indian subcontinent origin ethnic subgroups in Manchester (Rait *et al*, 1997).

The literature suggest that the prevalence of dementia among ethnic elders of Indian subcontinent origin in the UK is either similar or higher than among indigenous elders (Bhatnagar & Frank, 1997; Lindesay *et al*, 1997*a*; McCrakken *et al*, 1997). The prevalence of dementia among other ethnic groups in Liverpool, including Somali, Chinese, Arabic, Asian, Black African, Black Caribbean and Black other, was similar to that of the indigenous population (McCrakken *et al*, 1997). The prevalence of dementia, in the same study, was higher in those who were unable to speak English and this may be an artefact of their inability to speak English.

The prevalence of depression, in the Liverpool study, was higher among Black African elders than indigenous elders (McCrakken *et al*, 1997) and thought to be associated with seeing their families infrequently. The prevalence of depression was also high among Indian subontinent elders living in Bradford (Bhatnagar & Frank, 1997). Depression scores were higher among Bengali elders in east London (Silveira & Ebrahim, 1995), but this was not the case with Gujarati elders in north London (Ebrahim *et al*, 1991) and Leicester (Lindesay *et al*, 1997*a*). Levels of anxiety and simple phobias are low among Gujarati elders in north London (Ebrahim *et al*, 1991) and Leicester (Lindesay *et al*, 1997*a*).

If data on prevalence are absent they can be estimated from the country of origin; for example, several hospital and community prevalence studies have emerged from India (Venkoba Rao *et al*, 1972; Ramachandran *et al*, 1979; Venkoba Rao & Madhavan, 1983). However, such extrapolation is flawed because migration factors are not considered.

Data on illness severity and resultant disability provide information on the concept of need (Shah & Ames, 1994). However, such data on ethnic elders are only beginning to emerge now among Somalis and Bengalis in east London (Silveira & Ebrahim, 1995) and Gujaratis in north

London (Ebrahim *et al*, 1991) and Leicester (Lindesay *et al*, 1997*a,b*). These include severity of cognitive impairment, severity of depressive and anxiety symptoms, physical illness and functional ability.

Data on the location and distribution of patients allows targeting of services based on one index of need (Ebrahim *et al*, 1991; Manthorpe & Hettiarchy, 1993; Shah & Ames, 1994). Data on the availability and nature of social support in different locations allows estimation of the need for such support. Ethnic minority groups are concentrated in metropolitan and industrial areas (OPCS, 1993). Over 25% of the population in nine London boroughs and two districts outside London (Slough and Leicester) was from ethnic minority groups (OPCS, 1993). An elegant technique for developing a case register for older Caribbean people in south London had been described (Richards *et al*, 1996) and could be used for other groups of ethnic elders. Such case registers could provide data on the exact geographical distribution (e.g. which ward) of ethnic elders in a given geographical district.

Information on the natural history of psychogeriatric disorders is helpful for planning. However, such data for ethnic elders are limited. A recent 21-month follow-up study of Gujarati elders with dementia, originally identified in a general population survey in Leicester, confirmed subsequent decline in cognitive function and the stability of the original diagnosis of dementia (Shah *et al*, 1998).

Cooper (1991) has questioned the accuracy of the above-mentioned epidemiological approach because it assumes that the age distribution and location of patients is the same in the epidemiological study samples and the proposed service area, and different studies have reported differing prevalence rates. This argument is amplified for ethnic elders as basic data on many epidemiological facets are incomplete or absent.

Current services and their utilisation

Data on the availability and utilisation of the existing services are required because they will help identify deficiencies in service provision, avenues for stengthening and improving existing services and methods of integrating any new service development with the existing services. Information on current resources are published annually (Department of Health, 1992), but are flawed (Shah, 1992*a*). The accuracy of recording, the validity of recorded data and the completeness of the data sets acquired from the Korner statistics (collected by the Department of Health in England) are questionable. Moreover, until recently, such data were not collected for identified ethnic minority groups. Purchasers are increasingly requesting provider units to supply information on ethnicity of patients. Planners should gather this information first hand by visiting the existing services (Age Concern & Help the Aged Housing

Trust, 1984) irrespective of their availability in a published form. Furthermore, where such data are absent, experience of senior clinicians should be given considerable weight.

National or regional data on the use of health services, social services and voluntary services by ethnic elders are limited (Shah, 1998). This limited data suggests that the uptake of health and social services by ethnic elders is poor (Barker, 1984; Beliappa, 1991; Karseras, 1991; Spence & Atherton, 1991; Manthorpe & Hettiarchy, 1993; Richards *et al*, 1996; Lindesay *et al*, 1997*b*; Rait & Burns, 1997; Shah & Dighe-Deo, 1997; Jagger, 1998).

Almost all elders and their carers from the African–Caribbean, Asian, Chinese and Vietnamese ethnic groups were aware of services provided by general practitioners (GPs), utilised them effectively (Bhalia & Blakemore, 1981; Barker, 1984; McCallum, 1990) and had a high consultation rate (Bhalia & Blakemore, 1981; Gillam *et al*, 1989; Lindesay *et al*, 1997*b*).

There are several prevalence studies of physical illness among ethnic elders (Cruickshank *et al*, 1980; Bhalia & Blakemore, 1981; Donaldson, 1986; Ebrahim *et al*, 1991; Lindesay *et al*, 1997*b*). Data on the awareness and the utilisation of secondary care services by ethnic elders are emerging; one study of Gujarati elders in Leicester reported poor awareness and uptake (Lindesay *et al*, 1997*b*). African–Caribbean elders of both genders (Bhalia & Blakemore, 1981) and Asian women (Ebrahim *et al*, 1991) visited hospitals and were hospitalised more frequently than White elders in the preceding year. Ebrahim *et al* (1987) argued that there is no evidence to support the idea that ethnic elders underuse hospital resources. Very few ethnic elders and their carers were aware of community services including community nurses, bath nurses, incontinence advisors, health visitors, physiotherapists, occupational therapists, chiropodists and day centres (Bhalia & Blakemore, 1981; Atkin *et al*, 1989; McFarlane *et al*, 1989; McCallum, 1990; Lindesay *et al*, 1997*b*). Thus, it is not surprising that they received few services despite a high rate of untreated problems related to hearing, vision, feet, falling and teeth (Bhalia & Blakemore, 1981). However, many Asian elders acknowledged that they would use these services when made aware of their existance (Atkin *et al*, 1989). Many ethnic elders are unaware of the procedures for applying for these services and have been unsuccessful after applying (Lindesay *et al*, 1997*b*). Many of those who have succeeded in receiving services have been dissatisfied (Lindesay *et al*, 1997*b*).

A survey of Asians of all adult ages revealed lack of awareness of where to go with emotional or social difficulties (Beliappa, 1991). No data, other than lack of awareness and lack of utilisation of community psychiatric nurses and referrals to psychogeriatric services (McCallam,

1990; Abas, 1996; Lindesay *et al*, 1997*b*; Jagger, 1998), are available for use of psychogeriatric services by ethnic elders.

Ethnic elders are unaware of, and underuse, many social service resources (Bhalia & Blakemore, 1981; Age Concern & Help the Aged Housing Trust, 1984; Barker, 1984; McCallum, 1990). These include day centres, meals on wheels, home help, residential care (respite and long-term), housing departments and services of a social worker. There is a similar lack of awareness of voluntary services including the Citizen's Advice Bureau, Help the Aged, Age Concern and Dial-A-Ride. This is not always the case, as shown by a recent study of Indian subcontinent elders using a catchment area psychogeriatric service, where the rate of usage of all social service resources was similar in the ethnic and indigenous groups (Redelinghuys & Shah, 1997; Odutoye & Shah, 1999). In one survey of Asian adults of all ages, the need for improvement in statutory services including transport, services for the house-bound and treatment by Asian doctors or social workers were reported (Beliappa, 1991).

Diagnostic issues

Migrants have a higher rate of mental illness than the host population or the population of the country of their origin (Eitinger, 1960; Lipsedge, 1986). This has not been demonstrated in the elderly.

Psychiatric illness among ethnic elders is difficult to recognise (George & Young, 1991) for reasons listed in Box 1. Thus, greater awareness of transcultural psychiatry (Lipsedge, 1986) and clinical focus on personal, familial and cultural history at the level of migration, integration and adaption may help reduce diagnostic and treatment errors (Solomon, 1992).

BOX 8.1
Reasons for difficulties in diagnosing mental illness in ethnic elders

(a) Diagnosis complicated by cultural factors (Lipsedge, 1986: Solomon, 1992).
(b) Communication difficulties (George & Young, 1991; Shah, 1992*b*).
(c) Taboo topics such as sexual topics (Shah, 1992*b*).
(d) Stigma attached to mental illness.
(e) Bias and prejudice by the clinician (Lipsedge, 1986; Solomon, 1992).
(f) Institutional racism (Solomon, 1992).
(g) Lack of reliability screening and diagnostic instruments (Shah, 1992*b*; Solomon, 1992).
(h) Relative may be unfamiliar with symptoms of psychogeriatric disorders, as few people used to reached old age (Manthorpe & Hettiarachy, 1993).
(i) Illness may be viewed as a function of age.

In some ethnic groups (e.g. south Asians), depression may be characterised by somatic symptoms rather than by guilt, self-blame or suicidal ideation, which are more characteristic in White patients, and this can lead to diagnostic difficulties (Rack, 1982; Kleinman, 1987; Leff, 1988; Bhatnagar, 1997; Rait & Burns, 1997). Somatic symptoms are common among Gujarati elders elders in Leicester (Lindesay *et al*, 1997*b*), and Bengali and Somali elders in east London (Silveira & Ebrahim, 1995). These symptoms may reflect depression. However, in one study of all adult age groups, somatic symptoms were not more common in Asians than in their White counterparts (Mumford *et al*, 1991). Depression among Indians in India is similar to that in other countries (Venkoba Rao *et al*, 1972). Interestingly, younger Indians had more hypochondriacal features in the same study. Asian patients when asked in their mother tongue can report symptoms of mood disturbance (Mumford *et al*, 1991), although this has been questioned (Shah, 1992*b*). Similarly, West Indian patients may mean physical lassitude and disability by the term 'feeling low'. The symptom of 'sinking heart' among Punjabis (Krause, 1989) and Gujaratis (Lindesay *et al*, 1997*b*) is close to the Western concept of stress. Clearly, the diagnostic features of depression in ethnic elders are poorly understood (Abas, 1996; Abas *et al*, 1996; Bhatnagar, 1997) and culture-specific instruments are currently being developed for older Caribbeans (Abas *et al*, 1996). The few studies of ethnic elders are biased because they are of people who accessed the services (Blakemore, 1989). Furthermore, due to the heterogeneity of ethnic groups, findings for individual subgroups should not be generalised.

The aetiology of depression in ethnic elders may be multi-faceted (see Box 8.2). However, none of these factors has been systematically addressed.

Box 8.2
Possible aetiological factors for depression in ethnic elders

(a) Loss of home country and loved ones (Manthorpe & Hettiarachy, 1993).
(b) Reasons for migration (e.g. torture, political, economic).
(c) Stress associated with migration (Lipsedge, 1986).
(d) Alienation, isolation and powerlessness leading to low self-esteem (Manthorpe & Hettiarachy, 1993).
(e) Multiple deprivations leading to learned helplessness (Manthorpe & Hettiarachy, 1993).
(f) Individual and institutional racism (Boneham, 1989).
(g) Difficulties in accepting the reality of being unable to return home (Boneham, 1989)
(h) Concern about social values of younger generations (Boneham, 1989)
(i) Social isolation due to bereavement, retirement or rejection by family (Blakemore, 1989; Boneham, 1989).
(j) Alcohol misuse (Goodman & Ward, 1989).

Dementia is difficult to diagnose among ethnic elders. Many diagnostic systems place importance on the presence of cognitive impairment in the diagnosis of dementia (Fairburn & Hope, 1988). Many ethnic elders do not speak Western languages and many are illiterate in their own language (Bhalia & Blakemore, 1981; McCallam, 1990). Thus, simple cognitive tests involving language and writing or drawing as well as more sophisticated tests are of limited value. However, screening instruments are being developed in various ethnic languages including Hindi (Ganguli *et al*, 1995), Gujarati (Lindesay *et al*, 1997*a*) and other Indian subcontinent languages (Rait *et al*, 1997). Greater attention should also be paid to non-cognitive changes of dementia including personality change, behaviour change, affective features and psychotic features (Shah & Dighe-Deo, 1997).

Distressed people from some countries may report that they are bewitched, hearing voices of their ancesters or possed by spirits (Lipsedge, 1986). These should not necessarily be considered as psychotic phenomena because they may be normal features of the local culture.

Multiple jeopardy

The concept of double jeopardy due to age and race-related disadvantages was first developed in the USA (National Urban League, 1964) and later introduced to the UK (Dowd & Bengston, 1978). Sexism (Palmore & Manton, 1973) and social deprivation (Norman, 1985) have been added to develop a model of triple jeopardy. Boneham (1989) has developed a model of multiple disadvantage for elderly Asian women in Britain. This model can be equally applied to all ethnic elders (Rait *et al*, 1996).

Six factors contibute to this multiple jeopardy model including ageism, racism, gender disparities, restricted access to health and welfare services, internal ethnic divisions and class struggle. All these factors are discussed above and below in detail.

Planning psychogeriatric services for ethnic minority groups

Components of good contemporary ethnocentric psychogeriatric services are well described (Shah & Ames, 1994). These are equally important for ethnic minority groups. There has been a debate about integrating services or segregating services (Blakemore, 1985). One view is that segregated services for ethnic minority groups will lead to them being even more marginalised. Furthermore, in the present era of cut-backs and finite budgets they may not be able to compete for satisfactory funding (Blakemore, 1985; Patel, 1993). Thus, psychogeriatric services for ethnic elders should be integrated with the existing ethnocentric psychogeriatric services, otherwise ethnic elders will not receive comprehensive care. Purchasers can select and dictate the purchase and development of such integrated services; this is beginning to happen in many urban area with significant concentrations of ethnic minority groups. Similarly, social services should also integrate their services for ethnic elders with the mainstream services with inbuilt safeguards.

Sources of new referrals

Medical staff (GPs and other specialists), non-medical professionals (social workers, district nurses etc.), traditional healers and lay people (police, neighbours) may wish to refer patients. There has been a debate on the merits of receiving medical referrals (Cole *et al*, 1991; Dening, 1992) or open referrals (Tym, 1991) for indigenous patients and their advantages and disadvantages are well described (Shah & Ames, 1994). Ethnic elders have difficulty in accessing (Lindesay *et al*, 1997*b*; Jagger, 1998) and communicating (Shah, 1997*b,c*) with services. Thus, an open referral policy would be appropriate to avoid missing mental illness in this group.

Mode of referral

Referrals can be received via letter (post or facsimile) or over the telephone (Shah & Ames, 1994). Telephone referrals should always be accepted for ethnic elders as they have difficulties in accessing and communicating with services.

Ideally, all referrals should be seen within 24 to 48 hours to avoid waiting lists and routine referrals turning into emergencies (Lennon & Jolley, 1991). As ethnic elders have difficulty in accessing services, such rapid response time should be rigidly maintained to ensure a user-friendly service.

Other service innovations including an evening or a weekend service, although expensive, may allow a psychogeriatric service to be even more accessible to ethnic elders. Weekend community psychogeriatric nursing services in Melbourne and West London, catering for a significant number of ethnic elders, anecdotally appeared to be well received by patients, their carers and GPs.

Site of initial assessment

Initial assessment at the patients home, except for hospital in-patients, has been strongly advocated (Jolley & Arie, 1978; Arie & Jolley, 1982). The many advantages of a home visit for ethnic elders are listed in Box 8.3. Although these advantages also apply to indigenous elders, the advantages are amplified for ethnic elders because of the diffculties in assessing ethnic elders discussed in earlier sections. Home visits are suggested to have almost no disadvantage and their costs are similar to out-patient consultations (Shah, 1992c, 1994, 1997d).

Nature of initial assessment

The team should allocate two appropriate members to assess the patient for safety reasons (safety of staff from assaults and inappropriate accusations) and to enable a comprehensive assessment from the perspective of two disciplines (Shah & Ames, 1994). In traditional services one of the two staff members may be a doctor (Seidel *et al*, 1992) so a mental state and physical examination can be completed. In services with medical staff shortages (Dening, 1992), initial assessments might be performed by the CPNs. For ethnic elders, initial assessment should be done by the member of the team who can speak the patient's language and/or is culturally familiar. This member need not be a doctor. This will allow better understanding of the patient and remove barriers to accessing services. If such staff members are unavailable, then translation services should be used.

Each referral should be discussed with the whole team in a meeting similar to the traditional ward round (Cole *et al*, 1991; Dening, 1992). Subsequent management should be based on the principles

---

Box 8.3
Advantages of home visits for ethnic elders

(a) May be unable to use public transport due to physical illness, sensory deficits, language and communication difficulties and fear of racial harassment.
(b) Reduces the stigma of attending a psychiatric clinic.
(c) Ready access to relatives, friends and neighbours for a third-party history, which is particularly important.
(d) Direct observation of the quality and quantity of carer support.
(e) Patients are seen in a culturally appropriate environment.
(f) Patient is more likely to feel reassured when seen at home.
(g) Observation of Western and traditional medicines.
(h) Elderly Indian women may not leave home.

of care programme or case management (Thornicroft *et al*, 1992; Waterreus, 1992) where each care manager provides assistance from his or her discipline and coordinates the wider management package. If possible the care manager should speak the patient's language and/or be familiar with the culture. The care manager can then act a link between the referrer, the clinical team, the GP, the patient and the relatives.

Communication

Good communication between patients and professionals is paramount (Bhalia & Blakemore, 1981; Age Concern & Help the Aged Housing Trust, 1984; Shah, 1992*b*). Many ethnic elders do not speak English (Barker, 1984; Manthorpe & Hettiarchy, 1993; Lindesay *et al*, 1997*b*). This problem can be minimised if staff members can speak the patient's language (Shah, 1992*b*). However, bilingual health workers are uncommon (Phelan & Parkman, 1995), but valued when available (Redlinghuys & Shah, 1997). Translation services will be required when staff members are unable to communicate directly with patients (Shah, 1992*c* & 1997*b,c*). Relatives, non-clinical staff, clinical staff and professional translators with and without special training in mental health have been used (Phelan & Parkman, 1995; Shah, 1997*b,c*). Translations can be done in person or via a three-way telephone conversation.

Using relatives and friends as translators has advantages and disadvantages. They are readily available, are knowledgable about the patient and their presence may reassure the patient. However, translation in both directions may be biased due to good or unscrupulous intentions of the translator and a reluctance to reveal some problems to close relatives (Phelan & Parkman, 1995). Non-clinical staff may be unable to maintain an unbiased approach during translation (Phelan & Parkman, 1995).

The provision of professional interpreters in the UK is increasing but their utility and availability is patchy and poor (Atkin *et al*, 1989; Phelan & Parkman, 1995). The Australian state of Victoria provides an excellent translation service with interpreters trained in mental health translation (Shah, 1997*b*). An American study reported that the psychiatric interviewers felt that the interview was unhelpful but the patients felt they were understood (Kline *et al*, 1980). An Arabic study showed that the use of interpreters did not affect diagnosis (Dodd, 1983). However, interpreters can distort interpretation of mental states (Marcos, 1979). Shah (1992*b*) reported a number of difficulties in interviewing patients even when the psychogeriatrician was from the patients ethnic background and spoke the language.

Although there are no specific studies of the use of interpreters in psychogeriatrics, caution should be excercised. The interpreter should be given adequate warning of the interview, details of the venue, the duration of the interview, the name and address of the patient, details of the patient's language and dialect, and the purpose of the interview (Phelan & Parkman, 1995). Phelan & Parkman (1985) have described useful tips for interviewing using an interpretor. Ideally, the same interpreter should be used for subsequent interviews.

Site of follow-up

Patients requiring follow-up may be seen at home, out-patient clinic or day hospital (Shah & Ames, 1994). Novel forms of follow-up including home-visting clinics have been developed (Ratna, 1982; Benbow, 1990; Lennon & Jolley, 1991). These should be encouraged for ethnic elders for the reasons discussed in Box 8.3. The feasibility of such clinics will depend upon the geographical size of the catchment area, the travelling time and availability of staff. This is feasible as ethnic elders tend to live in geographical clusters (OPCS, 1993; Rait & Burns, 1997).

Out-patient clinic

Out-patient clinics and specialist memory clinics may complement home visits for detailed assessment including neuropsychometry, blood and radiological investigations. These are best provided in a general hospital with access to all their facilities (Tym, 1991; Jolley & Arie, 1992). Ethnic elders should have ready access to such clinics, particularly as psychogeriatric disorders are difficult to diagnose in this group.

Day hospitals

Despite the recent controversy (Fasey, 1994; Murphy, 1994) day hospitals are a vital component of psychogeriatric services (Arie, 1979; Howard, 1994). Day hospitals with different models have been proposed (Hettiarachy, 1985; Tym, 1991). These include separate functional and dementia day hospitals, a single central day hospital or several day hospitals closer to population clusters, and travelling day hospitals. They provide facilities for assessment, treatment, rehabilitation, long-term support, development of social networks, and support for carers; they also allow the patient to receive care while living at home (Shah & Ames, 1994).

Ethnic elders should have ready access to day hospitals. However, unless day hospitals are appropriately staffed and are culturally sensitive, uptake and utilisation will be poor. Currently, only 63% of day hospital places are utilised (Department of Health, 1991); thus, any cultural inappropriateness of the service should not be allowed further to reduce this low figure. Many ethnic elders, particularly Indian women, are reluctant to leave their home (Bhalia & Blakemore, 1981); here the day hospital provision may not be helpful. In rural areas travelling day hospitals have been developed (Hettiarachy, 1985; Tym, 1991). This reluctance of Indian women might be reduced if travelling day hospitals for ethnic elders were developed close to their homes; ethnic elders are more willing to attend day centres close to home (Bhalia & Blakemore, 1981). It is possible that once the purpose of such facilities is described to the community they may find it more acceptable to use them.

Transportation

Psychogeriatric services use taxis, ambulances and minibuses to transport patients (Shah, 1993, 1996), and their advantages and disadvantages have been well described. Elderly patients often require transportation to hospital-based facilities due to reduced mobility, sensory deficits, physical illness and mental illness. Also, ethnic elders are often reluctant to use public transport, owing to language and communication difficulties and fear of racial harassment on route (Barker, 1984). Ambulance and minibus staff should learn aspects of the patients culture and language. The minibus and the ambulance should have signs and notices in the patients' language, illustrated with symbols. Where taxis are hired from private companies it may be possible to stipulate that the driver comes from the same ethnic group; taxi companies are likely to comply with this request as they will receive business (Shah, 1996) and many have ethnic drivers available.

Psychiatric in-patient care

Hospital admission may be necessary if the patient cannot be managed at home. There are three types of admissions: assessment/treatment, respite and continuing care. Indications and objectives for admission have been well described (Jolley & Arie, 1978; Shah & Ames, 1994). It is often difficult to persuade elderly patients and their relatives to accept admission. Reasons for this include the stigma attached to psychiatry, poor insight into the illness, the belief that the illness is a function of old age and will not improve, the belief that they will get better anyway and the psychological defence mechanism of denial. These attitudes will be amplified in ethnic elders and their carers if the ward is perceived as culturally insensitive and unable to suit their needs. Thus, unless the wards are culturally sensitive their uptake and utilisation will be poor.

In catchment areas where there are likely to be significant numbers of ethnic elder admissions consideration should be given to designating some dormitories for ethnic elders. Anecdotal experience from psychogeriatric services in areas of significant ethnic elderly population suggests that placing ethnic elders in single rooms should be avoided, unless there are positive indications, because it may serve to increase their isolation. However, in the current era of community care and a general shortage of psychiatric beds in urban areas it will be difficult to have designated areas for ethnic elders on the ward unless ethnicity is considered important by service planners.

Role of the general practitioner

General practitioners play a vital role in the satisfactory functioning of psychogeriatric services. This is particularly important for ethnic elders as they are more aware and utilise their GP more than any other care provider (Bhalia & Blakemore, 1981; Barker, 1984). Moreover, 70% of Asians register with Asian GPs (Johnson *et al*, 1983). This may ease their access to psychogeriatric services. Ideally, all initial assessments should involve the GP on joint home visits and a significant number of GPs are satisfied with this (Orrell *et al*, 1992). Psychogeriatric teams should take a lead role in encouraging GPs to participate in such joint assessment as it will facilitate better management of ethnic elders and improve their access to the services, particularly for patients who never leave their home.

GPs see a significant amount of psychogeriatric morbidity (Royal College of General Practitioners, 1986), which they detect well, but undertreat. In Britain, this is further enhanced by legislation requiring GPs to offer an annual physical examination and mental examination to all patients over the age of 75 years (Secretaries of State for Health, Wales, Northern Ireland & Scotland, 1989). The uptake and usefulness of this exercise among ethnic elders is unclear. However, as very few ethnic elders are over 75 years, consideration should be given to reducing this to 65 years in geographical areas of high ethnic density. The low cost, wide availability and greater utility by ethnic elders of GP services suggest that much could be gained from improving GPs' competence in psychogeriatric assessments and promoting GP consultations as an important stage of assessment (Ames & Flynn, 1994). This could be facilitated by psychogeriatric services providing support and back-up, and education on cultural issues and diagnostic difficulties.

Liaison service

A liaison service should be available to departments of geriatric medicine, general hospitals, residential facilities for the elderly, social service and voluntary agency day facilities, voluntary organisations and other local government services (Tym, 1991; Dening, 1992; Jolley & Arie, 1992). Reasons for such links have been well described (Shah & Ames, 1994).

Services provided by social services, local government organisations and voluntary agencies to the general population should be encouraged to develop specialist components for ethnic elders (Age Concern & Help the Aged Housing Trust, 1984). In some urban districts social services are developing specialist day centres and residential homes for ethnic elders (Blakemore, 1985). Many ethnic elders may prefer such facilities as they may meet others from their background and be able to communicate. Supporting such developments and encouraging and improving the staff's ability to identify and manage mental illness can only be productive. Moreover, both sides may learn and be able to improve accessibilty of services to this vulnerable group.

Psychogeriatric services for ethnic elders should develop close links with voluntary agencies for the general population and with those catering for ethnic groups. Voluntary agencies catering for the general population should be encouraged to become ethnically sensitive. Many ethnic groups have their own cultural organisations, which may also provide a range of services. Liaison with such organisations is vital as this will allow dissemination of information about psychogeriatric services much more effectively and allow the service providers to learn about the ethnic culture (McCallum, 1990). It is possible that ethnic elders may be more likely to accept these services, particularly as such agencies are organised and staffed by their own community. Involvement of such local agencies has facilitated research among ethnic elders (Abas *et al*, 1996; McCrakken *et al*, 1997; Rait & Burns, 1997). Such organisations should act as advocates for ethnic elders, provide advice on service provision and develop translation services. There may be a case for outreach workers to disseminate information to the whole ethnic community through such organisations (Spence & Atherton, 1991). However, this should not be seen as a substitute for inadequate funding of satisfactory statutory services.

Liaison links should also be developed with practitioners of traditional medicine like faith healers because many ethnic elders may consult them in the first instance. Some South African doctors anecdotally accept that faith healers may help psychological problems (Kale, 1995), and for many in South Africa faith healers may be the first port of call. Health professionals should be aware of traditional medicine because symptoms related to cultural diseases may present late; as doctors are perceived as unhelpful, patients may present with interpretation rather than with symptoms, and traditional remedies may produce side-effects and interactions (Bhopal, 1986*a,b*).

The profile of carers for ethnic elders is similar to that of carers of indigenous patients with dementia (McCallum, 1990). However, where ethnic elders live in an extended family it is often erroneously assumed that the family provides care (Boneham, 1989; McCallum, 1990; Redelinghuys & Shah, 1997). Many carers do not speak English and are culturally isolated. Thus, the accepted role of psychogeriatric services to play a part in carer education (Brodaty & Gresham, 1992) and provide care, respite and other back-up services (Ames & Flynn, 1994) is even more important with carers of ethnic elders. The quality and quantity of informal support available to Black elderly people will have a profound effect on their long-term care (Gibson & Jackson, 1987).

Location of psychogeriatric services

The geographical size of the area, the expected distribution of morbidity within it, and the existing services and their distribution all need consideration. Ideally, all components of the service should be based in a general hospital within the catchment area (Jolley & Arie, 1978), where general psychiatry and geriatric medicine are located (Jolley & Arie, 1992). This will ensure access to all general hospital facilities (Jolley & Arie, 1992), reduce stigma attached to psychiatric hospitals and decrease hardship upon relatives (Cooper, 1991). Moreover, a liaison service to the hospital and links with GPs can be developed. The community component should based under the same roof. Tyrer (1985) suggested satellite centres close to population clusters in large catchment areas. This model may be effectively utilised for ethnic elders as they often live in such clusters (OPCS, 1993; Rait & Burns, 1997), thereby bringing the services closer to their home and improving accessibility.

Equipment, design and cultural sensitivity of facilities

All staff and the actual setting of psychogeriatric services should be culturally sensitive. This is more likely to be acheived if some of the staff originate from the same cultural group. Attention should be given to cultural attitudes towards sexual segregation (elderly Indian men and women rarely mix in public), bathing strategies, food (vegetarian, halal meat etc.), adequate washing and prayer facilities, signs and notices in ethnic languages, reality orientation cues in ethnic languages and culturally relevant reminiscence groups (Atkin *et al*, 1989). These issues need careful consideration in all arms of any psychogeriatric service. Any literature that is given to indigenous patients should ideally be available in the most common ethnic languages. The Mental Health Act Commission produces literature on various issues in several ethnic languages. However, it should be recognised that many ethnic elders and their carers may be illiterate (Atkin *et al*, 1989; Manthorpe & Hettiarchy, 1993), whereupon the contents should be read to them. Use of 'talking books' in the patients' mother-tongue may be worthwhile. Audio tapes, on aspects of dementia, in a few ethnic languages are available from the Alzheimer's Disease Society. Staff should understand the interaction between drugs and traditional remedies and medicines, patients' understanding of services, the expectations of families and the appropriateness of gender-specific behaviour (Manthorpe & Hettiarchy, 1993).

Staffing levels and mix

Complex medico-socio-psychological disorders in elderly people require multi-disciplinary staffing including psychiatrists (senior and junior), psychologists, nurses, occupational therapists, social workers, speech pathologists, physiotherapists, chiropodists and dieticians (Jolley & Arie, 1992). Ethnic minority staff are under-represented in all community services (Atkin *et al*, 1989). Many staff are unfamiliar with various cultural factors (Bhalia & Blakemore, 1981). The service can be made culturally more sensitive by employing more ethnic staff and improving awareness of cultural issues among indigenous staff. Inadequate staffing levels can lead to difficulties in accessing services by patients who need them most, like ethnic elders.

Appropriate staffing composition and an adequate environmental milieu for the service will allow integration of specialist services for ethnic groups into mainstream services. Clinical and non-clinical staff (domestics, secretaries, porters and gardeners) from the patients' ethnic background will facilitate integration, acceptability and accessibility of the service, translation services, communication, cultural sensitiveness, training of other staff on cultural issues, development of links with local ethnic organisations and advocacy. The West London Healthcare NHS Trust, which caters for a large Asian elderly population in west London, employs bilingual care workers.

Additionally, they employ a Punjabi-speaking CPN for the specific purpose of caring for this group. Many of the domestic staff are from similar ethnic backgrounds. Although this service has not been formally evaluated, it is well received by patients, carers, GPs and other staff. A similar approach was used at my former hospital (North Eastern Metropolitan Psychiatric Services) in Melbourne, Australia (Shah, 1997*a*).

Audit

All aspects of quality assurance monitoring should be applied to the psychogeriatric aspects of ethnic elders. Thus, the activities of both the overall service and the individual disciplines should be monitored. This audit can be internal and peer reviewed or external and reviewed by a governmental or other external agency (Jones, 1992*a,b*). It should employ the contemporary principles of integrated care pathways and variance tracking to identify problematic areas. It will also allow identification of flaws and areas of good practice. The latter can be strengthened and the former can be improved, if necessary by requesting further resources from the purchasers.

Education

Psychogeriatric services should be involved in education (Arie *et al*, 1985; Wattis, 1989; Mandeley & Wattis, 1994). This should include education on cultural aspects of psychogeriatrics for psychogeriatric staff, geriatricians, GPs, social service staff and voluntary sector staff. Psychogeriatric services should also play an important role in public education at a local level and this should involve ethnic elders and their carers. Public education programmes such as the Defeat Depression campaign by the Royal College of Psychiatrists could be implemented locally by psychogeriatric services particularly for ethnic elders.

Overview

The various components described are by no means comprehensive or exhaustive. Differing services with differing groups, proportions and geographical distribution of ethnic elders may have additional or fewer components and different modes of service delivery. The important ingredients of a satisfactory service are flexibility with ability to adapt and respond to changing needs, availability, home assessments and communication (Arie, 1970).

Future directions

Psychogeriatric services should have an ambition to provide an ideal service for all patients. Services for ethnic elders should be well advertised, readily accessible and user-friendly. There is little formal evaluation of psychogeriatric services (Draper, 1990). Such grandiose evaluations are unrealistic and costly (Shah & Ames, 1994). However, some aspects of service delivery to ethnic elders, including links with GPs, geriatricians and ethnic community organisations, could be examined. The accessibilty and friendliness of the service can also be examined. Such evaluations can form part of a clinical audit and also be supported by research and development funding from the Department of Health or regional health authorities. This will identify areas of good and bad practice, gaps in the service, avenues for improvement and inadequate resources.

Service planning needs support from epidemiological data. There are very few screening and diagnostic instruments for mental illness among ethnic elders. There is an urgent need to develop such instruments in ethnic languages with cultural sensitivity. This would allow clinical screening and formal prevalence studies in the community; at present both are lacking. Detailed data on the Goldberg & Huxley (1991) pathways to care are absent for ethnic elders. Studies designed to gather information in this area will be of great value to service planners and those interested in prevention.

Acknowledgements

Thanks are due to my patient wife and Dr Geetha Oommen for advice and encouragement.

References

ABAS, M. (1996) Depression and anxiety among older Caribbean people in the UK: screening, unmet need and the provision of appropriate services. *International Journal of Geriatric Psychiatry*, **11**, 377–382.

——, PHILLIPS, C., RICHARDS, M., *et al* (1996) Initial development of a new culture-specific screen for emotional distress in older Caribbean people. *International Journal of Geriatric Psychiatry*, **11**, 1097–1103.

AGE CONCERN & HELP THE AGED HOUSING TRUST (1984) *Housing for Ethnic Elders*. London: Age Concern.

AMES, D. & FLYNN, E. (1994) Dementia services: an Australian view. In *Dementia* (eds A. Burn & R. Levy). London: Chapman & Hall.

ARIE, T. (1970) The first years of the Goodmayes psychogeriatric services for old people. *Lancet*, ii, 1179–1182.

—— (1979) Day care in geriatric psychiatry. *Age & Ageing*, **8**, 87–91.

—— & Jolley, D (1982) Making services work: organisation and style of psychogeriatric services. In *The Psychiatry of Late Life* (eds R. Levy & F. Post), pp. 222–251. Oxford: Blackwell.

——, JONES, R. & SMITH, C. (1985) The educational potential of psychogeriatric services. In *Recent Advances in Psychogeriatrics* (eds T. Arie), pp. 197–208. London: Churchill Livingstone.

ATKIN, K., CAMERON, E., BADFGER, F., *et al* (1989) Asian elders' knowledge and future use of community social and health services. *New Community*, 15, 439–445.

BARKER, J. (1984) *Research Perspectives on Ageing: Black and Asian Old People in Britain* (1st edn). London: Age Concern Research Unit.

BELIAPPA, J. (1991) *Illness or Distress? Alternative Models of Mental Health.* Newcastle upon Tyne: Confederation of Indian Organisations (UK).

BENBOW, S. M. (1990) The community clinic: its advantages and disadvantages. *International Journal of Geriatric Psychiatry*, 5, 119–121.

BHALIA, A. & BLAKEMORE, K. (1981) *Elders of the Minority Ethnic Groups.* Birmingham: AFFOR.

BHATIA, S. C., KHAN, M. H. & MEDIRRATA, R. P. (1987) High risk suicide factors across cultures. *International Journal of Social Psychiatry*, 33, 226–236.

BHATNAGAR, K. S. (1997) Depression in South Asian elders. *Geriatric Medicine*, 27, 55–56.

—— & FRANK J. (1997) Psychiatric disorders in elderly from the Indian subcontinent living in Bradford. *International Journal of Geriatric Psychiatry*, 12, 907–912.

BHOPAL, R. S. (1986a) The inter-relationship of folk, traditional and western medicine within an Asian community in Britain. *Social Science & Medicine*, 1, 99–105.

—— (1986b) Bhye bhaddi: a food and health concept of Punjabi Asians. *Social Sciences and Medicine*, 7, 687–688.

BLAKEMORE, K. (1985) The state, the voluntary sector and new developments in provision for the old of minority racial groups. *Ageing & Society*, 5, 175–190.

—— (1989) Does age matter? The case of old age in ethnic minority groups. In *Becoming and Being Old, Sociological Approaches to Later Life* (eds B. Bytheway, T. Keil., P. Allat, *et al*). London: Sage.

—— & BONEHAM, M. (1994) *Age, Race and Ethnicity: A Comparative Approach.* Buckingham: Open University Press.

BONEHAM, M. (1989) Ageing and ethnicity in Britain: the case of elderly Sikh women in a midlands town. *New Community*, 15, 447–459.

BOWLING, B. (1990) *Elderly People from Ethnic Minorities: A Report on Four projects, Age Concern.* London: Institute of Gerontology.

BRODATY, H. (1991) The need for distinctive psychogeriatric services. *Royal Australian and New Zealand College of Psychiatrists News & Notes*, 24, 27–28.

—— & GRESHAM, M. (1992) Prescribing residential care for dementia – effects, side-effects, indications and dosage. *International Journal of Geriatric Psychiatry*, 7, 357–362.

COLE, R. J., VON ABENDORFF, R. & HERTZBERG, J. I. (1991) The impact of a new community mental health team on an inner city psychogeriatric service. *International Journal of Geriatric Psychiatry*, 6, 31–39.

COMMONWEALTH DEPARTMENT OF HEALTH, HOUSING AND COMMUNITY SERVICE (1991) *Aged Care Reform Strategy Mid-Term Review 1990–1991 Report.* Canberra: Australian Government Publishing Service.

COOPER, B. A. (1991) Psychiatric services for the elderly: principles of service provision in old age psychiatry. In *Psychiatry in the Elderly* (eds R. Jacoby & C. Oppenheimer), pp. 274–300. Oxford: Oxford University Press.

CRUICKSHANK, J. K., BEEVERS, D. G., OSBOURNE, V. L., *et al* (1980) Heart attack, stroke, diabetes, and hypertension in west Indians, Asians and whites in Birmingham, England. *British Medical Journal*, 281, 1108.

DARADEKH, T. K. (1989) Suicide in Jordan 1980–1985. *Acta Psychiatrica Scandinavica*, 79, 241–244.

DENING, T. (1992) Community psychiatry of old age: a UK perspective. *International Journal of Geriatric Psychiatry*, 7, 757–766.

DEPARTMENT OF HEALTH (1991) *NHS Day-Care Facilities in England Year Ending 31 March 1990.* London: HMSO.

—— (1992) *Health and Personal Social Service Statitics.* London: HMSO.

DODD, W. (1983) Do interpreters affect consultations? *Family Practitioner,* 1, 42–47.

DONALDSON, L. J. (1986) Health and social status of elderly Asians: a community survey. *British Medical Journal,* 293, 1079–1084.

DOWD, J. J. & BENGSTON, V.L (1978) Aging in minority populations: an examination of double jeopardy hypothesis. *Journal of Gerontology,* 3, 427–436.

DRAPER, B. (1990) The effectiveness of services and treatment in psychogeriatrics. *Australian and New Zealand Journal of Psychiatry,* 24, 238–251.

EBRAHIM, S., SMITH, C. & GIGGS, J. (1987) Elderly immigrants – a disdvantaged group?, *Age & Ageing,* 16, 249–255.

——, PATEL, N., COATES, M., *et al* (1991) Prevalence and severity of morbidity among Gujarati Asian elders: a controlled comparison. *Family Practice,* 8, 57–62.

EITINGER, L. (1960) The symptomatology of mental disease among refugees in Norway. *Journal of Mental Science,* 106, 947–966.

FAIRBURN, C. G. & HOPE, R. A. (1988) Changes in behaviour in dementia: a neglected area. *British Journal of Psychiatry,* 152, 406–407.

FASEY, C. (1994) The day hospital in old age psychiatry: the case against. *International Journal of Geriatric Psychiatry,* 9, 511–523.

FOLSTEIN. M. F., FOLSTEIN, S. E. & MCHUGH, P. R. (1975) "Mini Mental State": A practical method for grading the cognitive state of patients for the clinician. *Journal of Psychiatric Research,* 12, 189–198.

GANGULI, M., RATCLIFF, G., CHANDRA, V., *et al* (1995) A Hindi version of the MMSE: the development of a cognitive screening instrument for a largely illiterate rural elderly population of India. *International Journal of Geriatric Psychiatry,* 10, 367–377.

GEORGE, J. & YOUNG, J. (1991) In *The Physician In Multi-Cultural Health Care and Rehabilitation of Older People* (ed. A. J. Squires) London: Edward Arnold.

GIBSON, R. C. & JACKSON, J. S. (1987) The health, physical functioning and informal supporters of the black elderly. *Millbank Quaterly,* 65, 421–454.

GILLAM, S., JARMAN, B., WHITE, P., *et al* (1989) Ethnic differences in consultation rates in urban general practice. *British Medical Journal,* 299, 953–958.

GOLDBERG, D. & HUXLEY, P. (1991) *Common Mental Disorders: A Biosocial Model.* London & New York: Tavistock & Routledge.

GOODMAN, C. & WARD, M. (1989) *Alcohol Problems in Old Age.* London: Staccato Books.

HENDRIE, H. C., OSUNTOKUN, B. O., HALL, K. S., *et al* (1995) The prevalence of Alzheimer's disease and dementia in two communities: Nigerian Africans and African Americans. *American Journal of Psychiatry,* 152, 1485–1492.

HETTIARACHY, P. (1985) UK travelling day hospital. *Ageing International,* 12, 10–12.

HOWARD, R. (1994) Day hospitals: case in favour. *International Journal of Geriatric Psychiatry,* 9, 523–527.

JAGGER, C. (1998) Asian elders. An under studied and growing population. *Old Age Psychiatrist,* March 10, 8.

JOHNSON, M. R. D., CROSS, M. & CARDEW, S. (1983) Inner city residents, ethnic minorities and primary health care. *Postgraduate Medical Journal,* 59, 664–667.

JOLLEY, D. & ARIE, T. (1978) Organisation of psychogeriatric services. *British Journal of Psychiatry,* 132, 1–11.

—— & —— (1992) Developments in psychogeriatric services. In *Recent Advances in Psychogeriatrics, No. 2* (ed. T. Arie), pp. 177–185. London: Churchill Livingstone.

JONES, R. (1992*a*) Medical audit in geriatric psychiatry: more questions than answers. *International Journal of Geriatric Psychiatry,* 7, 1–3.

—— (1992*b*) Audit for old age psychiatry. In *Recent Advances in Psychogeriatrics, No. 2* (ed. T. Arie), pp. 187–200. London: Churchill Livingstone.

JORM, A. & HENDERSON, S. (1993) *The Problem of Dementia in Australia* (3rd edn). Canberra: Australian Government Publishing Service.

KALE, R. (1995) New South Africa's Mental Health. *British Medical Journal,* 310, 1254–1256.

KARSERAS, P. A. (1991) Minorities and access to health care, part 1: confronting myths. *Care of the Elderly*, Oct, 429–431.

KLEINMAN, A. (1987) Anthropology and Psychiatry. *British Journal of Psychiatry*, 151, 447–454.

KLINE, F., ACOSTA, F., AUSTIN, W., *et al* (1980) The misunderstood Spanish speaking patient. *American Journal of Psychiatry*, 137, 1530–1533.

KRAUSE, I. (1989) Sinking heart: a Punjabi communication of distress. *Social Science and Medicine*, 4, 563–575.

LEFF, J. (1988) *Psychiatry Around the Globe: A Transcultural View* (2nd edn). London: Gaskell.

LENNON, S. & JOLLEY, D. (1991) Psychiatric services for the elderly: an urban service in south Manchester. In *Psychiatry in the Elderly* (eds R. Jacoby & C. Oppenheimer), pp. 322–338. Oxford: Oxford University Press.

LINDESAY, J., JAGGER, C., MLYNIK-SZMID, A., *et al* (1997a) The mini-mental state examination (MMSE) in an elderly immigrant Gujarati population in the United Kingdom. *International Journal of Geriatric Psychiatry*, 12, 1155–1167.

——, ——, HIBBERT, M. J., *et al* (1997b) Knowledge, uptake and availability of health and social services among Asian Gujarati and White elders. *Ethnicity & Health*, 2, 59–69.

LIPSEDGE, M. (1986) Transcultural aspects of psychiatry. *Practical Reviews in Psychiatry*, 8, 1–2.

LLOYD, K. (1992) Ethnicity, primary care and non-psychotic disorders. *International Review of Psychiatry*, 4, 257–266.

MANDELEY, P. & WATTIS, J. P. (1994) Education in old age psychiatry. *International Review of Psychiatry*, 6, 119–125.

MANTHORPE, J. & HETTIARACHY, P. (1993) Ethnic minority elders in Britain. *International Review of Psychiatry*, 5, 173–180.

MARCOS, L. R. (1979) Effects of interpreters on the evaluation of psychopathology in non-English speaking patients. *American Journal of Psychiatry*, 136, 171–174.

MCCALLUM, J. A. (1990) *The Forgotten People: Carers in Three Minority Commmunities in Southwark*. London: Kings Fund Centre.

MCCRAKKEN, C. F. M., BONEHAM, M. A., COPELAND, J. R. M., *et al* (1997) Prevalence of dementia and depression among elderly people in black and ethnic groups. *British Journal of Psychiatry*, 171, 269–273.

MCFARLANE, E., DALTON, M. & WALSH, D. (1989) Ethnic minority needs and service delivery: the barriers to access in a Glasgow inner city area. *New Community*, 15, 405–415.

MORRIS, J., HEYMAN, A., MOHS, R. H., *et al* (1989) The consortium to establish a registry for Alzheimer's disease (CERAD). Part 1: Clinical and neuropsychological assessment of Alzheimer's Disease. *Neurology*, 39, 1159–1165.

MUMFORD, D. B., BAVINGTON, J. T. & BHAATNAGAR, K. S. (1991) The Bradford somatic inventory. A multiethnic inventory of somatic symptoms reported by anxious and depressed patients in Britain and the Indo-Pakistan sub-continent. *British Journal of Psychiatry*, 158, 379–386.

MURPHY, E. (1994) The day hospital debate. *International Journal of Geriatric Psychiatry*, 9, 517–518.

NATIONAL URBAN LEAGUE (1964) *Double Jeopardy: The Older Negro in America Today*. New York: National Urban League.

NORMAN, A. (1985) *Triple Jeopardy: Growing Old in a Second Homeland*. London: Centre for Policy on Ageing.

ODUTOYE, K. & SHAH, A. K. (1999) The clinical and demographic characteristics of ethnic elders from the Indian subcontinent newly referred to a psychogeriatric service. *International Journal of Geriatric Psychiatry*, 14, 446–453.

OFFICE OF POPULATION CENSUSES & SURVEYS (1983) *1981: Census Country of Birth: Great Britain*. London: HMSO.

—— (1987) *Population Projections 1985 to 2025*. London: HMSO.

—— (1993) *1991 Census: Ethnic Group and Country of Birth Great Britain*. London: Office of Population Censuses and Surveys.

OGUNLESI, A. O (1989) Psychogeriatrics in Nigeria. *Psychiatric Bulletin*, 13, 548–549.

ORRELL, M., HARDY-THOMSON, C. & BERGMAN, K. (1992) Comparison between general practitioners with high or low use of a psychogeriatric domiciliary visit service. *International Journal of Geriatric Psychiatry*, **7**, 885–889.

OSUNTOKUN, B. O., HENDRIE, H. C. & OGUNNIYI, A. O. (1992) Cross cultural studies in Alzheimer's disease. *Ethnicity & Disease*, **2**, 352–357.

PALMORE, E. & MANTON, K (1973) Ageism compared to racism and sexism. *Journal of Gerontology*, **28**, 363–369.

PATEL, N. (1993) Healthy margins: black elders' care- models, policies and prospects. In *Race and Health in Contemporary Britain* (eds W. I. U. Ahmad), pp. 114–134. Buckingham: Open University Press.

PHELAN, M. & PARKMAN, S. (1995) Work with an interpreter. *British Medical Journal*, **311**, 555–557.

PITT, B. (1974) *Psychogeriatrics*. London: Churchill Livingston.

QURESHI, K. N. & HODKINSON, H. M. (1974) Evaluation of a ten-question mental test in institutionalized elderly. *Age & Ageing*, **3**, 152–157.

RACK, P. (1982) *Race, Culture and Mental Disorder*. London: Tavistock.

RAIT, G., BURNS, A. & CHEW, C. (1996) Age, ethnicity and mental illness: a triple whammy. *British Medical Journal*, **313**, 1347.

—— & —— (1997) Appreciating background and culture: the South Asian elderly and mental health. *International Journal of Geriatric Psychiatry*, **12**, 973–977.

——, MORLEY, M., LAMBAT, I., *et al* (1997) Modification of brief cognitive assessments for use with elderly people from the South Asian sub-continent. *Ageing & Mental Health*, **1**, 356–363.

RALEIGH, V. S., BUSULU, L. & BALARAJAN, R. (1990) Suicides among immigrants from the Indian subcontinent. *British Journal of Psychiatry*, **156**, 46–50.

RAMACHANDRAN, V., SARADA MENON, M., & RAMAMURTHY, B. (1979) Psychiatric disorders in subjects over the age of fifty. *Indian Journal of Psychiatry*, **21**, 193–199.

RATNA, L. (1982) Crises intervention in psychogeriatrics: a two year follow-up study. *British Journal of Psychiatry*, **141**, 296–301.

REDELINGHUYS, J. & SHAH, A. K. (1997) The characteristics of ethnic elders from the Indian subcontinent using a geriatric psychiatry service in west London. *Ageing & Mental Health*, **1**, 243–247.

RICHARDS, M. & BRAYNE, C. (1996) Cross-cultural research into cognitive impairment and dementia: some practical experiences. *International Journal of Geriatric Psychiatry*, **11**, 383–387.

——, ——, FORDE, C., *et al* (1996) Surveying African Caribbean elders in the community: implications for research on health and health service use. *International Journal of Geriatric Psychiatry*, **11**, 41–45.

ROTH, M., TYM, E., MOUNTJOY, C. Q., *et al* (1986) CAMDEX: A standardised instrument for diagnosis of mental disorder in the elderly with special reference to the early detection of dementia. *British Journal of Psychiatry*, **149**, 698–709.

ROYAL COLLOGE OF GENERAL PRACTITIONERS (1986) *1981–1982 Morbidity Statistics from General Practice: Third National Survey*. London: HMSO.

SECRETARIES OF STATE FOR HEALTH, WALES, NORTHERN IRELAND AND SCOTLAND (1989) *Working for Patients*. London: HMSO.

SEIDEL, G., SMITH, C., HAFNER, R. J., *et al* (1992) A psychogeriatric community out-reach service: description and evaluation. *International Journal of Geriatric Psychiatry*, **7**, 347–350.

SEIDEN, R. H. (1981) Mellowing with age; factors influencing the non-white suicide rate. *International Journal of Ageing and Human Development*, **13**, 265–284.

SHAH, A. K. (1992*a*) *The Prevalence and Burden of Psychiatric Disorders. A Report to the Department of Health*. London: Institute of Psychiatry.

—— (1992*b*) Difficulties in interviewing elderly people from an Asian ethnic group. *International Journal of Geriatric Psychiatry*, **7**, 917.

—— (1992*c*) Home visits by psychiatrists. *British Medical Journal*, **304**, 780.

—— (1993) Taxi transportation to psychogeriatric day hospitals. *International Journal of Geriatric Psychiatry*, **3**, 270–271.

—— (1994) Cost comparison of psychogeriatric consultations: out-patient versus home based consultations. *International Psychogeriatrics*, **6**, 179–189.

—— (1996) Cost of transportation to a psychogeriatric day hospital: minibus versus taxi service. *International Journal of Geriatric Psychiatry*, **11**, 555–558.

—— (1997*a*) A British psychogeriatricians experience of working in Australia. *International Journal of Psychiatry*, **12**, 263–266.

—— (1997*b*) Interviewing mentally ill ethnic minority elders with interpreters. *Australian Journal on Ageing*, **16**, 220–221.

—— (1997*c*) Striaght talk. overcoming language barriers in diagnosis. *Geriatric Medicine*, **27**, 45–46.

—— (1997*d*) Cost comparison of out-patient and home-based geriatric psychiatry consultation in a service. *Ageing & Mental Health*, **1**, 372–376.

—— (1998) The psychiatric needs of ethnic minority elders in the United Kingdom. *Age & Ageing*, **27**, 267–269.

—— & AMES, D. (1994) Planning and developing psychogeriatric services. *International Review of Psychiatry*, **6**, 15–27.

—— & DIGHE-DEO, D. (1997) Elderly Gujaratis and psychogeriatrics in a London psychogeriatric service. *Bulletin of the International Psychogeriatric Association*, **14**, 12–13.

—— & GANESVARAN, T. (1994) Suicide in the elderly. In *Functional Psychiatric Disorders of the Elderly* (eds E. Chiu, D. Ames & T. Arie), pp. 221–244. Cambridge: Cambridge University Press.

——, LINDESAY, J. & JAGGER, C. (1998) Is the diagnosis of dementia stable over time among elderly immigrant Gujaratis in the United Kingdom (Leicester)? *International Journal of Geriatric Psychiatry*, **13**, 440–444.

SHIMUZU, M. (1990) Depression and suicide in late life. In *Psychogeriatrics: Biomedical and Social Advances* (eds K. Hasegawa & A. Homma), pp. 330–334. Amsterdam: Excerpta Medica.

SILVEIRA, E. & EBRAHIM, S. (1995) Mental Health and health status of elderly Bengalis and Somalis in London. *Age & Ageing*, **24**, 474–480.

SOLOMON, A. (1992) Clinical diagnosis among diverse populations: a multicultural perspective. *Family in Society: The Journal of Contemporary Human Services*, June, 371–377.

SPENCE, S. A. & ATHERTON, C. R. (1991) The black elderly and social service delivery system: A study of factors influencing the use of communirty based services. *Journal of Gerontological Social Work*, **16**, 19–35.

SURTEES, P. G. & DUFFY, J. C. (1989) Suicide in England and Wales 1946–1985: an age period cohort analysis. *Acta Psychiatrica Scandinavica*, **79**, 216–223.

THORNICROFT, G., WARD, P. & JAMES, S. (1992) Carer management and mental health. *British Medical Journal*, **306**, 768–771.

TYM, E. (1991) Psychiatric services for the elderly in East Anglia. In *Psychiatry in the Elderly* (eds R. Jacoby & C. Oppenheimer), pp. 313–321. Oxford: Oxford University Press.

TYRER, P. (1985) The hive system: a model for psychiatric services. *British Journal of Psychiatry*, **146**, 571–575.

VENKOBA RAO, A. & MADHAVAN, T. (1983) Geropsychiatric morbidity survey in a semi-urban area near Madurai. *Indian Journal of Psychiatry*, **24**, 258–267.

——, VIRUDHAGIRINATHAN, B. S. & MALATHI, R. (1972) Mental illness in patients aged fifty and over. *Indian Journal of Psychiatry*, **14**, 319–332.

WATERREUS, A. (1992) Community psychiatric nursing in primary care. *International Review of Psychiatry*, **4**, 317–322.

WATTIS, J. (1989) Old age psychiatry in the United Kingdom: their educational role. *International Journal of Geriatric Psychiatry*, **4**, 361–363.

9 Effective services? Understanding the care of the ethnic minority elderly

NAINA PATEL and NAHEED R. MIRZA

Editors' introduction

Patel & Mirza provide the theoretical underpinning of the practical approach to developing psychiatric services for the ethnic minority elderly described by Shah in Chapter 8. They argue that social demographic factors and economic positions play a key role in the development of symptoms and health care seeking. Using evidence from UK and European studies they offer solutions and challenges to care of the ethnic minority elderly. Access and appropriateness of services are key to successful engagement of this group.

"Who has sent old age?
Strength in the body disappears,
Work progresses in slow motion
But I like the 'ladoos' (cakes)
And the idea of visiting places
  – an adventure.
Faith in god and belief in oneself
will see that this adventure comes –
There is so much to see and learn!"
    Shantaben, aged 78 years

"The elderly! What elderly?
My legs are only a little
tired and death is due, but
do I think about it? No!"
    *M. K., a 92-year-old man
    from the Maghreb*

The above quotations are among the UK and French contributions to the publication *Living and Ageing as a Minority in Europe* (Patel & Mertens, 1998). They illustrate the reality of many ethnic minority older people, who are neither passive nor inactive as they age. Many will have been involved in the struggles for racial and social justice in the 1950s and 1960s. Some will even have pioneered services for their group as they approached old age in the 1980s and 1990s. Even if they do not belong to these categories, the ordinary aspects of raising their families in a 'second home', often facing unfriendly workplaces, and of living in a cold, cold place have been sufficient challenges. They have met such challenges with remarkable success, as is witnessed by their extraordinary management of ordinary living in the UK, where life for minorities and refugees is affected by racism and disadvantage. The European Parliament's declaration of 1997 as the European Year against Racism and the resulting Action Plan implemented in 1998 (European Commission, 1998) gave recognition to the problem. Psychiatric professionals are no more immune than others to such wider forces in society: how they view people influences the type of care they do (or do not) provide.

Fernando (1991), in analysing the approach of psychiatrists to Black, Asian or other minority ethnic groups, which include the elderly (hereafter referred to as 'minority elderly'), says:

> "psychiatric treatment is seen as being directed at biological disease or illness which, by definition, cannot have a racial or cultural component in a social sense. Thus, a colour-blind, culture-blind approach is perceived as an objective approach – a 'scientific' approach. An approach that incorporates race and culture implies a need for a radical rethinking of psychiatry – something that the profession is probably not ready for at present" (p. 138).

In the years since Fernando wrote this there have been some signs of improvement, no doubt in part due to the efforts of psychiatrists like himself. Referring to Patel *et al*'s book *Visions of Reality* (1998*b*), Paul Boateng MP, the former Junior Health Minister, gave his views on how psychiatrists and related care professionals should view the minority elderly:

> "It is important to recognise, as we work for example with the elderly, that they have a need – whatever their faith, tradition, or none, they have a need to work with people who understand the search they are beginning to make at that time of their life for a spiritual context ... Whether or not we share their faith, whether we have any faith, if we are to deliver to the elderly we need that sense of where they are coming from, where they are at.
>
> We need to recognise when we are working with people suffering mental distress that we need to shed some of our own stereotypes and preconceptions. ... We need to recognise the gifts of the spirit and how they manifest themselves to different people in different ways. We need to recognise that those who are genuinely in the grip of delusions also have a right to religion" (in Patel & Amin, 1999).

The critical question for care professionals is whether they can discharge their duties in a non-discriminatory way encompassing all the aspects that define our humanity. Their conduct should be guided as much by the Race Relations Act 1976 as by professional and medical ethics. The organisations in which health and social care professionals work have much to do to set the appropriate ethos. When we are considering the care needs of the minority elderly, for example, the historical and cultural context of their early and later life matters as much as the professionals' understanding and competence.

The management culture in which care professionals operate is also significant. The overrepresentation of Black people in psychiatric hospitals, children's homes, prisons and remand centres is due not to some coincidence, but to coercive practices in the 'control' aspects of care (Sashidharan & Francis, 1993). The underrepresentation of Black people in utilisation of health and social care services reflects inequalities in dispensing the 'caring' aspects of care. Francis points to the effect psychiatrists and other care system professionals have: "by the time the various agencies are through with you, you may well be crazy" (in Torkington, 1991).

This chapter outlines some of the key developments in the care of the minority elderly and the growing challenge presented by their increasing number in the population. The challenges relate not only to differences in culture, language and faith, but also to differences in experiences arising from being a minority, immigrant or refugee. These factors generate external forces in society that determine the opportunities that such people have and the consequent adjustment they must make, successfully or not. Our approach is not to list the tools available to old age psychiatrists working with the minority elderly. Such tools are, of course, important, but we wish here to consider issues of race, culture, racism and power that are central to the reality of the minority elderly.

Context, content and conduct are therefore significant in the determination of an effective approach to psychiatric work with the minority elderly. It is to be hoped that the increasing collaboration between health and social care services aimed at providing a 'seamless service' will have some positive spin-offs: for example, in seeing users in their entirety, rather than just within our respective clinical and non-clinical categories and approaches. For the minority elderly, who have only recently been 'discovered' by the health and social care research and professional community, this may take time. Our hope is that their 'discovery' will yield better results in the care they receive from professionals and the health and social care system in general. After all, they have been heavily researched, and a population census (Office of Population Censuses and Surveys, 1996) revealed that there were 130 000 minority elderly aged 65 years or over in the UK in 1991. Yet the CNEOPSA (Care Needs of Ethnic Older Persons with Alzheimer's) project on dementia and the minority elderly (Patel *et al*, 1998*a*) constituted the first publications on dementia and ethnicity (CNEOPSA, 1999). Other research studies have been highly restrictive, focusing on analysing the needs of the minority elderly.

We set out below the themes that we regard as important to a full understanding of the subject of minority elderly care and reveal the apparent trend of ad hoc, patchy and piecemeal developments over the past two decades. If this trend continues it will, sadly, confirm the marginalisation of this growing number of people in the UK.

Demographic trends

An ethnic minority presence in the UK is not a recent phenomenon – for example, our history has seen the immigration of Irish between the 16th and the 18th centuries, Jews and Poles in the late 19th and 20th centuries and people from the Caribbean and Indian subcontinent mainly since the mid-20th century. According to the 1991 Census there were about 3.2 million ethnic minority people in the UK (about 5.5% of the total population), living in most areas of Great Britain and Northern Ireland.

Table 9.1 shows the population distribution for Great Britain according to age and ethnicity. It shows the relative youth of the ethnic minority population compared to the White population and the diversity in patterns of ageing among different ethnic groups. Nevertheless, over 4% of ethnic minority people were over 65 years of age, compared to 16% of the White population. That is, of the 8.8 million people aged 65 years or over, 130 000 were from ethnic minority groups. Of those aged 85 years or over, ethnic minority groups accounted for 3871 people (about 0.005%) from a total population of 830 678. Of the total population aged 65 and over and 45–64 years, ethnic minority groups made up 1.3 and 4% respectively, compared to 98.7 and 96% for the corresponding age ranges for White groups (Owen, 1996; Warnes, 1996). This means that in the next decade there will be an increased percentage of ethnic minority people reaching retirement age, resulting in a considerable change in the profile described above.

Moreover, there are variations in the ageing profile in ethnic minority groups depending upon location and gender. In his analysis of the 1991 Census data, Warnes states that "females [were] more numerous but the sex ratio of 1.006% was slight in comparison to the ratio of 1.069 in the White population" (1996, p. 161). As regards location, in the London borough of Brent, for example, 26% of the ethnic minority population were aged 60–74 years, and 9% were aged 75–85, compared to 11 and 4% respectively in Harrow. However, in both boroughs the projected increase in 2011 for both age ranges is more than double: 49 and 44% respectively for Brent and 35 and 23% for Harrow (PRIAE, 2000).

The socio-economic position

The diversity in distribution by age, location – some 45% of all ethnic minority groups in Great Britain live in Greater London (Owen, 1996) – and gender reflect the pattern of migration and settlement. This process has also determined the social and economic position of today's minority elderly. Their social and health care needs cannot be understood without reference to their experience of employment, housing and income.

TABLE 9.1
Age breakdown of ethnic groups in Great Britain, 1991,
based on data adjusted for Census under-renumeration

Ethnic group	Total population (1000s)	Percentage of total population in age ranges (years)					
		0–4	5–15	16–24	25–44	45–64	65+
White	52,893.9	6.5	13.0	12.9	29.3	19.2	19.3
Ethnic minority groups	3,117.0	11.1	21.7	16.4	32.9	13.6	4.2
Black	9255	11.1	18.0	16.5	33.8	15.4	5.1
Caribbean	517.1	7.6	14.1	15.3	33.4	21.8	7.7
African	221.9	11.8	17.1	17.0	42.7	9.5	1.8
Other	186.4	20.1	29.6	19.3	24.6	4.4	1.6
South Asian	1524.3	10.9	24.6	16.5	30.5	13.5	3.9
Indian	865.5	8.9	20.5	15.5	34.9	14.9	5.2
Pakistani	491.0	13.2	29.2	17.9	26.1	11.3	2.4
Bangladeshi	167.8	15.1	31.9	17.9	20.8	12.7	1.5
Chinese and other	667.2	11.6	20.1	16.1	36.9	11.4	3.8
Chinese	162.4	7.1	16.0	18.4	41.4	12.7	4.4
Other Asians	204.3	8.0	16.2	15.1	43.6	13.7	3.1
Other	300.5	16.4	25.0	15.5	29.9	9.2	3.9
Entire population	55,969.2	6.7	13.5	13.1	29.5	18.9	18.5

Source: Owen, 1996: p. 116.

Early surveys by the Policy Studies Institute (Smith, 1977; Brown, 1984) explained the unequal distribution of ethnic minority workers in the 1970s (that is, the minority elderly of today) by sector and industry as being due to differences in labour requirements between various industries and discrimination by employers and unions. Once in jobs, minority workers were paid less. The disparity in earnings as regards 'working period' (period of work at lower pay) as well as the length of working life, coupled with known underclaiming of welfare benefits, account for differences in pensionable income (Askham *et al*, 1995). For the emerging generation of minority elderly we must add the effects of long-term unemployment resulting from the decline of the manufacturing industries (foundries, textile mills, car manufacturing) where many ethnic minorities had worked. These factors may contribute to the use of services by people in this emerging generation as young as 55 years. This has serious implications for policy, since there may be 'early ageing' among this group.

The minority elderly face a range of health problems, and mainstream health and social services have been inadequate in meeting their needs (Bhalla & Blakemore, 1981; Patel 1990; Askham *et al*, 1995; Pharoah, 1995; Lindesay *et al*, 1997; Nazroo, 1997). These authors also show evidence that elderly African–Caribbeans and Asians use health services, including general practitioners (GPs), more frequently than elderly White people. However, frequency of contact with GPs and hospitals says nothing about the quality of treatment received.

Murray & Brown (1998) undertook a survey of policies, strategies and practice in the care of Black elderly people by social services departments. Their survey adds to the empirical studies conducted over the past two decades. Considerably less information is available on health care, although the CNEOPSA study (Patel *et al*, 1998*a*) presents country and practice data on dementia and a summary of the health profile of Black elderly people from various surveys. Askham *et al* (1995) and Pharoah (1995), at the Age Concern Institute for Gerontology, provide a range of information on the responsiveness of health professionals to the 'appropriate' care of Black elderly people.

Developments, solutions and challenges in care

Evidence from the 1980s

This section summarises the main points of Patel's (1990) analysis of 10 empirical studies of social services for Black elderly people from 1980 to 1989.

First, the experiences of the minority elderly reflect both racial and cultural stereotyping in their care and welfare. When adjustments to the existing mainstream care have been called upon to respond to variations in culture, statements such as "we treat everyone the same", "our service is open to all" and "providing special needs is discriminatory – it is racism in reverse" have all been used. However, treating everyone the same is often inappropriate and may leave some with no service at all.

Let us briefly consider the continuing racial stereotype of "extended families take care of their own". Here the popular image that an extended network of 'families within families' provides care and socio-psychological support is activated when calls for referrals and assessments are made. It might be noted that family structures are continually changing in our society as the families adjust to internal and external conditions, and ethnic minority families are not immune from this process. However, the important question is not whether extended family structures exist, but whether the minority elderly are receiving the necessary care from the social, health and housing services, irrespective of the family within which they live. "They look after their own" is a useful and cost-effective evasion, maintaining the status quo in services. It is used by many professional staff (including doctors), who do not refer the minority elderly to existing services in the belief that their needs are best met by their extended families. Unfortunately, 'no referrals' means 'no assessment of needs', and hence 'no services'. Thus, this belief essentially determines the eligibility criteria for services, not the rights or needs of the minority elderly.

The above experiences need to be understood in the context of consistent evidence from empirical studies in the 1980s, which indicate the following:

(a) There is a growing recognition that Black, Asian and other ethnic minority people also grow old, and like the majority population in old age, they require specific social and health care services. Their needs and demands for such services are well documented (see Chapter 8, this volume).

(b) The elderly (and their carers) lack information not only on social and health services, but also on financial benefits.

(c) There is a low take up on a range of mainstream services (day centres, residential housing, health programme activities) geared for older people generally.

Why is this the case? It may be claimed that the minority elderly do not use services because they do not need them. However, the following examples of the concerns expressed by minority elderly themselves suggest a different answer:

(a) speaking and understanding English, in the absence of staff with the appropriate languages;
(b) culturally inappropriate food and facilities;
(c) social and health care facilities that make the practice of faith and beliefs difficult to observe;
(d) finding it difficult to establish relationships, in the absence of a common background with other, non-minority people in day care, residential or hospital services;
(e) being subjected to racist abuse and hostility from other residents and users.

The studies in 1980s showed that the minority elderly have needs and would use social and health care services if they were accessible and appropriate to their social and cultural situation. Such needs are not 'special': they are basic to fulfilling daily life. This distinction is important since the emphasis placed on 'special' is not only inaccurate, but also suggests that somehow they are over and above 'normal' human needs. Unfortunately, when planning the effective care of the minority elderly, the debate and practices have been couched in terms of special needs rather than the ordinary needs of diverse groups.

The studies also confirmed that it is self-help organisations in the voluntary sector, rather than mainstream providers, that meet the care needs of the minority elderly. Voluntary projects are often started up by the minority elderly themselves, with or without the help of professionals. Patel (1990) documented the characteristics of such organisations and described them as the "primary providers of care" (i.e. substitutes for mainstream provision). Two facts emerged. First, the majority of such projects are day care centres attempting to meet basic care needs on temporary and small budgets. Their particular position and poor infrastructure limit their ability to cover all sectors of the minority elderly community and to provide a comprehensive range of services. Second, there have been some successful examples of sheltered housing projects led by ethnic minority organisations that address the changing patterns in families and the preferences of the elderly to age independently. Again demand exceeds supply, resulting in long waiting lists.

Evidence from the 1990s

The National Health Service and Community Care Act 1990, implemented in 1993, introduced a mixed economy of care with a purchaser–provider split in the health services. The key objective was to make sure that users live in the community as independently as possible. Flexibility, choice and users' and carers' involvement were some of the principal aims of this policy, as was the intention to consult with minority groups in developing a purchasing strategy (the commissioning role). This emphasis follows from the 1989 White Paper, *Caring for People*, which stated:

> "The Government recognises that people from different cultural backgrounds have particular care needs and problems. Minority communities may have different concepts of community care and it is important that service providers are sensitive to these variations. Good community care will take account of the circumstances of minority communities and will be planned in consultation with them" (Department of Health and Social Services, 1989: pp. 10–11).

How does this work in reality?

We turn to two main reports, both published in 1998, for the answer. We will first consider the Government's own report on the inspection of social services, *They Look After Their Own, Don't They?* (Murray & Brown, 1998). There is no comparable report for health services, but both sectors share aspects of commissioning and provision of 'appropriate cultural services' to the minority elderly. We briefly summarise the report's findings below.

Regarding policies, strategies and planning, the inspection found that there was reference to minorities, but specific issues relating to the elderly were often absent. Where they were mentioned, best practice included examples of effective joint planning between health services, social services and minority elderly organisations; ethnic record-keeping and monitoring systems routinely used by staff; and the treatment of race and ethnicity as integral to policy planning and delivery.

As regards communication and information, it found that some organisations had produced information in languages accessible to minorities, had developed channels of communication with minority communities and had issued clear guidelines for staff. These are all essential to enable minority elderly who cannot communicate in English to gain access to services.

Assessment and care management are critical if the minority elderly are to receive adequate care services. The report stated that assessors' skills in anti-discriminatory practice, cultural sensitivity and confidence-building (to enable elderly people and their carers to exercise choice) are significant in selecting appropriate services and care packages. Here it found that best practice included advocacy for the elderly and their carers, participation of the elderly in their assessments and discussion of care plans, and ethnic minority staff working in the assessment and management-decision teams.

The effect of the Community Care Act was to ensure that the users have effective services. For our target group, cultural, social, linguistic and spiritual considerations are ordinary, not special, needs that must be met to ensure effective care. The report noted "genuine" attempts by mainstream authorities to respond appropriately to the needs of the minority elderly, but success was variable. For example, it was noted that:

> "service choice was limited in the majority of LA [local authority] areas and the euro-centric nature of the service provision meant ... basic services like meals-on-wheels were provided in an inappropriate manner" (p. 12).

The report recognised the critical role played by ethnic minority organisations in service provision, acknowledging restrictions in its funding and infrastructure. As to best practice, it found examples of residential care homes where staff spoke the residents' languages and food was prepared in accordance with their cultural requirements; of direct participation in service delivery by staff who shared the same cultural background as their clients; and of the therapeutic use of reminiscence work.

These examples from the report give some idea of the scale of work still required to meet the principles outlined in the Government's 1989 White Paper legislation on ethnic minority communities mentioned above. Patel (1999) summarises the situation in the late 1990s as follows: "some authorities are making good progress, while others are slow and some are not doing anything at all".

It would be instructive to compare the record of the health sector with this report on social services inspection. It is felt by some that the pace of developments in the health care of the minority elderly generally lags behind social services care. If this is so, there is considerable scope for transfer of learning on how health care professionals can make a difference in referrals, assessments and developments in services for the minority elderly.

The CNEOPSA study (Patel *et al*, 1998*a*) on dementia and the minority elderly, which considered the UK, Denmark and France, found that "the world of dementia is colour-blind and the world of ethnic minority organisations is dementia-blind" (Marshall, 1998). In the UK, Marshall identified an urgent need for investment in organisations dealing with dementia in the minority elderly, and for a planned and managed programme to enable health and social care professionals to respond appropriately from diagnosis to effective care. The Government acknowledged the importance of Patel *et al*'s study and its recommendations for a 'satellite model' to generate specialist developments in a selected number of ethnic minority organisations.

The present and the future

In 1998 the Government set up a Royal Commission to look at the long-term care needs of older people for the next 50 years. The Policy Research Institute on Ageing and Ethnicity (PRIAE) was asked by the Commission to produce a UK report on the perspectives of the minority elderly and their carers. It gathered data in seminars with minority elderly groups and their carers focusing on four key areas:

(a) *the appropriateness of current models of care*: users' and carers' experiences and views on the choice and quality of current service provision in day care, residential, sheltered and nursing homes;

(b) *access to services*: the experience of carers, the elderly and managers engaging and coordinating services with the social, health and housing services;

(c) *planning and paying for long-term care*: the experience and effect of means testing and the practice of capped local budgets;

(d) *reducing dependency*: alternative models of care under consideration for the future.

The results of PRIAE's work are highly consistent with the research findings illustrated above.

The Royal Commission's report was released in March 1999 (Royal Commission on Long Term Care, 1999), and it included a summary of PRIAE's recommendations that "it should be a priority for Government to improve cultural awareness in services offered to black and minority elderly" (p. 92).

Following publication of the Commission's report the Government undertook to enage in further consultations and to consider the Commission's recommendations: a result met by many with dismay.

Two specific recommendations from PRIAE's report to the Commission which have direct connections with the Government's White Papers on health and social care and the MacPherson Report into the murder of Stephen Lawrence, also released in March 1999, are discussed below.

On appropriateness of care, we recommended urgent examination of why mainstream health, housing and social care organisations appear to have difficulties in responding effectively to the ordinary (not 'special') needs of the minority elderly and their carers. If they continue with the present approach of "ad hoc, patchy and piecemeal developments" (Patel, 1999), they will by default create a system of centres offering the minority elderly segmented long-term care on minimal resources, endorsing *de facto* racism. The settlement of the minority elderly in concentrated areas simply presents planners with less difficulty in implementing PRIAE's proposals to the Royal Commission (Patel, 1999) and those of the Ethnic Minorities Steering Group, Age Concern in PRIAE (1999*a*). Government departments must take action now to prevent the structuring of the above scenario, which could have serious social and race relations policy implications.

On access to services, we recommended that information on services must be made publicly available and that there should be a planned strategy in marketing services. Good quality translated leaflets are only one part of this communication programme.

Barriers relating to information, choice, culturally responsive care and underlying discriminatory processes that affect assessments must be eliminated. The minority elderly of tomorrow will demand an equal, but perhaps different, service and the authorities must be prepared for this and be flexible in their approach to care (Patel 1999, pp. 258–259).

When considering fair access, how professionals interpret eligibility criteria when making referral decisions (and the effective gate-keeping role of GPs regarding referrals) is as important as having the appropriate services to which to refer. This is critical to breaking the cycle of 'no referrals mean no assessments mean no services', since "any criterion, which is good for minority use, will also be good for majority users"(PRIAE, 1999*a*).

The combined policy drives of the National Service Framework on Older People, Fair Access and the Inter-Departmental Group on Ageing should give us hope. The fact that the issue of old age is gaining prominence and that attempts are being made to address the problems of the minority elderly are hopeful signs of change. Issues of ageing and ethnicity have been well rehearsed over the past century, so now it is a matter of commitment and implementation. The old and new structures for the minority, including PRIAE as a national body, are focusing their resources on specific themes to advance the area generally. A particular issue is the economics of ethnic demography, which may make 'ageing and ethnicity' an important business for public, private and voluntary sectors. We should also not underestimate the effect of the Macpherson Report and the Government's response to its recommendations.

As *The Economist* commented:

> 'the Macpherson Report represents a defining moment in race relations ... by exposing the cancer of racism ... it has stripped away any complacency that all is well' (27 February 1999).

Conclusion

Many elderly people from Black, Asian and other ethnic minority groups wish independence as they age, and they are in urgent need of support to build a solid foundation of day care, sheltered living schemes and culturally sensitive professional health and social care. They regard organisations for the minority elderly as the main suppliers of care and see the future in terms of diversity within unity. They also recognise that their children, the elderly of tomorrow, have the same expectations and aspirations to be treated as citizens with rights, responsibilities and the need to live and age with dignity, free from racial discrimination. The work of CNEOPSA in dementia care suggests that many professionals in health and social care regard ethnicity as an important factor in care. Yet how this is conceptualised (Patel, 1990) and acted upon are determinants of what progress the minority elderly can expect in the twenty-first century. This will require a flexible approach, sensitive to the needs of the minority elderly: "being receptive to situations rather than putting situations in a pre-designed framework is the good that we should strive for" (Patel *et al*, 1998*a*: 65). This indeed is a challenge for us all.

References

ASKHAM, J., HENSHAW, L. & TARPEY, M. (1995) *Social and Health Authority Services for Elderly People from Black and Ethnic Minority Communities*. London: HMSO.

ATKIN, K. (1996) An opportunity for change. In *'Race' and Community Care* (eds W. Ahmad & K. Atkin). Abingdon: Open University Press.

BHALLA, A. & BLAKEMORE, K. (1981) *Elders of the Ethnic Minority Groups*. All Faiths for One Race.

BLAKEMORE, K. & BONEHAM, M. (1994) *Age, Race and Ethnicity*. Abingdon: Open University Press.

BROWN, C. (1984) *Black and White: The Third PSI Survey*. Oxford: Heinemann.

CNEOPSA (1999) *Dementia Matters: Ethnic Concerns in the UK, Finland, Netherlands and Spain* (videofilm and booklet). Bradford: Policy Research Institute on Ageing and Ethnicity (PRIAE).

DEPARTMENT OF HEALTH (1998) *Modernising Social Services: Promoting Independence, Improving Protection and Raising Standards*. Cm 4169. London: HMSO.

—— (1999) *Saving Lives: Our Healthier Nation*. Cm 3807. London: Stationery Office.

DEPARTMENT OF HEALTH AND SOCIAL SERVICES (1989) *Caring for People: Community Care in the Next Decade and Beyond*. Cm 849. London: HMSO.

EUROPEAN COMMISSION COUNCIL OF MINISTERS (1998) *An Action Plan Against Rascism*. Brussels: European Commission.

FERNANDO, S. (1991) *Mental Health, Race and Culture*. Basinstoke: Macmillan Press.

LINDESAY, J., JAGGER, C., HIBBETT, M. J., *et al* (1997) Knowledge, uptake and availability of health and social services among Asian Gujarati and White elderly persons. *Ethnicity and Health*, **2**, 59–69.

MACPHERSON, W. (Chair) (1999) *Enquiry into the Murder of Stephen Lawrence*. Cm 4262-1. London: Stationery Office.

MARSHALL, M. (1998) Foreword. In *Dementia and Ethnic Minority Older People: Managing Care in the UK, Denmark and France* (Patel, N., Mirza, N., Linblad, P., *et al*). CNEOPSA study. Lyme Regis: Russell House.

MURRAY, U. & BROWN, D. (1998) *They Look After Their Own, Don't They?* London: Department of Health.

NAZROO, J. Y. (1997) *The Health of Britain's Ethnic Minorities.* London: Policy Studies Institute.

NORMAN, A. (1985) *Triple Jeopardy: Growing Old in a Second Homeland.* London: Centre for Policy on Ageing.

OFFICE OF POPULATION CENSUSES AND SURVEYS (1996) *Ethnicity in the 1991 Census.* London: HMSO.

OWEN, D. (1996) Size, structure and growth of the ethnic minority populations. In *Ethnicity in the Census* (eds D. Coleman & J. Salt), vol. 1. London: HMSO.

PATEL, N. (1990) *A 'Race' Against Time? Social Services Provision to Black Elders.* London: Runnymede Trust.

—— (1999) Black and minority ethnic elderly: perspectives on long term care. In *With Respect to Age* (Royal Commission on Long Term Care). London: Stationery Office.

—— & Amin, K. (1999) *Faith, Communities and Social Work.* Symposium report. London: CCETSW and DETR.

—— & Mertens, H. (eds) (1998) *Living and Ageing as a Minority in Europe: Profiles and Projects.* Utrecht: NIZW.

——, Mirza, N., Linblad, P., *et al* (1998a) *Dementia and Ethnic Minority Older People: Managing Care in the UK, Denmark and France.* CNEOPSA study. Lyme Regis: Russell House.

——, Naik, D. & Humphreys, B. (eds) (1998b) *Visions of Reality – Religion and Ethnicity in Social Work.* London: CCETSW.

PHAROAH, C. (1995) *Primary Health Care for Elderly People from Black and Ethnic Minority Communities.* London: HMSO.

PRIAE (1999a) *Fair Access – Who Gets What Service?* Report to the Department of Health. London: Department of Health.

—— (1999b) *Ageing Matters: Ethnic Concerns.* Millennium Debate of the Age. London: Age Concern.

—— (2000) *The Changing Face of London's Black and Minority Ethnic Elders.* Report. London: City Parochial Foundation (in press).

ROYAL COMMISSION ON LONG TERM CARE (1999) *With Respect to Age.* London: Stationery Office.

SASHIDHARAN, S. P. & FRANCIS, F. (1993) Epidemiology, ethnicity and schizophrenia. In *'Race' and Health in Contemporary Britain* (ed. W. I. U. Ahmad). Abingdon: Open University Press.

SMITH, D. J. (1977) *Racial Disadvantage in Britain: the PEP Report.* Harmondsworth: Penguin Books.

TORKINGTON, N. (1991) *Black Health – A Political Issue.* London: CARJ and LIHE.

WARNES, T. (1996) The age structure and ageing of the ethnic groups. In *Ethnicity in the Census* (eds D. Coleman & J. Salt), vol. 1. London: HMSO.

10   Child psychiatry

ANULA D. NIKAPOTA

Editors' introduction

The multiple needs of children and adolescents from Black and other ethnic minority groups are discussed. Cultural influences and parenting styles can influence the growth, identity and self-esteem of children and adolescents. In addition, there is evidence that functioning at school may also be affected. The interaction between personal, family and school factors complex. Nikapota considers the influence of race, ethnicity and culture on individual differences, family and social factors and subsequently on coping, poor mental health and maladaptive behaviour. Using case materials she suggests that any management plan must be multi-factorial. Cultural factors influence presentation and diagnosis, and service development must take into account the rates of different disorders in different communities. It is tempting to believe that certain mental disorders have an early onset and that aetiological factors may be biological. Nikapota warns us against this assumption and shows how similar environments may have different psychological impacts.

Understanding differences and recognising similarities in terms of need, experience and patterns of response are important for developing culturally sensitive and appropriate mental health services for children, adolescents and their families. Recognition of similarities helps prevent a stereotyped response dictated by race, ethnicity or religious affiliation. Reviews of international analyses of child mental health (Sartorius & Graham, 1984) and cross-cultural data on child development and behaviour (Minde & Nikapota, 1993) highlight the fact that rates of both disorder and symptomatology follow similar patterns, with few culture-specific syndromes.

Research in the UK has focused mainly on Asian and African–
Caribbean ethnic minority groups and there is little information on
immigrant groups from Europe, such as the Irish, Polish, Hungarian
and Greek communities. Existing studies, whether of clinical
prevalence (Graham & Meadowes, 1967; Cochrane, 1979; Stern
et al, 1990; Jawed, 1991; Goodman & Richards, 1995) or community-
based epidemiology (Rutter *et al*, 1974; Richman *et al*, 1975; Hackett
et al, 1991), have demonstrated similar rates and patterns of disorder,
although there is some difference between ethnic minority groups
and the native White population in terms of age of onset and type
of disorder. Initial studies focused on rates and types of disorder,
with identification of associated individual, family and social factors.
More recent work has included issues relating to attendance at and
compliance with child mental health services (Stern *et al*, 1990;
Subotsky & Berelowitz, 1990; Hillier *et al*, 1994), parents' attitudes
to behaviour (Hackett & Hackett, 1993; Newth & Corbett, 1993)
and identification of risk factors (Goodman & Richards, 1995).
Rates for problems among Asian (Newth & Corbett, 1993) and
African–Caribbean pre-school children (Richman *et al*, 1975)
and associated factors such as family dysfunction, relationship
problems and social situation are similar to those found in the
White population in the UK (Richman *et al*, 1982) and elsewhere
(Campbell, 1995). Studies of school children in African–Caribbean
populations have consistently shown higher rates of conduct
disorder among boys, pervasive developmental disorder and
psychosis (Rutter *et al*, 1974; Goodman & Richards, 1995). There
appears to be a comparatively lower rate of conduct disorder
and higher rate of emotional problems and somatisation among
school children from Bangladesh, Pakistan and India (Hackett *et
al*, 1991; Jawed, 1991). However, clinical audit data from east London
suggests an increasing trend towards conduct problems and
substance misuse among Asian adolescents boys in deprived inner-
city locations.

The relative importance of genetic and psychosocial factors
in the psychopathology of disorder is currently under debate, and
the evidence for an interaction between them is too strong to
be ignored (Rutter, 1999). The purpose of this chapter is to
consider the influence of race, ethnicity and culture on
individual differences, family and social factors, and hence on
coping, resilience, maladaptive behaviour and poor mental health,
and to highlight issues relevant to culture-sensitive clinical practice
and service provision.

Racial characteristics are biologically determined and I will not
discuss disorders for which there may be biologically determined

vulnerabilities within certain racial groups. I will, however, mention issues relating to attitudes that are bound up in biologically determined attributes such as skin colour.

Culture and child psychiatry

The concept of culture is integral to understanding and knowledge within child psychiatry. A wealth of data from work done largely in the European and North American White culture reveals the way in which family, school and social factors influence the emergence of coping styles and behaviour patterns, highlights the interactive nature of these variables, and shows the impact of repeated stress and differences associated with age, developmental stage, gender, temperament, self-esteem and so on (Rutter, 1981, 1985; Goodyer, 1990; Garmezy & Masten, 1994). The fact that significant variables relating to family type, attitude or practices often represent cultural or subcultural variations is implicit in discussion, but not emphasised. Any clinician who has worked among indigenous White working- and upper-middle-class families is aware of dealing with different subcultures.

The term 'culture' tends to be used to describe family and social issues pertaining to foreign countries, or the lifestyle of ethnic minority groups. While this serves to highlight difference, it could lead to acceptance of the norms of one culture as the yardstick of measurement of other cultures in a way that is potentially unhelpful or discriminatory. This does not mean that many significant variables are not applicable cross-culturally. There is ample evidence that factors such as poor quality maternal relationships, marital conflict, marital disruption and divorce, bereavement and academic failure are stressful for children everywhere (Sartorius & Graham, 1984; Goodyer, 1990; Minde & Nikapota, 1993).

The influence of culture on psychopathology is primarily due to the way that cultural factors alter the context and meaning of a situation, resulting in diverse interactions or transactional effects. Experiences related to racial or ethnic issues are also involved. Risk factors may be similar cross-culturally, but the patterns of risk or definition of the level of risk may differ (Goodman & Richards, 1995). There will also be factors specific to certain ethnic groups, such as the trauma of refugees of civil war or the higher risk of physical illnesses such as sickle cell anaemia or maternally transmitted HIV infection. Discussion of specific examples may serve to illustrate the points made.

Family type and size

Family size is often an expression of the family's perception of its need for children and it relates to beliefs about survival rates. These have changed for the indigenous White population in the UK over the past 50 years, with the very significant reductions in infant and child mortality. However, this is not the experience that immigrants from countries with high mortality rates will bring with them; furthermore, the pressures of social survival within an alien environment might also encourage larger families. Therefore a culturally determined trend for large families may persist (Garcia-Coll, 1990). Thus, although family size may be a risk factor across cultures, the family size that constitutes risk may vary.

Family structure can have different meanings according to culture. An African–Caribbean single mother who identifies with the matrifocal culture of the Caribbean may view her role differently than a White mother left single by desertion or divorce. In a comparison of immigrant Gujerati and English families, there was different meaning attached to two-parent families in which one or both parents had divorced and remarried (which was far more common in the English group than in the Gujerati sample) (Hackett *et al*, 1991).

While extended families may be the norm in the countries in which many ethnic minority groups in the UK originated, relatively few first-generation parents from immigrant families benefit from their support. For example, there is a trend for families from the Caribbean to disperse, with adult siblings or parents moving to the USA or returning to the Caribbean. This loss of the extended family is a feature of the second and third generations, whether from Europe, Ireland, Africa, the West Indies or Asia. Studies of the effect of parental depression, particularly depression in young mothers, on the development and behaviour of their children (Cox, 1988) highlight the role of culturally appropriate support, and equally the greater risk of social isolation and depression, among refugee groups and recent immigrants.

Extended family support is not always a positive feature. A recent study of suicide within three cultural groups points to the pressures on older adolescent and young adult Asian females from within the family: this was not a feature for the African–Caribbean and White females (Raleigh & Balarajan, 1992).

Parenting style

A parent's response to a child's behaviour will be determined by beliefs, attitudes, expectations and social norms. A recent study of White and Asian pre-schoolers by Newth and Corbett (1993) illustrating some of these issues reflects the clinical prevalence of problems found among Bangladeshi families in Tower Hamlets (Stern *et al*, 1990). Newth and Corbett found a striking difference in the frequency with which sleep and conduct problems were reported in the Asian children. It was suggested that one reason why Asian mothers seemed to have less difficulty controlling their pre-school children was that their attitude was less confrontational. White mothers tended to feel that their 3-year olds were old enough to have firm boundaries set for them. Social habits also differed, with Asian children going to bed when their parents did. These practices do not mean there are no limits set for the children, nor that learning through limit setting is not important across cultures. Limit setting may be done in relation to other aspects of the child's life that are considered more important. For example, there may be greater emphasis on the young child's compliance with socially accepted norms of behaviour towards family elders. Primary health care professionals working with families from different backgrounds should therefore look for limit setting in general, rather than in specific situations such as a bedtime.

Where problems were reported, Newth and Corbett (1993) found similar pressures on both Asian and White mothers, although the percentage of single mothers was lower in the Asian group. The lower rates for conduct disorder and aggression found among Asian children seem to derive from the parenting attitude and style, with disapproval of aggression and an insistence on conformity (Stopes-Roe & Cochrane, 1990; Hackett & Hackett, 1993). A study of parental perceptions and use of services in London across four cultural groups (Nikapota *et al*, 2000) indicated variations in parenting styles that may explain observed differences in the behaviour of the index group in school. For example, Asian parents tend to expect that children will respect all adults, whereas many African–Caribbean parents expect only that reasonable instructions be obeyed. Thus, it may be easier for Asian children to conform to a teacher's dictates. The work of Weisz *et al* (1993) in the USA, Thailand and Kenya further illustrates the links between parental attitude and the prevalence of under- or overcontrolled behaviours in their children. The issue of control might explain the lower clinical prevalence of conduct problems among Asian children observed both in the UK and in Asia: such problems are seen as 'badness' or disobedience requiring control (Stern *et al*, 1990; Jawed, 1991; Nikapota, 1991).

We cannot ignore the impact on children of institutional racism, which can be felt either directly or, through parental experience, indirectly. Many parents seek to compensate for this in ways that can be stressful for the children. For example, families may strive for success, sending children to private schools to offset disadvantages due to race or ethnicity, or they may encourage particular attitudes in their children. One Black British (self-declared ethnicity) mother said to me, "You know how it is if you are Black -- I have taught him to fight for himself, not let anyone put him down". A cross-cultural study of child mental health services in South London (Nikapota *et al*, 2000) found that ethnic minority parents perceived the impact of racism on their role as parents in many ways, and had different strategies for compensating for racial discrimination. African–Caribbean parents and mothers of mixed-race children thought it important that their children be confident, look smart and present themselves well. Mothers of mixed-race children expressed the greatest feelings of vulnerability in relation to their role as parents, because of social isolation and perceptions of racial discrimination from White and Black groups.

Limit setting and control are major issues in child psychiatry and the links between harsh, authoritarian, inconsistent and inadequate parenting styles and mental disorder have been extensively researched and reviewed (Goodyer, 1990). An authoritarian and punitive parenting style is the norm in some cultures. A mother from Sierra Leone said, "The African culture is different to the English. We teach children to behave through making them fear a punishment". There is no praise when parental expectations are met, only if something "brilliant" is achieved. This may not be so very different from the attitudes prevailing in the UK a century ago. Clinicians need to consider whether such attitudes (which are different from the use of positive or negative reinforcement for control or limit setting) play a part in the problems a child presents. The following excerpts from case studies illustrate this point.

> B was 9 years old and referred for oppositional behaviour in school. He came from a Nigerian background with professional parents. There were no problems reported at home. Parenting style was very authoritarian but not punitive.

B's problem was mostly a difficulty in adapting to the different styles of control and limit setting that he experienced at home and in school.

T was 11 years old and very bright. His parents, Chinese from Hong Kong, worked very hard themselves and expected a high degree of performance from him. He was able to cope with this pressure without evident problems until his mother developed breast cancer. Her illness was not terminal, but it caused great anxiety in the family and in T. T refused to go to school and his father entered a cycle of negative attitudes to which T responded by stealing.

The authoritarian parenting style of T's father might have been due in part to the father's anxiety about his wife.

N, a 15-year-old Greek Cypriot, was referred for conversion reactions. Her mother prevented her from going anywhere without an approved escort, as the mother feared that N would form inappropriate peer group friendships, which would lead to criticism from the family and N's rejection within their social network.

Different cultures will have varying coping strategies, and there is little evidence on the way these differences affect children's resilience or vulnerability.

Separation

There are qualitative differences in the separation experiences of different groups. Many children who enter the UK from abroad have been separated from carers to whom they are attached in order to be reunited with parents whom they may not remember. Where such shared care within extended families is a cultural norm the negative effect on children is not always considered, either by the families themselves or by agencies (such as schools) with which the child has contact.

J was 15 years old and from Ghana. He rejoined his parents after a separation of 7 years, during which he was looked after by his maternal grandmother. He missed her greatly. He was unhappy at home, resented by two younger brothers, who did not want an older brother, and felt excluded from a close relationship with his parents. Adapting to school was also difficult, although his knowledge of English was good.

How do parents' experiences of separation influence their own parenting? Few studies have looked at the impact of separation and reunion undergone by parents on their relationships with their own parents and on the quality of the relationship they have with their children.

Marital conflict, separation and divorce

Marital problems are an acknowledged source of stress, which may be greater for parents (usually mothers) and children if culture-based values insist on the preservation of the marital relationship because it gives stability to the larger family and social network. While offering consultative support for an Asian refuge for women I have witnessed the psychosocial distress and alienation from family (both their own and their in-laws) and the harsh and punitive attitudes of an extended family that face women who have left their husbands.

> A Maltese mother who wanted help for her children after leaving a violent husband said, "My family take his side, they feel I should have stayed for the children's sake – that is what is expected of wives. They will not help me".

Children can be placed in a conflict that involves not only their parents, but the whole family network. Supportive and meaningful contact with the separated parent may become almost impossible, and children are seen clinically who resolve this conflict by refusing to see the non-custodial parent, or by developing extremely avoidant behaviour patterns.

Poverty

Many ethnic minority immigrants live in socially disadvantaged and deprived regions, often the inner-city areas to which they came initially (Rack, 1982). Poverty in itself can be a risk for mental ill health where associated with deprivation and disadvantage, although relative levels of poverty or indicators by which it is measured vary enormously between countries. The association between poverty and raised rates of conduct disorder has been discussed frequently (see, for example, Rutter, 1985; Goodyer, 1990). A study in the USA has shown the effect of poverty on increased rates of conduct disorder across cultures, irrespective of ethnicity (Conger *et al*, 1992; Bolger *et al*, 1995).

Higher levels of social stress in terms not only of socio-economic factors, but also family factors were reported among Black adolescents presenting to psychiatric services in south-east London than in a comparable White group (Goddard *et al*, 1996). Poverty and social disadvantage also predispose adolescents to substance misuse, which presents a significant risk for youngsters from socially disadvantaged minority groups (Farrell & Strang, 1991).

M was a 12-year old from Portugal. He was the seventh of eight children. The family lived in overcrowded, privately rented lodgings. He and a Portuguese friend regularly played truant, during which time both boys were threatened and sexually abused by a family friend. The family sought professional help after this episode, and as a result his school responded more actively to his needs.

School factors

School has a significant influence on the behaviour and development of all children (Rutter, 1985; Sylva, 1994). Children from minority cultures may face problems in school (not least of which may be academic problems resulting from language limitation) and their ability to cope and maintain self-esteem may be influenced by ethnic and cultural factors. Not all schools adequately address these problems, and some schools are better than others in involving parents.

The value of Headstart and other early-intervention programmes in promoting greater self-competence of socially disadvantaged young children in inner-city areas should not be ignored (Sylva 1994).

Another important variable is teacher attitude. Differences in teacher bias and perception of culture-appropriate behaviour have been demonstrated in teacher ratings of hyperactivity in Asian and White children (Sonuga-Barke *et al*, 1993). The teachers' belief that Asian children are very controlled seemed to influence their ratings. Many African–Caribbean parents feel that teacher bias contributes to reports of their children's aggressive behaviour in school, but it appears that this belief has not been systematically researched.

Individual differences

There has been relatively little research on the impact of institutional racism on the self-concept of children or on the success of parental and family strategies to combat this. Similarly, few studies have examined the conflicting feelings that arise in children and adolescents who have to move between very different attitudes and values. There are no data on how much racism, racist attitudes or, indeed, the perception of racism (imagined or actual) affect young people's self-esteem and feelings of control over their destiny, nor of the defences they may use against such feelings and experiences. However, the relationship between racial identity and mental health among adolescents has been examined in the USA, for example, in Arroyo and Zigler's (1995) study of identity, academic achievement and well-being.

I do not propose to deal with issues of identity in detail (see Chapter 4, this volume), but I will note that identity confusion can contribute to stresses in children. Children of dual heritage (mixed race) or children in reconstituted families where there are racial or ethnic differences are often most vulnerable.

A was 7 years old and was referred for oppositional behaviour in school. His White mother was a professionally employed single parent. His father was African–Caribbean and had died 2 years earlier. His mother kept him in touch with his paternal grandparents, but the relationship was uneasy, with critical and ambivalent feelings on both sides. To help him with his heritage his mother had formed a close friendship with a Black single mother and had emphasised his Black heritage to him. A was an intelligent child, and it became apparent that he felt insecure, uncertain if he could belong to a White mother. He also found it difficult to understand the relevance of people being described as Black and White in relation to his own mixed-race background. To his therapist he described his colour as "black and white – grey".

While epidemiological study has demonstrated gender differences in rates of mental disorder in children, evidence on parental expectations of gender roles comes, in the main, from clinical information.

One Nigerian mother, a professional, said of her 11-year-old son "Of course there are high expectations for him – he is a son and the first. In our culture that is how it is".

J, a 15-year-old girl with parents of Greek Cypriot origin, said, "I don't count, my mother only listens to my brother because he is the boy -- I must be obedient and do whatever she says".

Mental disorder and cultural beliefs

Anorexia nervosa and bulimia nervosa have long been held as examples of culture-specific disorders in societies that place a value on being slim. Food scarcity is an important dimension contributing to the relative absence of these disorders in many non-Western countries (Bryant-Waugh & Lask, 1995). The prevalence of eating disorders in Japan is linked to Japanese, not Western, values favouring small build (Mukai *et al*, 1994). Data on anorexia among Asian schoolgirls in the UK, however (Bryant-Waugh & Lask, 1991; Mumford *et al*, 1991), implicate a conflict between generations or between Western and Asian value systems.

A study examining cross-cultural differences in maternal evaluation of children's body shape reported that South-Asian mothers were significantly more likely to present at paediatric clinics with worries that their children were not gaining weight (Hodes *et al*, 1996). The authors comment that this could influence how children evaluate their bodies and might reflect maternal anxiety about under-nutrition.

Problems: how do they present?

Parents' perceptions of disorder vary and this inevitably affects expression of parental concern (Nikapota, 1991). Somatisation may present more commonly in some cultures because it is a way of expressing distress, elicits greater attention from parents, or is a successful method of avoiding school or, in the case of Embu children, work (Weisz *et al*, 1993). Emotional problems or conflicts can present as somatic symptoms or conversion reactions. A review of somatisation disorders in child psychiatry examined evidence linking factors leading to distress with disorder type (Gerralda, 1992). It may be that there are culturally determined patterns linking different types of stress with somatisation disorders.

Mention has already been made of the fact that parental concerns when presenting for help vary according to cultural attitudes about the significance of observed behaviour. In one Asian sample fears among young children were increased, but as they did not arouse parental concern there was a low report rate of phobias in this group (Hackett & Hackett, 1993).

Beliefs about the causes of problems will also affect the type of problems brought to child mental health services for help. Behaviour problems may be viewed as 'disobedience' requiring control by family or community elders, or may be attributed to inauspicious planetary influences or possession by evil spirits. Conversion reactions may also be interpreted as possession states, for which help will be sought from traditional sources.

A service for a multicultural community

Service development that is appropriate across cultures and ethnic groups must follow basic principles of provision for need and effective use of resources. Recent Government publications have advocated a tiered approach depending on the type of problem, with planned inputs at a primary care level (Department of Health, 1995; Health Advisory Services, 1995). This follows principles for the development of services for child mental health advocated by the World Health Organization (WHO) (1977). It is certainly both practical and feasible for developing countries (Nikapota, 1991), as it uses resources available in the community, allows integration of child mental health service activities with ongoing activities at a primary care level and is the best way of ensuring access for high-risk and needy groups. It is a system equally valuable for developed countries, particularly in regions of high need such as the inner-city areas in the UK.

Current pressures within the National Health Service make the adoption of a tiered approach almost a requirement from the point of view of purchasers. Such an approach is likely to be the most effective in terms of provision for ethnic minority groups: it should facilitate contact with them, meeting their needs using resources from within the groups themselves. The process of service organisation and the liaison network developed will have to vary to fit the ethnic composition and multicultural characteristics of each community. A cross-cultural study looked at parents' perceptions of services available to help them deal with their children's behavioural problems. Asian and African mothers were most likely to approach schools first for help. Asian parents were least likely to approach specialist child mental health services, even when they thought that their child had a problem (Nikapota *et al*, 2000).

Preventive action must be relevant for particular ethnic minority groups. Parent education on children's needs, for example, must present concepts of successful parenting that can be incorporated into different cultures, rather than imposing the single style of the majority culture.

Cohen *et al* (1992) comment that the development of treatment modalities has not been accompanied by service structures that reach disadvantaged young people and their families. Ethnic minority cultures may be high-risk, high-need groups if their minority status is combined with a limited knowledge of English, socio-economic disadvantage and social isolation. There is anecdotal evidence that self-help groups to assist children and adolescents to function better in school have been most successful among cultural minorities, where a degree of group solidarity has developed.

There is a particular need for contact points for adolescents in difficulty or crisis. Many young people from ethnic minority groups will not approach helping agencies if they believe that their race or ethnicity will place them at a disadvantage. There is a considerable body of data on the prevalence of psychiatric disorder in various ethnic and cultural groups. This reveals different cultural attitudes towards mental illness, as well as higher rates of serious mental illness among certain minority groups. These differences highlight the need for effective liaison between children's services and adult psychiatric services, particularly in areas with high rates of disorder among minority population groups, and for projects such as support groups for parents with mental health problems.

Should community-based specialist child mental health services be clinic/centre based, or outreach to facilitate access by minority groups? The decision to see a child or family within a primary care facility, rather than a specialist child mental health facility, must be determined by clinical need. However, meeting a family for the first time at home or in a primary care facility may help them in their acceptance of the service. This is the case not only for ethnic or cultural minorities, so the principles of good practice form the framework for a culturally sensitive service. For example, contact with families is a useful pre-assessment activity to facilitate engagement (Cox, 1994). Hence, if a clinic has good communication with referrers about each family's acceptance of the referral, it becomes easier to identify those families requiring reassurance and to arrange pre-assessment contact.

Several aspects of service organisation are emphasised for culture-friendly services, for example, they should be accessible and welcoming. However, it is important that making services welcoming cross-culturally does not make indigenous White families feel out of place. We should also ask whether cultural diversity is required among specialist teams. Certainly where services are within multicultural areas, cultural diversity within the team can contribute to the insights shared by the team as a whole. This depends on team members' willingness be open-minded in understanding and appreciating differences in approach, child care style, family values, structures and systems. It is reinforcing a stereotype to assume that a team member who is Asian or African–Caribbean will serve the needs of all ethnic minorities who attend the clinic or that families from minority groups will always prefer a staff member who is also from a minority group. However, it is true that having an obviously mixed staff group does help some families engage.

Working across cultures

The essential requirement for therapists where there is a cultural dissonance between therapist and family is a readiness to see things differently and explore what is unknown. "I don't know enough, I need to know more" is a statement often made by clinicians from White Western backgrounds when talking of cross-cultural work.

This is usually because training in child psychiatry has insufficiently emphasised the fact that careful and thoughtful use of interviewing and assessment techniques are the primary requirement for cross-cultural work.

Children, adolescents and their families are usually the best informants on their own culture. A comprehensive child psychiatric history allows for communication from both the child and the family about attitudes and values. A context that encourages expression of need must be created (Burnham & Harris, 1996; Maitra & Miller, 1996). Open-ended questions can be used to obtain relevant information without the family feeling devalued or misunderstood. It may be that more time for assessment will need to be incorporated in clinical schedules to accommodate this. Vyas (1991) describes a process of information gathering from Asian families that gives the family confidence to express their ideas and concerns. It is also essential to confirm meanings, even with families whose English language is fluent, as there may be a different usage of idiom. Asking for examples of what is meant by a word, phrase or behaviour is a good way of doing this and is a useful practice irrespective of the background or ethnic origin of the family.

Where a family is defensive or reticent it is useful for the therapist to consider whether this may be due to the family members' sensitivity about describing their situation to a therapist from a different background, from fear that they will be misunderstood.

Interpreters may at times be required, and when a clinical service is based in a multicultural area the first language of the family should be determined as part of routine pre-referral data collection. There is consensus that a well-trained independent interpreter is better than a family member or friend, but at times an interpreter brought by the family will help acceptance of therapy. It is important even in these instances to ask for an opportunity to talk to the interpreter, to explain the role required and negotiate an informal contract of work, which can in turn be explained to the family.

Working with an interpreter is never easy: interviews will take significantly longer and there will be occasions when the clinician feels loss of control over them. The question of whether a child from the family can act as interpreter always arises and in principle this is undesirable. However, refusal can sometimes alienate the family and the relative risk of doing so has to be considered. In my experience there have been occasions when having the index adolescent act as interpreter has been useful therapeutically.

> K was 14 years old and was referred for conduct problems at home and school. He was the second in a Somalian family of five children

and had an older, capable brother who had settled well in school. K had very poor reading skills and was of average intelligence. The family had come to the UK as refugees 5 years earlier. The mother's knowledge of the English language was limited. The interpreter assigned to them was not acceptable because of tensions between the tribes of origin of the family and the interpreter. K was chosen as interpreter and the role and responsibility of interpreting truthfully what was said was explained to him. He had admitted to very low self-esteem, and took great pride in his interpreting role.

Information acquisition for a minimum data set is an important aspect of administrative and clinical information gathering. Ethnic monitoring is one component of a minimum data set that is demanded by purchasers of services and is mandatory for in-patient units. Aspinall (1995) gives an excellent summary of the present categories of ethnicity used by the health services. Ethnicity and ethnic identity may derive only in part from racial origin and be associated with culture of origin. However, there is cultural diversity within ethnic groups, and other factors such as site of residence and culture of peer group will contribute to both ethnicity and cultural diversity. There is no reason to suppose that White people are similar from an ethnic or cultural standpoint. Adolescents from second- or third-generation immigrant families need to be able to describe themselves as British, Black British or Asian irrespective of race. In fact, it is clinically significant if they do, especially if their self-declared ethnicity differs from that of their parents. Regardless of how data may later be collated, this information when obtained from children and their families needs to allow for self-declared ethnicity and for encouraging mixed-race children to declare a dual heritage, i.e. their own ethnicity and that of each parent. The inadequacy of current ethnic monitoring categories is highlighted by a study, albeit a small one, by a child psychiatry department in central London. Of children born in the UK, just over half were described by their parents (who were from many parts of the world) as "White British": there is no Black British category within most systems. The authors comment on the need for other cultural variables to be used to gather meaningful data on culture (Hodes *et al*, 1998).

There are no therapeutic approaches that should never be used within particular cultures. However, some therapies, such as behavioural approaches, are more easily used and adapted within different cultures. Family therapy requires sensitivity to avoid pitfalls such as erroneous assumptions about family relationships and the appropriateness of family structures or systems made on the basis of meanings derived from a White indigenous culture, or a therapeutic plan that does not respect the families' views (Lau, 1996). Programmes of parent training, increasingly popular as an approach for oppositional behaviour and conduct problems in younger children, may not be effective or accepted if not sufficiently adapted to parenting styles in different cultures.

When working with families it is useful to address their concerns, obtain an idea of the type of intervention they expect and explain common approaches used in child mental health care. Negotiating an agreed goal ensures that the family is comfortable with it. A Nigerian mother, a nurse, reacted with anxiety and some hostility to the thought that her 14-year-old daughter would be seen alone in some sessions: "surely as I am responsible for her I should be present". Her view was reasonable and cannot be considered over-intrusive within that context. An explanation and discussion to reassure her were all that was required for positive compliance.

There are times when a cultural interpreter may be required. One particular instance will be when making assessments about child residence and contact after parental separation and divorce.

There are two situations that sometimes place clinicians in conflict with local authorities over cultural issues. One is child abuse. Sensitivity to cultural norms should not lead to collusion with adults in situations that are abusive by standards based on the welfare of children irrespective of culture. Punishment that is irrational, excessive or inflicts physical injury is abuse, even in a culture where discipline is authoritarian and punishments are used as aversive conditioning. More difficult are patterns of family care that are claimed to be culture-appropriate.

> Mr S was a well-educated Asian father, suffering from increasingly severe paranoia. On his wife's death he kept his teenage children at home, teaching them himself and allowing no social contact. His argument that he was Buddhist and he was ensuring a culturally appropriate education prevented the local authority from taking any action although there was great concern about his mental health and the welfare of the children.

The second problem area is that of adoption and fostering. Department of Health Social Services Inspectorate (1990) guidelines request that race and culture be taken into account, but local authority policies on same-race placement can deny children the placement that would best meet their needs. Inter-country adoptions can work (Tizard, 1991), and although trans-racial placements require careful consideration they cannot be ruled out, as for many children a *same-race* placement could end up being a *transcultural* one. This is a point made by Tizard & Phoenix (1989), who highlight the need to recognise cultural and ethnic diversity. The most vulnerable in this regard are children who have dual heritage (where one parent is White and the other non-White, i.e. politically Black) or children whose culture and ethnicity place them in the politically Black category but for whom foster parents of their own background are not available. Child mental health clinicians and local authority agencies need to discuss these issues, to find a solution that acknowledges pressures on local authority services but results in a decision-making process in which the well-being of the child as paramount.

Research issues

Before much-needed research can be done on child mental health in ethnic minority populations appropriate research methodologies are required. Research in the UK and abroad has tended to use screening lists, behavioural checklists developed in one culture and validated for use in another. The problems of these methods and their potential bias have been discussed elsewhere (Rutter & Sandberg, 1985; McGuire & Richman, 1986). An initiative to develop a screening instrument for Asian pre-school children is not yet complete.

The processes leading to mental disorders require more study across cultures. Issues that must be considered in cross-cultural research are now better understood and basic principles have been outlined (Verhulst & Achenbach, 1995; Bird, 1996). Areas still to be researched include: patterns of family functioning; coping styles; culturally relevant risk assessment; strengths within cultures in relation to protective factors or resilience; the relationship between childhood coping, perceptions of identity and self-competence; cross-cultural evaluation of therapeutic techniques; and identification of cross-culturally sensitive outcome indicators.

Conclusion

While some significant family, school and social factors that influence childhood behaviour patterns are similar across cultures, the context and meaning of others vary according to culture. The technology needed to develop culture-appropriate child mental health services is available, but it must be used in a way that is culture-aware. Of particular importance among the service development and training issues still to be addressed is the need for a shift of viewpoint that acknowledges the role of culture and culture bias in the present knowledge base.

References

ARROYO, C. G. & ZIGLER, E. (1995) Racial identity, academic achievement, and the psychological well-being of economically disadvantaged adolescents. *Journal of Personality and Social Psychology*, **69**, 903–914.

ASPINALL, P. (1995) Department of Health's requirement for mandatory collection of data on ethnic groups of inpatients. *British Medical Journal*, **311**, 1006–1009.

BIRD, H. R. (1996) Epidemiology of childhood disorders in a cross-cultural context. *Journal of Child Psychology and Psychiatry*, **37**, 35–50.

BOLGER, K. E., PATTERSON, C. J. & THOMPSON, W. W. (1995) Psychosocial adjustment among children experiencing persistent and intermittent family economic hardship. *Child Development*, **66**, 1107–1129.

BRYANT-WAUGH, R. & LASK, B. (1991) Anorexia nervosa in a group of Asian children living in Britain. *British Journal of Psychiatry*, **158**, 229–233.

—— & —— (1995) Eating disorders in children. *Journal of Child Psychology and Psychiatry*, **36**, 191–202.

BURNHAM, J. & HARRIS, Q. (1996) Emerging ethnicity. In *Meeting the Needs of Ethnic Minority Children* (eds K. N. Dwivedi & V. P. Varma). London: Jessica Kingsley.

CAMPBELL, S. B. (1995) Behaviour problems in pre-school children: a review of more recent research. *Journal of Child Psychology and Psychiatry*, **36**, 113–150.

COCHRANE, R. (1979) Psychological and behavioural disturbance in West Indians, Indians and Pakistanis in Britain. A comparison of rates among children and adults. *British Journal of Psychiatry*, **134**, 201–210.

COHEN, R., SINGH, N., NIRBHAY, N., *et al* (1992) Implementing a responsive system of mental health services for children. *Clinical Psychology Review*, **1**, 819–828.

CONGER, R. D., CONGER, K. J., ELDER, G. H., *et al* (1992) A family process model of economic hardship and adjustment of early adolescent boys. *Child Development*, **63**, 526–541.

COX, A. D. (1988) Maternal depression and impact on children's development. *Archives of Disease in Childhood*, **53**, 90–95.

—— (1994) Interviews with parents. In *Child and Adolescent Psychiatry: Modern Approaches* (eds M. Rutter, E. Taylor & L. Hersov), 3rd edition, pp. 34–50. Oxford: Blackwell Scientific.

DEPARTMENT OF HEALTH (1995) *Handbook on Child Mental Health*. London: DoE.

DEPARTMENT OF HEALTH SOCIAL SERVICES INSPECTORATE (1990) *Issues of race and culture in the family placement of child*. Circular 1. London: DoH.

FARRELL, M. & STRANG, J. (1991) Substance use and misuse in childhood and adolescence. *Journal of Child Psychology and Psychiatry*, **32**, 109–128.

GARCIA-COLL, C. T. (1990) Developmental outcome of minority infants: a process-oriented look into our beginnings. *Child Development*, **61**, 270–289.

GARMEZY, N. & MASTEN, A. (1994) Chronic adversity. In *Child and Adolescent Psychiatry: Modern Approaches* (eds M. Rutter, E. Taylor & L. Hersov), 3rd edition, pp. 191–206. Oxford: Blackwell Scientific.

GERRALDA, M. E. (1992) A selective review of child psychiatric syndromes with a somatic presentation. *British Journal of Psychiatry*, **161**, 759–773.

GODDARD, N., SUBOTSKY, F. & FOMBONNE, E. (1996) Ethnicity and adolescent deliberate self-harm. *Journal of Adolescence*, **19**, 513–521.

GOODMAN, R. & RICHARDS, H. (1995) Child and adolescent psychiatric presentations of second generation Afro-Caribbeans in Britain. *British Journal of Psychiatry*, **167**, 362–369.

GOODYER, I. M. (1990) Family relationships, life events and childhood psychopathology. *Journal of Child Psychology*, **31**,161–192.

GRAHAM, P. J. & MEADOWES, C. E. (1967) Psychiatric disorder in the children of West Indian immigrants. *Journal of Child Psychology and Psychiatry*, **8**, 105–116.

HACKETT, L. & HACKETT, R. (1993) Parental ideas of normal and deviant child behaviour: a comparison of two ethnic groups. *British Journal of Psychiatry*, **162**, 353–357.

———, ——— & TAYLOR, D. C. (1991) Psychological disturbance and its associations in the children of the Gujerati community. *Journal of Child Psychology and Psychiatry*, **32**, 851–856.

HEALTH ADVISORY SERVICES (1995) *Child and Adolescent Mental Health Services: Together We Stand – The Commissioning, Role and Management of Child and Adolescent Mental Health Services.* London: DoH.

HILLIER, S. A., LOSHAK, R., RAHMAN, S., *et al* (1994) An evaluation of child psychiatric services for Bangladeshi parents. *Journal of Mental Health*, **3**, 327–337.

HODES, M., JONES, C. & DAVIES, H. (1996) Cross-cultural differences in maternal evaluation of children's body shapes. *International Journal of Eating Disorders*, **19**, 257–263.

———, CREAMER, J. & WOOLLERY, J. (1998) Cultural meanings of ethnic categories. *Psychiatric Bulletin*, **22**, 20–24.

JAWED, S. H. (1991) A survey of psychiatrically ill Asian children. *British Journal of Psychiatry*, **158**, 268–269.

LAU, A. (1996) Family therapy and ethnic minorities. In *Meeting the Needs of Ethnic Minority Children* (eds K. N. Dwivedi & V. P. Varma). London: Jessica Kingsley.

McGUIRE, J. & RICHMAN, N. (1986) Screening for behaviour problems in nurseries: the reliability and validity of the Pre-school Behaviour Checklist. *Journal of Child Psychology and Psychiatry and Allied Disciplines*, **27**, 7–32.

MAITRA, B. & MILLER, A. (1996) Children, families and therapists: clinical considerations and ethnic minority cultures . In *Meeting the Needs of Ethnic Minority Children* (eds D. N. Dwivedi & V. P. Varma), pp. 111–129. London: Jesscia Kingsley.

MINDE, K. & NIKAPOTA, A. D. (1993) *Child Psychiatry and the Developing World: Recent Developments.* Transcultural Psychiatric Research Review. London: Sage.

MORTON, J. & BAGLEY, C. (1975) Children of West Indian immigrants: 111 home circumstances and family pattern. London: Sage.

MUKAI, T., CARGO, M. & SHUSSLAK, C. (1994) Eating attitudes and weight pre-occupation among high school students in Japan. *Journal of Child Psychology and Psychiatry*, **35**, 677–688.

MUMFORD, D., WHITEHOUSE, A. & PLATTS, M. (1991) Sociocultural correlates of eating disorders among Asian school girls in Bradford. *British Journal of Psychiatry*, **158**, 222–228.

NEWTH, S. J. & CORBETT, J. (1993) Behaviour and emotional problems in three year old children of Asian parentage. *Journal of Child Psychology and Psychiatry*, **34**, 333–352.

NIKAPOTA, A. D. (1991) Child psychiatry in developing countries: A review. *British Journal of Psychiatry*, **158**, 743–751.

———, Cox, A. D., Sylva, K., *et al* (2000) *Development of Culture Appropriate Child Mental Health Services: Perceptions and Use of Services* . Final Report submitted to the Department of Health. London: Department of Health (in press).

RACK, P. (1982) *Race Culture and Mental Disorder.* London: Tavistock.

RALEIGH, V. S. & BALARAJAN, R. (1992) Suicide and self burning among Indians and West Indians in England and Wales. *British Journal of Psychiatry*, **161**, 365–368.

RICHMAN, N., STEVENSON, J. E. & GRAHAM, P. J. (1975) Prevalence of behaviour problems in 3 year old children: an epidemiological study in a London borough. *Journal of Child Psychology and Psychiatry and Allied Disciplines*, **16**, 222–287.

——, —— & —— (1982) *Pre-School to School: A Behavioural Study.* London: Academic Press.

RUTTER, M. L. (1981) Stress, coping and development: some issues and some questions. *Journal of Child Psychology and Psychiatry.* **22**, 323–356.

—— (1985) Family and school influences on behavioural development. *Journal of Child Psychology and Psychiatry,* **26**, 349–368.

—— (1999) Psychosocial adversity and child psychopathology. *British Journal of Psychiatry,* **174**, 480–493.

—— & SANDBERG, S. (1985) Epidemiology of child psychiatric disorders. Methodological issues and some substantive findings. *Child Psychiatry and Human Development,* **15**, 209–233.

——, YULE, W., BERGER, M., *et al* (1974) Children of West Indian immigrants: 1. Rates of behaviour deviance and psychiatric disorders. *Journal of Child Psychology and Psychiatry,* **15**, 241–262.

SARTORIUS, N. & GRAHAM, P. (1984) Child mental health: experience of eight countries. *WHO Chronicle,* **38**, 208–211.

SONUGA-BARKE, E. J. S., MINOCHA, K., TAYLOR, E., *et al* (1993) Inter-ethnic bias in teachers' ratings of childhood hyperactivity. *British Journal of Developmental Psychology,* **11**, 187–200.

STERN, G., COTTRELL, D. & HOLMES, J. (1990) Patterns of attendance of child psychiatry out-patients with special reference to Asian families. *British Journal of Psychiatry,* **156**, 384–387.

STOPES-ROE, M. & COCHRANE, R. (1990) The child-rearing values of Asian and British parents and young people: an inter-ethnic and inter-generational comparison in the evaluation of Kohn's 13 qualities. *British Journal of Social Psychology,* **29**, 149–160.

SUBOTSKY, F. & BERELOWITZ, G. (1990) Consumer views at a community child guidance clinic. *ACPP Newsletter,* **12**, 8–12.

SYLVA, K. (1994) School influences on children's development. *Journal of Child Psychology and Psychiatry,* **35**, 135–170.

TIZARD B. (1991) Inter-country adoption: a review of the evidence. *Journal of Child Psychology and Psychiatry,* **32**, 743–756.

—— & PHOENIX, A. (1989) Black identity and transracial adoption. *New Community,* **15**, 427–437.

VERHULST, F. C. & ACHENBACH, T. M. (1995) Empirically based assessment and taxonomy of psychopathology: cross cultural applications. *European Child and Adolescent Psychiatry,* **4**, 61–76.

VYAS, I. (1991) Emotional problems in Asian children – a practical approach. *ACPP Newsletter,* **13**, 10–14.

WEISZ, J. R., SIGMAN, M., WEISS, B., *et al* (1993) Parent reports of behavioural and emotional problems among children in Kenya, Thailand, and the United States. *Child Development,* **64**, 98–109.

WORLD HEALTH ORGANIZATION (1977) *Child Mental Health and Psychosocial Development.* Technical Report Series 613. Geneva: WHO.

11 Learning disabilities in multicultural Britain

ZENOBIA NADIRSHAW

Editors' introduction

As with child and adolescent psychiatry, psychiatry of learning disability in Black and other ethnic minority groups has multiple complex factors at play. Not only that, biological and neuropsychiatric factors play a role, and cultural factors in diagnosing and accepting the diagnosis are equally important. In some cultures individuals with learning disability are seen to have special powers and are worshipped, whereas in others they are marginalised. The perceptions of normalisation/social role valorisation philosophy that now influences many of the services for people with learning disabilities should benefit all those who use the service. Nadirshaw argues that in spite of the idea that the learning disabled should aspire to be 'normal', people also make the assumptions that the values and mores of white majority society are equally appropriate to all people irrespective of their ethnic and cultural backgrounds. It is argued that an extra dimension – the achievement of a satisfactory racial identity – needs to be added to the dominant models of service development.

Learning disability is a lifelong impairment of the mind caused by incomplete development of or damage to the brain and nervous system resulting in learning and performance limitations, behavioural problems and social disadvantages. Learning disability is not a specific disease, but a behavioural syndrome reflecting the level of a person's functioning. People with learning disabilities are not a homogeneous group, but represent a wide spectrum of abilities, clinical presentations and behaviour, and require a multi-disciplinary and multi-agency approach for help and assistance to live in the community (Macadam & Rodgers, 1997).

211

There is no accepted definition of the term 'learning disabilities' (previous known as 'mental handicap'). The Department of Health & Home Office Working Group (Deaprtment of Health, 1992) on services for people with special needs officially defined it as "a state of arrested or incomplete development of mind, which includes significant disabilities of intelligence and social functioning".

It is likely that the term is confused with other terms and used interchangeably by many health professionals. It is, therefore, important to present a glossary of terms to clarify the confusion that might exist.

Mental deficiency

This term was introduced in the early 1900s and was legalised in the Mental Deficiency Acts 1913–1927. It defines a condition of "arrested or incomplete development of mind, whether arising from inherent causes or induced by disease or injury". This term was replaced by the words 'mental subnormality' in 1959.

Mental subnormality

This term was introduced in the Mental Health Act 1959 and was synonymous with the terms 'mental retardation' and 'mental handicap', though not with mental impairment as defined in the Mental Health Act 1983.

Mental handicap

This term was introduced by relatives and professionals as an alternative term to 'mental subnormality' and it described people who have significant impairment of intellectual skills.

Mental impairment

This term is defined in the Mental Health Act 1983 as "a state of arrested or incomplete development of mind (not amounting to severe impairment) which includes significant impairment of intelligence and social functioning and is associated with abnormally aggressive or seriously irresponsible conduct on part of the person concerned".

Mental retardation

The ICD–10 (World Health Organization (WHO), 1992) defines this as "a condition of arrested or incomplete development of the mind which is especially characterised by impairment of skills manifested during the development period, which contributes to the overall level of intelligence, i.e. cognitive, language, motor and social abilities".

Intellectual impairment

A term often preferred by medical scientists to distinguish biological faults in tissues or organs from the disabilities and handicaps that these create for individuals. In general while impairment describes any loss or abnormality of psychological, physiological and anatomical structure or function, disability describes limitations of personal activity or ability, while handicap refers to person and social disadvantages resulting from impairment or disability.

Learning difficulty

A term used by certain public agencies in the context of special education, as distinct from the health needs of people with intellectual impairments. This term is preferred by some due to the de-emphasis on disability which is thought to arise as much from environmental as birth factors.

Learning disability

This term was introduced by the Department of Health in 1991 to replace the term 'mental handicap'. It is described as "a change of emphasis in the philosophy of care and in the values which inform our thinking". This term emphasises learning potential and equality of citizenship and "a commitment to thinking of people with learning disabilities as individuals in their own right".

Classification and incidence of learning disabilities

The classification of impairments, disabilities and handicaps developed by World Health Organization (1980) provides a good model for considering the needs of people with learning disabilities.

By this classification, general characteristics of individuals with leanring disabilities include an IQ below 50 (as scored on standardised tests of intelligence), clear signs of significant disabilities in the acquisition of adaptive behaviours from early in age and the need for considerably more support than their other peers to participate successfully in everyday activities, evidence of damage to the central nervous system and additional physical or sensory handicaps (Emerson, 1995). There is no precise information available nationally about the number of people with learning disabilities or the degree of those disabilities. Similarly, no precise information is available nationally about the number of Black and other ethnic minority people with learning disabilities and their degrees of disability. Through the introduction of databases and registers, the estimated prevalence of learning disabilities can be made for individual districts, based on the number of people with learning disabilities known to agencies. In an average district of 250 000 people, 5000 will have a learning disability, and of those 750–1000 will have a severe or profound learning disability.

However, current estimates suggest that there are probably 150 000 adults in the UK with a learning disability sufficiently severe for them to need significant help with the tasks of ordinary life. In addition, there are probably about 30 000 children under the age of 16 years with severe or profound learning disabilities. Other adjectives such as mild or moderate are also given to this condition, based on the severity of the disability. It is estimated that moderate learning disabilities may have 10 times the prevalence rate of severe learning disabilities. The boundaries between these 'levels' are imprecise and cannot always be relied upon for accurate assessments of ability or special needs (see Assessment of Learning Disability). In general, people with mild learning disabilities do not necessarily have 'special' needs, though they may require remedial education and psychosocial support. Those with more severe disabilities often require long-term support in terms of specialist health, education and social support.

Causes of learning disability

Despite significant recent advances in molecular biology and genetics, medical scientific knowledge about the causes of learning disability remains incomplete. Broadly speaking, two types of causes are responsible for the majority of learning disabilities: those that have a genetic origin and those which arise as a result of external or environmental factors affecting the mother and child during pregnancy, delivery or shortly after birth. Table 11.1 (pp. 216–217) shows, in summary form, the aetiology of learning disability with some examples and estimated incidence (where available).

People with learning disabilities have lifelong needs, requiring a complex interplay of the fulfilment of responsibilities of several statutory agencies on one hand versus society's response to them on the other. They need access to generic health, educational and social care systems, and specialist systems where required – for example, in work with people who present with psychiatric, behavioural and other problems to service providers.

Incidence and prevalence of learning disabilities in Black and other ethnic minority communities

There is no national information on the prevalence of learning disabilities among Black and other ethnic minority communities. However, Emerson & Hatton (1999), in predicting future trends in the ethnic composition of British society and among British citizens with learning disabilities, state that by 2021 one in 10 of all people with a learning disability will belong to a non-White ethnic minority group with a predicted 70% increase in the number of non-White people with a learning disability. Local studies can provide some useful but controversial information at this point in time.

An area of concern has been the higher prevalence of learning disabilities among Black and other ethnic minority families than among their White counterparts. In a study of Asian people with learning disabilities living in two metropolitan boroughs of north-west England, Azmi *et al* (1996*a–c*) found the prevalence of severe learning disabilities in children and adults between 5 and 34 years of age to be approximately three times greater in the Asian community than in the non-Asian community. This picture is consistent with the relatively young age profile of the Asian population as a whole and from information from other areas regarding the age structure of Asian service users. Comparing these figures with the Sheffield case register confirms, at least on a small scale, an increased prevalence of learning disabilities and severe learning disabilities in the Asian Community (Emerson, 1999). Baxter (1998) draws attention to the long-running debate about the cause of the apparently higher prevalence of learning disabilities in some ethnic minority communities. Those factors which have been suggested as specifically relevant are: a higher incidence of congenital rubella syndrome and a higher frequency of first-cousin marriages within some Asian communities. The latter is a particularly emotive and controversial issue. First-cousin marriages may increase the risk of autosomal recessive conditions, but many of

Table 11.1. Aetiology of learning disability (from Sperlinger, 1997)

Prenatal causes	Some examples	Estimated incidence
Genetic disorders		
Chromosomal disorders		
Autosomal	Down's syndrome (Trisomy 21)	1:660–700 live births
Autosomal + microdeletions	Prader–Willi syndrome (Ch 15)	5–10:10 000
Gender-linked	Klinefelter syndrome (47XXXY)	2:1000 live male births
	Turner's syndrome (XO)	1:4000 live female births
Single gene disorder (dominant)	Neurofibromatosis	1:3000
	Tuberous sclerosis	1:30 000 (60% have a learning disability)
Single gene disorder (recessive)	Inborn errors of metabolism, e.g. phenylketonuria	1:14 000 newborns
X-linked	Lesch–Nyhan syndrowm (hyperuricaemia), Fragile X syndrome (Xq27) (most common inherited cause of learning disability)	1:1500 male births
		1:2500 female births
Multi-factorial	Neural tube defects	1:500 births
Infections	Cytomegalovirus	0.4–2.2% all live births
	Toxoplasmosis	480 births per year in UK
	Rubella virus	Fewer since introduction of MMR vaccine
Physical/nutritional	Syphilis	Not available
	Irradiation, drugs, severe malnutrition, smoking, injury	Not available
Maternal factors involving abnormalities in pregnancy	Hypothyroidism	Not available
	Placental insufficiency, diabetes, toxaemia	
	Foetal alcohol syndrome	20–50% risk in alcohol dependent mothers
Other	Cerebral palsy	1:500 live births

Causes at birth (perinatal)	Some examples	Estimated incidence
Early delivery or problems during delivery	Prematurity	5–10% of all births
	Birth injury, asphyxia, anoxia	Not available
	Infection at birth	Not available
	Intra-uterine growth retardation	Not available
Immediate postnatal disorders	Hypoxia	Not available
	Intraventricular haemorrhage	Not available
	Rhesus incompatibility	Not available

Following birth (postnatal, infancy, childhood and adolescence)	Some examples	Estimated incidence
Severe physical injury	Abuse (non-accidental injury)	Not available
	Accidents	Not available
	Neurotoxins (e.g. lead)	Not available
	Post status epilepticus	Not available
Infections	Meningitis, encephalitis	Not available
	Severe gastroenteritis (e.g. typhoid), brain abscess	Not available
Progressive neurological disease	Sturge–Weber syndrome	Not available
Deprivation	Maternal, sensory, cultural, environmental	Not available

these conditions are rare so that 50% consanguinity would be required before a significant number would appear in the population. Furthermore, studies which have explored association between consanguinity and incidence of congenital malformations, have failed to find an established significantly high correlation (Rao & lnbaraj, 1980; Terry *et al*, 1985; Rosenthal *et al*, 1988; Pearson, 1991). Other factors need to be explored to avoid the approach which blames the victim and to explain the relatively higher than expected proportion of ethnic children and young adults with learning disabilities. Poverty, diet, effects of poor housing and environmental pollution, lack of knowledge about and unfamiliarity with the methods of genetic counselling, antenatal services, poorer maternal health care, mis-classification as a result of the confounding effects of language and bilingualism, higher incidences of non-genetic factors such as intrauterine infection, and secondary perinatal complications may be other factors which may contribute to this on-going debate. Need and demand for services for adults with learning disabilities will sharply increase as the population of Asian adults is expected to more than double over the next 10 years. No such figures exist nationally for African–Caribbean communities in Britain, although a Department of Health project refers impressionistically to high levels of autism in African–Caribbean children with learning disabilities (CVS Consultants and Asian People's Disability Alliance, 1998). A number of field studies in this project describe a process whereby awareness of autism within the general population as a whole has increased and a significant number of people from African–Caribbean backgrounds have been coming forward for help, advice, guidance and support for their autistic children.

Learning disabilities and challenging behaviour

The label 'challenging behaviour' within learning disabilities has come to provoke anxiety, guilt and stress to paid and unpaid carers within the statutory, independent and private sectors. Clements (1997) states that behaviour can be problematical in the mind and heart of the beholder. A person's behaviour will be defined as challenging and problematical when it is judged by another to be socially unacceptable and evokes significant negative emotional responses (e.g. fear, anger, despair, embarrassment). There is a strong subjective element in its identification, and this label does not sit comfortably within a clinical diagnostic framework. However, there are certain behaviours which are commonly identified as challenging: physical and verbal aggression, sexually abusive behaviours, self-injury, property damage and stealing. The following criteria are used to classify theses behaviours as challenging or problematical:

(a) unacceptability relating to social standards and to the person's age, class and cultural background;
(b) imposing a significant cost on the person (i.e. physical damage, social rejection, limiting opportunities for learning);
(c) imposing a significant cost to others.

It should be emphasised that such behaviours represent a challenge to the services and that the definition is based on social judgements, that is, what challenges one service may not challenge another.

Challenging behaviour is both relatively common and relatively persistent among people with learning disabilities. Kiernan & Qureshi (1993) have suggested that at any one time between 15 and 20% of those in contact with services for people with learning disabilities will present significant, active challenges to those who live and work with them – with most engaging in more than one type of behaviour. Depending on the different behaviours considered and definitions used, in one area with a population of 220 000 between 31 and 56 people could be expected to present significant challenging behaviours. The challenging behaviours appear to be more common among people with certain characteristics, including severe disabilities, additional sensory impairments and deficits in social and expressive language.

Over recent years, there has been a proliferation of approaches and models aimed at reducing the incidence of challenging behaviour. Primitive and harsh forms of individual treatment (e.g., unnecessary/excessive medication, physical or mechanical restraints, social deprivation, neglect and abuse) have fortunately given way to ones which are more 'benign' in nature (Donnellan *et al*, 1988; Durand, 1990; Scott *et al*, 1991; Zarkowska & Clements, 1994; Clements, 1997; Emerson, 1999). The development of community-based support teams for people with learning disabilities and challenging behaviours, with a running cost in excess of £10 million, serve the majority of these service users – but only with some degree of success. Detailed analysis suggests that the majority of cases seen by teams are 'successfully' closed due to factors such as: acceptance of the team's recommendations; referral of the person to another service; or completion of assessment rather than reduction in challenging behaviour. Frameworks for understanding challenging behaviour have become more sophisticated over time, with important implications for assessment and intervention practice. People whose needs are complex and challenging will need service response to match – it must be right to resource people according to their level of need and to serve need before wants. Relevant skills from health, local authority and private and voluntary agencies are essential so as to develop a sound knowledge base of the resulting individual care packages for this group of people.

Black and other ethnic minority people with learning disabilities are additionally vulnerable in this area (Baxter *et al*, 1990). Stereotyped views and perceptions make it possible that they stand a higher risk of being diagnosed as having challenging behaviour and/or other forms of mental illness. Black people are still often thought to be violent and aggressive and are perceived with a great deal of suspicion. Service providers must take into account the prevalence of racial stereotypes, long-held prejudices and labelling process which lead providers and professionals to treat them from a pathological perspective, rather than with a systematic and constructive approach. The effects of the labelling process should be considered in terms of the consequences for people diagnosed as having challenging behaviour. It cannot be over-emphasised that services must act responsibility, humanely and in an acceptable way in meeting the needs of Black and other ethnic minority people with learning disabilities in this group, rather than locating the problem within the individual and his or her family's cultural and religious context. This has usually led to exclusion or other undesirable sanctions (e.g. locked wards). Supporting the Black and other ethnic minority carers in looking after their son or daughter with challenging behaviours is a key factor in the overall intervention strategy. In Azmi *et al*'s (1996*a–c*) study 53% of the sample surveyed had challenging or 'problem' behaviours (physical aggression to others or self-injury). The lack of either formal or informal support had overstretched the resources of many mothers, who reported substantial stress-related health problems, and these levels of stress put them at increased risk of developing mental health problems.

Dual diagnosis

Far-reaching changes have occurred in psychiatric provision for people with learning disabilities. Psychiatric services for people with learning disabilities in the new millennium look very different to the institution-based services of the 1970s. These changes have not occurred smoothly. Many questioned whether psychiatry had any relevance to the needs of people with learning disabilities and whether learning disabilities should remain as a separate entity from mental illness. Many professionals believed that people with learning disabilities were incapable of developing emotional disorders that could be characterised as mental illness. Behaviour problems were often attributed to the impaired development that characterised learning disability and behaviours which challenged services (Holland & Murphy, 1990). The last decade has witnessed increasing attention in research and in service provision for people with dual diagnosis indicating a co-existence of learning disability and mental health disorder. An in-depth review of the service needs for this group carried out by a study team of the Department of Health in 1989 underpinned a major policy statement by the Minister of Health in 1991 (Dorrell, 1991). Such is the level of interest that policy-makers and clinicians in the field of psychology and psychiatry have become particularly concerned with meeting this group's mental health needs. Training of psychologists as well as psychiatrists (Day & Jancar, 1991) in the area of learning disabilities is now established and treatment is no longer limited to psychopharmacy. Psychiatrists are now redefining their role to enable them to develop more specific diagnostic and therapeutic skills.

Bouras (1994) provides a comprehensive overview of contemporary developments in psychiatric assessment, diagnosis and treatment and new patterns of service delivery. A short section on 'special issues' highlights recent research. A reading list on dual diagnosis based on the DSM–III–R classification is also available (Sturmey & Levin, 1993). A teaching/training pack on mental health and learning disabilities is also available for carers and service providers (Bouras & Holt, 1997). Studies reporting prevalence rates give figures ranging from 8 to 15% and these rise to over 50% when emotional disorders are included. Prevalence rates of mental illness in people with learning disability vary from 14.3 to 67.3% according to the definition of the population under consideration and the criteria used for determining the presence of a psychiatric disorder. There are concerns, however, in terms of methodology used in the interpretation and generalisation of the data from epidemiological studies. Reasons for the variation in reported prevalence are to due to: methodological differences between studies, including differences in characteristics of the sample; the types of psychiatric disorders measured; and both the diagnostic criteria and the assessment methods used for determining the presence of a psychiatric disorder. Evidentially, these inconsistencies substantially limit comparisons between studies and pose difficulties in interpreting overall prevalence.

People with learning disabilities experience the full range of psychiatric disorders found in the non-disabled population and are probably at increased risk of developing mental health problems (Borthwick-Duffy, 1990, 1994). Fraser & Nolan (1994) report that the prevalence of schizophrenia in the former is at least three times that in the latter. People with learning disabilities also have higher levels of autism. The age of onset is earlier in the population with learning disabilities but the reasons for this are unclear. The precise impact of these disorders in this population is also not clear. Other frequently reported mental health problems include other psychotic states, emotional disorders, anxiety states, sleep disorder, dementia, suicidal and self-injurious behaviour, and inappropriate sexual behaviours.

Attempts to distinguish 'challenging' behaviour or behaviour disorders from the so-called emotional disorders or mental illness have been made. In some cases, challenging behaviour may reflect a deficiency in an individual's skill development without underlying psychopathology, but in others the same behavioural difficulties and stunted social development may be symptoms of underlying mental health disorder. There is a tendency to assume that inappropriate or challenging behaviour is a manifestation of learning disability rather than an indication of an accompanying mental health disorder or an extreme manifestations of anger and distress as part of an emotional response. The phenomenon of diagnostic overshadowing which refers to instances in which the presence of learning disability decreases the diagnostic significance of an accompanying behaviour problem clouds this issue further (Reiss, 1994*a,b*).

In addition to the effects of brain damage, epilepsy, motor abnormalities and sensory impairments, other explanations for the increased prevalence might include: communication difficulties; repeated loss; low intelligence leading to poor coping mechanisms and vulnerability to exploitation; failure to acquire social, inter-personal and recreational skills, which predisposes a person to mental ill health; low self-esteem from repeated failures, unattractive appearance and rejection from family or significant others; social isolation; adverse life events; labelling; and adverse environmental factors. The most widely used measures for detecting mental illness in people with learning disabilities are the Reiss Screen for Maladaptive Behaviour (Reiss, 1987) and the Psychopathology Instrument for Mentally Retarded Adults (Kazdin *et al*, 1983). The Psychiatric Assessment Schedule for Adults with Development Disabilities PAS–ADD (Moss *et al* 1998; Prosser *et al*, 1998) is gaining popularity. Difficulties in diagnosis include: the traditional reliance on self-reported symptoms; the need for reliable reports from informants; the need to rely on direct observation, disentangling those features which may be part of the person's learning disability from those which are not; and the need to consider symptoms within a developmental and environmental context. Recent research on offenders with learning disabilities (Hayes, 1996) shows that they are typically over-represented in Western criminal justice systems. Research also shows that when questioned in detail about the mental health status of people with learning disabilities, carers were able to give very good symptom information (Patel *et al*, 1993). This suggests that carers have a key role to play in identifying mental health problems.

For a comprehensive review of the different mental health problems and their management and treatment, the reader is referred to Bouras (1999). Historically, Black and ethnic minority people with mental health problems have had a very poor deal with the mental health caring system (Fernando, 1995, 1998). For example, differential treatment received by certain minority groups, such as African–Caribbean men, is often explained by mental health professionals as attributable to the greater 'dangerousness' of this group of users. This perception is not borne out by any body of empirical evidence, but does result in oppressive treatment regimes. Dutt & Ferns (1998) report in a study that over 75% of the professionals from all agencies interviewed concurred that Black service users were more likely to be perceived as dangerous. In hospital, Black people are more likely to 'require' physical restraint prior to or on admission, are more likely to have had medication used as a sedative, are likely to be treated with greater precautions by approved social workers and are more likely to preciptiate a call to the police for help. Psychiatry and Western cultures have consistently portrayed Black people as dangerous and those around them as 'at risk'. Given the context of notions of risk and dangerousness, Fernando (1998) presents a useful model of how the association between racialised assumptions and diagnosis emerges. Myths become confused with (scientific) facts, and categories with stereotypes in the construction of psychosis and in perpetuating the association with 'dangerousness'. Fernando states that as a result of Black people being seen as "disturbed", "alien" and "undesirable" they become alienated, feel unwanted and feel angry. This is then followed by a scientific diagnosis of their behaviour as a formal diagnosis of 'bizarre, psychotic and aggressive' behaviour (Fernando, 1998). Racialised assumptions inform practice, for those identified as 'fitting particular cultural stereotypes'.

Although there is no formal research evidence, Black and ethnic minority people with learning disabilities could also be 'treated' in a similar manner, being especially vulnerable to being diagnosed as 'bad', 'mad' or irrational within particular sub-classifications of mental illness. 'Treatment' could consist largely of sedation and restraint without any research undertaken into the efficacy and potency of the medication and the increased risks of side-effects, the lack of understanding about consent issues, the use of appropriate drugs based on sound pharmacological principles and the ability to acquiesce during police interviews. There are now an increasing number of anecdotal reports and single case studies that suggest the possible success of psychological treatment for emotional difficulties such as depression, anxiety and anger in people with mild and moderate learning disabilities (Matson, 1982; Black *et al*, 1997; Lindsay *et al*, 1997). However, the authors remain cautious in their conclusions due to the lack of systematically conducted controlled outcome studies. The use of the Mental Health Act 1983 and its various sections applicable to Black and other ethnic minority people with learning disabilities needs to be carefully monitored, as does the psychiatrist's role and responsibilities in this area.

Community care framework

The publication of the 1971 White Paper *Between Services for the Mentally Handicapped* (Department of Health and Social Security, 1971) saw a widespread move away from hospital-based care towards community services and residential facilities. This move was furthered by the human rights movement of the 1960s, the work of Goffman (1961) on asylums and stigma, several scandals and public inquiries into hospitals, and the principles of 'normalisation' (Wolfensberger, 1972) and 'an ordinary life' for this service user group. The NHS and Community Care Act 1990 heralded a new way delivering services in the community. Local authorities were given lead responsibility to develop services in the community and to provide community-based alternatives to hospital care. The 1990 Act and its subsequent guidance to purchasers offered a commitment to the needs and rights of those people who needed support in the community by emphasising the importance of assessment of need at both a population and individual level and in the purchasing of services which were cost-effective.

Community-based alternatives to hospital care have gone through several changes in emphasis. There was an implicit assumption that living in the community would guarantee a high quality of life and to date research indicates that people with learning disabilities (including those with more severe learning disabilities) can be supported in the community in a way that improves their quality of life significantly. However, outcome measures also show that, in many domains (e.g. choice, income, employment, friendships), the quality of life of people in all residential settings is impoverished when compared with the general population (Emerson & Hatton, 1994; Mental Health Foundation, 1996). The role of key players in health and social care agencies in providing services in a way to support, facilitate and enable the lives of people with learning disability is particularly highlighted in the latest NHS Executive document *Signposts for Success* (Lyndsey, 1998). This document sets out the core features and components of good quality health services for people with learning disabilities – particularly as epidemiological data suggest that the increased life expectancy of these groups, ageing family carers, and increased survival rates of children with severe and complex physical disabilities are likely to combine to increase demand for service provision in the next two decades. However, it is unfortunate that yet another opportunity has been missed in addressing a similar picture for the Black and other ethnic minority population with learning disabilities (Emerson, 1999).

Azmi *et al*'s study (1996*a–c*) shows the overall extent of need for services for Asian adults with learning disabilities is also increasing, with a significant amount of 'hidden' need among these communities. Their studies also reveal that services appeared to target wealthier families rather than those in greatest need.

Philosophy and principles underlying service planning

The role played by social values and cultural ideologies in shaping the form of services for people with learning disabilities has received extensive attention over the past two decades. A value base nowadays underpins the very existence of welfare services and exerts a pervasive and powerful influence upon everyday practice with people with learning disabilities. The concepts and ideas of Normalisation (Wolfensberger, 1972, 1980; Perrin & Nijre, 1985), Social Role Valorisation (Wolfensberger, 1983) and service accomplishments (O'Brien, 1987) have had a profound impact upon the way services are organised, delivered and managed and in the development of the advocacy movement with Britain.

The underlying principles of Normalisation and Social Role Valorisation (Wolfensberger, 1983) and the five O'Brien Service Accomplishments (O'Brien, 1987) are intended to guide managers, staff and others in their interactions with people with learning disabilities and in the planning and delivery of care services. They are based on the belief that people with learning disabilities (like other vulnerable people) should have the same rights as others, should be socially accepted and valued as are other, non-handicapped people and should have the same rights of choice, dignity and respect, development of personal competencies, community participation and integration as other citizens living in mainstream society.

Community care issues for Black and other ethnic minority people with learning disabilities

The introduction of assessment and care management contained within government legislation, the structured process used to identify peoples' needs, the introduction and development of care planning and service provision, and separating the needs and views of individuals and their carers can all be helpful to people with learning disabilities. 'Autonomy', 'empowerment' and 'choice' are key seductive words. However, the system has a long way to go before the individual with learning disabilities can exert real control and bring about real changes to their life, particularly when consideration of services for Black and other ethnic minority people is confined to two sentences in the White Paper. It states:

> "minority communities may have different concepts of community care and it is important that service providers are sensitive to these variations. Good community care will take into account the circumstances of minority communities and will be planned in consultation with them"

The White Paper's recognition of the differing needs and circumstances is acknowledged and the community care policies and procedures in themselves are reasonable, but the impact of these policies on the different minority groups for Black people with learning disabilities is negligible (Nadirshaw, 1991, 1997, 1998). Black people and other minority people with learning disabilities and their carers continue to be doubly disadvantaged by the following.

(a) The maintenance of a colour-blind approach and the lack of acknowledgement of the diverse and varied needs of Black and other ethnic minority communities.

(b) The obsession on the part of most authorities in creating uniform procedures to meet the needs of service user groups. In doing this, they may have lost some of the unique features needed to meet individual needs of Black people with learning disabilities in the assessment forms.

(c) The continuation of establishing policies and procedures which reflect mostly White norms and which fail to uncover unprofessional standards in care and service delivery; this results in the maintenance and perpetuation of racist and prejudiced beliefs and attitudes about Black and other ethnic minority people with learning disabilities and their ability levels.

(d) The lack of information produced in different languages about access to services, including the care management process which remains inaccessible to Black people with learning disabilities and their carers. They are completely dependent on professionals completing the assessment and 'talking them through the process'.

(e) Assuming that Black people with learning disabilities even know about the existence of legislation, little information is provided about it and their rights contained within it, how to access these services, what these services can really offer, their rights to satisfactory alternatives, etc. Little or no time is provided for preparation and understanding of the system and procedures (including the appeal process).

(f) Pressure of work on the part of care managers and the care management team to fit Black and other ethnic minority people with learning disabilities into the traditional menu of day and residential services rather than taking time to explore and get to know the Black and ethnic minority person with learning disabilities and his or her unique religious and cultural features. In addition, high workload demands do not allow individual care managers to listen carefully or develop rapport with the Black and ethnic minority people with profound disabilities or those who cannot communicate verbally, or those whose ways of communicating are different to the norm.

(g) The shortfall of and lack of Black advocates or independent care managers, which indicate that the majority of Black and other ethnic minority people with learning disabilities do not appear to have any form of independent support through the assessment and care management process. Apart from carers who may speak limited English and professional workers who are mainly White, there are not enough advocates or 'brokers' to identify whether the appropriate or best care package is being provided or to clarify and determine what specific service and support will be offered and at what frequency and quality, adherence to previous recommendations, etc.

(h) Assessment forms, which are normally thick and bulky and inaccessible to people who are illiterate. They make 'heavy going' for an already vulnerable group of people in society who may define their needs differently from people with learning disabilities coming from the majority culture. Similarly, confusion about terminology and phrases (e.g.

'unmet need' and 'service shortfalls') used interchangeably which confound the problem further for the Black or other ethnic minority people with learning disabilities and their carers. 'Unmet need' in areas such as social stimulation, help with personal care and help to become more mobile is different to 'service shortfalls', which are to do with inappropriate and unacceptable day care, residential care and respite home care services. Black and other ethnic minority people with learning disabilities may be unable to differentiate between these deficits, remaining unclear about eligibility criteria. as a result they may feel under pressure to use existing resources and services, and are grateful for whatever services they have for fear of disturbing the status quo. Unmet need for Black and ethnic minority people with learning disabilities remains unidentified and not fed back into the planning process.

(i) Confusing purchaser and provider roles within the assessment and care management system, between the roles and functions of social workers versus those of other health professionals, community nurses, psychologists and psychiatrists. The division between health and social care, and disputes about finances (that is, who finances what), who takes overall responsibility and other similar issues lead to greater stress and tensions for the Black or other ethnic minority person with learning disabilities and his or her carer. It is important to recognise that these act as additional problems to an already disadvantaged and disempowered group of people in the community.

Normalisation philosophy and its impact on Black and other ethnic minority people with learning disabilities

Potentially, the Normatisation and Social Role Valorisation philosophy should be a tremendous force in service provision and development. However, it encompasses and reflects strong entrenched beliefs about and makes blanket assumptions on what is considered 'normal' or 'valued' in society. According to Ferns (1992), human services operate in an inherently racist society and as a set of principles, Normalisation and Social Role Valoriszation must take into account the fact that White societies are racist in covert ways and not least in their value systems and norms. Despite Britain being a multiracial, multilingual and multicultural society, authority and decision-making power rests mainly in the hands of White people who cater on the whole to the needs, wants and wishes of the White majority, who are considered 'normal' and 'valued'. The needs of Black and other ethnic minority service users do not fit into standard service provision and therefore run the risk of being ignored or devalued. The principles have been implemented and interpreted in many different ways and in fact are sometimes misused, abused or subverted to continue to perpetuate oppressive services. Although the theory purports to revalue people with learning disabilities, it is "rooted in a hostility to a denial of difference" (Mesibov, 1990). Blommaert & Verschueren (1988) note the construction of an idea of the 'threshold of tolerance', which in essence asserts that there is a threshold (limit) beyond which it is not reasonable to expect majority populations to continue with their 'normal' level of tolerance. The valued roles that Wolfensberger expressed do not defend individuals, for example Black and other ethnic minority people with learning disabilities, against being devalued. They are discriminated against regardless of the social roles they hold in society (Elks, 1994).

Black and other ethnic minority people with learning disabilities remain as an oppressed and vulnerable group in society – suffering discrimination and disadvantage in the course of their everyday lives through socially constructed concepts of 'differences' and 'differentness'. The resulting effects of a negative self-concept, feelings of rejection and stigmatisation, confusion about one's sense of group belongingness, its long-term implications for emotional and psychological well-being and the resulting limited life opportunities and experiences are only just beginning to be addressed. The idea inherent within the philosophy of Social Role Valorisation, that people with learning disabilities must aspire to the 'normal', presupposes many judgements, for example that the current values held within mainstream British society are worth aspiring to and that these values are pertinent, appropriate and useful to all individuals. According to the philosophy, people with learning disabilities, so as to decrease further devaluation, must be encouraged to adopt the culture, expectations, attitudes and behaviours of the dominant group in society. They must ascribe to and adopt a value set which might be clearly inappropriate for them. For Black and other ethnic minority people with learning disabilities, it might be even more damaging – particularly when it appears that value is conferred only to people who look, behave and perform within an established norm, thereby relinquishing their 'differentness' (of diet, clothing, appearance, lifestyles, family grouping etc.). The pressure to 'fit' into the dominant cultural norms and value systems with little real choice to stand out and be counted is a reality for a lot of Black people with learning disabilities. To take responsibility for society's irresponsibilities is further oppression and harassment for an already vulnerable group.

Newland (1999) argues for the inclusion of a further accomplishment, that of personal racial identity, to the existing O'Brien framework. With this addition, he believes the needs of Black and other ethnic minority people with learning disabilities would be addressed within policy statements and through the care management and assessment of need procedures. Included within this addition, he also argues for a shift away from a social work-based care management model to the use of more psychological models of Personal Construct Theory (Fransella, 1990; Kelly, 1995) and of Social Psychological Theories of Identity (Hutnik, 1991). Translating this additional accomplishment into good practice is a challenge to service providers and should go beyond the mere encouragement of dressing according to traditional stereotypical patterns or eating traditional foods or being surrounded by ethnic people and artefacts.

Assessment of learning disability

The changes within government legislation, the policy context and philosophies underlying services for people with learning disabilities has had clear implications for the way in which professionals meet their obligations in the areas of assessment of people with learning disabilities. A plethora of assessment tools abound in this area, reflecting an attitudinal change that has occurred since the 1970s. Although learning disability is still regarded as pervasive, in that a wide range of specific functions and competencies will be slow, fail to develop or are impaired, attitude changes have resulted in: moving learning disabilities from global to more specific characteristics of the impairments/conditions; emphasising the shift from within the person to person–environment interactions; and viewing 'mental deficiency' in terms of behavioural competence, which has resulted in a continuum along which classes of assessment can be ranged. Hogg & Raynes (1986) identify four broad classes of approach in assessing people with learning disabilities, namely: (a) norm-referenced tests; (b) assessment of adaptive behaviour; (c) criterion-referenced tests; (d) techniques of behaviour observation. The early enthusiasm, particularly by psychiatrists, for identifying learning disability through the use of norm-referenced psychometric intelligence tests has fortunately eased. Thankfully, the days when results of IQ were used and relied upon as the sole basis upon which to make decisions about the classification and diagnosis are now past. The criteria for diagnosing learning disabilities remains complex and complicated, with the testing of intelligence being filled with misunderstanding, controversy and criticism, particularly in their use with ethnic minority communities.

Nadirshaw (1991) questions the assessment tools that are used in the process of assessing ethnic minority people with disabilities. She believes that intelligence tests are heavily biased in favour of and reflect the values of White, middle-class society and therefore cannot adequately assess intelligence and personality when applied to Black and other ethnic minority groups. Using norm-referenced psychometric tests in cultures other than where the tests were developed requires evidence of reliability, validity and a lack of discriminatory bias. The basic issue lies in determining whether the tests are as valid for ethnic minority groups as for non-minorities and whether the differences when they do exist can be attributed to causes other than hereditary determinations. Assessment should be done *with* the person rather than *to* the person (Emerson, 1999). Identification of other variables within the examiner, the varied ways in which the corresponding cut-off IQ points are used to define categories of functioning, the motivational and emotional state of the person being tested, the examiner's expectations, set stereotyped perceptions (and like or dislike of the service user), and the resulting bias in scoring can be identified as additional factors which can confound the issues further for Black and other ethnic minority people with learning disabilities. In addition, the definition of mental retardation in the new American Association of Mental Retardation (Reiss, 1994*a*) has been criticised on the basis of it being culturally biased (MacMillan, *et al*, 1993). This is a further indictment against labelling individuals who run the risk of being triply disadvantaged in their lives.

The British Psychological Society (1991, 1995) and the American Psychological Association (1985) are very clear that IQ testing and scoring needs to be interpreted within the overall context of other available non-verbal test information alongside sensitive interviewing, observations, understanding of the cultural milieu and the application of the individual professional's clinical judgement and responsibilities in this area of work. Beecham & Childress (1983) remind us of the ethical principles of professional practice in this context via the principles of beneficence and non-maleficence, each professional's need to actively contribute to the service user's welfare and health versus the duty to actively prevent harming the service user. This includes ensuring that any potential harmful consequences of professional action are acknowledged and weighed against their potential beneficial consequences. In my view the major purpose of assessment of learning disability is to identify the service user's strengths and weaknesses in order to decide an appropriate day or residential placement and to design an optimal programme of teaching. Areas besides intellectual functioning, such as development of cognitive processes, achievement and adaptive skills, environmental demands, reactions of others to the service user's difficulties, fear of failure, uncertainty with the testing requirements and interpersonal adjustments should also be addressed (for a more detailed discussion of these issues and their relevance to ethnic minority communities, the reader is referred to Groth-Marnat, 1990).

Steps forward – an agenda for action

In keeping with the government's *Signposts for Success* document (Lyndsey, 1998), the following are some possible solutions or steps forward to meet the community care needs of Black and other ethnic minority people with learning disabilities and their carers. The issue of implementing these steps is critical to all professionals who have a vision in which people with learning disabilities – including those from ethnic communities – have the power, opportunities and support to make decisions and choices about their lives. However, implementing these steps requires radical changes to social policy and to the service delivery map involving the interplay of complex social, political and economic variables. Change is often anathema to those who enjoy status and power. Opposition can go 'underground' from individuals and groups who do not want to disturb the status quo.

Development of the Black voluntary sector

The mainstream voluntary sector, which is based largely on Victorian philanthropy and charitable works, appears to have neglected Black communities. There are:

(a) a failure to publicise services effectively;
(b) inadequate resources;
(c) assumptions made about ethnic minority lifestyle/cultures ('they look after their own', 'no tradition of membership of voluntary organisations');
(d) language difficulties;
(e) problems related to services offered (services geared to Western culture, 'inexperience in race field');
(f) under-representation;
(g) cultural misunderstanding.

Against the background that the White voluntary sector has failed Black communities, it is now imperative to acknowledge and validate the role and strengths of Black and other ethnic minority voluntary organisations in their ability to offer a 'whole'/combined community care service to people with mental and physical disabilities (Ahmed & Webb-Johnson, 1995; CVS Consultants and Asian People's Disability Alliance, 1998). Services should be offered in a flexible manner (help and support being provided at certain times and places, job descriptions being defined in ways best suited to the needs of Black and other ethnic minority people etc.), acknowledging the diverse and differing needs of the multi-ethnic population in Britain. Ongoing financial support, training on purchaser contracts and service specification, consultation and active participation with health agencies and local authorities, planning and providing services sensitive to the norms and values of Black and other ethnic minority users and their families, consultation with community members on planning and resourcing issues, providing information to community groups, and validating the employment and experiences of Black and other ethnic minority workers are some of the key features that need to be addressed for the future.

People from Black minorities have different needs from the majority White population. They do not necessarily have special needs. To consider that they do implies that their 'distinctiveness' is identified as a problem. The needs of Black and other ethnic minority people with learning disabilities and their cultures can no longer continue to be identified as a 'problem' or be 'pathologised' (Nadirshaw, 1997). They must no longer be classified as 'special' needs requiring special people to work in specialist segregated settings. Until recently, the Social Services Abstracts printed by the Department of Health and Social Security Libraries included literature on ethnic minorities under the special needs heading. This section also included poverty, homelessness, violence, probation, alcohol and drug dependency! This form of classification may state a social reality, but when placed within the context of an inherently racist society, this kind of thinking can be used to further oppress an already disadvantaged group.

A note of caution on the predicament that may be suffered by the Black voluntary organisations needs to be made. There is the danger on the one hand of being seduced into providing direct-care services without adequate back-up resources versus on the other hand focusing time and energy on lobbying for the substantive changes needed at policy level within mainstream service provision. A system needs to be created that genuinely centres on Black and other ethnic minority people with learning disabilities and/or their carers. Services need to work towards their benefit and to accord them their rightful status and rights as consumers.

Research and policy

New research committed to an antiracist methodology must be undertaken using findings connected to practice. In my experience, recipients of research (mainly carers) express considerable scepticism about the usefulness of research studies, suggesting that research has often been a substitute for action and a way of diverting attention from Black peoples' problems. Research must be seen as a way of achieving change for this group of people in society. A general exploration of the policy, practices and service delivery to Black and other ethnic minority people with learning disabilities within health education and social services settings exists (Baxter *et al*, 1990). Azmi *et al*'s (1996*a*–*c*) study provides a good picture of service utilisation and service barriers as perceived by Asian people with severe learning disabilities living in the Rochdale and Thameside areas of the northern England. There is, however, no detailed exploration at a national level of the experiences of Black and other ethnic minority people with learning disabilities using statutory community health and social care services. Psychiatrists and other health care professionals could be involved in detailed research in the community into the identification of factors relating to severe learning disabilities in ethnic communities. Information is also needed on: informal care among Black and other ethnic minority communities on a nationwide scale, determining the incidence and nature of care-giving, the incidence of learning disabilities within the Black communities, the experience and, organisation of care-giving and the needs of carers in communities with children and adults with learning disabilities; in the needs of Black and other ethnic minority individuals with learning disabilities as identified by themselves and by professionals appropriately trained in the awareness of understanding and knowledge about learning disability issues (stigmatisation, oppression, the labelling process, etc.). These needs could then inform care managers on the appropriate and relevant care packages that are meaningful to the Black and other ethnic minority people with learning disabilities and their carers. Similarly, against the backdrop that current services on the whole remain inappropriate and unacceptable to Black and other ethnic minority people with learning disabilities and their carers, research could be undertaken to look at barriers to access and service use, not only about what is provided but about how it is provided, its impact on the service user, the implications of racism within existing service provision and delivery, the views and attitudes of Black and other ethnic minority parents about learning disabilities (Fatimilehin & Nadirshaw, 1994), the employment and experiences of Black staff working in statutory service organisations, implementation of and evaluating ethnic monitoring, assessing within the local profile the demographic statistics of Black and other ethnic minority people with learning disabilities, and the way in which they access present services, etc. The Black voluntary sector providing services for minorities also needs to be the subject of research, particularly as current government policy promotes future contracting out of community services. Questions such as how these organisations operate, their role and strength in community care, the type, level and character of service provided, their relationship with statutory service provision, and monitoring the effect on Black voluntary organisations are clearly some important research questions for the future.

Working towards race equality and change

Black and other ethnic minority people with learning disabilities and their carers have been ill-served by existing statutory health and social care provision. Traditional care services have ignored the wishes of this group. Many have and many still continue to experience oppression, devaluation and discrimination in their lives. Statutory service providers need to address more fully the mechanisms by which services become achievable, accessible and more appropriate for this group of people. It is incumbent upon them that they be committed to equal-opportunity policies in both service delivery and employment issues by looking at their existing ways of working and the system in which the services operate.

Professionals working in the health and social care section for people with learning disabilities should lobby their respective department to review their present equal-opportunities policies which affect service delivery and employment practices. They need to redefine and re-adopt such policies for which a named senior person in management is directly held responsible. They need to re-evaluate normalisation principles as the guiding ideology in learning disability services for Black and other ethnic minority people. Furthermore, they should develop employment practices which recruit more Black staff, interpreters and advocacy services and to develop ethnic monitoring standards. However, all these steps, although commendable, are only a partial answer to this inequity. There are general limitations to all these approaches used singly or partially. The importance of a strategic approach to achieve real change in services for Black and other ethnic minority people with learning disabilities highlights the fact that the debate on inequality and inequity of services has to be placed within a wider context. Understanding how institutional racism operates in all its guises for this vulnerable, disadvantaged group of people, not perceiving race primarily as a Black person's responsibility, redefining and refocusing normalisation theory to autonomy, empowerment, self-determination, citizenship, racial and cultural identify as basic guiding human values and principles, and the rights of Black and other ethnic minority people with learning disabilities all need to be undertaken if service provision is to have a meaningful impact on Black people's lives (Nadirshaw, 1999). The debate should not simply be about input (recruiting more Black staff, basic ethnic monitoring, interpreting and translating services), but about outputs, that is, changed outcomes for the Black or other ethnic minority individuals with learning disabilities and their carers. (Nadirshaw, 1998).

Needs-led service

As stated before, statutory services need to address the colour-blind approach that manifests itself in offering a uniform service to everyone – including Black and other ethnic minority people, who may describe their needs as different to the mainstream population. To my knowledge there are a few authorities who are keen to improve the services and the quality of services offered to Black and other ethnic minority people with learning disabilities against the reality that their current services do not reflect the concerns and needs of their local Black and other ethnic minority communities. However, lack of knowledge and foresight, fear of the threat of additional financial and other resource implications, and anxiety of being considered racist immobilises them into offering services '*en bloc*' rather than in an individualised manner. It is, therefore, essential that a person-oriented approach which acknowledges and validates the wishes and interests of Black and other ethnic minority people with learning disabilities and their carers as the centre of the whole process is undertaken. Developing individual plans which take full account of the experiences, circumstances and wishes of the Black person with learning disabilities and his or her family within the care management framework is a sound way forward for changing the devaluing and oppressive experiences that many Black service users face within the system. The personal qualities of Black and other ethnic minority persons with learning disabilities, their carers, their community network and other social and support systems, the individuals' strengths and talents, their preferences within their religious, cultural and family context should all be identified. Similarly, emphasis on the impact of significant events that have occurred within an ethnic minority person's life, their impact on the person's self-esteem (the labels and stereotypes that the Black person with learning disabilities has carried around over previous years), the loss of confidence in one's racial and cultural identity due to the lack of people's attention and lack of experience of being listened to, being unsure of one's rights in not being able to stand up to complain, having family and community ties weakened when placed in residential homes far away from familiar environments, and no recourse to objective interpreters and advocates within patient–care management meetings are some of the other factors that need to guide the care planning system. The principles of an individual needs-led service based on a joint collaborative partnership with the Black person with learning disabilities and his or her family, working with Black-led service providers, can lead to more creative care packages that encompass the basic principles of valuing cultural diversity and working positively with 'the difference'. This will increase the influence of Black and other ethnic minority people with learning disabilities on decision-making, including monitoring of the quality of services received. For a more practical focused discussion see Nadirshaw (1997).

Other practical steps

Some practical steps that could be addressed by service planners and providers to meet the needs of this group in society who have no choice other than to work and live in a White environment are:

(a) Diet and food preferences to be catered for in all these settings. Asian parents remain concerned about the lack of halal meat provided to their children in respite care services.

(b) Environment and general decor (for example posters, music, videos, reading material) for day and residential units to reflect the positive images of the different cultural and racial background of the user groups it serves.

(c) Activities to be geared to the needs of the Black and other ethnic minority clientele; for example, single-gender swimming and dancing sessions, preparation of food other than English or European, and use of cooking utensils/equipment which are familiar and relevant to the lifestyles of Black and other ethnic minority service users. In addition, visits to places of worship other than churches, etc. The activities offered must positively reflect and cater for Black and other ethnic minority leisure pursuits, dietary preferences and cultural norms.

(d) An appropriate curriculum design, including courses relating to personal care, washing and dress, care of skin and hair, assertiveness training to deal with racism faced by Black service users with learning disabilities within the units as well as outside these places, support for people whose mother tongue is not English, and confidence building to gain meaningful employment.

(e) Equal opportunity policies and the use and implementation of a proper complaints procedure which is monitored by senior management in health, education and social services authority establishments in terms of racial discrimination, verbal and physical abuse and harassment. A booklet in the form of a code of conduct could be devised which clearly sets out what is acceptable and unacceptable behaviour.

(f) Units/centres to be located in multiracial neighbourhoods with other Black and ethnic minority communities living near by and to access local ethnic facilities and networks of interest, for example, social centres, relevant places of worship.

(g) Recruitment of Black and other ethnic minority staff and advocates so as to reflect the multiracial nature of the population the units serve and to act as appropriate role models in terms of providing skills and knowledge on antiracist practice and having the seriousness to influence decision-making at every level of service provision and management positions.

(h) Care plans which reflect individuality and personal differences, respect and values about people's religious wishes and cultural needs within the assessment procedures, and their translation into relevant languages – including the use of audio and visual material and of the ethnic press if necessary. Trained Black advocates to be employed.

(i) Antiracist training and support to be provided to all staff as part of their mandatory training. It would be incumbent for senior management to take overall responsibility for such an undertaking. This should include the development of an action plan with clear targets and delegated responsibilities for the development of an antiracist strategy.

(j) Communication systems and the use of professional jargon to be avoided. Trained interpreters to be employed to ensure that all staff can communicate with all their service users. This should include monolingual, English staff to be given training on working effectively with interpreters and link workers.

(k) The establishment of joint commissioning processes and practical collaboration between health, education and social services within individual localities. The practice of joint commissioning between health and social services is relatively common, but joint commissioning with educational services is most unfamiliar. Bearing in mind the incidence of severe learning disabilities within Black and other ethnic minority children and young adolescents, joint working and coordination of care and service responses can reduce learning disabilities and minimise their effects in later life.

Conclusion

It is hoped that as community care moves into the 21st century, the arrangements within it create new opportunities to eradicate pockets of inequality and to develop meaningful and relevant services for previously unserved groups of people in the community. One can identify the changes which have to take place to achieve equality and fairness. One can identify problems of finite resources, the constraints and counter-interests, and the problems within one's own organisations and those that can be anticipated within the wider system of which we are all a part. We should be aware that community care legislation is the outcome of a political ideology, rather than the ethos of social equality, and that as the issue of 'race'-related changes is taken on board the social inclusion agenda it will become institutionalised within the health and welfare system. It will inevitably become less and less informed by the experiences of Black and other ethnic minority users which it seeks to redress.

References

AHMED, T. & WEBB-JOHNSON, A. (1995) Voluntary Groups. In *Mental Health in a Multi-Ethnic Society. A Multi-Disciplinary Handbook* (ed. S. Fernando). London: Routledge.

AMERICAN PSYCHOLOGICAL ASSOCIATION (1985) *Standards for Educational and Psychological Tests.* Washington, DC: American Psychological Association.

ANASTASI, A. (1985) *Psychological Testing* (3rd edn). New York: Macmillan.

AZMI, S., EMERSON, E., CAINE, A., et al (1996a) *Improving Services for Asian People with Learning Disabilities and their Families.* London: Hester Adrian Research Centre, University of Manchester & Mental Health Foundation.

——, Hatton, C., Emerson, E., et al (1996b) *Asian Staff in Services for People with Learning Disabilities.* London: Hester Adrian Research Centre, University of Manchester & Mental Health Foundation.

——, ——, CAINE, A., et al (1996c) *Improving Services for Asian People with Learning Disabilities. The Views of Users and Carers.* London: Hester Adrian Research Centre, University of Manchester & Mental Health Foundation (available from the Mental Health Foundation).

BAXTER, C., (1998) Learning Difficulties. In *Assessing Health Needs of People from Minority Ethnic Groups* (eds S. Rawaf & V. Bahl). London: Royal College of Physicians & Department of Health.

——, POONA, K., WAD, L., et al (1990) *Double Discrimination. Issues and Services for People with Learning Difficulties from Black and Ethnic Minority Communities.* London: King's Fund Centre & Commission for Racial Equality.

BEECHAM, T. L. & CHILDRESS, J. F. (1983) *Principles of Biomedical Ethics* (2nd edn). Oxford: Oxford University Press.

BESWICK, J., KEMP, F. & MULLEN, E. (1991) Should psychologists use IQ tests to categorise people with learning disabilities? *BPS/DCP Special Interest Group in Learning Difficulties Newsletter,* March, 4–6.

BLACK, L., CULLEN, C. & NOVACCO, R. W. (1997) Anger assessment for people with mild learning disabilities in secure settings. In *Cognitive Behaviour Therapy for People with Learning Disability* (eds B. Sternfert Kroese, D. Dagnan, & K. Loumidis), London: Routledge.

Bloomaert, J. & Verschueen, J. (1988) *Debating Diversity.* London: Routledge.

BORTHWICK-DUFFY, S. A. (1990) Who are the dually diagnosed? *American Journal of Mental Retardation*, **94**, 586–595.

—— (1994) Epidemiology and prevalence of psychopathology in people with mental retardation. *Journal of Consulting and Clinical Psychology*, **4**, 17–27.

BOURAS, N. (1994*a*) Epidemiology and prevalence of psychopathology in people with mental retardation. *Journal of Consulting & Clinical Psychology*, **462**, 17–27.

—— (ed.) (1994*b*) *Mental Health and Mental Retardation: Recent Advances and Practices.* Cambridge: Cambridge University Press.

—— (1999) *Psychiatric and Behavioural Disorders in Developmental Disabilities and Mental Retardation.* Cambridge: Cambridge University Press.

—— & HOLT, G. (1997) *Mental Health in Learning Disabilities. A Training Pack for Staff Working with People Who Have a Dual Diagnosis* (2nd edn). Brighton: Pavilion Publishing.

BRITISH PSYCHOLOGICAL SOCIETY (1991) *Mental Impairment and Severe Mental Impairment: A Search for Definitions.* Leicester: British Psychological Society Professional Affairs Board.

—— (1995) *The Mental Health Order 1986: Mental Handicap, Severe Mental Handicap and Severe Mental Impairment. Definition and Operational Guidelines.* Leicester: British Psychological Society.

CLARIZIO, H. F. (1982) Intellectual assessment of Hispanic children. *Psychology in Schools*, **19**, 61–77.

CLEMENTS, J. (1997) Challenging needs and problematic behaviour. In *Adults with Learning Disabilities. A Practical Approach for Health Professionals* (eds J. O'Hara & A. Spertinger). Chichester: John Wiley & Sons.

CVS CONSULTANTS AND ASIAN PEOPLE'S DISABILITY ALLIANCE (1998) *Ethnicity and Learning Difficulty. Moving Towards Equity in Service Provision.* London: CVS Consultants & Department of Health.

DAY, K. & JANCAR, J. (1991) Mental handicap and the Royal Medico-Psychological Association. A historical association 1841–1991. In *150 Years of British Psychiatry. 1841–1991* (eds G. E. Berrios & H. Freeman). London: Gaskell.

DEPARTMENT OF HEALTH (1992) *Review of Services for Mentally Disordered Offenders and Others Requiring Similar Services. Official Working Group on Services for People with Special Needs.* London: Home Office.

DEPARTMENT OF HEALTH AND SOCIAL SECURITY (1971) *Between Services for the Mentally Handicapped.* White Paper. London: DHSS.

DICKENS, P. & STALLARD, A. (1981) *Assessing Mentally Handicapped People: A Guide for Care Staff.* Oxford: NFER-Nelson.

DONNELLAN, A. M., LAVIGNA, G. W. & NEGRI-SHOULTZ, N. (1988) *Progress Without Punishment. Effective Approaches for Learners with Behavioural Problems.* New York: Teachers College Press.

DORRELL, S. (1991) *Statement on Services for People with Learning Disability.* London: Department of Health.

DURAND, V. I. M. (1990) *Severe Behaviour Problems: A Functional Communication Training Approach.* New York: Guildford Press.

DUTT, R. & FERNS, P. (1998) *Letting Through Light. A Training Pack on Black People and Mental Health.* London: Race Equality Unit & Department of Health.

ELKS, M. (1994) Valuing the person of valuing the role? Critique of Social Role of Valorisation theory. *Mental Retardation*, **32**, 265–271.

EMERSON, E. (1999) Assessment. In *Clinical Psychology and People with Intellectual Disabilities* (eds E. Emerson, C. Hatton, J. Bromley, *et al*). Chichester: John Wiley & Sons.

—— & HATTON, C. (1994) *Moving Out Relocation from Hospital to Community.* London: HMSO.

——, CULLEN, C. & HATTON, C. (1996) *Residential Provision for People with Learning Disabilities. Summary Report.* Manchester: Hester Adrian Research Centre, University of Manchester.

—— & HATTON, C. (1999) Future trends in the ethnic composition of British society and among British citizens with learning disabilities. *Tizard Learning Disability Review*, **4**, 28–32.

FATIMILEHIN, I. & NADIRSHAW, Z. (1994) A cross-cultural study of parental attitudes and beliefs about learning disability. *Mental Handicap Research*, **7**, 202–227.

FERNANDO, S. (1995) *Mental Health in a Multi-Ethnic Society. A Multi-Disciplinary Handbook.* London: Routledge.

—— (1998) Part 1: Background. In *Forensic Psychiatry, Race and Culture* (eds S. Fernando, D. Ndegwa & M. Wilson). London: Routledge.

——, NDEGWA, D. & WILSON, M. (1998) *Forensic Psychiatry, Race and Culture.* London: Routledge.

FERNS, P. (1992) Promoting race equality though normalisation. In *Normalisation. A Reader for the Nineties* (eds H. Brown & H. Smith). London: Routledge.

FRANSELIA, F. (1990) Personal Construct Therapy. In *Individual Therapy. A Handbook* (cd. W. Dryden). Milton Keynes: Open University Press.

GOFFMAN, A. (1961) *Asylums.* New York: Anchor.

GROTH-MARNAT, G. (1990) Handbook for Psychological Assessment (3nd edn). Chichester: John Wiley & Sons.

HAYES, S. (1996) Recent research on offenders with learning disabilities. *Tizard Learning Disability Review,* 1.

HOGG, J. & RAYNES, N. (1986) *Assessment in Mental Handicap.* London: Croom Helm.

HOLLAND, T. & MURPHY, G. (1990) Behavioural and psychiatric disorders in adults with mild learning disabilities. *International Review of Psychiatry,* **2,** 117–137.

HUTNIK, N. (1991) *Ethnic Minority Health. A Social Psychological Perspective.* Oxford: Clarendon Press.

JENSON, A. R. (1969/1980) How much can we boost IQ and scholastic achievement. *Harvard Educational Review,* **39,** 1–23.

JENSON, J. (1972) *Genetics and Education.* New York: Harper & Row.

KELLY, G. (1995) *The Psychology of Personal Constructs.* Vols 1 & 2. New York: Morton.

LINDSAY, W. R., NEILSON, C. & LAWRENSON, H. (1997) Cognitive therapy for anxiety in people with learning disabilities. In *Cognitive Behaviour Therapy for People with Learning Disabilities* (eds B. S. Kroese, D. Dagnan & K. Loumidis). London. Routledge.

LYNDSEY, M. (1998) *Signposts for Success.* Department of Health.

MACADAM, M. & RODGERS, J. (1997) A multi-disciplinary, multi-agency approach. In *Adults with Learning Disabilities. A Practical Approach for Health Professionals* (eds J. O'Hara & A. Sperlinger). Chichester: John Wiley & Sons.

MACMILLAN D. L., GRESHAM F. M. & SIPERSTEIN, G. N. (1993) Conceptual and psychometric concerns about the 1992 AAM definition of mental retardation. *American Journal on Mental Deficiency,* **98,** 325–335.

MANSELL, J., HUGHES, H. & McGILL, P. (1994) Maintaining local residential placements. In *Severe Learning Disabilities and Challenging Behaviours: Designing High Quality Services* (eds E. Emerson, P. McGill & J. Mansell), pp. 260–281. London: Chapman & Hall.

MATSON, J. L. (1982) The treatment of behavioural characteristics of depression in the mentally retarded. *Behaviour Therapy,* **13,** 209–218.

—— (ed) (1990) *Handbook of Behaviour Modification with the Mentally Retarded.* New York: Plenum.

MENOLASCINO, F. J. (1998) Mental illness in the mentally retarded: diagnostic and treatment issues in mental retardation and mental health. In *Mental Retardation and Mental Health: Classification, Diagnosis, Treatment, Services.* (eds J. A. Stark, F. J. Menolascino, M. H. Albarelli, *et al*). Berlin: Springer-Verlag.

MENTAL HEALTH FOUNDATION (1995) *Don't Forget Us. Results of a National Inquiry into Services for Children with Learning Disabilities and Severe Challenging Behaviour.* London: MHF.

—— (1996) *Building Expectations: Opportunities and Services for People with Learning Disability.* London: Mental Health Foundation.

MESIBOV, G. (1990) Normalisation and its relevance today. *Journal and Autism and Development Disorders,* **20,** 379–390.

MOSS, S. C., PROSSER, H., COSTELLO, H., *et al* (1998) Reliability of Validity of the PASS–ADD Check-list for detecting psychiatric disorders in adults with intellectual disability. *Journal of Intellectual Disability Research,* **42,** 173–183.

NADIRSHAW, Z. (1991) Assessment of learning difficulties in ethnic minority clients. In *Ethnic Minority Health. A Current Awareness Bulletin.* Vol. 2. Bradford: Bradford Community Health.

—— (1997) Cultural issues. In *Adults with Learning Disabilities. A Practical Approach for Health Professionals*. (eds J. O'Hara & A. Sperlinger). Chichester: John Wiley & Sons.

—— (1998) Community care. For whose benefit? *Learning Disability Practice*, **1**.

—— (1999) Editorial. *Tizard Learning Disability Review*, **4**.

NAYLOR, L. & CLIFTON, E.(1993) People with learning disability. Meeting complex needs. *Health & Social Care in the Community*, **6**, 343–353.

NEWLAND, J. (1999) A method for assessing personal cultural identity in services for people with learning disabilities. *Tizard Learning Disability Review*, **4**, 20–24.

O'BRIEN, S. (1987) A guide to life-style planning: using the Activities Catalogue to integrate services and natural support systems. In *The Activities Catalogue: An Alternative Curriculum for Youth and Adults with Severe Disabilities* (eds B. Wilcox & G. T. Bellamy). Baltimore, MD: P.H. Brookes.

O'HARA, J. & SPERLINGER, A. (1997) *Adults with Learning Disabilities. A Practical Approach for Health Professionals*. Chichester: John Wiley & Sons.

PATEL, P., GOLDBERG, D. P. & MOSS, S. C. (1993) Psychiatric morbidity in older people with moderate and severe learning disability (mental retardation). Part II: The prevalence study.

PEARSON, M. (1991) Ethnic differences in infant health. *Archives of Diseases in Childhood*, **66**, 88–90.

PERRIN, B. & NIRJE, B. (1985) Setting the record straight: a critique of some frequent misconceptions of the normalisation principle. *Australian & New Zealand Journal of Development Disabilities*, **11**, 69–74.

PROSSER, H., MOSS, S., COSTELLO, U., *et al* (1998) Reliability & validity of the mini PASS–ADD for assessing mental health problems in adults with intellectual disability. *Journal of Intellectual Disability Research*, **42**, 264–272.

RAO, P. S. S. & INBARAJ, S. G. (1980). Inbreeding effects of foetal growth and development. *Journal of Medical Genetics*, **7**, 27–31.

REISS, S. (1987) *Reiss Screen for Maladaptive Behaviour.* Chicago, IL: Internadon Diagnostic Systems Inc.

—— (1994a) Issues in defining mental retardation. *American Journal of Mental Retardation*, **99**, 1–7.

—— (1994b) Psychopathology in mental retardation. In *Mental Health and Mental Retardation. Recent Advances and Practices* (ed. N. Bouras). Cambridge: Cambridge University Press.

ROCHERON, Y. (1988) The Asian mother and baby campaign; the construction of ethnic minorities health needs. *Critical Social Policy*, **22**, 4–23.

ROSENTHAL, M., ADDISON, G. M. & PRICE, D. A. (1988) Congenital hypothyroidism. Increased incidence in Asian Families. In *Archives in Disease in Childhood*, **63**, 790–793.

SCOTTI, J. R., EVANS, I. M., MEYER, L. H., *et al* (1991) A meta-analysis of intervention research with problem behaviour: treatment validity and standards of practice. *American Journal on Mental Retardation*, **96**, 233–256.

STURMEY, P. & LEVIN, J. (1993) Dual diagnosis. An annotated bibliography of recent research. *Journal of Intellectual Disability Research*, **37**, 437–448.

TERRY, P. B., BISSENDEN, J. B. G., CONDIE, R. G., *et al* (1985) Ethnic differences in congenital malformations. *Archives of Disease in Childhood*, **60**, 866–888.

WORLD HEALTH ORGANIZATION (1980) *International Classification of Impairments, Disabilities and Handicaps*. Geneva: WHO.

—— (1992) The Tenth Revision of the International Classification of Diseases and Related Disorders. Geneva: WHO.

WOLFENSBERGER, W. (1972) *The Principle of Normalisation in Human Services*. Toronto: National Institute on Mental Retardation.

—— (1980) The definition of Normalisation: update, problems, disagreements and misunderstandings. In *Nomalisation, Social Integration & Community Services* (eds R. J. Flynn & K. E. Nitsch). Baltimore, MD: University Park Press.

—— (1983) Social Role Valorisation a proposed term for the principle of normalisation. *Mental Retardation*, **21**, 234–239.

ZARKOWSKA, E. & CLEMENTS, J. (1994) *Problem Behaviour and People with Severe Learning Disabilities*. London: Chapman & Hall.

12 Substance misuse and ethnic minorities: issues for the UK

SHAMIL WANIGARATNE, SUJATHA UNNITHAN and JOHN STRANG

Editors' introduction

Different cultural groups accept intoxication with alcohol and other chemical substances to varying degrees. Within each culture religious and ethnic factors also influence rates of substance misuse and hence associated mental health disorders. The levels of misuse identified as problematic differ across cultural and clinical settings. Social acceptance to total exclusion can be seen around the world. In this chapter, Wanigaratne et al highlight comorbidity of substance misuse and mental disorders as well as their association with various social and economic factors. Having illustrated the levels of substance misuse from existing epidemiological data, they go on to suggest that several problems remain while interpreting this data. Within the African–Caribbean community, Wanigaratne et al suggest, prevalence of abuse of different substances varies; for example, rates of alcohol dependency and misuse are low. Among certain religious groups in the south Asian communities, however, levels of alcohol misuse are high, while those of opiates are remarkably low. Wanigaratne et al highlight the treatment needs of special groups such as the young within the ethnic minority groups. They conclude by suggesting a way forward in answering some research questions.

Substance use and misuse

The use of intoxicants or mind-altering substances by man is as old as the history of humanity. The history of every civilisation is rich in records of substance use and intoxication. The best evidence for problems of misuse of mind-altering substances can be seen in the ethical codes of all the major world religions. Substance use and misuse continues to the present day in every society and country. The cultural and religious structures together with the availability of different substances have created a complex picture of substance use and misuse across communities.

In Britain, the tapestry of race and culture includes most of the major religions of the world and the cultural fabrics of second- and third-generation immigrant communities continue to have religion as their focus. Apart from Christianity and Judaism, the majority of ethnic minority communities in Britain have Islam, Hinduism, Sikhism and Buddhism as the central focus of their culture. The attitude to substance misuse in a particular culture will be largely governed by religious teachings. For example, Islam gives clear guidance in those things which are lawful (*Halal*) and unlawful (*Haram*) based on the teachings of the *Quran* and *Sunnah*. Wine-drinking, taking alcohol or any intoxicating drug is forbidden in Islam. Islamic views on substance misuse are outlined in detail in *Al-Halal Wal Haram Fil Islam* (*The Lawful and Prohibited in Islam*) by Yusuf Al-Qaradawi. The Hindu scriptures also instruct individuals not to indulge in intoxicants. The Sikh code of discipline also instructs individuals not to partake of alcohol, tobacco, drugs or any other intoxicants. Buddhist teachings, on the other hand, can be interpreted as advocating the 'middle path'; it avoids the position of prohibition with the instructions that intoxicants are harmful and should be used in moderation. Christian teachings can also be interpreted to take a 'moderation' stance.

Problematic substance use or misuse has a separate history, in terms of how it has been perceived and defined within cultures. An individual who misuses substances has been perceived as being everything from a 'moral degenerate', to being afflicted by an illness, to someone who has made the choice, for reasons of personal history and genetic make-up among other things, to use substances excessively as a compensatory mechanism (Brickman *et al*, 1982). Socio-economic and political factors as well as the existing knowledge base at any given time have dictated the definitions or more broadly the perception of problematic substance use. The disease concept that emerged in 19th century North America and Europe, although having undergone a number of changes, has endured to the present time with the adoption of a broader 'biopsychosocial' framework. Several of the major international disease categorising or diagnostic systems now include substance misuse within psychiatric classifications as a behavioural disorder of control.

There is no doubt that choice and pattern of substance use is heavily influenced by religious, cultural and historical factors. While it would be illuminating to compare the patterns of substance misuse of the various ethnic minority communities in Britain with that in their countries of origin, the diversity of ethnic communities would make this task beyond the scope of this chapter. The generational differences in patterns of substance misuse further complicate the picture, although this has been illustrated with respect to some communities.

Substance misuse and mental health

The position of substance misuse as a mental disorder, a behavioural disorder or a normal behavioural pattern that has become excessive or problematic will continue to be debated. Notwithstanding the academic debate as to whether it is a mental disorder or is a symptom of underlying mental disorders, there is a large co-incidence of both these phenomena.

The issues surrounding the over-diagnosis of certain types of mental disorders in Black and other ethnic minority communities has been described by a number of writers (McGovern & Cope, 1987; Littlewood & Lipsedge, 1989; see Chapters 1, 3 and 7, this volume). The over-diagnosis of cannabis psychosis in Black and African–Caribbean patients is probably the most striking example of this (Ranger, 1989). Based on an assumption that most Black people misuse cannabis, there was a tendency to diagnose any psychotic phenomena seen in these individuals as cannabis psychosis (Thornicroft, 1990). However, the work of Lewis *et al* (1994) contradicts this.

The association between common stressors experienced by immigrant populations (such as poor housing, living in deprived areas, unemployment and hostile environments) and the incidence and prevalence of mental illness and substance misuse is a complex one. There is little understanding of the perpetuation of these problems in subsequent generations and the phenomenon of 'ghetto cultures'.

Epidemiology of substance misuse in ethnic minority communities

The real extent of substance misuse or problematic drug and alcohol use in the UK is unknown. Epidemiologists using various methods to estimate the size of the problem have come up with various prevalence figures. This has led one commentator to conclude that:

> "assessing the prevalence of drug misuse in Britain is more like piecing together a jigsaw – with most of the pieces missing and the rest fitting poorly or not at all – than an exercise in statistics" (Baker, 1997).

It is estimated that at least 25% of the general population have used some illicit drugs at some point in their lives, a figure of 10 million people between the ages of 15 and 69 years. Of the general adult population, it is estimated that at least four million people (10%) will have used illicit drugs in the last year and two million people will have used these drugs in the last month (Baker, 1997).

When it comes to estimating the drug use in ethnic minority communities within the UK, the data are sparse. The consequences of lack of reliable statistics on substance misuse in Britain have been described as leaving the field open to "wishful thinking, anecdotal assertions, propaganda, rumour, exaggeration and potentially wildly inaccurate guesswork" (Baker, 1997). Generalisations and misperceptions such as 'most drug users are Black people' are an example of this. The Four City Study (Leitner *et al*, 1993) found that in one location over half the White respondents had taken illicit drugs compared to only one-third of the Black respondents. The British Crime Survey (Ramsay & Percy, 1996) found that White and African–Caribbean lifetime drug use was identical (29%).

In estimating figures for substance misuse for ethnic minorities there is a real danger of generalisations or blanket figures that could have the effect of hindering, rather than helping, planning and appropriate service development. While it can be argued that broad-brush general figures are important in a national context, particularly for resource allocation, it can have the opposite effect on appropriate service development for ethnic minorities in a local context. To be helpful, epidemiological data on ethnic minority substance misuse need to be precise, with appropriate sensitivities to subtle variations in the picture. The same applies to service development and provision.

Examining the broad picture first, the 1991 Census revealed that Black and other visible minorities made up 6% of the population (Office of National Statistics, 1996). Geographically, the majority of the visible minorities live in urban areas. Nearly half the minority population (45%) is distributed in the greater London area, with the rest mainly concentrated in the West Midlands, Manchester, Liverpool, Leeds and Bradford. Similar to the pattern seen in most Western developed countries, immigrant populations tend to be concentrated in urban areas that are in decay, where housing is cheaper. Historic links are established and particular communities are concentrated in certain areas, for example, the Bangladeshi community in Tower Hamlets (East London), the African–Caribbean community in Brixton and several other parts of south London.

It is important to note that in these areas of urban decay and deprivation it is not only substance misuse but also other independent and associated behaviours such as criminal activities which are often more frequent in general. So there may be a tendency to overestimate the extent of substance misuse within these visible minority groups. The association between indices of social inequalities or forms of social exclusion and substance misuse is well established (Pearson, 1993; Advisory Council on the Misuse of Drugs, 1998). A higher proportion of Black and other ethnic minority groups are represented in indices of inequality such as unemployment, poor housing, education and health, compared with their White counterparts (Jones, 1996; Office of National Statistics, 1996). The relationship between social disadvantage and drug misuse in the general population may not be reflected in the same way in Black and other ethnic minority groups, and the nature of this relationship must be determined. Broad-brush generalisations without this information could lead to misconceptions and inappropriate service provision.

These same limitations apply to the examination of the health and social needs of people within these groups who misuse drugs. In the absence of detailed, comprehensive nationwide surveys, the picture of needs of Black and other ethnic minority substance misusers has to be constructed from small-scale local studies. These local studies enable us to construct a varied picture with some common themes emerging. The needs highlighted and the emergent themes are then helpful in developing appropriate responses as well as giving direction to policy planning and development. The available information is best summarised in terms of the different ethnic groups on which the studies have focused.

African and African–Caribbean communities

A number of studies have identified that cannabis is the main illicit drug used in this community in the UK, as is the case with their White counterparts (Mirza *et al*, 1991; Perera *et al*, 1993; Castleton & Francis, 1996). Crack/cocaine use is emerging as the second most used drug and the most problematic from the perspective both of service providers and drug users (Daniel, 1992; Perera *et al*, 1993; Castleton & Francis, 1996). In some African–Caribbean communities, crack use has also observed to be a route to heroin use (Perera *et al*, 1993). The prevalence of heroin use in African–Caribbean community is estimated from different studies to range from 2 to 4% (Castleton & Francis, 1996).

Some African communities, particularly some clearly defined groups such as the Somali community living in the UK, are known to chew a plant known as *khat* or *qat* that contains a drug with stimulant properties. Khat is legal in Britain, but illegal in the USA. In a study investigating patterns of Khat use among 207 Somalis living in

London, using a particularly culturally sensitive methodology known as privileged access interviewing (Griffiths *et al*, 1993), it was found that 78% of the sample had used khat at some stage in their life and 67% had used the substance the week prior to the interview (Griffiths *et al*, 1997). The figures for khat use were similar in both men and women and 76% of the sample reported using more of the substance while living in the UK than when living in Somalia.

Alcohol consumption and alcohol-related problems among the African–Caribbean communities in the UK appear to be comparatively lower than that of their White counterparts (Balarajan & Yuen, 1986). This trend has been confirmed by several other studies. Cochrane & Howell (1995), Cruikshank & Jackson (1985) and Haines *et al* (1987) all showed findings demonstrating lower "average alcohol consumption levels" among African–Caribbean communities, compared with the White population. Balarajan & Yuen, 1986), Cruikshank & Jackson (1985) and Haines *et al* (1987) have shown that this trend is consistent among both men and women; for example, Cruikshank & Jackson (1985) found the weekly average consumption of their African–Caribbean sample to be 18 units of alcohol for men and four units for women compared to the White sample which was 22 units for men and seven units for women. Cochrane & Bal (1990) found that first-generation African–Caribbean men were more likely to be regular drinkers than those of the second-generation, but the unit consumption of alcohol was the same, suggesting that members of the second-generation drink less often, but consume more when they do (Alcohol Concern, 1995). McKeigue & Karmi (1993), in their review of the available evidence on alcohol consumption and alcohol-related problems, concluded that "rates of heavy drinking and alcohol-related problems appear to be about 50% lower in Afro-Caribbean men and women than in the native British population".

Asian communities

Asian communities, as with African–Caribbean communities, are not a homogeneous group. In Britain there are Asian communities originating from India, Pakistan, Bangladesh, Hong Kong, Vietnam and Sri Lanka, to name a but few. Each community has a distinct identity and the religious focus may also vary. Some areas in Britain have large concentrations of Indian, Pakistani and Bangladeshi communities and the few studies on drug use have been conducted in these areas (Awiah *et al*, 1992; Khan *et al*, 1995).

Obtaining an accurate picture of Asian drug use is more difficult than with some other communities because of the concept of *izzat* or 'respectability' that governs much of the Asian way of life (Khan *et al*, 1995). The potential damage to the respectability of a family by the identification of a member as someone who misuses substances is considerable and this factor makes the detection of drug use in the community much more difficult. This may explain the consistently low level of self-reported drug use in this group in available studies, which has been summarised by Pearson & Patel (1998). The exceptions to this trend are the findings of the *British Crime Survey* (Ramsay & Percy, 1996) and a study involving outreach work in Bradford (Patel *et al*, 1995).

Studies indicate that cannabis is the main drug of misuse in the Asian community in general, particularly among young people (Khan *et al*, 1995; Sangster, 1997). The *British Crime Survey* (Ramsay & Percy, 1996), found that 4% of young Asians (aged 16–29 years) from the Pakistani and Bangladeshi communities sampled had used heroin. A similar percentage of the sample had used crack and cocaine and a smaller percentage steroids. Patel *et al* (1995) in their study in Bradford found recreational cannabis use among young Asians and drug use associated with the Bhangra music scene, similar to the wider rave scene where dance drugs such as 3,4-methylenedioxymethamphetamine (MDMA/Ecstasy) and lysergic acid diethylamide (LSD) were used. They also found differing patterns of heroin use, including injecting, in different neighbourhoods in the city. Pearson & Patel (1998) describe a phenomenon they call the "Pakistan holiday habit" where young men appeared to have picked up a heroin habit while on holiday in Pakistan. The increasing trends in heroin use in Pakistan (Ahmed & Ali, 1993) giving rise to a cheap and plentiful supply of heroin used in a holiday context is suggested as an explanation for the development of a dependent pattern of use.

Sections of the Asian community, particular older members, as in the case of some African communities who use khat, chew betel leaves and betel nuts, in a similar way. The effects of chewing betel concoctions are similar to khat in that they produce a stimulant effect. Chewing preparations of betel leaves, tobacco and betel nuts, particularly after meals, is a practice that has been known for centuries in the Indian subcontinent and in South-east Asia and there is general acceptance that it is habit-forming. As in the case with khat, betel preparations are legal in Britain and seen as part of the Asian culture, particularly among the older generation. It does not warrant a discussion in a chapter on illicit drug use; nevertheless it forms part of drug use in the Asian community and it is a practice with known health hazards, particularly oral cancer and tooth decay (Raman *et al*, 1996).

There is little available data on the patterns of substance misuse in the Chinese community.

Studies on alcohol consumption and alcohol problems in the Asian community in Britain is sparse (Alcohol Concern, 1995). The available literature points to a number of trends.

Cochrane & Bal (1990) found that Sikh men formed the largest group to consume more than the recommended 21 units per week. They also found that when it came to heavy drinking (consumption over 40 units per week) Sikh men were second only to White men and that older Sikh men drank more than White men of equivalent age. Cochrane & Bal (1990) also found that Sikh men were more likely to drink alone than any other group and that both Sikh and Hindu men born in India were more likely to be regular drinkers than those born in the UK. Cochrane & Bal (1990) and McKeigue & Karmi (1993) found that around 90% of Asian Muslims did not drink alcohol and only 0.5% consumed over 41 units of alcohol per week. In terms of alcohol-related problems, Mather & Marjot (1992) and Cochrane & Bal (1989) have found that Indian-born men are significantly over-represented in alcohol-related hospital admissions compared with UK- and Caribbean-born men.

Other minority groups

Among other ethnic minorities in Britain, the Cypriot community forms one of the largest groups. Abdulrahim *et al* (1994) studied the drug using patterns and service use among the Cypriot population in north London and found a pattern of drug use similar to that of the Black and Asian groups, with cannabis being the drug most used and stimulants and opiates taking second and third places, respectively. These investigators identified that many of the barriers to uptake of services that are experienced by Black and Asian groups were common to this group as well. There were particular similarities with the Asian community in that individuals with problematic substance use did not want members of their community to find out about their problem. Being seen by members of their community if they approached services was a particular concern.

Barriers to uptake of services

The under-representation of Black and other ethnic minority service users presenting at substance misuse services both in the statutory and non-statutory sectors is a major concern for clinicians, managers and policy-makers (Mirza *et al*, 1991; Abdulrahim, 1992; Perera *et al*,

1993). The statistics of under-representation are calculated by comparing the racial breakdown of service users with that of the adult population in the area served. In general, ethnic minorities are under-represented among service users. An exception to this trend was found in the Kensington, Chelsea and Westminster area of London, where the Regional Drugs Misuse Database figures showed that the proportion of the ethnic minority population seen by the agencies was higher than than that of the White population for that area (26.4% compared with 21.8%), although the author advised extreme caution in interpreting the data (Daniel, 1992, 1993). If this anomaly was due to a particular intervention by services in the area, then it should be carefully evaluated and applied in other parts of the country.

Studies in other parts of the country have identified a number of barriers that prevent Black and Asian drug users using services. There is a widely held perception that these services are run for, and by, White people (Mirza *et al*, 1991; Awiah *et al*, 1992; Butt, 1992; Perera *et al*, 1993). The perception that the services are for White male opiate users is difficult to dispute, as this is the case in most services. The view that drugs services are not geared to helping people with problems other than opiate dependence is another barrier. This view is also difficult to counter, as the main service providers have been very slow to develop interventions for cannabis users or stimulant users (Tippell *et al*, 1990). Unlike the treatment of opiate addiction, the available treatments for stimulant use and cannabis use are less explicitly medical and more psychological or psychosocial in their approach. Statutory services that have evolved around the prescription of substitute opiates in general have a medical model as their *modus operandi* and appear to have difficulty in readily assimilating alternative therapies and approaches. This can act to further alienate Black and other ethnic minority patients, for whom these approaches may be more attractive.

Perera *et al* (1993), in their study in west London, identified a number of barriers: the perception of lack of understanding and empathy by staff; fears about confidentiality; lack of practical support and solutions to problems; and the lack of Black and other ethnic minority staff. They also found perceptions of institutionalised racism a major barrier for Black and other ethnic minority service users accessing services.

Fears about confidentiality as a barrier to uptake of services has been identified in a number of studies and this factor alone differentiates Black and other ethnic minority service users from their White counterparts, who were less concerned about confidentiality (Perera *et al*, 1993; Abdulrahim *et al*, 1994). Many respondents in surveys have expressed their negative experience of being asked a lot of questions during assessment that have seemingly very little to do with the help they were seeking and their fear that the services were linked to agencies such as the police, Home Office and social services.

Overcoming barriers, the provision of appropriate services

The report of the Task Force to Review Services for Drug Misusers (1996) concluded that dependent drug users from ethnic minority communities in England are reluctant to establish contact with drug agencies. Interventions to overcome each of the possible factors contributing to a reluctance of ethnic minority groups to engage with the substance misuse services referred to in earlier sections are suggested below – for consideration by clinicians, managers of statutory and non-statutory sector services, and policy-makers. They are by no means an exhaustive list of solutions, but rather a limited number of practical measures that may start to address the problem.

Perception that substance misuse services are run by White staff for White opiate users

This theme has emerged in most of the studies looking at Black and Asian substance misuse. Basic measures that can be adopted include the recruitment of Black and Asian staff, creating an accepting and friendly environment, and having Black and Asian images and symbols in the waiting areas and counselling rooms. Publicity material about the services should be designed to contain Black and Asian images with text that gives out positive messages. If the service is in an area where there is a particularly large community of a particular racial group and it is known that there is a substance misuse problem, then services should be developed with this group as a target. This may involve recruiting members of staff, if appropriate, from that community to be responsible for developing services. Publicity material could then be specifically targeted for that community, for example, posters in an appropriate language.

Is the answer to the 'services are for Whites only' perception the creation of race-specific services or projects? There are those who advocate that Black- or Asian-specific services are the only answer to the problem: "two Black workers in an all White project, does not a black service make" (Ahmun, 1997). The desire for race-specific services have been expressed by participants in a number of surveys (Butt, 1992; Khan *et al*, 1995), even from Asian respondents who would find the discovery by a member of their own community that they misuse substances unacceptable. These findings cannot be ignored by service planners. In areas where there are large communities of a particular race, where there is evidence for substance misuse problems, developing race-specific services may be the most effective response in accessing individuals with substance misuse problems within that community. While there should always be a goal of changing the perceptions regarding 'White only' services and in some instances changing the culture within these services to be more competent in providing in race-sensitive services, it is acknowledged that these processes take time. An alternative strategy may be the development of race-specific services which can later be integrated into the main services.

Services are for opiate users only

Drugs services in Britain evolved around providing services for opiate users and this has set a strong tradition (Strang & Gossop, 1994). It has in general had the unintended effect of making services less responsive to the changing pattern of drug use in Britain. In recent years services have made attempts to keep pace by developing services for stimulant users. For example, all data on drug misuse in Britain points to the fact that cannabis is the most commonly used drug, but no specific service has yet been developed to help individuals with cannabis-related problems. Attempts to develop services for non-opiate drugs such as stimulants or benzodiazepines have also suffered from the problem of circularity in perception. That is, individuals are reluctant to take up the services provided within mainline services on the presumption that they are for 'junkies', and this perception reinforces the reality that the services do, in fact, have opiate users as most of their 'clientele'. This then affects the uptake of newly developed services, undermining the establishment of a broader scope for these services.

A considerable switch in resource allocation and work is needed to develop services for individuals whose drugs of choice are not opiates (Tippell *et al*, 1990). Since much of the existing resources and expertise may be found within mainline services, new and innovative strategies have to be developed to access non-opiate drug users. Different opening times, satellite clinics and projects, and liaison clinics in other health care settings are all potential methods of overcoming the barriers. Publicity material that emphasises the difference may help, as may targetting specific racial and age groups.

Western medical model

The perception that treatments offered by substance misuse services are not appropriate for the particular needs of individuals from ethnic minority groups has emerged in a number of studies (Perera *et al*, 1993). Help for psychosocial problems, practical forms of help, counselling and alternative therapies such as acupuncture emerged as approaches which were more acceptable than Western medical treatment, as these individuals did not see their problems as a disease. The strong medical tradition with its considerable reliance on substitute prescribing, has prevented the assimilation of alternative treatment approaches that may be more acceptable to individuals from Black and other ethnic minority groups. To make services attractive to these groups, it is essential that a broad menu of treatment options are provided for users of the services: these might include treatments such as acupuncture, aromatherapy, massage, hypnotherapy and meditation, to cite but a few examples. This would also enable systematic evaluation of the effectiveness of these approaches for substance misuse problems – a much-neglected area of research.

The evidence points to (as in the case of White service users) ethnic minority service users expecting services to provide practical help with, for example, housing, social services and legal problems. Providing these services or helping individuals access these services may go a long way in attracting and retaining service users from ethnic minority groups.

Fears of confidentiality

To what extent do fears about confidentiality stand as a barrier to uptake of services? This has emerged as a factor in most studies looking at ethnic minorities and substance misuse (Perera *et al*, 1993; Abdulrahim *et al*, 1994). As outlined above, there is a perception that services are linked to the police, Home Office, social services, social security and other authorities, and that just by attending services, these authorities will find out about the illegal drug use. This anxiety is perhaps not reduced by the failure to adequately explain and introduce the assessment procedure in most services, which often requires the collection of extensive data for the information requirements of the regional databases, Home Office and purchasers, and sometimes exceeds the requirements for clinical decision-making. This experience alone may account for some of the failure to retain individuals in treatment following the initial interview. Positive interventions to lower this barrier may involve a flexible approach being adopted by services when they are assessing individuals from Black and other ethnic minority groups. It may necessary for assessment procedures to be shortened for these individuals, for example. Explaining the rationale for each piece of information collected during assessment should be regarded as good clinical practice regardless of the race of the individual being assessed, although extra attention often needs to be given to this when assessing individuals from minority groups.

Describing the service provided as a 'confidential service' may not convey the same meaning to every one. When advertising services, and prior to assessing individuals, it may be necessary to explain exactly what confidentiality means in this context and precisely who would have access to any information given by the user. It may also be necessary to state explicitly that the police and Home Office or social services would not have access to the information – or under what circumstances they could. Overcoming such elements of the 'suspicion barrier' may itself help to increase access to services for individuals from Black and other ethnic minority groups.

Institutional racism

Institutional racism is perhaps the most fundamental reason why individuals from Black and other ethnic minority groups do no access services. The perception may exist, based on individuals' own experience of racism in Britain, that services are intrinsically prejudiced against them, and this may not be an easy perception to shift. A token gesture of a 'Black member of staff or two' to alter superficial perceptions will not be adequate without commitment to systematic change and vigilance for institutional racism. Eradication of institutional racism requires action at different levels — at a policy level where 'equal opportunity' policies are carefully thought out and at a management level where these policies are made explicit and communicated – with implementation carefully monitored by senior managers. Particular attention should be paid to this issue during staff recruitment, so that as far as possible the staff in a service are representative of the ethnic mix in the area. Additionally, there should be a clear equal access strategy with specific targets and an individual or group responsible for the implementation of the strategy. At a staff level, in accordance with a strategy, there should be regular 'race awareness' or 'anti-racism' training, including the development of codes of conduct or guidelines for working with Black and other ethnic minorities. An outline of the code developed by Teteh *et al* (1994) is given in Box 12.1.

Measures should also be taken to obtain feedback from Black and other ethnic minority service users as to their experience of the service. This can be done, for example, by means of an anonymous survey, or

Box 12.1
Guidelines for cross-cultural work (from Teteh *et al*, 1994)

There is no doubt that culture needs to be taken into account when providing adequate and equitable substance misuse services. However, peoples' lives are also affected by a multitude of other social, economic and political factors, and over-emphasising 'culture' may lead to simplistic, unhelpful stereotypes. While the following guidelines are therefore important in cross-cultural working, they also provide the basis of general good practice.

(a) **Do not stereotype the service user**
Do not make assumptions about a service user as a result of his or her cultural background, for example, lifestyle, personality, class or attitude to services. This could be very detrimental to the service user's response to any interventions made.

(b) **Make an effort to understand the service user's cultural background**
Assess the service user's understanding of his or her problem and consequent services offered. Do not assume that the service user is aware of the services on offer, what they imply and how they can be accessed and used. It is essential that any type of work undertaken with the service user takes into account the individual's medical, psychological, social, spiritual and political beliefs. An in-depth assessment will highlight a service user's needs as conveyed by him or her.

(c) **Assess the different socio-economic and cultural influences on the service user**
In any assessment take into account the service user's different life experiences. These could include racism, feeling 'labelled' or being disempowered due to race or class discrimination. The emphasis should always be on the service user as an individual.

(d) **Share your interest in and knowledge of the service user's culture and lifestyle**
Be willing to learn from the service user about the multiplicity of issues that affect people's lives.

(e) **Do not be judgemental, and show respect for the service user's background**
Avoid being condescending, over-enthusiastic, phoney and prescriptive.

(f) **Provide boundaries for your interactions**
Provide safe and effective boundaries during any interventions with the service user in a warm manner regardless of the service user's race or ethnicity.

(g) **Acknowledge and respect the religious/spiritual beliefs that some may hold**
The outcome of any work done with service users may be adversely affected if issues around religious/spiritual beliefs are ignored, when important to the service user. Workers must acknowledge their own limitations and call on the help of others, e.g. priests, clergy, if appropriate and necessary for the service user.

(h) **Show appreciation of the service user's own dialects and language**
The service user's own dialect, be it 'patois', slang, street talk, etc. ,should be taken into account as a valid form of language enabling the service user to express a rich cultural heritage and deep emotions. If necessary and relevant resort to advocacy services, books or visual aids, particularly if English is a second language.

cont.

Box 12.1 (*cont.*)

(i) **In marital and family work allow parties to overcome fear of losing face**
Take into account different cultural family structures, arranged marriages, mixed relationships, etc., when they exist. Allow family members individual space to air their grievances and explore values and roles within the family. Consider the influences of different value systems, authoritarianism and communication between the genders and generations.

(j) **Assess any additional stress factors**
Take into account additional stress a service user may experience as a result of conflict between cultural heritage and the need to conform to peer pressure.

alternatively by using an independent researcher. Focus groups with external facilitators are also a valuable method. Explanation of complaints procedures and having a visible suggestions box are all methods of encouraging user feedback.

Beyond the immediate service level, there is much that could be done by substance misuse services in their teaching and training role. Substance misuse services are often required to teach in schools and other settings and also to train and raise awareness in other health care and service settings. These are excellent opportunities to raise and discuss access issues and outline steps taken to address barriers. Professionals within services, for example, psychiatrists, physicians, nurses, psychologists, occupational therapists and social workers, could also, through their professional bodies and training courses, take steps to overcome institutional and unintentional racism, and thereby increase the potential of access to services by Black and other ethnic minority groups. A good example of this is the British Psychological Society's development of a Race and Culture Module for training in clinical psychology with a special section on substance misuse (Patel *et al*, 2000).

Outreach work

The most practical and effective measure that a service can take to increase access to Black and other ethnic minority individuals is to target outreach work. Instead of waiting for individuals with substance misuse problems to approach services, it is possible to take services to individuals, or to help individuals overcome some of the perceptual barriers by doing outreach work. This approach, also termed the 'community development approach', is now being used increasingly by services as a way of accessing hard-to-reach groups (Henderson, 1995). This approach is similar to the privileged access interview (Griffiths *et al*, 1993) described earlier, a method developed by researchers to access and study hard-to-reach groups. An effective strategy for doing outreach work is to target a particular ethnic group or community and have a dedicated worker or workers from the same community or speaking the appropriate language, to systemically work their way into, and establish themselves within, the community as a helper or helpers. By building trust and a positive reputation and using social networks, such workers can access the hidden populations of problem substance misusers, provide help and, where appropriate, encourage individuals to attend mainline services. Outreach work is also a good vehicle through which to do preventive work.

Young people

All the evidence points to an increase in drug use among young people of all ethnic backgrounds (Home Office, 1997). Reaching young people early with preventive messages and getting help to them earlier is an urgent priority: indeed, this was highlighted in the recent UK government drug strategy for the next 10 years *Tackling Drugs to Build a Better Britain* (Department of Health, 1998). Mainline services designed for older, chronic substance misusers may not be the most appropriate settings in which to provide services for young people from all racial groups, and it may be particularly difficult to reach young people from Black and other ethnic minority groups with the existing credibility gap. A detailed strategy for working with young people from ethnic minority groups has been outlined by Abdulrahim *et al* (1994), in which the need for coordinated agency and multi-disciplinary efforts are emphasised. The report calls for collaboration between drugs services, health promotion departments, education authorities, schools and special schools, youth services, the police, juvenile justice teams and other relevant bodies in the statutory and voluntary sectors. Implementation of these recommendations should be a priority of drug action teams in all areas. Prevention work outlined in the next section should also follow the same directives if it is to have an impact.

Prevention work

The alarming statistics of increasing illicit drug use in Britain, particularly among young people, highlights the importance and urgency of prevention work and this issue has been taken up by politicians and policy planners (Department of Health, 1995). Prevention work is one aspect of the 'Rubic Cube' of illicit drug use and is in essence the largest area of intervention since it covers areas ranging from law enforcement and customs to health promotion, education and small community-based interventions to treatment. Policy-makers have been criticised for placing too great an emphasis on law enforcement and interruption of supply rather than emphasising the education and treatment aspects of prevention. It is argued that the American 'War on Drugs' approach has failed to stem the increase in illicit drug use in the USA and a more creative approach is needed with a different emphasis. It is also argued that preventing illicit drug use and associated behaviours requires a fundamental change in the social and economic fabric of the country. There is little scope in this chapter to explore the area of prevention with its many complexities, conflicting priorities and dilemmas. Many of the issues are national ones with implications for all ethnic groups. Nevertheless, there are aspects of prevention such as interventions at community and individual levels that are relevant here. The inadequacy of the broad-brush approaches to suit all communities discussed earlier applies in this area too. It requires precision and sensitivity, and lessons learnt from innovative interventions in other areas such as HIV prevention as well as from other countries need to be taken into consideration (Gordon, 1994; Johnson & Carroll, 1995; Abdulrahim, 1998). Interim outcomes of the Home Office Drugs Prevention Initiative, launched in 1990, include the identification of examples of good practice in racially and culturally diverse communities. In their excellent review Johnson & Carroll (1995) concluded that:

(a) direct action should be targeted at ethnic minority groups to meet their specific needs;
(b) all activity must take into account the very real diversity in the population in general;
(c) minority communities and service providers have needs which must be met if prevention work is to be relevant and effective. These conclusions are identical to those in the treatment and service provision area.

A cautionary note must be added here that when searching for innovative prevention initiatives, all initiatives should follow the principle of evidence-based practice. In a review of HIV prevention initiatives, where £15 million is spent every year, Oakley *et al* (1995) found only one initiative that was satisfactorily evaluated. The substance misuse field is no different. In an environment where resources are scarce and there is competition for funding, the need for strict evaluation of interventions is all the more salient. The failure to do so may undermine this crucial sphere of activity.

Other measures

Overcoming barriers and increasing access to services for Black and other ethnic minority individuals is a difficult and challenging task for politicians, policy planners and service managers as well as for clinicians. It requires commitment to the principle and a great deal of institutional and personal support. The support element may be the one crucial factor in achieving the objectives, and it is the workers who perhaps need the most support. Appropriate clinical and managerial supervision for working with Black and other ethnic minority people is a key element of support. Collective support in the form of locally organised groups or forums and national organisations, such as the Black Drug Workers Forum, can also be crucial. Such groups can provide support for the workers, an opportunity to discuss issues and problems, and a platform to present new and innovative ideas as well as achievements.

Research horizons

Perhaps the most urgent need from a research perspective is for the subject of ethnicity and drug use to be seen as a legitimate area of scientific study – rather than just as an area of political consciousness or correctness. As in some other areas, such as the influence of gender upon drug misuse, the wish to correct perceived misunderstanding of the extent of the problem and miscarriages of justice can often interfere with the necessary clarity of purpose and vision in objective, scientific study. Such objective study can and should, of course, be informed by an understanding of the nature of the condition under study (and any perceived associated disadvantage), but a firm grip must nevertheless be retained on the same principles of scientific enquiry as would be applied in other areas of investigation and exploration.

Particular sensitivity will be required in exploring the true extent of such hidden populations – especially in areas where there are compound reasons for its concealment. One such issue is drug use by women from some ethnic minority communities, which, on the face of it, appears extremely rare, but which may be particularly taboo and hence particularly determinedly hidden. Furthermore, even when findings are made and relationships established, it will be crucial to explore the extent to which these findings are generalisable to other ethnic minority groups, or to the same ethnic group who are geographically located elsewhere. With recent advances in methods of biological study, future research will increasingly require collaboration between investigating scientists from different areas of scientific study so as, for example, to identify the proportions of the variants of drug taking behaviour which may be assigned to genetic and familial factors, to childhood and developmental influences, and to the influence of peers and of the drug itself on the individual in his or her social and biological context. Until such time as these areas are recognised and accepted as legitimate areas of research study, the subject of ethnicity and drug misuse is in danger of being dismissed with token acknowledgement, an appeasing development grant, and a continued failure to address the relevant scientific, policy and practice issues.

References

ABDULRAHIM, D. (1992) *Working with Diversity: HIV Prevention and Black and Ethnic Minority Communities.* London: North East and North West Thames Regional Health Authorities.
—— (1998) Power, culture and the 'hard to reach': the marginalisation of minority ethnic populations from HIV prevention and harm minimisation. In *Meddling with Mythology: The Social Construction of Post-AIDS Knowledge* (eds R. Barbour & G. Huby). New York: Routledge.
——, WHITE, D., PHILLIPS, K., *et al* (1994) *Ethnicity and Drug Use: Towards the Design of Community Interventions.* Vol. 1. London: AIDS Research Unit, University of East London.
ADVISORY COUNCIL ON THE MISUSE OF DRUGS (1998) *Drugs and the Environment.* London: The Stationery Office.
AHMED, S. M. & ALI, M. R. (1993) *National Survey on Drug Abuse in Pakistan.* Islamabad: Ministry of Health.
AHMUN, V. (1997). Taking things forward: underpinning issues faced by Black professionals. *Black Drugs Workers Forum News*, **3**, 3–4.
ALCOHOL CONCERN (1995) *Alcohol and the Asian, African and Caribbean Communities: Research and Practice.* London: Alcohol Concern.
AWIAH, J., BUTT, S. & DORN, N. (1992) *Race, Gender and Drugs Services.* ISDD Monograph 6. London: Insititute for the Study of Drug Dependence.
BAKER, O. (1997) *Drug Misuse in Britain.* London: Institute for the Study of Drug Dependence.
BALARAJAN, R. & YUEN, P. (1986) British smoking and drinking habits: variation by country of birth. *Community Medicine*, **8**, 237–239.
BRICKMAN, P., RABINOWITZ, V. C., KARUZA, JR., J., *et al* (1982) Model of helping and coping. *American Psychologist*, **37**, 368–384.
BUTT, S. (1992) Asian males and access to drug services in Bradford. In *Race, Gender and Drug Services* (eds J. Awiah, S. Butt & N. Dorn). London: Institute of the Study of Drug Dependence.
CASTLETON, J. & FRANCIS, R. (1996) *African-Caribbean Drug Use, Risk Behaviour and Attitudes to Drugs.* Dudley: Warehouse.
COCHRANE, R. & BAL, S. (1989) Mental hospital admission rates of immigrants to England: a comparison of 1971 and 1981. *Social Psychiatry and Psychiatric Epidemiology*, **24**, 2–11.
—— & —— (1990) The drinking habits of Sikh, Hindu, Muslim and white men in the West Midlands: a community survey. *British Journal of Addiction*, **85**, 759–769.

—— & HOWELL, M. (1995) Drinking patterns of black and white men in the West Midlands. *Social Psychiatry and Psychiatric Epidemiology*, **30**, 139–146.

CRUIKSHANK, J. & JACKSON, S. (1985) Similarity of blood pressure in blacks, whites and Asians in England: the Birmingham study. *Journal of Hypertension*, **3**, 365–367.

DANIEL, T. (1992) *Drug Agencies, Ethnic Minorities and Problem Drug Use. Executive Summary.* London: Centre for Research on Drugs and Health Behaviour.

—— (1993) Ethnic minorities use of drugs services. *Drug Link*, Jan/Feb, 16–17.

DEPARTMENT OF HEALTH (1995) *Tackling Drugs Together. A Consultation Document on a Strategy for England 1995–98.* London: The Stationery Office.

—— (1998) *Tackling Drugs to Build a Better Britain; A Ten-Year Strategy for Tackling Drugs Misuse.* London: HMSO.

GORDON, J. U. (1994) *Managing Multiculturalism in Substance Abuse Services.* London: Sage.

GRIFFITHS, P., GOSSOP, M., POWIS, B., *et al* (1993) Reaching hidden populations of drug users by privileged access interviewers: Methodological and practical issues. *Addiction*, **90**, 607–614.

——, ——, WICKENDEN, S., *et al* (1997). A transcultural pattern of drug use: qat (khat) in the UK. *British Journal of Psychiatry*, **170**, 281–284.

HAINES, A., BOOROFF, A., GOLDENBERG, E., *et al* (1987) Blood pressure, smoking, obesity and alcohol consumption in black and white patients in general practice. *Journal of Human Hypertension*, **1**, 39–46.

HENDERSON, P. (1995) *Drugs Prevention and Community Development: Principles of Good Practice.* London: Home Office.

HOME OFFICE (1997) *British Crime Survey.* London: HMSO.

JOHNSON, M. & CARROLL, M. (1995) *Dealing with Diversity: Good Practice in Drug Prevention Work with Racially and Culturally Diverse Communities.* London: HMSO.

JONES, T. (1996) *Britain's Ethnic Minorities.* London: Policy Studies Institute.

KHAN, K. (1997) *Race and Drugs Project: Race, Drugs, Europe.* London: City University.

——, SHABIR, G. & AHMED, I. (1995) *An Investigation into Drugs Issues in the Asian Community in Dudley.* Blackheath: Catalyst Community Services Agency.

LEITNER, M., SHAPLAND, J. & WILER, P. (1993) *Drug Usage and Drugs Prevention: the Views and Habits of the General Public.* London: Home Office.

LEWIS, G., CROFT-JEFFREYS, C. & DAVID, A. (1990) Are British psychiatrists racist? *British Journal of Psychiatry*, **157**, 410–415.

LITTLEWOOD, R. & LIPSEDGE, M. (1989) *Aliens and Alienists: Ethnic Minorities and Psychiatry.* London: Unwin Hyman.

MATHER, M. & MARJOT, D. (1992) Alcohol-related admissions to a psychiatric hospital: a comparison of Asians and Europeans. *British Journal of Addiction*, **87**, 327–329.

McGOVERN, D. & COPE, R. V. (1987) First psychiatric admission rates of first and second generation African Caribbeans. *Social Psychiatry*, **22**, 139–149.

McKEIGUE, P. & KARMI, G. (1993) Alcohol consumption and alcohol-related problems in African/Caribbean and South Asians in the UK. *Alcohol and Alcoholism*, **28**, 1–10.

MIRZA, H., PEARSON, G., & PHILLIPS, S. (1991) *Drugs, People and Services in Lewisham. Drug Information Project.* London: Goldsmiths College, London University.

OAKLEY, A., FULLERTON, D. & HOLLAND, J. (1995) Behavioural interventions for HIV/AIDS prevention. *AIDS*, **9**, 479–486.

OFFICE OF NATIONAL STATISTICS (1996) *Provisional Rebased Mid-1995 Resident Population: By Single Year and Age and Sex.* London: ONS.

PATEL, K., PEARSON, G. & KHAN, F. (1995) *Outreach Work Among Asian Drug Injectors in Bradford. A Report to the Mental Health Foundation.* London: Goldsmiths College, London University.

PATEL, N., BENNETT, E., DENNIS, M., *et al.* (2000) *Clinical Psychology, Race and Culture: A Training Manual.* Leicester: BPS Books.

PEARSON, G. (1993) Varieties of ethnography: limits and possibilities in the field of illegal drug use. In *Illegal Drug Use: Research Methods of Hidden Populations* (eds H. F. L. Garretsen, L. A. M. van de Goor, C. D. Kaplan, *et al*). Rotterdam: Netherlands Institute on Alcohol and Drugs.

—— & PATEL, K. (1998) Drugs, deprivation and ethnicity: outreach among Asian drug users in a northern English city. *Journal of Drug Issues*, **28**, 199–224.

PERERA, J., POWER, R. & GIBSON, N. (1993) *Assessing the Needs of Black Drug Users in North Westminster*. London: Hungerford Drug Project & Centre for Research on Drugs and Health Behaviour.

RAMAN, B., BHAL, B. V. & RAYAN, R.R. (1996) *Dentists, Patients and Ethnic Minorities*. London: Department of Health.

RAMSAY, M. & PERCY A. (1996) *Drug Misuse Declared: Results of the 1994 British Crime Survey*. London: Home Office.

RANGER, C. (1989) Race, culutre and "cannabis psychosis": the role of social factors in the construction of disease category. *New Community*, **15**, 357–369.

SANGSTER, D. (1997) *Peer Education and Young Black People. Drugs Edition* (No. 13). London: Release Publications.

STRANG, J. & GOSSOP, M. (1994) *Heroin Addiction and Drug Policy: The British System*. Oxford: Oxford University Press.

TASK FORCE TO REVIEW SERVICES FOR DRUG MISUSERS (1996) *Report of an Independent Review of Drug Treatment Services in England*. London: Department of Health.

TETEH, N., LANGLIS, Y., WANIGARATNE, S., JOB, N., *et al* (1994) *Guidelines for Cross-Cultural Work*. London: North London Race and Culture Substance Misuse Forum, Camden and Islington Substance Misuse Service.

THORNICROFT, G. (1990) Cannabis and psychosis. Is there epidemiological evidence for an association? *British Journal of Psychiatry*, **157**, 25–33.

TIPPELL, S., ASTON, F., HUNTER, A., *et al* (1990) *Cocaine Use: the US Experience and the Implications for Drug Services in Britain*. London: Community Drug Project.

13 Forensic psychiatry

ROSEMARIE COPE

Editors' introduction

Black people of African–Caribbean heritage are more likely than any other ethnic minority group to be in prisons and secure psychiatric facilities. Various reasons for this have been postulated. Cope argues that direct discrimination may not play an important role in explaining this increase but the perception by such communities must be taken into account. Differential rates of criminal activity in Asian and African–Caribbean communities may be explained by social networks and cultural cohesiveness. However, as Cope suggests, assimilation may influence these rates. The relatively high numbers of mentally disordered offenders among the African–Caribbean communities have been attributed to mental illness, existing comorbidity and differential pathways into care. Cope suggests that racial stereotyping may influence some of the increase in both prison and health care systems. She argues for culturally sensitive forensic psychiatry services with active promotion of racial equality in both clinical assessment and service delivery. The observation that traditional in-patient and community services have failed the African–Caribbean community, in particular contributing to increased rates of imprisonment of Black mentally disordered offenders and increased marginalisation into the more coercive secure parts of the system, are sobering thoughts indeed.

Forensic psychiatry services offer assessment, treatment and rehabilitation for two main groups of patients: first, mentally disordered offenders in the criminal justice system, and second, non-offender patients who present significant behavioural and management problems. African–Caribbean people are greatly over-represented, particularly in the first group, among admissions to forensic psychiatry facilities (Cope, 1990). A similar increased proportion of Black people (of African and Caribbean descent) is found among the prison population. Asian and other minority ethnic groups are either found in expected proportions or are under-represented in both the forensic psychiatry services (Cope & Ndegwa, 1990) and the criminal justice system (Home Office, 1997*a*). For this reason, this chapter will largely focus on the experiences of African–Caribbean people. It is divided into two parts: the first describes ethnic minorities' experience of the criminal justice system and the second deals with African–Caribbean mentally disordered offenders and their treatment.

Ethnic minorities and the criminal justice system

Prison population

Since the Home Office began publishing details of the ethnic composition of the prison population in 1986, there has been a gradual increase in the proportion of prisoners from ethnic minorities. This over-representation is largely made up of Black people, of African or African–Caribbean origin. In 1996, 18% of the male prison population and 24% of the female prison population were from ethnic minorities; of the total population, 12% of males and 19% of females were Black (Home Office, 1997*a*). This compares with an ethnic minority population of 6% in Great Britain. The proportion of Black women prisoners is inflated by substantial numbers of women normally resident in Africa and the West Indies who have been convicted for the importation of drugs (Maden *et al*, 1992). People of south Asian ethnic origin (Bangladeshi, Indian and Pakistani) make up less than 3% of the prison population, approximately representative of their numbers in the general population. However, within this statistic, Pakistanis (but not Indians or Bangladeshis) are over-represented (Walmsley *et al*, 1992). At the end of the criminal justice process, Black people are about seven times as likely to be in prison as White people or Asians (Smith, 1994).

Criminal justice process

Criminal conviction and sentencing are the result of a lengthy and complex process. Many offences do not come to the attention of the police, and of those that do, only a proportion will lead to arrest, and an even smaller proportion result in a criminal conviction.

Of all offences committed, the 1996 British crime survey estimated that less than half are reported to the police and only a quarter are recorded (Mirrlees-Black *et al*, 1996). About 26% of recorded offences are cleared up, of which only 5% result in a criminal conviction (Home Office, 1997*b*). These statistics form a useful reference point when considering ethnic minorities' experience of the criminal justice process.

There is now considerable research and statistical evidence of disparity between ethnic groups at different points in the criminal justice system. The most striking is the over-representation of African–Caribbean people in British prisons, described above. In a study for the Royal Commission on Criminal Justice, Fitzgerald (1993) reviewed the available research findings at successive stages of the criminal justice process.

These are summarised below:

(a) Black youths are especially likely to be stopped by the police and to be arrested (although only a small proportion of these stops result in arrests); Asian individuals are less likely than White individuals to be stopped (Willis, 1983; Skogan, 1990).

(b) Once arrested, Black people are less likely to be cautioned than White people and are less likely than Asians to have no further action taken against them (Landau & Nathan, 1983). A combination of these two factors may push Black people more than Whites towards the full criminal justice process, but it has the reverse effect on Asians.

(c) The overall pattern of charges brought against Black people differs from that of White and Asian people. For example they are accused of more victimless crimes and are charged with more serious offences than Whites.

(d) African–Caribbeans are more likely to be remanded in custody than Whites. This in itself further increases the likelihood of a custodial sentence.

(e) African–Caribbean people are more likely than Whites to plead not guilty to the charges against them and are more likely to be tried at Crown Court.

(f) African–Caribbeans are more likely than Whites to be acquitted.

(g) African–Caribbeans found guilty of crimes are more likely than Whites to receive punitive disposals with a higher use of custody and longer sentences; they are less likely to receive probation (Walker, 1989).

These findings raise three fundamental questions. First, is the rate of criminal activity higher among African–Caribbean people than among similarly placed White people? Second, do they represent the effects of racial bias and discrimination? Third, do both these factors apply, and if so, to what degree?

There is evidence of higher offending rates among Black people compared with Whites and Asians, resulting in higher rates of arrest and imprisonment. There are a number of socio-demographic factors that would lead us to expect a difference between Black and White crime rates. The Black population is, on average, younger than the White population and there is, therefore, a higher proportion of Black people among the peak ages for offending, that is, 16–25 years. Black people, especially males, are strongly characterised by socio-economic factors linked with higher offending rates such as high levels of unemployment, lower educational achievement and residence in inner city areas where crime rates are high. There are policing factors too, such as higher levels of policing in ethnic minority inner city areas and more proactive law enforcement that targets Black people. It is also important to remember that the statistics relate to the small proportion of offences for which arrests are made. A self-report study of crimes admitted by a random sample of young people aged 15–24 years found that White and African–Caribbean people reported similar rates of offending, while Asian people reported lower rates (Graham & Bowling, 1995).

Racial differences in sentencing

The most comprehensive study of racial disparities in sentencing in the UK is the multivariate analysis by Hood (1992) of West Midlands Crown Courts. This found that the over-representation of African–Caribbean men and women in the prison system was largely a product of their over-representation among those convicted and sentenced in the Crown Courts. Hood estimated that 80% of the over-representation of Black male offenders in the prison population was due to their over-representation among those convicted at the Crown Court and to the type and circumstances of their offences. For men only, the remaining excess appeared to be due to differential treatment and other factors, which influenced the nature and length of the sentence imposed. Two-thirds of the non-legal causes of the over-representation of convicted Black men resulted from the higher proportion of Black defendants who pleaded not guilty and were therefore more liable to receive longer prison sentences on conviction. For women, no differences were found between Black and White women regarding the rate and duration of imprisonment when the seriousness of the offence was taken into account.

Discrimination in the criminal justice system

Although there is little conclusive evidence of direct discrimination in the criminal justice system, with the exception of police action, there is a perception of racial bias by Black people. Smith & Gray (1983) found that a much higher proportion of young Black males than Whites or Asians believed that the police did not treat ethnic minorities fairly. Racial hostility from the police and antagonism towards authority by Black people may become mutually reinforcing; this in turn may act on actual crime rates, causing a cycle of deviance amplification (Smith, 1994). Racial stereotyping has been found to be common in pre-sentence reports prepared by probation officers, although the main disadvantage to Black people is the failure to prepare a report at all (Waters, 1988). Race relations problems have also been found in prisons, with evidence of discriminatory policies and practices (Genders & Player, 1989).

Racial discrimination persists in all the areas covered by the Race Relations Act 1976 (Fitzgerald, 1993) and therefore it would be implausible to assert that the criminal justice system was uniquely immune from demonstrating discrimination. Fitzgerald also noted that African–Caribbean people were likely to suffer disproportionately from the criminal justice system's capacity for inequitable treatment, with some inevitable consequences for:

> "their faith in the system, their respect for it and, in turn, for their willingness to engage cooperatively with it, whether as suspects, as victims of crime, as witnesses or as potential recruits to the agencies it comprises".

Ethnic minorities, except within the criminal bar, are considerably under-represented among professionals within the criminal justice system, which is overwhelmingly White. Although efforts are being made to expand their numbers, Smith (1994) points out that this will not, in itself, secure equal treatment for ethnic minorities and that it will be necessary for the majority of White police officers, magistrates and judges to demonstrate equality of treatment.

Differential crime rates in Asians and African–Caribbeans

There are striking differences between Asians and African–Caribbeans in terms of both their involvement in and processing by the criminal justice system. When Asian people do become involved in the criminal justice system, there is no evidence of discrimination against them and, if anything, they tend to be favoured compared with White and Black people (Smith, 1994). To understand the possible reasons for these findings, criminologists and sociologists have found it helpful to trace the relative experiences and expectations of Asians and African–Caribbeans following migration to Britain in the 1950s and 1960s. It has been suggested that south Asians and African–Caribbeans adopted radically different survival strategies (Daniel, 1968). Both ethnic minority groups have suffered racial discrimination and socio-economic disadvantage; however, African–Caribbeans it is argued, whose language was English, expected to be assimilated and were unprepared for the hostility and rejection they experienced, leading to inevitable conflict. By contrast, south Asians continued to speak their own languages, to practise their religions and expected to rely upon their families and communities.

African–Caribbean and Asian people were under-represented among offenders in the earliest research on race and crime (e.g. Lambert, 1970). Concern about Black crime developed in the 1970s when claims about Black youths' involvement in street crime were amplified in an emotive way by the press into the new crime of 'mugging'. Mawby & Batta (1980) accurately predicted that:

> "... this new social problem could lead to an escalation in the violence and a deterioration in race relations".

There was an increase in disturbance and high-profile confrontations between the police and Black people. At the same time, African–Caribbeans became associated in the public mind with predatory crime and were perceived as a threat to law and order, unlike Asians. Smith (1994) suggests that high offending rates in young Black people may be linked to the interaction between racial hostility and discrimination on one side and antagonism to authority on the other. This can become mutually reinforcing, leading to escalation in offending and more discrimination. With regard to south Asians, it has been suggested that the low crime rates reflect strength and stability within the Asian communities, allowing them to withstand the pressures towards integration and assimilation (Mawby & Batta, 1980). It is argued that Asian culture exerts control and support through the power of the family and the wider community, which counteracts deviant behaviour.

Ethnic minorities as victims of crime

It has been found that ethnic minorities are more likely than Whites to be victims of crimes and serious threats. This is mainly related to their youth, their socio-economic characteristics and the type of area in which they live. Disadvantages that disproportionately affect ethnic minorities also increase their risk of being victims of crime. The information derives from the British Crime Survey (BCS) of 1992 (Aye Maung & Mirlees-Black, 1994), a large sample survey, which estimated the extent of crimes and threats, and also whether incidents had been racially motivated. The 1992 BCS reported that some of the relatively high crime victimisation rates of African–Caribbeans was associated with the relatively high local crime rates and was mostly accounted for by Black on Black crime. For racially motivated incidents, Pakistanis seemed to be most vulnerable, nearly one-third of victims stating that incidents were racially motivated, compared with one-fifth for Indians and 14% for African–Caribbeans (Fitzgerald & Hale, 1996). Reporting of incidents to the police was variable, but minority groups were less satisfied with the police response to racial incidents than with their response to other types of crime and threats. It has been suggested that ethnic minorities have an incidence of racial attacks 10 times that revealed by statistics from police records (Brown, 1984; also see Chapter 5).

African–Caribbean mentally disordered offenders

In the same way that African-Caribbean people are over-represented in the criminal justice system as suspects, those arrested and as remand and sentenced prisoners, there are increased proportions of African–Caribbean people with psychiatric disorders presenting via the police, to the courts and in the prisons as mentally disordered offenders. As a consequence, they are over-represented among admissions to the specialist forensic services for assessment and treatment. To put the findings relating to African–Caribbeans into context, it is important to remember that the very great majority, that is over 90% of admissions to psychiatric hospitals, are informal. For those patients detained under the Mental Health Act 1983, the majority are detained on civil sections under Part II of the Act; this figure was 92% (including Section 136) in 1996–97; the remainder, 8%, were detained under Part III of the Act (the criminal sections) by the order of a court or the direction of the Home Secretary after they had been accused of criminal offences (Department of Health, 1998). Thus, less than one in a 100 psychiatric admissions are mentally disordered offenders.

It is well documented that African–Caribbean people are over-represented among admissions to psychiatric hospitals, especially as compulsorily detained patients (McGovern & Cope, 1987; Owens *et al*, 1991; Davies *et al*, 1996). Whatever their legal status, high rates of schizophrenia are diagnosed (Harrison *et al*, 1988; Wessely *et al*, 1991).

However, the most striking finding is the very great over-representation of African–Caribbeans as offender patients detained under Part III of the Act. A study of ethnic differences in psychiatric hospital admissions found that African–Caribbean men were 25 times more likely than Whites to be detained on criminal sections (McGovern & Cope, 1987). This finding could be related, in part, to the high numbers of African–Caribbean prisoners with psychotic disorders.

Ethnicity of mentally disordered prisoners

High rates of mental disorder are found in the prison population. A national study of convicted prisoners reported that over one-third suffered from mental disorders (Gunn *et al*, 1991) and even higher rates were found in a more recent national study of unconvicted prisoners, with two-thirds receiving a diagnosis of psychiatric disorder (Brooke *et al*, 1996). Diagnoses of neurosis, personality disorders and substance misuse account for most of the psychiatric morbidity, but 2% of convicted prisoners and 5% of unconvicted prisoners are reported to have psychotic disorders. African–Caribbean prisoners, both male and female, remand and sentenced, have lower rates than Whites of non-psychotic disorders, including substance misuse, but a higher prevalence of psychosis. Overall, in sentenced Black prisoners the prevalence of psychosis is 4% compared with 2% in Whites. Gunn *et al* (1991) also reported that White prisoners were significantly more likely to report 'hard' drug use and to have evidence of drug dependence, but also half of the Black prisoners and one-third of the Whites admitted to using cannabis. This accords with findings from the 1996 British Crime Survey (Ramsay & Spiller, 1997). This reported that, irrespective of age, drug misuse, including cannabis, is significantly more widespread in White than African–Caribbean people. Table 13.1 shows diagnoses in male and female sentenced prisoners, based on the reports of Gunn *et al* (1991) and Maden (1996).

TABLE 13.1.
UK residents serving a prison sentence 1988/9. Psychiatric diagnosis by ethnicity (Maden, 1996)

	Male (%)		Female (%)	
	White	Black	White	Black
Psychosis	2	4	1	6
Neurosis	6	5	16	12
Personality disorder	11	5	18	18
Substance abuse	26	9	39	15
Any diagnosis	39	22	59	42

Of adult men remanded in prison about 5% will require transfer to psychiatric hospitals because of psychotic illness, of whom half will need a medium secure bed (Maden *et al*, 1995). Unpublished data from this remand prison study (personal communication, Brooke 1999) showed that 30% of male prisoners diagnosed as having a psychosis were African–Caribbean. A similar proportion of men with mental illness remanded to Brixton Prison during one year were African–Caribbean (Bhui *et al*, 1998). They were significantly more likely than Whites to receive a diagnosis of schizophrenia and as a consequence they were more often sent to hospital under Part III of the Mental Health Act. This study and two other London studies of mentally disordered remand prisoners requiring transfer to hospital reported that between one-third and one-half were African–Caribbean (Banerjee *et al*, 1995; Murray *et al*, 1997).

Why are excessive numbers of African–Caribbeans with severe mental illnesses entering prison when it is current policy to divert mentally disordered offenders out of the criminal justice system and into health care (Home Office, 1990)? Psychiatric assessment is now well established not only at police stations, but also via court liaison schemes at many magistrates' courts (Blumenthal & Wessely, 1992). A large proportion of referrals to court diversion schemes, up to two-thirds in some studies, have committed relatively minor offences (James & Hamilton, 1991; Joseph & Potter, 1993). These cases are more likely to be diverted from custody than those charged with more serious offences. However, there is evidence that diversion services fail to act as filters for mentally disordered Black offenders to the same extent as Whites even though they are charged with offences of equivalent or lesser seriousness. The next section explores why this occurs.

Ethnic differences in contact with psychiatric services

Very few mentally disordered offenders are unknown to psychiatric services. By any measure, be it contact with the police via Section 136 (Turner *et al*, 1992), referral to court liaison schemes (Joseph & Potter, 1993), or admission to a regional secure unit (Cope & Ndegwa, 1990), between 70 and 80% of cases have a previous psychiatric history. However, between one-third and a half of mentally disordered offenders are not in contact with psychiatric services at the time of arrest. This is of particular relevance for Black patients whose previous experience of compulsory admissions, coupled with their perception of psychiatric services as racist and coercive (McGovern & Hemmings,

1994), may contribute to their dropping out of contact with community services. Black patients are in any case less likely to seek voluntary contact, both before admission and after discharge (McGovern & Cope, 1991). They may be less likely than Whites to access appropriate help. A supportive relative or friend and the presence of a general practitioner are important factors in avoiding an adverse pathway to care. Absence of these factors has been associated with police involvement and compulsory admission for Black patients (Cole *et al*, 1995).

Racial stereotyping

Criticisms of the criminal justice system with regard to discriminatory practice could equally apply to psychiatry. Practice in psychiatry has not yet been subjected to the same degree of scientific scrutiny as the criminal justice system. However, there is indirect evidence of racism, particularly institutional racism and racial stereotyping in psychiatric practice (Lipsedge, 1994). This could play a significant part in the restrictive outcome of the psychiatric process for many African–Caribbean patients. Black patients are undoubtedly perceived by some psychiatric professionals as more uncooperative, difficult, violent and dangerous. When they offend, this may contribute towards their rejection by local psychiatric services, because of a fear of violence or disruptive behaviour. Ndegwa (1998) suggests that psychiatrists tend to overpredict dangerousness in Black people and that biases in information processing may adversely affect risk assessment, leading to a more restrictive outcome. A vignette study of British psychiatrists (Lewis *et al*, 1990) reported that African–Caribbean males were perceived as potentially more violent than White males, and that psychiatrists thought that criminal proceedings were more appropriate than hospital admission. Earlier claims of racial bias contributing to over-diagnosis of schizophrenia in African–Caribbeans have not been substantiated (McGovern *et al*, 1994). Despite the violent and dangerous stereotype, there is no consistent evidence for an association between violence and Black ethnicity when diagnosis is controlled (Shah *et al*, 1991; Kennedy *et al*, 1994; also see Chapter 4).

Police contact with the mentally disordered

As a group, mentally disordered people, especially those suffering from schizophrenia, are more vulnerable to detection and arrest, unlike the majority of offenders who are either unreported or undetected (Robertson, 1988). The presence of schizophrenia has been found to increase the risk of conviction in young Black men (Wessely *et al*, 1994), who have increased arrest rates irrespective of any mental disorder. The police are extremely good at recognising mental disorder when they encounter it (Turner *et al*, 1992) and as the gatekeepers to the criminal justice system, they act as the first filter for mentally disordered offenders. Decision-making by the police at the point of detection is crucial to subsequent events. Section 136 of the Mental Health Act may be used to take suspected mentally disordered persons to a place of safety, they may be allowed to enter hospital voluntarily, under a civil section of the Act, or they may be cautioned, prosecuted or released without charge. Black people with mental disorders are more likely than Whites to have contact with the police in the community. Their relatives and friends may summon the police rather than the general practitioner if they suspect someone has a mental illness (Harrison *et al*, 1989); African–Caribbean people are more likely to present with a public disturbance when psychotic, attracting involvement of the police (Harrison *et al*, 1989; McGovern & Cope, 1991) and to be removed to a place of safety under Section 136 of the Act (Dunn & Fahy, 1990; Turner *et al*, 1992).

Although African–Caribbean people with mental disorders are more likely than Whites to present via the police, significantly fewer are diverted at the police stage. Despite obvious mental illness, they are processed by the police into the criminal justice system more often than Whites (Robertson *et al*, 1996). Remand in custody is more likely to occur if there has been violent behaviour at the time of arrest, or a serious offence has been committed. Legal factors, including previous convictions, are taken into account. Black mentally disordered offenders are more likely to have a previous criminal history (Wessely *et al*, 1994) but the reasons for remanding some Black mentally disturbed offenders into custody may be obscure. More Black offenders than Whites were remanded despite more stable housing conditions and more favorable indices of lifetime criminality, violence and substance misuse (Bhui *et al*, 1998)

Thus, the consequence of failure to divert mentally disordered Black offenders from custody is an excess of African–Caribbeans with psychosis in remand prisons. They are eventually transferred from prison to hospital under Part III of the Mental Health Act. Mentally disordered offenders may be rejected for treatment by consultants responsible for their care (Coid, 1988; Robertson *et al*, 1994) but we do not know if this occurs more frequently for Black patients. As a group, mentally disordered offenders transferred from prison are more likely to be admitted to regional secure units (RSUs) and locked wards. Inevitably, African–Caribbeans are over-represented as offender patients in secure psychiatric facilities.

Psychiatric services for mentally disordered offenders

A large proportion of mentally disordered people who present to psychiatrists through the criminal justice system never come to the attention of the forensic psychiatry services. In addition to community services, general psychiatry services provide some facilities for mentally disordered offenders and behaviourally disturbed non-offender patients in open or locked wards and in intensive care units. Specialist forensic services provide intensive psychiatric care through a high staff/patient ratio in units with locked external doors.

Patients are considered to require admission to medium secure units for one or more of the following factors:

(a) they present a significant risk of harm to others;
(b) they require a level of security provided by the medium secure unit;
(c) where the level of risk cannot be adequately assessed without admission;
(d) the patient has a mental disorder and is detainable under the Mental Health Act (informal admission may sometimes occur, e.g. on a condition of bail or readmission of former patients with their agreement);
(e) estimated length of stay is less than two years.

A large majority of patients are admitted from the courts and from prison (up to 60%) and a smaller proportion, of about 20%, of mostly non-offender patients who present management problems are transferred from local psychiatric units. Up to 15% of patients are admitted, for rehabilitation, from the high-security hospitals, Broadmoor, Rampton and Ashworth. The remainder are admitted from the community, frequently via the community forensic service.

The high-security hospitals provide maximum security through high perimeter walls, security cameras and escorting of patients and visitors. They provide care for patients with severe mental disorders who are liable seriously to endanger others through their behaviour and require treatment and care that cannot be provided at a lower level of security. Up to 75% of admissions are from the criminal justice system and the remainder mostly from NHS hospitals, including RSUs. For a detailed account of the specialist forensic services see Snowden (1995).

African–Caribbeans and forensic psychiatry services

Regional secure units

An early survey of medium secure units found that 20% of patients were from ethnic minorities, mostly African–Caribbean (Jones & Berry, 1986). This proportion is even higher in later studies. Over one-third (38%) of admissions to the Reaside Clinic, the RSU in the West Midlands, were African–Caribbean (Cope & Ndegwa, 1990). A similar proportion of first admissions to the North-West Thames RSU were African–Caribbean (Mohan *et al*, 1997). In the Reaside study significantly more African–Caribbean patients were living alone at the time of referral, had a previous criminal history and had a history of previous compulsory admissions. They were also significantly more likely to receive a diagnosis of schizophrenia and to be referred from the prison system while on remand, for urgent psychiatric treatment. In contrast, White patients were more likely to come from local psychiatric hospitals because of problems in management and from high-security hospitals for rehabilitation.

Although the African–Caribbean patients as a group had not committed more serious offences than the White patients, they were perceived by the courts as being more dangerous. Thus, they were more likely to receive a hospital order with restrictions on discharge (Sections 37/41 of the Mental Health Act 1983) because the judge considered it was necessary "to protect the public from serious harm". A recent study of offenders who had restricted hospital orders imposed by the courts reported that African–Caribbeans were over-represented, comprising one-fifth of the total sample (Street, 1998). This was partly explained by the finding that Black offender patients were significantly more likely than those from other ethnic groups to have previous convictions for violent and sexual offences. A follow-up study of conditionally discharged restricted patients found that one-quarter were recalled to hospital by the Home Office because of concerns about mental state or risk. Of this group proportionately more Black patients than Whites or Asians were recalled, having been regarded by their supervisors as causing problems with supervision (Street, 1998).

Although equal proportions of White and Black patients are previously known to their local services, African–Caribbeans are significantly more likely to progress from open to secure care. A long-term follow-up study of patients with a first admission diagnosis of schizophrenia reported that a quarter of the Black cohort, but none of the White cohort, were admitted to an RSU or high-security hospital (McGovern *et al*, 1994).

TABLE 13.2
*Ethnicity of high-security hospital patients in England, 1993
(Department of Health 1994)*

Ethnicity	n	%
White	1372	82.3
Black		
Caribbean	162	
African	19	
Other	14	
Total		11.7
Indian subcontinent	28	1.7
Other/mixed race	73	4.3
Total	1668	

High-security hospitals

The three high-security hospitals in England, Broadmoor, Rampton and Ashworth, together provide about 1600 beds for patients who require treatment in maximum security. In 1993, 84% were men and 17% were from ethnic minorities (Department of Health, 1994). Table 13.2 shows their ethnicity.

African–Caribbean patients in high-security hospitals and RSUs are almost exclusively detained under the Mental Health Act category of mental illness, mostly with a diagnosis of schizophrenia. Very few are in the legal category psychopathic disorder, in keeping with the findings in medium secure units (Cope & Ndegwa, 1990). Shubsachs *et al* (1995) suggest that the under-representation of African–Caribbeans with a classification of psychopathic disorder reflects either a bias against diagnosing the condition in African–Caribbeans or a bias against offering them treatment. White and African–Caribbean patients with mental illnesses in high-security hospitals are similar on most variables. These include age, forensic and psychiatric histories, source of admission, legal status, pharmacological treatment and length of stay (Shubsachs *et al*, 1995).

The deaths in Broadmoor Hospital of three male African–Caribbean patients between 1984 and 1991 led to three separate inquiries (Ritchie, 1985; Special Hospitals Service Authority (SHSA), 1989, 1993). The most recent report, the Prins Report (SHSA, 1993) is subtitled *"Big, Black and Dangerous?"*, referring to the common stereotype of Black psychiatric patients. It also examined the other two inquiries with the aim of identifying any significant common factors between all three deaths and making appropriate recommendations. Each of the three patients had died in a seclusion room after being placed there following disagreements with staff or other patients, resulting in violence. The inquiry examined whether racism was a factor in the treatment of the three patients. Although no overt evidence of this was found, the existence of institutional racism was identified. The inquiry also suggested that Broadmoor Hospital was a White, middle-class institution in rural Berkshire, which was an alien environment for African–Caribbean patients from poor inner-city areas. The report made a number of recommendations regarding the use of medication, seclusion and restraint as well as comments on race and cultural issues. Among the latter were: the development of an equal opportunities policy that dealt explicitly with the problem of racism in the forensic psychiatric system as a whole; the monitoring of diagnosis and medication levels and prescription among ethnic minority groups; ethnic monitoring in recruitment of staff; and the appointment of a senior manager from the ethnic minority community with responsibility for tackling racism in the special hospitals, to develop race awareness training and an effective equal opportunities policy.

A recent publication, produced under the auspices of Broadmoor Hospital (Kaye & Lingiah, 2000), examines many of the above issues. There are contributions on the experience of being a Black patient at Broadmoor, experiences of Black staff and a discussion of progress made since the Prins report (Special Hosptials Service Authority, 1993).

Future provision for mentally disordered offenders from ethnic minorities

A government review of health and social services for mentally disordered offenders (Department of Health & Home Office, 1992*a*), known as the Reed Report, listed five guiding principles which stated patients should be cared for:

(a) with regard to the quality of care and proper attention to the needs of individuals;

(b) as far as possible in the community, rather than in institutional settings;

(c) under conditions of no greater security than is justified by the degree of danger they present to themselves or others;

(d) in such a way as to maximise rehabilitation and their chances of sustaining an independent life;

(e) as near as possible to their own home or family, if they have them.

A discussion paper on issues of race and culture (Department of Health & Home Office, 1992*b*) pointed out that meeting these principles for mentally disordered offenders from Black and other ethnic minority groups would pose particular demands, given their experience of both the criminal justice system and the mental health services. Among the recommendations in the discussion paper was the establishment of strong, proactive equal opportunities policies relating to race and culture in all agencies dealing with mentally disordered offenders, as well as appropriate multi-agency training for professionals; also it was recognised that local ethnic minority communities should be involved in the planning, development and monitoring of services for mentally disordered offenders; research priorities should be discussed with ethnic minority communities and a coordinated system of ethnicity data collection should be established within all agencies concerned with minority disordered offenders.

Psychiatric patients who have committed an offence will come into contact with a wide range of mental health professionals and different agencies. Their needs will vary over time and should be met by a flexible combination of general and specialist forensic psychiatry services together with support from social services and sometimes other agencies. Regardless of ethnicity, a comprehensive service for mentally disordered offenders should contain the following elements (Chiswick, 1998):

(a) an effective emergency service to deal with police referrals;
(b) court liaison services, including provision for early diversion;
(c) liaison with probation and community services for offenders;
(d) access to a range of in-patient facilities, including open wards, intensive care and medium security;
(e) liaison with high-security hospitals for patients being transferred from or admitted to high-security care;
(f) access to supported accommodation in the community.

To this list should be added effective community aftercare and support, including assertive outreach services.

Forensic psychiatry services should take into account cultural differences, with active promotion of racial equality. This is of importance throughout psychiatry but is especially relevant to forensic psychiatry, in view of its role in social control and its association with the criminal justice system. Ethnic monitoring is crucial at all stages of contact by mentally disordered offenders with criminal justice agencies as well as the psychiatric services. This includes contact with the police, courts, diversion services and referral of remand and sentenced prisoners to general and forensic psychiatry services. Monitoring should also reveal the ethnicity of mentally disordered offenders rejected for treatment by general psychiatry services as well as patients who have lost contact with services. The aim of collecting this information is to identify problems in local service provision for Black and ethnic minority patients, so that organisation and provision of services can be more relevant and acceptable. Those in regular contact with primary care, psychiatric and social services are less likely to become mentally disordered offenders and present to forensic services. Inter-agency working is an integral part of forensic psychiatry. Steering groups that oversee inter-agency work, for example court liaison schemes, should have ethnic minority representation. Systems of risk assessment should be culturally sensitive and rely on objective observation and assessment, including collateral information that can be verified. It is essential to eliminate racial stereotyping. Training of staff from all psychiatric disciplines should include ethnic and cultural issues. This equally applies to criminal justice agencies, including the police, probation service, the magistracy and the judiciary. Ready access to advocacy services is of particular importance to Black and ethnic minority patients detained in forensic units. Secure psychiatric institutions are at particular risk of exploiting and abusing patients in their care (Cope & Chiswick, 1995).

Unless general in-patient and community services are more racially and culturally sensitive and are found to be acceptable by the African–Caribbean community, Black patients will continue to be marginalised to the more restrictive and secure parts of the psychiatric services. Being Black, male, arrest-prone and having a mental illness combine to produce the excessive numbers of African–Caribbean mentally disordered offenders described. However, the relationship between offending, psychiatric disorder and processing by the criminal justice system and psychiatric services is a complex one; it is influenced by socio-demographic factors, culture, offence characteristics and the configuration of local services as well as legal factors. Further research is needed to shed light on the intricacies of the process as it affects ethnic minorities.

References

AYE MAUNG, N. & MIRLEES-BLACK, C. (1994) *Racially Motivated Crime: a British Crime Survey Analysis*. London: Home Office.

BANERJEE, S., O'NEILL-BYRNE, K., EXWORTHY, T., *et al* (1995) The Belmarsh Scheme. A prospective study of the transfer of mentally disordered remand prisoners from prison to psychiatric units. *British Journal of Psychiatry*, **166**, 802–805.

BHUI, K., BROWN, P., HARDIE, T., *et al* (1998) African–Caribbean men remanded to Brixton Prison. Psychiatric and forensic characteristics and outcome of final court appearance. *British Journal of Psychiatry*, **172**, 337–344.

BLUMENTHAL, S. & WESSELY, S. (1992) National survey of current arrangements for diversion from custody in England and Wales. *British Medical Journal*, **305**, 1322–1325.

BROOKE, D., TAYLOR, C., GUNN, J., *et al* (1996) Point prevalence of mental disorder in unconvicted male prisoners in England and Wales. *British Medical Journal*, **313**, 1524–1527.

BROWN, C. (1984) *Black and White Britain: the Third Policy Studies Institute Survey.* London: Heinemann.

CHISWICK, D. (1998) The relationship between crime and ethnicity. In *Companion to Psychiatric Studies: 6th Edition* (eds E. C. Johnstone, C. P. L. Freeman & A. K. Zeally), pp. 807–832. Edinburgh: Churchill Livingstone.

COID, J. W. (1988) Mentally abnormal patients on remand: I. Rejected or accepted by the NHS. *British Medical Journal,* 296, 1779–1782.

COLE, E., LEAVEY, G., KING, M., *et al* (1995) Pathways to care for patients with a first episode of psychosis. A comparison of ethnic groups. *British Journal of Psychiatry,* 167, 770–776.

COPE, R. (1990) Psychiatry, ethnicity and crime. In *Principles and Practice of Forensic Psychiatry* (eds R. Bluglass & P. Bowden), pp. 849–861. London: Churchill Livingstone.

—— & CHISWICK, D. (1995) Ethical issues in forensic psychiatry. In *Seminars in Practical Forensic Psychiatry* (eds D. Chiswick & R. Cope), pp. 329–346. London: Gaskell.

—— & NDEGWA, D. (1990) Ethnic differences in admission to a regional secure unit. *Journal of Forensic Psychiatry,* 1, 365–366.

DANIEL, W. W. (1968) *Racial Discrimination in England.* Harmondsworth: Penguin Books.

DAVIES, S., THORNICROFT, G., LEESE, M., *et al* (1996) Ethnic differences in risk of compulsory psychiatric admission among representative cases of psychosis in London. *British Medical Journal,* 312, 533–537.

DEPARTMENT OF HEALTH (1994) *Report of the Working Group on High Security and Related Psychiatric Provision.* London: Department of Health.

—— (1998) *In-Patients Formally Detained in Hospitals Under the Mental Health Act 1983 and Other Legislation, England: 1991–92 to 1996–97.* Statistical Bulletin 1998/1. London: Department of Health.

—— & HOME OFFICE (1992a) *Review of Health and Social Services for Mentally Disordered Offenders and Others Requiring Similar Services.* The Reed Report. London: HMSO.

—— & —— (1992b) *Services for People from Black and Ethnic Minority Groups – Issues of Race and Culture. A Discussion Paper.* London: HMSO.

DUNN, J. & FAHY, T. A. (1990) Police admissions to a psychiatric hospital. Demographic and clinical differences between ethnic groups. *British Journal of Psychiatry,* 156, 373–378.

FITZGERALD, M. (1993) *Ethnic Minorities and the Criminal Justice System.* Royal Commission on Criminal Justice Research Study No. 20. London: HMSO.

—— & HALE, C. (1996) *Ethnic Minorities, Victimisation and Racial Harrassment.* Home Office Study No. 154. London: Home Office.

GENDERS, E. & PLAYER, E. (1989) *Race Relations in Prisons.* Oxford: Clarendon Press.

GRAHAM, J. & BOWLING, B. (1995) *Young People and Crime.* London: Home Office.

GUNN, J., MADEN, T., & SWINTON, M. (1991) *Mentally Disordered Prisoners.* London: Home Office.

HARRISON, G, OWENS, D., HOLTON, A., *et al* (1988) A prospective study of severe mental illness in Afro-Caribbean patients. *Psychological Medicine,* 18, 643–647.

——, HOLTON, A., NEILSON, D., *et al* (1989) Severe mental disorder in Afro-Caribbean patients: some social, demographic and service factors. *Psychological Medicine,* 19, 683–696.

HOME OFFICE (1990) *Provision for Mentally Disordered Offenders.* Circular 66/90. London: Home Office.

—— (1995) *The Entry of Mentally Disordered People to the Criminal Justice System.* London: Home Office Research and Planning Unit.

—— (1997a) Ethnic minorities in Great Britain. *Research and Statistics Directorate for the Home Office for the Ethnic Minorities Advisory Committee of the Judicial Studies Board.* London: Home Office.

—— (1997b) *Criminal Statistics England and Wales 1996.* Cm 3764. London: Home Office.

HOOD, R. (1992) *Race and Sentencing.* Oxford: Clarendon Press.

JAMES, D. V. & HAMILTON, L. W. (1991) The Clerkenwell Scheme: assessing efficacy and cost of a psychiatric liaison service to a magistrates' court. *British Medical Journal,* 303, 282–285.

JONES, G. & BERRY, M. (1986) Regional secure units: the emerging picture. In *Current Issues in Clinical Psychology, Volume 4* (ed G. Edwards), pp. 111–119. London: Plenum.

JOSEPH, P. L. A. & POTTER, M. (1993) Diversion from custody. I: Psychiatric assessment at the magistrates' court. *British Journal of Psychiatry*, **162**, 325–334.

KAYE, C. & LINGIAH, T. (eds) (2000) *Race, Culture and Ethnicity in Secure Psychiatric Practice. Working with Difference.* London & Philadelphia: Jessica Kingsley.

KENNEDY, J., HARRISON, J., HILLIS, T., *et al* (1994) Analysis of violent incidents in a regional secure unit. *Medicine, Science and Law*, **35**, 255–260.

LAMBERT, J. R. (1970) *Crime, Police and Race Relations.* London: Oxford University Press.

LANDAU, S. F. & NATHAN, G. (1983) Selecting delinquents for cautioning in the London metropolitan area. *British Journal of Criminology*, **23**, 128–149.

LEWIS, G., CROFT-JEFFREYS, C. & DAVID, A. (1990) Are British psychiatrists racist? *British Journal of Psychiaty*, **157**, 410–415.

LIPSEDGE, M. (1994) Dangerous stereotypes. *Journal of Forensic Psychiatry*, **5**, 14–19.

MADEN, A. (1996) *Women, Prisons and Psychiatry: Mental Disorder Behind Bars.* Oxford: Butterworth-Heinemann.

——, SWINTON, H. & GUNN, J. (1992) The ethnic origins of women serving a prison sentence. *British Journal of Criminology*, **32**, 218–221.

——, TAYLOR, C. J. A., BROOKE, D., *et al* (1995) *Mental Disorder in Remand Prisoners.* London: Home Office.

McGOVERN, D. & COPE, R. (1987) The compulsory detention of males of different ethnic groups, with special reference to offender patients. *British Journal of Psychiatry*, **150**, 505–512.

—— & —— (1991) Second-generation Afro-Caribbeans and young Whites with a first admission diagnosis of schizophrenia. *Social Psychiatry and Psychiatric Epidemiology*, **26**, 95–99.

—— & HEMMINGS, P. (1994) A follow-up of second-generation Afro-Caribbeans and White British with a first-admission diagnosis of schizophrenia. *Social Psychiatry and Epidemiology*, **29**, 8–19.

——, ——, COPE, R., *et al* (1994) Long-term follow-up of young Afro-Caribbean Britons and White Britons with a first admission diagnosis of schizophrenia. *Social Psychiatry and Psychiatric Epidemiology*, **29**, 8–19.

MAWBY, R. I. & BATTA, I. D. (1980) *Asians and Crime. The Bradford Experience.* Southall: National Association for Asian Youth.

MIRRLEES-BLACK, C., MAYHEW, P. & PERCY, A. (1996) *The 1996 British Crime Survey.* Home Office Statistical Bulletin, 19/6. London: Home Office.

MOHAN, D., MURRAY, K., TAYLOR, P., *et al* (1997) Developments in the use of regional secure unit beds over a 12-year period. *Journal of Forensic Psychiatry*, **8**, 312–335.

MURRAY, K., AKINKUNMI, A., LOCK, M., *et al* (1997) The Bentham Unit: a pilot remand and assessment service for male mentally disordered remand prisoners. I: Clinical activity in the first year and related ethical, practical and funding issues. *British Journal of Psychiatry*, **170**, 456–461.

NDEGWA, D. (1998) Clinical practice. In *Forensic Psychiatry, Race and Culture* (eds S. Fernando, D. Ndegwa & M. Wilson). London & New York: Routledge.

OWENS, D., HARRISON, G. & BOOT, D. (1991) Ethic factors in voluntary and compulsory admissions. *Psychological Medicine*, **21**, 185–196.

RAMSAY, S. & SPILLER, J. (1997) *Drug Misuse Declared in 1996: Latest Results from the British Crime Survey.* Home Office Research Study 172. London: Home Office.

RITCHIE, S. (1985) *Report to the Secretary of State for Social Services Concerning the Death of Mr Michael Martin at Broadmoor Hospital on 6th July 1984.* London: Department of Health and Social Security.

ROBERTSON, G. (1988) Arrest patterns among mentally disordered offenders. *British Journal of Psychiatry*, **153**, 313–316.

——, DELL, S., JAMES, K., *et al* (1994) Psychotic men remanded in custody to Brixton Prison. *British Journal of Psychiatry*, **164**, 55–61.

——, G., PEARSON, R. & GIBB, R. (1996) The entry of mentally disordered people to the criminal justice system. *British Journal of Psychiatry*, **169**, 172–180.

SHAH, A. K., FINEBERG, N. A. & JAMES, D. V. (1991) Violence among psychiatric in-patients. *Acta Psychiatrica Scandinavica*, **84**, 305–309.

SHUBSACHS, A. P. W., HUWS, R. W., CLOSE, A. A., *et al* (1995) Male Afro-Caribbean patients admitted to Rampton Hospital between 1977 and 1986 – a control study. *Medicine, Science and the Law*, **35**, 336–346.

SKOGAN, W. (1990) *The Police and Public in England and Wales. A British Crime Survey Report*. Home Office Research Study No. 117. London: HMSO.

SMITH, D. J. (1994) Race, crime and criminal justice. In *The Oxford Handbook of Criminology* (eds M. Maguire, R. Morgan & R. Reiner). Oxford: Oxford University Press.

—— & GRAY, J. (1983) *Police and People in London. IV: The Police in Action*. London: Policy Studies Institute.

SNOWDEN, P. (1995) Facilities and treatment. In *Seminars in Practical Forensic Psychiatry* (eds D. Chiswick & R. Cope), pp. 164–209. London: Gaskell.

SPECIAL HOSPITALS SERVICE AUTHORITY (1989) *Report of the Inquiry into the Circumstances Leading to the Death in Broadmoor Hospital of Mr Joseph Watts on 23 August 1988*. London: HMSO.

—— (1993) *Report of the Committee of Inquiry into the Death in Broadmoor Hospital of Orville Blackwood and a Review of the Deaths of Two Other Afro-Caribbean Patients. "Big, Black and Dangerous?"* The Prins Report. London: HMSO.

STREET, R. (1998) *The Restricted Hospital Order: From Court to the Community*. Home Office Research Study. London: Home Office.

TURNER, T. H., NESS, M. N. & IMISON, C. T. (1992) 'Mentally disordered persons found in public places' diagnostic and social aspects of police referrals (Section 136). *Psychological Medicine*, **22**, 765–774.

WALKER, M. A. (1989) The court disposal and remands of White, Afro-Caribbean and African men (London 1983). *British Journal of Criminology*, **29**, 353–367.

WALMSLEY, R., HOWARD, L. & WHITE, S. (1992) *The National Prison Survey 1991: Main Finding*. Home Office Research Study No. 128. London: HMSO.

WATERS, R. (1988) Race and the criminal justice process: two empirical studies on social enquiry reports and ethnic minority defendants. *British Journal of Criminology*, **28**, 82–94.

WESSELY, S., CASTLE, D., DER, G., *et al* (1991) Schizophrenia and Afro-Caribbeans. A case control study. *British Journal of Psychiatry*, **159**, 795–801.

——, ——, DOUGLAS, A. J., *et al* (1994) The criminal careers of incident cases of schizophrenia. *Psychological Medicine*, **24**, 483–502.

WILLIS, C. F. (1983) *The Use, Effectiveness and Impact of Police Stop and Search Powers*. Home Office Research Study No. 70. London: HMSO.

14 Training and supervision in cross-cultural mental health services

KAMALDEEP BHUI and DINESH BHUGRA

Editors' introduction

The training and supervision needs of those members of multi-disciplinary teams who deal with Black and other ethnic minority groups are often ignored by service providers. It is essential that these are encouraged, especially now that self-regulation and personal and continuing professional development plans are being encouraged. In this chapter the authors examine cross-cultural training for multi-disciplinary teams. It is self-evident that training is an essential component in the development and sustenance of ethnically sensitive services, yet there are a number of cultural and organisational barriers which inhibit the implementation of effective training strategies. Bhui & Bhugra suggest that only locally owned teams with genuinely multi-disciplinary team training can integrate service development and training requirements to the benefit of all service users, including those from ethnic minority groups.

In recent times, the Royal College of Psychiatrists, the Department of Health, the Institute of Psychiatry, the King's Fund Institute and the Mental Health Foundation have all hosted conferences to raise the profile of the mental health needs of Black and other ethnic minority groups in the UK (Mental Health Foundation, 1995; Royal College of Psychiatrists, 1996; Bell, 1997; Bhui, 1997; Bhugra & Bahl, 1999). In September 1997, the Department of Health hosted an international conference where professionals, managers and policy-makers from the USA and the UK met in order to share their experiences about health care for ethnic minorities. Despite this persistent political activity, there has been an inadequate level of pragmatic change to local psychiatric unit policies, procedures and clinical practice. The hasty series of legislative responsibilities directed at psychiatric practice distracted providers from any systematic scrutiny of the service provision requirements of ethnic minorities (Bhui *et al*, 1995*b*). Only where there have been tragedies or crises which involve ethnic minorities are policy-makers and providers more engaged with ethnic minority mental health. Hence, the Ritchie Report highlights race and culture as a legitimate focus of omissions in the care of Christopher Clunis (Ritchie *et al*, 1994). This is mirrored in the response of at least one purchasing authority which emphasises that over 70% of their regional secure unit admissions were Black and over 80% were men (Lambeth, Southwark and Lewisham Health Commission, 1994). Such concerns are often compounded by a realisation that racism in society is inevitable and manifest within institutional structures and that mental health services structures might perpetuate the inadequate delivery of care to patients from Black and other ethnic minority groups (Wilson, 1993; Fernando, 1996; Institute for Public Policy Research, 1997).

Clinical assessment and management of individuals belonging to different cultures from that of the mental health professional cannot be undertaken in isolation from the atmosphere and mores of the society in which these two key participants meet. The professional–patient interaction is built upon patients' previous experience of services and their culturally derived idiom of distress, as well as their socio-economic and educational status. Similarly, mental health professionals bring their own educational background, their unique training experiences, profession-based beliefs and expectations, their cultural background and their real or perceived understanding of the individual's cultural values and experiences (Leff, 1988; Bhugra, 1993). Training about ethnicity, culture and the interaction with illness is especially pertinent in psychiatric practice, where assessment and management are so heavily informed by subjective judgements. These are always patterned by the observer's (professional's) and patient's individual culturally embedded health beliefs and value systems (Helman, 1990; Mezzich, 1995).

Racism and prejudice are but two of the key processes which might be enacted in the interaction between service users and service providers. Others include ignorance of cultural norms, emphasis on colour-blindness (i.e. seeing all patients as being equal irrespective of their needs and ethnic and cultural factors), undue emphasis on diagnosis rather than needs, inability to distinguish between demands and unmet need, and unrealistic expectations placed on the individual rather than on the provider. Although this list is not comprehensive, it highlights key areas which can be usefully addressed within professional training, team-based training, and in the context of educational and clinical supervision. Although training in cultural psychiatry for existing service providers and policy-makers is essential, there is little information to guide providers about the specific profile of topics that should be included in training. The variety of formats that can be selected further complicate the selection of training formats (see Box 14.1).

Box 14.1
Training for cross-cultural mental health services

Duration	Single event
	Series of events
	A rolling programme to suit organisation, group, individuals
Modality	Conference – national, regional, trust, locality team level
	By attendance or correspondence course
Trainers	Mental health professionals: single professions or multi-disciplinary
	Independent consultancies
	Voluntary sector
	Academies in anthropology and sociology, ethnic relations, ethics, philosophy
Theoretical model	Self-reflective and experiential
	Behavioural: change behaviour without thinking about motivations
	Cognitive: questioning belief systems that appear to cause inequality
Trainees	Individuals
	Groups
	The organisation's 'culture'
Material	Socio-demographics of ethnic groups in the UK
	Racism and anti-racism
	Culture, lifestyle and interpersonal behaviour
	Culturally determined health beliefs and help seeking
	Religious belief systems
	Alternative healing (including medical) systems
	Alternative psychological systems
	Which ethnic or cultural groups?
Evaluation	None
	Exams – written, oral
	Literature review or thesis to be prepared
	Case studies
	Formal diploma
	Formal postgraduate degree
Crises in the programme	Tutors provide individual supervision
	Line manager supervision
	Group supervision

Efforts to improve the quality of care for ethnic minorities

Organisational and government policy

Significant proportions of purchasers (54%), family health service authorities (35%) and providers (42%) have an equal opportunity policy and provide regular training on anti-discriminatory policy and cultural awareness (48%, 46% and 73% respectively; National Association for Health Authorities and Trusts, 1996). Forty-five per cent of undergraduates, 25% of postgraduates and 59% of general practitioners reported the inclusion of health and culture in medical training (British Medical Association, 1995). These are modest gains and more needs to be done. Furthermore, policy alone does not lead to better practice without an operationalisation of managerial activity, clinical skill acquisition and competency assessments.

The experience from the USA, although not always directly applicable to the British context, shows that an overall strategy requires the commitment of local and national government as well as provider units (see Box 14.2). Only through policies that support multicultural initiatives in public mental health will multicultural populations improve in their overall health status (Cassimir & Morrison, 1993). The general principles of adapting local services have previously been discussed (Bhui *et al*, 1995*b*). Individual provider units should determine the most locally suitable infra-structural requirements to optimally implement their chosen models of 'culture work'. These models can never be 'picked off

---

Box 14.2
Issues in service design and utilisation from the USA

Assessing needs
Importance of auspice and location
Staff competence and training
Need for policy and administrative support
Federal government award to National Institute of Mental Health for research
New York State government commits funding
Multicultural advisory committee appointed by commissioner of mental health
Minority education, research and training
Institute trains the trainers

the shelf'. They can only be assembled after full consultation of local communities; this requires a more sophisticated approach than the 'take me to your leader' syndrome (Chandra, 1996). Although the 'local' initiative has all these advantages, it leaves responsibility for progress to individual providers and purchasers. If all purchasers and providers take local action there would be no need for government directives. However, the experience to date is that little pragmatic action takes place unless there is a clear top-down policy that enables a bottom-up strategy to flourish. Charting progress carefully is a minimum requirement of all strategies. Audit tools to examine the cultural sensitivity of community- and hospital-based psychiatric services are being developed (Sathyamoorthy & Ford, 1997). However, they are not being routinely applied in provider units.

Ethnic monitoring

The introduction of ethnic monitoring is the only visible statutory sector response to date that demonstrates inequalities of health care for Black and other ethnic minorities. Even this is poorly performed and early returns have been less than adequate. Ethnic monitoring, although well intentioned, is bedevilled by the widely acknowledged instability of self-rated ethnicity as a meaningful proxy measure of health and lifestyle and culture (Singh, 1997); hence the data will give an indication of the patient's self-rated ethnic origin, but say little of their cultural identity or health-related lifestyle and belief systems. This information may have no scope to influence health promotion and interventions at a clinical and managerial level. For example, information on first language is invaluable as it is known that psychiatric diagnostic evaluations and health education can only be complete if the diagnostic assessment is in the patient's first language (Collins *et al*, 1984; Westermeyer & Janca, 1997). A similar use for ethnicity is not readily identified; to what end ethnic data collection is useful, beyond monitoring ethnic under- and over-representation in psychiatric service planning, remains unresolved.

The Patient's Charter: effective for ethnic minorities?

Patients' culturally grounded rules concerning the expression of dissatisfaction with services and lodging complaints has been little examined. If interpreters are required to seek health care and to complain, then a grievance procedure will take longer and make greater demands on a service's resources. Do service providers advertise the provision of interpreters for complaints procedures and do they have in place procedures which ensure the rapid translation and communication of dissatisfactions? There are cultural sanctions which determine a readiness to complain or even to assertively ask for a better care package. Cultures which hold the helping professions in high esteem would deem any expectation beyond what is available as 'ungrateful'. Specific cultures that are from deprived and disenfranchised groups feel grateful for any care, even if it others would judge it to be a minimum or inadequate level of health care. Intense needs therefore manifest as overwhelming dependency even on an incompetent service. This constellation of factors is unlikely to favour assertive communications of dissatisfaction for fear of help being withdrawn.

Comprehensive education and training for the workforce

There is no global package to meet the training needs of the diversity of mental health professionals; psychiatrists, nurses, psychologists, managers, administrators, researchers and social workers all have distinct 'professional cultures' which include a 'profession-determined' psychological template for how one works with colleagues and patients. Professional-directed training packages can not accurately convey the complex nuances of language and behaviour for all potential ethnic, linguistic and racial groups. A multitude of information packs have been compiled, but their impact on the quality of care, satisfaction and clinical outcome is unknown (Good Practices in Mental Health, 1995). Our experience is that integrating training and service development strategies affords a valuable opportunity to deal with these problems.

The history of cross-cultural mental health services

Moffic & Kinzie (1996) have traced the development of cross-cultural psychiatric services (see Table 14.1). In Britain it seems that statutory sector service adaptation is the most mature stage and the only affordable and practically viable option which could become operative immediately (Bhui, 1997). It is the least likely to unnecessarily deplete scarce resources from other priority services. It is also the most easily regulated, such that the quality of care can be assured. It does require that the independent, voluntary and statutory providers and the local ethnic communities share their grievances and pool their aspirations for local mental health services.

TABLE 14.1
Phases of including culture in service development

Phase 1	Recognition of difference	An awareness that ethnic minority populations have different health care needs.
Phase 2	Treatment variations	An awareness that desired treatments vary across racial and ethnic groups and that there is a differential use of services.
Phase 3	Treatment changes	Altering staff and service characteristics. Using bilingual staff and non-Western modes of healing.
Phase 4	Cultural biology	Demonstration that not only are some groups psychologically and culturally different but that they have unique race- and culture-based responses to interventions. This can be understood not only from a biomedical model (different rates of metabolism of drug), but also from a socio-cultural response (different expectations and degrees of adherence to interventions).
Phase 5	Newer directions	These seek innovation in service structures and styles of care delivery such that the service optimally manages distress in the targeted cultural groups. Thus, the involvement of family, offering physical investigations and assessments, and services suited to specific refugee groups which are still integral to generic service. Essentially broadening the remit to achieve more.

In the realm of appropriate health service research for ethnic minorities, the statutory sector and the research institutions have responded in a rather fragmented way. All that is known is that existing services are found to be inadequate and Black and other ethnic minority patients are less satisfied the longer they remain in contact with these services (Wilson, 1993; Leavey *et al*, 1997). Primary care is less often effective in preventive efforts or as a source of early intervention for Black and other ethnic minorities. Hence, the conclusion is often that ethnic minorities present through crisis services later in the natural history of their illness episode (Bhui, 1997). One consequence of this apparent ineffectiveness of statutory services is the emergence of independent separate services for Black people; these are usually on short-term funding as pilot projects and rarely become integral to a comprehensive and ongoing service (Bhui *et al*, 2000). Only recently has there been an emphasis in statutory services and academic centres on high-quality health service research and service provision to explore and eradicate inequalities in health and health care. The future of separate services for ethnic minorities is under close scrutiny. The voluntary sector and independent organisations have developed good practice models but their efforts and ideology remain firmly bounded with little impact on service planning in the statutory sector (Ahmad & Atkin, 1996; Gauntlett *et al*, 1996; Bhui, 1997; Bhui *et al*, 2000). Certainly qualitative data have suggested that 'Black only' projects are more attractive (Wilson, 1995) as they provide non-stigmatising care that is packaged in the context of patients' unique circumstances; it is argued that these cultural contexts are only understood by the voluntary and independent sector (Gray, 1999). There is actually little quantitative research evidence to favour any specific independent, voluntary or statutory sector model of culturally sensitive service. Specifically no innovative service evaluations take account of clinical outcomes, satisfaction and the economics of alternative service provision (Bhui *et al*, 2000).

Comprehensive cross-cultural mental health service models

We now turn to some models of multiculturally sensitive and effective service delivery. These models can resolve the training dilemmas in the context of service development and the multi-disciplinary team approach. Each approach has advantages and disadvantages which will influence whether it is a viable option for any specific service in the UK. "The therapist/health professional must try and assume the internal frame of reference of the client and perceive the world as the client sees it, as well as seeing the client as he/she sees himself" (Cassimir & Morrison, 1993). Even with an adequate cultural knowledge base, the professional's skills and competencies can only be progressively upgraded by ongoing service-based training. High-quality clinical and managerial supervision can reinforce the gains of training and education initiatives. These models assume that community psychiatric teams carry and retain responsibility to address the needs of local Black and other ethnic minority patients. Relying on voluntary and separate services to address the needs of these populations denies the statutory sector's responsibility to serve all citizens.

One team-wide strategy involves each member of the team accepting a liaison role for a specific community; the named individual makes contact with and explores the health beliefs and

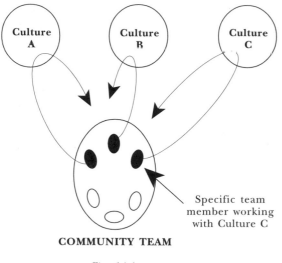

COMMUNITY TEAM

Fig. 14.1
Model of cross-cultural service delivery

the problems of a specific community in a broad context (Fig. 14.1). Mental health issues are then understood in the context of this background information which is acquired slowly and after gaining the trust of the community. As the named professional becomes more accessible and culturally skilled to serve the targeted community so his or her knowledge and skills are communicated to other team members. An alternative model involves culture-, race- or ethnic-group-specific voluntary and independent providers to participate fully in regular service provision, training and supervision (Bhui *et al*, 1995*a*). This requires that such organisations are functionally integrated with the statutory sector. Inherent in this model are potential tensions and rivalries to do with autonomy, funding, and the possibility that the voluntary sector may have to compromise its way of working in order to accommodate the procedures and regulations of the funders and the more powerful statutory provider (Jennings, 1996). None the less, the gains for the statutory provider and the voluntary provider are considerable in terms of mutual education, support, shared risk assessment and supervision. Joint work with more traditional healers who use acupuncture, stress reduction, dietary advice, exercise advice, spiritual healing and religious interventions might be considered unorthodox. These treatments are sought by Black and otherethnic minority patients (Mental Health Foundation,

1995). More substantial joint working with such providers is, therefore, one step towards a more holistic service which might successfully engage peoples who do not currently engage with statutory services because of objections to more traditional models of psychiatric practice.

Some services deploy members from the targeted population after giving them suitable training and ongoing supervision (Timpson, 1984). This approach has been successful in involving the local Native American community in planning committees such that they prioritised the local needs, sanctioned the types of interventions to be offered and offered directive guidance on community taboos and prohibitions. The only problem was that only a small proportion of the cases seen (1.4%) had severe mental illnesses. However, as local non-mental health professionals were acting as carers, the resources of the local services could be more effectively concentrated on those with severe mental illness. This approach has the advantage of educating the local community but not compromising their own beliefs. Clearly there will be disagreements if the professional disagrees with an indigenous intervention or fears that unless a medical intervention is delivered there will be a deterioration. Furthermore, should the professional then act in accord with legislative requirements but in defiance of the local community's preferred plans, any alliance is likely to be challenged. Clearly, such scenarios should be anticipated and openly discussed before they take place. A willingness to re-examine a treatment plan and service development strategy and to continue to engage the community in dialogue and decision-making is essential.

Creative approaches such as these could succeed in engaging alienated groups once their trust in the service and the individual link person increases. Patients can then negotiate with the clinician in an air of mutual respect and without the anticipation of being powerless to influence their care. The use of alternative and voluntary sector practitioners will challenge the more biomedically minded psychiatric professionals. Non-pharmacological healing treatments are notoriously difficult to evaluate. If only evidence-based interventions are sanctioned, then potentially valuable interventions will be overlooked (Ernst, 1995; Vincent & Lewith, 1995). Finding complementary practitioners, their fees and a venue to evaluate such treatments among patients who do not engage or who really do not benefit from standard packages of care might be fruitful. Extensive use of these more natural and less medicalised interventions is only possible if they prove to be clinically and economically sensible treatment options.

Clinical and educational supervision

Clinical supervision is virtually mandatory for trainees regardless of profession. Psychiatrists, psychologists, social workers and managers all share in this approach to appraise one's work, modify practice and ensure informed decision-making by consulting with a senior colleague. Even qualified professionals have a line management structure which allows them to seek help and discuss complex cases along with some level of pastoral counselling. This process of supervision involves constructing a bridge between what the supervisees have learnt in didactic teaching and course work and what they need to do in practical clinical situations (Gopaul-McNicoll & Brice-Baker, 1998). However, the key to this bridge remains the service user whose needs, problems and possible solutions to these problems are being discussed. Where such patients are from an ethnic minority, or do not share a culture with the health professional, supervision requires these dimensions to be actively scrutinised. The individual supervisee's and supervisor's cultural and ethnic identity play an important role in the discussion about the patient–professional interaction and conclusions about favoured interventions or strategies to ensure the best health outcome for the patient.

The interaction between the supervisee and the supervisor is often unequal, in terms of both profession-based hierarchy and experience. The supervisor usually dictates the duration, place and type of supervision, as well as the number and types of patients handed to the supervisee and often makes some formal report of the supervisee's competence. The quality and the type of supervision is variable as with psychotherapy supervision there will be a need to understand transference and counter-transference responses. As patients from minority groups bring their expectations to consultations, so the minority trainee may experience conflict between their cultural and ethnic identity and their profession-based role which carries responsibilities and expectations that are inculcated from the majority culture. If the trainer is from an ethnic minority group and the trainee is not, the latter might be surprised by feelings of alienation, lack of confidence in the trainer and concern about the quality of supervision by seeing a minority member in a position of power. If such issues are not discussed openly with ethical responsibility to the patient taking precedence, then there might be rebellion or selective reporting of clinical material to which the supervisee anticipates a favourable or unfavourable response from the trainer (Remington & Da Costa, 1989). It must be emphasised that these phenomena are not straightforward, unidimensional or this clear. Cook (1994) argues very cogently that if individuals are being seen as not belonging to a homogeneous racial or ethnic group, it is only fair to see the interaction between the trainee and the trainer in a multi-faceted, multi-level manner beyond the dichotomous categorisation of race. Supervision might fail if there is an active denial and avoidance of such strong feelings for fear that more powerful feelings might emerge. These would, and should, test the critical thinking faculties of the supervisory dyad; however, such a process might inadvertently result in the patient's material being regarded as a subsidiary or separate issue. Such a derailment should not be allowed – as whatever the reaction in supervision, it must be understood in terms of the patient's material as well as the personal development of the trainer and trainee. Neither is exempt from a new learning experience. For the trainees, cross-cultural competence in assessment, management, dealing with conflict, awareness of their own prejudices as well as those of the society, the generation of research questions and improvements of research data interpretation are absolutely crucial outcomes. Gopaul-McNicoll (1997) has described a cross-cultural competency instrument which is designed to provide trainers and trainees with information to determine their effectiveness as cross-cultural mental health workers. Although this is not a test or an examination, it is likely to be seen as such by employers and employees alike. However, it provides a very clear way forward.

Multi-disciplinary teams as a focus for effective training

The interaction between the trainees and the trainers takes place in the context of the multi-disciplinary team and the attitudes of participants to multi-disciplinary functioning, leadership within the team and demands of other members on the team. The issues pertinent to the supervision dyad must be anticipated in the group context also. Indeed, group supervision is likely to yield a more diverse range of feeling and responses to clinical material.

Profession-based cross-cultural training for social work, psychology and psychiatry and nursing core professional training are in their infancy (Central Council for Education Training and Social Work, 1991; Nadirshaw, 1993; Campinha-Bacote, 1994; Royal College of Psychiatrists, 1996). The multi-disciplinary team must equip itself with the necessary skills, competencies and knowledge essential for the effective and appropriate provision of high-quality treatment for individuals from any ethnic group (Bhui *et al*, 1995*a*). The difficulties of doing this in an economically unfavourable time and of maintaining progress despite the evolving locality based ethnic, cultural and social demography compounds the cautious commitment to any specific strategy. Community teams require careful organisation, clear boundaries and leadership in order to manage transactions between multiple agencies (Richards, 1996) and to maintain autonomy to function effectively.

At a local level, there is a dilemma as to who should take the lead on race, culture and ethnicity as a training need: the professional bodies, local managers or the individuals themselves. Even if profession-based training is provided it probably would not address the populations or working environment in which professionals might find themselves several years after qualification.

The models outlined here interweave local training and service delivery agendas. Local hospital trusts bear some responsibility to train their staff in order to optimally serve local patients. The strength of adopting a multi-disciplinary team model is that each member will acquire locally relevant theoretical knowledge and skills alongside other members of their team. The effectiveness of their training experience as a group will constantly be revisited in the joint care of their patients. Ethnic minority mental health is an emotive issue perhaps most subject to conflict between biomedical, psychological, social and spiritual models of health care (Mental Health Foundation, 1995). There is no conflict if a team-wide strategy is adopted in preference over a profession-based one. A team-wide approach includes sharing operational styles, risk management, assessment strategies, alliance building and engagement strategies. A team-wide policy for biomedical, social, psychological, complementary and religiously appropriate treatment can then be realised, taking full account of economic limitations.

Risk management

African and Caribbean populations are more often admitted on Mental Health Act sections in comparison with White samples (Bebbington *et al*, 1981; Moodley & Perkins, 1991; Wessely *et al*, 1991; King *et al*, 1994; Davies *et al*, 1996). Medication is more often administered at higher doses and by injection for Black patients (Littlewood & Cross, 1980; Lloyd & Moodley, 1992). Each provider unit must revisit the inequalities of health and health care delivery across ethnic groups by systematic audit to examine local practice. Part of the difficulty is that clinicians lack skills in risk assessment; they might respond more to fears of litigation and stereotype rather than to a patient's actual clinical and biographical details. Specific audits about culture, race and treatment practice, and educational training about cultures and risk management are essential in a culturally competent service. For example, body language and aggression sanctions differ across cultures and misreading these can result in detrimental and more restrictive treatment (Bhugra & Bhui, 1997). A regular audit could form the foundation of locally appropriate in-service training informed by each team's and trust's strengths and weaknesses. Risk management strategies owned by the team are favourable as a 'profession-free' procedure to assess risk and to be resilient to changes of staff and the loss of charismatic team enthusiasts.

Within the multi-disciplinary team the question of who provides supervision to whom and how it is done must be clarified. For example, the medical staff may provide supervision to junior doctors, medical students as well as nurses or occupational therapists, but the line management in the latter two groups may well be quite different. Special expertise ought to be the main indicator of who should be sought out to supervise a specific issue. In community settings such a process becomes even more complex and an openness to seek supervision outside of established and perhaps restrictive structures should be considered and sanctioned at the outset. Similarly the individual supervisor or the group supervision activity must have the courage to recognise the limits of competence and seek specialist supervision when necessary from an independent person or organisation.

Conclusions

Training is a recommendation from the majority of conferences, consultation exercises and research reports, but no universal training strategy exists. We have presented a range of in-service training and service development models; statutory sector service adaptation is the only practically viable option that could become operative immediately. Local action to reach national targets seems the only way to make progress beyond collecting and hoarding more data.

References

AHMAD, W. & ATKIN, K. (eds) (1996) *Race and Community Care.* Buckingham: Open University Press.

BEBBINGTON, P., *et al* (1981) Psychiatric disorders in selected immigrant groups in Camberwell. *Social Psychiatry*, **16**, 43–51.

——, FEENEY, S. T., FLANNIGAN, C. B., *et al* (1994) Inner London collaborative audit of admissions in two health districts. II: Ethnicity and the use of the mental health act. *British Journal of Psychiatry*, **165**, 743–749.

BELL, A. (1997) Are mental health services bad for black (African Caribbean) people? *Share*, **17**, 6–7.

BHUGRA, D. (1993) Influence of culture. In *Principles of Psychiatry* (eds D. Bhugra & J. Leff). London: Blackwell Science.

—— & BAHL, V. (eds) (1999) *Ethnicity: an Agenda for Mental Health.* London: Gaskell.

—— & BHUI, K. (1997) Cross-cultural psychiatric assessment. *Advances in Psychiatric Treatment*, **3**, 103–110.

BHUI, K. (1997) London's ethnic minorities and the provision of mental health services. In *London's Mental Health Services* (eds Johnson *et al*), London: King's Fund Institute.

——, FOULDS, S. G., BAUBIN, F, *et al* (1995*a*) Developing culturally sensitive community psychiatric services. *British Journal of Health Care Management*, **1**, 817–822.

——, CHRISTIE, Y. & BHUGRA, D. (1995*b*) The essential elements of culturally sensitive psychiatric services. *International Journal of Social Psychiatry*, **41**, 242–256.

——, BHUGRA, D. & McKENZIE, K. (2000) *Specialist Services for Ethnic Minority Groups?* Maudsley Discussion Paper no. 8. London: Institute of Psychiatry.

BRITISH MEDICAL ASSOCIATION (1995) *Multicultural Health Care. Current Practice and Future Policy in Medical Education.* London: British Medical Association.

CAMPINHA-BACOTE, J. (1994) Cultural competence in psychiatric mental health nursing. A conceptual model. *Nursing Clinics of North America*, **29**, 1–8.

CASSIMIR, G. & MORRISON, B. J. (1993) Re-thinking work with multicultural populations. *Community Mental Health Journal*, **29**, 547–559.

CENTRAL COUNCIL FOR EDUCATION TRAINING AND SOCIAL WORK (1991) *Setting the Context for Change: Anti-Racist Social Work Education.* London: Central Council for Education and Training Social Work.

CHANDRA, J. (1996) Roles and models for purchasing health for black and ethnic minority communities. In *Locating the Goal Posts. Health Promotion and Purchasing for Black and Minority Ethnic Health.* London: Health Education Authority.

COLLINS, J. L., MATHURA, C. B. & RISHER, D. L. (1984) Training psychiatric staff to treat a multicultural patient population. *Hospital and Community Psychiatry*, **35**, 372–376.

COOK, D. (1994) Racial identity in supervision. *Counsellor Education and Supervision*, **34**, 132–141.

DAVIES, S., Thornicroft, G., Leese, M, *et al* (1996) Ethnic differences in risk of compulsory psychiatric admission among representative cases of psychosis in London. *British Medical Journal*, **312**, 533–537.

ERNST, E. (1995) Complementary medicine: common misconceptions. *Journal of the Royal Society of Medicine*, **88**, 244–247.

FERNANDO, S. (1996) *Mental Health in Multi-Ethnic Society.* London: Routledge.

GAUNTLETT, FORD, R. & MUIJEN, M. (1996) *Teamwork. Models of Outreach in Urban Multi-Cultural Settings.* London: Sainsbury Centre for Mental Health.

GOOD PRACTICES IN MENTAL HEALTH (1995) *Not Just Black and White. An Information Pack About Mental Health Services for People from Black Communities.* London: Good Practices in Mental Health.

GOPAUL-McNICOLL, S. (1997) *Multicultural, Multi-Modal Multi-Systems Approach in Working with Culturally Different Families.* Westport, CT: Praeger.

—— & BRICE-BAKER, J. (1998) *Cross-Cultural Practice: Assessment, Treatment and Training.* New York: John Wiley.

GRAY, P. (1999) Voluntary organisations' perspectives on mental health needs. In *Ethnicity: an Agenda for Mental Health* (eds D. Bhugra & V. Bahl), pp. 202–210. London: Gaskell.

HELMAN, C. (1990) *Culture, Health and Illness.* Oxford: Butterworth-Heinemann.

INSTITUTE FOR PUBLIC POLICY RESEARCH (1997) *IPPR Attitudes to Race Survey.* London: Institute for Public Policy Research.

JENNINGS, S. (1996) *Creating Solutions. Developing Alternatives in Black Mental Health.* London: King's Fund.

KING, M., COKER, E., LEAVEY, G., *et al* (1994) Incidence of psychotic illness in London: comparison of ethnic groups. *British Medical Journal*, **309**, 1115–1119.

LAMBETH, SOUTHWARK & LEWISHAM HEALTH AUTHORITY (1994) *Local Responses to the Ritchie Report of Three Borough-Based Conferences held July/August 1994*. London: Lambeth Southwark & Lewisham Health Authority.

LEAVEY, G. KING, M. COLE, E., *et al* (1997) First-onset psychotic illness: patients' and relatives' satisfaction with services. *British Journal of Psychiatry*, **170**, 53–57.

LEFF, J. (1988) *Psychiatry Around the Globe. A Transcultural View*. London: Gaskell.

LITTLEWOOD, R. & CROSS, S. (1980) Ethnic minorities and psychiatric services. *Sociology of Health and Illness*, **2**, 194–201.

LLOYD, P & MOODLEY, P. (1992) Psychotropic medication and ethnicity: an inpatient survey. *Social Psychiatry and Psychiatric Epidemiology*, **27**, 95–101.

MENTAL HEALTH FOUNDATION (1995) *Mental Health in Black and Minority Ethnic People. Time for Action. The Report of a Seminar on Race and Mental Health. "Towards a strategy"*. London: Mental Health Foundation.

MEZZICH, J. (1995) Cultural formulation and comprehensive diagnosis. Clinical and research perspectives. *Psychiatric Clinics of North America*, **18**, 649–657.

MOFFIC, H. S. & KINZIE, J. D. (1996) The history and future of cross cultural psychiatric services. *Community Mental Health Journal*, **32**, 581–592.

MOODLEY, P. & PERKINS, R. (1991) Routes to psychiatric inpatient care in an inner London borough. *Social Psychiatry and Psychiatric Epidemiology*, **26**, 47–51.

NADIRSHAW, Z. (1993) The implications of equal opportunities in training in clinical psychology: a realist's view. *Clinical Psychology Forum*, **54**, 27–28.

NATIONAL ASSOCIATION FOR HEALTH AUTHORITIES AND TRUSTS (1996) *Good Practice and Quality Indicators in Primary Health Care. NHS Ethnic Health Unit in Conjunction with Kensington and Westminster Health Authority*. Bradford: NHS Ethnic Health Unit.

REMINGTON, G. & DA COSTA, G. (1989) Ethnocultural factors in resident supervision: black supervisors and white supervisees. *American Journal of Psychotherapy*, **43**, 398–404.

RICHARDS, H. (1996) Managing boundaries and spaces: leadership in mental health. *British Journal of Health Care Management*, **2**, 375–382.

RITCHIE, H., DICK, D. & LINGHAM (1994) *The Report of the Inquiry into the Care and Treatment of Christopher Clunis*. London: HMSO.

ROGERS, A., PILGRIM, D. & LACEY, R. (1993) Experiencing psychiatry. Users' views of services. London. Macmillan.

ROYAL COLLEGE OF PSYCHIATRISTS (1996) *Report of the Working Party to Review Psychiatric Practices and Training in a Multi-Ethnic Society*. Council Report 48. London: Royal College of Psychiatrists.

SATHYAMOORTHY, G. & FORD, R. (1997) *Audit Tool to Assess the Cultural Sensitivity of Mental Health Services: Staff and User Interview Schedules*. London: Sainsbury Centre for Mental Health.

SINGH, S. P. (1997) Ethnicity in psychiatric epidemiology: the need for precision. *British Journal of Psychiatry*, **171**, 305–308.

TIMPSON, J. (1984) Indian Mental Health: changes in the delivery of care in North Western Ontario. *Canadian Journal of Psychiatry*, **29**, 234–241.

VINCENT, C. & LEWITH, G. (1995) Placebo controls for acupuncture studies. *Journal of the Royal Society*, **88**, 199–202.

WESSELY, S., CASTLE, D., DER, G., *et al* (1991) Schizophrenia and Afro-Caribbeans: a case control study. *British Journal of Psychiatry*, **159**, 795–801.

WESTERMEYER, J. & JANCA, A. (1997) Language, culture and psychopathology: conceptual and methodological issues. *Transcultural Psychiatry*, **34**, 291–311.

WILSON, M. (1993) *Britain's Black Communities*. London: NHS Management Executive Mental Health Task Force & King's Fund Centre.

—— (1995) *Alternatives in Black Mental Health. The Sanctuary Model*. London: King's Fund Centre.

15 Needs assessment and service evaluation

DINESH BHUGRA, SASHI SASHIDHARAN and MARTIN COMMANDER

Editors' introduction

Concepts of mental health and mental illness tend to vary across cultures. Mental illness is seen as a conglomeration of symptoms and signs of dysfunction. The starting point for the provision of high-quality services of any kind is an accurate assessment of the needs of the population to be served. Needs assessment is not an easy task – even in a culturally homogenous population – the difficulties are multiplied in an ethically diverse catchment area. Not only does the definition of need (and the extent to which it is unmet) vary from group to group and service user to service user and different disciplines in a multi-disciplinary team, the definition of ethnic groups must be clearly understood as well. In this chapter Bhugra et al put forward some of the options for identifying needs and also argue that evaluation of services is crucial. Such a requirement is all too often overlooked or attempted in a scientifically unconvincing fashion which can only result in potentially promising innovations being ignored or discredited.

As has already been discussed in this volume, there is little doubt that the concepts of mental health and mental illness differ across cultures, nations and ethnic groups. Any emotional distress can be defined according to an individual's social status, previous experiences, education and religious and cultural background. This allows the individuals and their carers to seek help from folk or social sectors even before they reach the professional sector. However, an array of personal concepts also means that an individual's health cannot be truly measured as an epidemiological exercise.

Mental illness may be seen as a conglomeration of symptoms and signs of dysfunction which are deviating from the societal norms, and often the society or the culture decides what is abnormal and what is normal behaviour.

Hence, it is likely that culture itself will determine the needs as well as clinical outcomes. It is incredibly important that needs are identified clearly and carefully, but it is also equally valid that a host of social and cultural issues present fundamental obstacles to the satisfactory attainment of consensus over the definitions and domains of needs assessment. There is often a discrepancy between what the individual sees as needs which must be met and what their carers and society at large identify as needs. The needs must be differentiated from demands. We will highlight some of the questions which are important in identifying and measuring need and provide an overview of the role of ethnicity in the process of needs assessment.

Definition of needs

Assessing needs (both health and social), especially in regard to mental illness, is an integral part of planning and delivering high-quality health care to individuals and the ethnic cultural groups to which they belong. The pressure on finite resources available for health care suggests that needs can and should be measured to prioritise delivery of health care.

Needs can be defined in a number of ways – needs are, when fulfilled, something that people can benefit from. These reflect the services which are being asked for. Whereas demands can fluctuate and are affected by various socio-demographic factors on the part of those who are making them, such as higher socio-economic status, education, available knowledge of health services and prevalent fashion and trends, needs are related to the overall aim of a healthier population. Stevens & Galsbay (1990) highlight differences between needs, demands and wants (what people desire whether or not they are translated into demands). Rawaf (1998) suggests that the purpose of any health (and social) needs assessment is to determine the range of services required to meet the identified needs of diverse populations exposed to or suffering from a condition, but also to improve service planning and resource allocation, to identify potential areas for improvement in health care delivery, to identify the most effective interventions and to monitor changes in relation to factors which influence health. In addition, such processes of needs assessment have been used for generating information for advocacy, responding to central directives and advance research and development.

The actual process of assessing health needs is more than the collection of routine data to measure the extent of disease or disability in any given community. Such a process is not static. In the assessment, any impact of disease or disability on health and social care needs must be measured. Rawaf (1998) argues that in the health needs assessment population profile (population structure, environment, life styles, cultures and religions), disease and disability, effectiveness of intervention (primary, secondary and tertiary preventions; treatment and management), measurements of perceptions and expectations, and social values are key factors to be assessed.

Measurement of needs

Three common approaches in the measurement are epidemiological, comparative and corporate. Each of these approaches yields a different set of factors which contribute to fuller and comprehensive needs assessment; for example, any epidemiological data will yield rates of a condition and the expected disease burden can then be measured. The comparative approach will measure process and outcome indicators to compare the services across different groups and identify patterns of service utilisation, risks of exposure and levels of morbidity and mortality. The corporate approach provides an overall view following consultations with professional, public and other interested parties. Several sources can be utilised for such data collection.

Problems with measurement

In measuring health needs for ethnic minority groupsa key problem is in the definitions of ethnicity and mental health itself (Sashidharan & Commander, 1998). The second problem is the current vogue of emphasising number-crunching from existing data rather than assessing these needs in terms of value, evaluation and priority ranking. As Rawaf (1998) emphasises, this numerical counting, in order to be a meaningful process for needs assessment measurements, has to be expanded to help in deciding against competing priorities within an acceptable social value framework. In real terms, he argues, needs will depend upon benefits as well as costs and such an assessment will obviously be more difficult in cases of mental health where cost-benefit analysis is very much in its early stages of development.

The ethnic differences depend upon different social, cultural and ethnic identities (as discussed in Chapter 5) and also on different patterns of disease and perceptions and expectations of health services and institutional racism. Although the socio-economic and ethnic or cultural factors that underlie such discrepancies have been investigated, less attention has been paid to institutional and cultural factors in the appropriate recognition of the mental health needs of ethnic minority groups.

In the delivery and planning of mental health services factors determining the pathology are perhaps less important than those that influence the definition and subsequent recognition of such pathology. Cultural factors may play a more important role in the recognition of mental disorders and therefore using categories from other cultures may add another dimension of disservice to ethnic minority groups.

Conflicts

The question posed by Sashidharan & Commander (1998) in that expressions of mental disorders are culturally or otherwise variant and whether the very concept of mental illness has any validity outside particular discourses and specific social and cultural milieu is a valid one. Once mental illnesses are established as cultural categories in that pathological significance is attributed to (culturally determined) deviant behaviour, then the dangers of applying such models across other cultures without recognition of cultural relativism makes any needs assessment totally inadequate. In addition, cultural biases in management then come into play. These differences attributed to category fallacy (Kleinman, 1980; see also Chapter 2) suggest that any needs assessment in a given ethnic minority group must follow a 'bottom-up' approach. Based on such a distinction the questions about diagnosis and managing mental illness, in the context of understanding mental health experiences of Black people, need to be reassessed and revised. An additional conflict often ignored in public discussion is the role psychiatry plays in managing mental illness (deviant behaviour) in the context of maintenance of social order (Mercer, 1984). The complex relationship between gender, race, socio-economic status and discrimination (social as well as economic) is difficult to untangle, especially when mental health needs are being assessed. Thus, the high levels of psychiatric morbidity in some ethnic minority groups cannot be seen in isolation from prevailing social and cultural norms.

Quantity or quality of assessment

As noted above, epidemiological and comparative data can be collected in a quantitative manner, whereas corporate data have to be collected using qualitative measures. The problems associated with the validity and reliability of psychiatric diagnosis and the multitude of factors mentioned earlier may mean needs assessment based purely on diagnosis or service usage is likely to be inadequate. The established practices of needs assessment based on professional opinion or service evaluation are likely to be highly misleading. There is a general problem with establishing the nature of psychiatric morbidity or different levels in the pathways to psychiatric care (Thornicroft *et al*, 1992), although exceptions exist (Nazroo, 1997).

Furthermore, qualitative differences in the presentations of mental illness in the general population and in primary care must be addressed prior to setting out to measure needs assessment. A service-led approach is unlikely to further our understanding about the nature and extent of mental health in Black and other ethnic minority groups. Bhugra *et al* (1997) have recommended using qualitative methods of approach such as focus groups to identify health needs as well as determining models of explanation in primary care.

The difficulty often lies in identifying mental health care needs perceived by the users and the providers. On the one hand the professionals view continuing and unrecognised health care needs as being best addressed by more health care interventions, whereas the majority of health service users see a need for more preventive and supportive strategies and less treatment (Institute of Race Relations, 1993).

Service evaluation and economics

Science has long been able to establish methods of basic research when evaluating an isolated aspect of psychiatric treatment, such as a drug trial, but evaluative research, trying to measure the effectiveness of complex treatment processes, services or even a section of the care system, has been neglected (An der Heiden & Hafner, 1996) and the process for ethnic minority groups is virtually non-existent.

The development and use of measurement instruments to evaluate services and health economics is relatively recent. The study of service evaluation for Black and other ethnic minority groups has yet to be developed beyond service planners and purchasers.

What is being evaluated?

The term evaluative research can be used for different approaches depending upon the process being assessed (Milne, 1987). Of these, effort evaluations examine the relationship between the characteristics and activities of a service (e.g. expenditure, staff–patient ratio). The process evaluation in the traditional sense can be seen to be limited to a simple outline of services over time, for example, recording the number of patients receiving a particular treatment. Such an evaluation is descriptive. The third type of evaluation is efficiency evaluation establishing a relationship between the cost of service and the goal it aims to achieve. Psychiatric care is efficient when better results are being achieved on the same budget or same results are achieved on a lower budget. Service user satisfaction evaluation examines the patient's acceptance of treatment measures. Outcome evaluation is the core of evaluation in that the results of a measure or service of measures are the focus of the study.

Before any meaningful evaluation can take place it is necessary to define the goals by which the effectiveness is being measured. It is crucial that the goal of a procedure or service is clear. As An der Heiden & Hafner (1996) suggest, ideally, a treatment measure is adapted to the patient and therefore evaluation must allow for individual goals. Thus, for one case successful treatment may mean that symptoms have been significantly reduced. Wing (1986) suggested that three methodological approaches within evaluation must be included: monitoring, descriptive surveys and evaluation. For Black and other ethnic minority groups in monitoring and evaluation the problems of heterogeneity and poor definition highlighted above must be considered very carefully.

Who is being evaluated?

The evaluation of the process must be differentiated from the evaluation of the individual. Economic evaluation is concerned only with measuring value for money, using techniques linking costs and benefits and providing objective data as to what is being bought (Jackson & Goldberg, 1996). The evaluation of service is a complex task and a clear aim and precise hypothesis will focus the data collection.

When setting up an economic appraisal, Jackson & Goldberg (1996) recommend that design of the study must follow the hypothesis to be tested. A register of patients and basic information about the service are established and only their monitary effects are measured by administering the economic questionnaire, counting the items of service used and estimating unit costs.

For Black and other ethnic minority groups these evaluative procedures must be identified in relation to models of illness which encourage individuals to seek help. In the step when the use of services by patients is being studied ethnic minority groups' use of primary care and other levels of care may show a differential, hence making any comparisons problematic.

Once again, a useful solution may be through observation of the unit being evaluated. Jackson & Goldberg (1996) suggest that although the process is expensive, the research team may need to spend time observing the work of the unit to measure the resource used per item of care – this may show that costs are different for different groups of patients. For example, detailed observation of the resources used by in-patients in a general psychiatric ward showed that patients received more staff time in the first few days of their admissions (Hyde *et al*, 1985).

Assessing the quality of care

The quality of care being delivered can be assessed by ascertaining environmental and other factors. The patient's views of services are important components of quality of care. Dissatisfaction with treatment has been shown to be a correlate of non-adherence (Ley, 1982). Measuring quality and consumer satisfaction can have methodological problems in sampling, timing of assessment and questions being asked.

The outcome of care has several dimensions: mental state, physical health, behaviour, social skills, quality of life and employment – all have to be studied. Quality of life, although advantageous in that comparisons can be made across cultures, still needs to be monitored very carefully across ethnic groups as their expectations of treatment and explanations of illness may differ (Chisholm & Bhugra, 1997). Health economics can provide a framework but cultural differences must be studied very carefully.

Next steps

From this brief overview three key themes can be drawn out. First, that any needs assessment must use both qualitative and quantitative data. Second, that the perspectives of users and their carers and those of professionals often differ and need to converge. Third, and perhaps most importantly, the discrepancy between psychiatric diagnosis and definitions of needs across cultures must be borne in mind in ascertaining needs.

The focus of needs assessment must shift to populations – rather than users of primary or secondary care. Unless such studies are underway the needs of ethnic minority groups cannot be judged accurately much less met appropriately. Alternative explanations for the use of mental health services must be remembered. It is possible that the models that Asian people use, for example, are less likely to be medical; hence developing psychiatric services which do not take these models into account may result in services being underutilised. If service users see depression as a life-related event where the medical professional has little to offer, is it fair to force individuals into taking antidepressants and making them comply with medical models, thereby reducing any sense of adherence and cooperation? As Sashidharan & Commander (1998) have previously demonstrated, the use of five levels of Goldberg & Huxley's (1980) model does indicate a differential use of different levels according to ethnicity and other factors. Thus, a series of factors must be taken into account while measuring mental health care needs and also in planning of health care delivery.

Conclusions

The current preoccupation with needs assessment – especially for Black and other ethnic minority groups – suggests that this is a golden opportunity to highlight the problems with the current 'blunderbuss' approach and develop qualitative and quantitative models of assessment which are user-friendly and yield information which is genuine that can be utilised to benefit those whose needs are greatest. For this endeavour to succeed, both clinicians and planners must work together to develop instruments which are culturally sensitive and applicable and make the services more accessible.

References

AN DER HEIDEN, W. & HAFNER, H. (1996) Evaluating the effectiveness of services by means of mental health care information systems. In *Handbook of Mental Health Economics and Health Policy*, Vol. 1 (eds M. Moscarelli, A. Rupp & N. Sartorius), pp. 335–345. Chichester: John Wiley.

BHUGRA D., BALDWIN, D & DESAI, M. (1997) Focus groups: implications for primary and cross cultural psychiatry. *Primary Care Psychiatry*, **3**, 45–50.

CHISHOLM, D. & BHUGRA, D. (1997) Sociocultural and economic aspects of quality of life measurement. *European Psychiatry*, **12**, 210–215.

GOLDBERG, D. & HUXLEY, P. (1980) *Common Mental Disorders: A Biopsyhcosocial Model.* London: Tavistock.

HYDE, C., BRIDGES, K., GOLDBERG, D., *et al* (1985) The evaluation of a hostel ward: a controlled srudy using cost-benefit analysis. *British Journal of Psychiatry*, **151**, 805–812.

INSTITUTE OF RACE RELATIONS (1993) *Community Care: the Black Experienced.* London: IRR.

JACKSON, G. & GOLDBERG, D. (1996): Methodology of economic evaluations of mental health services: the clinician's perspective. In *Handbook of Mental Health Economics and Health Policy*, Vol. 1 (eds M. Moscarelli, A. Rupp & N. Sartorius), pp. 373–383. Chichester: John Wiley & Sons.

KLEINMAN, A. (1980) *Patients and Healers in the Context of their Culture.* Berkely, CA: University of California Press.

LEY, P. (1982) Satisfaction, compliance and communications. *British Journal of Clinical Psychology,* **21**, 241–254.

MERCER, K. (1984) Black communities experience of psychiatric services. *International Journal of Social Psychiatry,* **30**, 22–27.

MILNE, D. (1987) *Evaluating Mental Health Practice.* London: Croom Helm.

NAZROO, J. (1997) *Ethnicity and Mental Health.* London Policy Studies Institute.

RAWAF, S. (1998) Theoretical framework. In *Assessing Health Needs of People from Minority Ethnic Groups* (eds S. Rawaf & V. Bahl). London: Royal College of Physicians of London.

SASHIDHARAN, S.P. & COMMANDER, M. (1998). Mental Health. In *Assessing Health Needs of People from Minority Ethnic Groups* (eds S. Rawaf & V. Bahl), pp. 281–290. London: Royal College of Physicians of London.

STEVENS, A. & GALSBAY, J. (1990) Needs assessment needs assessment. *Health Trends,* **23**, 20–23.

THORNICROFT, G., BREWIN, C. R. & WING, J. K. (1992) *Measuring Mental Health Needs.* London: Gaskell.

WING, J. K. (1986). The cycle of planning and evaluation. In *The Provision of Mental Health Services in Britain: The Way Ahead* (eds G. Wilkinson & H. Freeman), pp. 35–48. London: Gaskell.

16 Primary prevention and ethnic minority mental health: a path for the future?

KWAME McKENZIE

Editors' introduction

Strategies for prevention of mental illness are less well known and less frequently used with Black and other ethnic minority groups. The public health problems posed by psychiatric disorders are numerous, and not only are they common, but they are also a considerable drain on human and financial resources. Using the prevalence of schizophrenia in African–Caribbeans as a model for developing and discussing preventive strategies, McKenzie highlights the role of biological and social factors, including social exclusion, in the genesis of schizophrenia. He proposes that primary prevention is possible, especially in a social and cultural context. These contexts also have implications for a number of risk factors relating to other psychiatric conditions. Some of these, such as housing and education, will require political action, but others, such as an increase in family and social support, are attainable by the community. Social and cultural factors are inextricably linked and this relationship must be understood in the context of any prevention strategies.

Public health measures, including better education, housing and sanitation, have been the most potent forces in improving life expectancy in the UK in the recent past (Acheson, 1990). Newer public health initiatives aimed at behavioural change, such as stopping smoking, improving diet and incouraging exercise, are our best chance to decrease mortality and morbidity rates over the next 50 years. Preventive strategies are a key factor in improving the nation's health (Secretary of State for Health, 1998).

There are three types of prevention (Caplan, 1964).

(a) Primary prevention is directed at reducing the incidence of an illness in a community. It attempts to help well people who are believed to be at risk.
(b) Secondary prevention is directed at reducing the prevalence of a disorder. This is usually achieved by reducing its duration, for instance by early detection and treatment.
(c) Tertiary prevention efforts try to decrease the severity of disability caused by a disorder.

Prevention in psychiatry

Psychiatric disorders are important public health problems. They are common, they cause considerable personal and family distress and they are very costly. Worldwide 1500 million people suffer from mental, neurological and psychosocial disorders (World Health Organization, 1998). The World Health Organization(WHO) claims that a considerable proportion of mental ill health could be avoided by the use of effective and affordable simple methods (World Health Organization, 1998). In a speciality where there are few cures, prevention is of the utmost importance.

Secondary and tertiary prevention are considered part of good clinical care in UK psychiatric practice, but primary preventive strategies have been slow to develop (Paykel & Jenkins, 1994). Although primary prevention is increasingly discussed, programmes are few and far between (Paykel & Jenkins, 1994; World Health Organization, 1998). A number of reasons have been cited for this, including the current low level of understanding of the causes of mental illness and fears that the types of intervention required would be beyond the scope of normal psychiatric competence.

The slow development of primary prevention in psychiatry has important implications for ethnic minority groups. Because there is little or no primary prevention there are few tools or strategies available to be aimed at decreasing the disparities in the incidence of mental ill health. Secondary and tertiary prevention through the improvement of existing services and the development of new services have been the main strategy to counter disparities in prevalence, service use, satisfaction and outcome between ethnic minority and ethnic majority populations in the UK (Bhugra & Bahl, 1999), but they will not reduce disparities in the incidence of illness (unless, of course, the services themselves are responsible for the increased incidence).

Wide disparities between ethnic groups in the incidence of some illnesses offer a huge potential for improvement through primary prevention. The WHO has concluded that where there is a difference in incidence between two comparable groups there is potential for primary prevention that is at least as large as the difference (World Health Organization, 1998).

Here I will discuss one area in which the incidence of mental illness in one ethnic minority group is higher than in the ethnic majority group. I will discuss possible reasons for the increased incidence and then outline how the epidemiological research to date could inform a primary prevention strategy. It is hoped that a more detailed analysis of one group will illuminate areas of more general concern.

The increased incidence of psychosis in African–Caribbeans

The increased incidence of psychotic illness in UK African–Caribbeans has been one of the most keenly researched areas of psychiatry in the country (Wessely *et al*, 1991; King *et al*, 1994; Bhugra *et al*, 1997; Harrison *et al*, 1988). Estimates of the size of the increase compared to incidence in Whites vary and the research has many shortfalls, However, even the most sceptical of commentators would concede that there is an higher incidence of psychosis in African–Caribbeans in the UK conservatively placed at between 2 and 3 times that of the White population (McKenzie & Murray, 1999).

The incidence debate has now moved on from whether there is an increased incidence to what may be causing the increase. In keeping with the dominant research paradigms of the time, biological risk factors were the first to be studied in detail. Factors such as genetic make-up, neurodevelopmental problems and substance misuse were considered as possible candidates.

Biological risk factors

Genes

If African–Caribbeans have some particular genetic susceptibility to developing schizophrenia, then one would expect an increased incidence of schizophrenia on Caribbean islands. There is no evidence of this. Incidence studies on a number of Caribbean islands have reported rates for schizophrenia similar to those of the

White population in the UK (Hickling & Rodgers-Johnson, 1995; Bhugra *et al*, 1996). The UK African population also have an increased risk of psychosis (Castle *et al*, 1998) and genetic hypotheses have been proffered. However, the African Centre in the WHO's International Pilot Study of Schizophrenia (Sartorius *et al*, 1986) similarly showed no increased incidence of schizophrenia in Africa. These facts confound arguments that there is a simple genetic explanation for the increased incidence of schizophrenia in UK African–Caribbeans.

The neurodevelopmental hypothesis

Neurodevelopmental problems are an important risk factor for psychosis in the White population (Murray & O'Callaghan, 1991). Research suggests that schizophrenia can be a consequence of aberrant brain development during foetal and neonatal life. Insults to the growing brain predispose to later psychosis when the final maturational changes in brain organisation occur in teenage and early adult life.

Increased rate of premorbid neurological illness, perhaps due to poorer antenatal or intrapartum care or maternal viral infections, could be a factor in increasing the rate of psychosis in African–Caribbeans. However, a recent UK study has shown that premorbid neurological illness is actually less common in African–Caribbeans than in Whites (McKenzie *et al*, 2000*a*). The usual characteristics of neurologically mediated psychotic illness are less common in African–Caribbeans than Whites, and brain scanning stigmata of neurodevelopmental illness may be less common in African–Caribbean patients (Nigaonkar *et al*, 1988). Furthermore, obstetric complications are actually less commonly reported by the mothers of African–Caribbeans with psychosis (Hutchinson *et al*, 1997).

Cannabis

Cannabis may be aetiologically important in the genesis of psychosis (Andreasson *et al*, 1989 McKenzie and Murray, 1999). Research has shown that regular use of cannabis when young doubles the risk of developing schizophrenia and other research claims that it brings forward the age of onset of the illness (Andreasson *et al*, 1989; McKenzie & Murray, 1999). There is little evidence of increased use of cannabis in African–Caribbeans compared to Whites in the UK . In The Netherlands, where there is a similarly higher rate of psychosis in people of Caribbean origin than in Whites, cannabis consumption has actually been shown to be less prevalent in the Caribbean population (Selten *et al*, 1997).

Environment

Research into the biological risk factors of schizophrenia has pointed to the important role that the environment plays in the increased incidence of schizophrenia in African–Caribbeans.

Genetic studies have concluded that the genetic risk is the same in both African–Caribbean and Whites, but that the increased incidence of psychosis is due to environmental factors affecting African–Caribbeans in the UK (Sugarman & Craufurd, 1994; Hutchinson *et al*, 1996). Furthermore, the fact that neurodevelopmental risk factors are less common in African–Caribbeans has led researchers away from a classical neurodevelopmental hypothesis, which argues for factors affecting the developing brain, towards factors in the environment that may act much later in life.

This is supported by work that compares the course of illness in African–Caribbeans and Whites. Classically, illness mediated by neurological factors is chronic in nature and illness with social or environmental precipitants has a more benign course. A number of analyses have shown that the course of the illness is more benign for African–Caribbeans (McKenzie *et al*, 1995; Callan, 1996; Harrison *et al*, 1999), hence they may have illnesses with more social or environmental precipitants.

This has led some to question whether the types of psychosis associated with or precipitated by social factors are the same as the types associated with biological risk factors (McKenzie *et al*, 1995).

A unifying hypothesis is that there is no point of rarity between schizophrenia and affective psychosis and that risk factors in this spectrum disorder are diverse. Those at the more 'schizophrenic' end have illnesses with more neurodevelopmental or genetic risk factors and those at the 'affective' end have illnesses with more social risk factors (van Os *et al*, 1998). The increased rates of illness in African–Caribbeans could be due to an increase in psychoses that have a strong affective component. Illnesses with identifiable precipitants have a better prognosis than those due to constitutional factors in the individual (Vaillant, 1964). The better prognosis for patients of Caribbean origin may be because more illness in this group is precipitated or mediated by social or environmental factors (McKenzie *et al*, 1995).

Social factors and psychosis

A number of social factors are linked to mental illness. Below I have described those that are more likely to be experienced by African–Caribbeans than by Whites in the UK.

Racism

Racism is a social factor of great importance to the African–Caribbean population (see Chapter 4, this volume). Racism has been shown to have effects on the physical, social and psychological environment (Williams, 1996), across generations (Laviest, 1993). It compounds the effects of gender and social class (Lillie-Blanton & Laviest, 1996). Its influence on the perception of self and the perception of community may have a deleterious effect on the structures of minority communities and society as a whole. Institutional racism may also be important. Disparities in the rate of illness could be due to the lack of detailed multi-disciplinary and longitudinal investigation of the social dimension of psychiatric problems because of the perceived importance of other issues or types of study (McKenzie & Murray, 1999). This could lead to poorer public health interventions to reduce risks.

Migration

One of the first social factors to be proffered as a cause of the increased incidence of psychosis in UK African–Caribbeans was migration (Littlewood & Lipsedge, 1997; Chapter 6, this volume). However, it is important to emphasise that migration is a complex event: different groups migrate for different reasons and have different experiences. Worldwide, the number of studies showing higher rates of mental disorder in migrants is the same as the number showing lower morbidity in migrants (Canadian Task Force on Mental Health Issues, 1988). Warner (1985) concluded that the incidence of schizophrenia is higher in immigrants who encounter harsher labour conditions in the country they go to and that the rate of schizophrenia is higher in the gender that faces harsher labour market conditions. It is not migration itself, but sociocultural, political and economic factors that dictate rates of mental illness among migrants.

Macro-economics

In a review of the causes of schizophrenia, Warner (1985) concluded that the number of first-time admissions increased at times of high unemployment; that the prevalence of schizophrenia was lower in parts of the non-industrialised world where wage labour had not developed, and higher in parts of the developed world where there was high unemployment; and that the prevalence rates of schizophrenia were not only higher in developing countries that had wage labour, but were highest in those that were most negatively affected by labour conditions and unemployment (Warner, 1985).

African–Caribbeans suffer high unemployment levels and are more vulnerable to changes in labour conditions than Whites (Bahl, 1999).

Socio-economic class and work

The links between social class and mental health are complex (Perry, 1996). Lower social class is generally associated with a higher prevalence of illness and worse outcome, but the association between the incidence of specific mental illnesses and social class varies. Some studies have found that the incidence of schizophrenia is higher in higher social classes (Jones *et al*, 1994) and that of depression is higher in lower social classes (Brown & Harris, 1975; Perry, 1996).

Movement up and down the social scale changes an individual's risk of developing an illness: in general, moving down leads to worse mental health and moving up improves mental health (Timms, 1996).

However, there is some evidence that moving up the social class ladder may not improve the mental health of ethnic minority groups. Those who move to an area with a lower concentration of ethnic minorities can experience higher levels of stress and worse mental health, possibly due to increased exposure to racism (Halpern, 1993).

Mental disorder is more common in those with financial difficulties, those who are unemployed and those who are uncertain about their future. More recently, studies have shown that financial worries are linked to the incidence of illness as well as its prevalence (Weich & Lewis, 1998).

Social class is linked to educational attainment. In the UK, African–Caribbeans have less access to good education than Whites. Furthermore, African–Caribbean males are more likely to be excluded from school and to be referred by schools for psychological help (Goodman & Richards, 1995).

Unemployment is linked to anxiety and depression, but work itself can be a risk factor for mental ill health. The work environment and the type of job (stress *v.* autonomy) are related to mental and physical health (Marmot *et al*, 1991).

Many African–Caribbeans are of lower social class and so are less autonomous in their work. They are more likely to be unemployed (Bahl, 1999) and first-generation African–Caribbeans are more likely to have taken a job at a level lower than they had before they emigrated (Fryer, 1984). It might be supposed that they will therefore be more likely to have financial worries. Given these facts, higher rates of mental illness would be expected.

The urban environment

The link between low socio-economic status and health is due in part to the physical environment. Poor housing, high traffic levels, accidents and overcrowding are related to low life expectancy and poorer health. Limited access to transportation, parks and recreational facilities increase isolation and fear, which are associated with both psychological morbidity and increased violence (Freeman, 1985; Task Force on Adolescent Assault Victim Needs, 1996).

Living in an urban environment is associated with higher blood pressure and poorer general health. Inner-city residents are more likely to be exposed to air and water pollution. Carbon monoxide fumes, which are high in poor inner-city areas, may add to stress physiologically by adrenal activation. Carbon monoxide levels in the air are related to the rate of presentation to emergency services for psychological problems (Freeman, 1985). There is a striking association between city life and schizophrenia and a number of other psychiatric illnesses. African–Caribbeans are very likely to live in cities.

Children

Children who live in cities are more likely to become criminals and to be victims of criminals (Task Force on Adolescent Assault Victim Needs, 1996). They are more poorly supervised and they suffer higher rates of accidents both in and outside the home (Quinton, 1988).

In urban areas there is an increased rate of conduct and emotional problems in children. The mechanism for this has been difficult to pin down, but the effects of the urban environment have been shown to be separate from that of socio-economic class (Quinton, 1988).

Although adaptation to an urban environment leads to psychological changes that may produce stress, their link to psychiatric disorder in childhood has not been firmly established. There are, however, good reasons for the current belief in a link between the urban environment and both childhood and adult mental illness. In the USA, levels of substance misuse are related to social status and social environment (National Household Survey on Drug Abuse, 1990. Lillie-Blanton *et al* (1993) have shown that in the USA neighbourhood characteristics are a better predictor of crack cocaine use than is ethnic group.

Exposure to cocaine during foetal development may lead to subtle, but significant, deficits in later childhood (Vogel, 1997). Behaviours crucial to success, such as concentrating for long periods and blocking out distractions, are particularly affected, and these deficits may lead to conduct disorders (Vogel, 1997).

Lead poisoning is now mainly an urban problem. The link between lead poisoning and attention deficit disorder is a matter of debate (Rice, 1996; Winneke & Kramer, 1997). Symptoms resembling conduct disorder may be due to low-level lead poisoning in some children.

Adults

Living in a city is one of the most powerful risk factors for schizophrenia. African–Caribbeans are more likely to live in cities. There is also evidence of an association between being brought up in a city and an increased risk of schizophrenia, but the mechanism is unclear (Lewis *et al*, 1992). The increased incidence is not accounted for by higher levels of obstetric complications. But recent work on those who develop schizophrenia before the age of 23 has shown that environmental factors seem to act before the onset of the illness (van Os *et al*, 1998). This may be due to urban deprivation or to social selection and migration (Freeman, 1985).

There is some evidence of an increased risk of schizophrenia in those born in cities and those born in the winter, and an interaction between these two risk factors. An as yet unidentified agent, such as a virus, may link being born in a city, winter birth, poverty and schizophrenia. However, if this were the case the pathway cannot be obstetric complications or classical neuro-developmental psychosis, as the rates of these are low in the UK African–Caribbean population.

Two other possible reasons for the high rates of mental illness in those born and living in cities are overcrowding and overstimulation. Both of these have been linked to mental illness, but they have proved difficult to study (Freeman, 1985). Each is influenced by an individual's perception of the environment as well as by the environment itself. Both are also influenced by the stability of the area. In areas with rapidly changing populations people feel more crowded and suffer from more overstimulation than in areas with stable populations (Freeman, 1985).

Social isolation

Social isolation is linked to psychosis. As it is also a pre-morbid factor it is difficult to assess. Social isolation is associated with depression (Brown & Harris, 1975), and those who live in cities are more likely to be socially isolated, partly due to the social architecture of the city and partly through choice (Freeman, 1985).

Life events

General and racial life events have been discussed in Chapter 5 and will not be discussed in detail here. I would simply state that stressful events are linked to both the incidence of new and the relapse of existing psychiatric illness (Dohrenwend & Dohrenwend, 1974); that the individual's perception of the event is important; and that recent work has linked high levels of maternal stress during pregnancy to psychosis in the offspring in adulthood (Huttumen, 1989; Walker & Diforio, 1997; van Os & Selten, 1998).

Violence and mental disorder

There are long-term psychological sequelae of witnessing violence that include both psychiatric disorders (such as antisocial personality disorder, borderline personality disorder, brief reactive psychosis, conversion disorder, dissociative amnesia, dissociative fugue, dream anxiety disorder, multiple personality disorder and somatisation disorder) and effects on social relationships and addictive behaviour (Bell & Jenkins, 1993). Victims of violence are more likely subsequently to misuse alcohol and drugs. In turn, alcohol and drug misuse are involved in the majority of homicides and non-fatal assaults (Task Force on Adolescent Assault Victim Needs, 1996).

Violence may also have positive effects on individuals exposed to it (such as greater avoidance of high-risk behaviours and spiritual development), but these have not been well researched (Task Force on Adolescent Assault Victim Needs, 1996).

Multiple losses, violent death or imprisonment of a family member are known risk factors for substance misuse (Task Force on Adolescent Assault Victim Needs, 1996) and other mental illnesses. All of these factors are more likely in a city.

Family and mental illness

Loss of parent is a risk factor for mental illness (Brown & Harris, 1975), but its predictive value may depend on the subsequent social environment. It may not be the loss of a parent *per se*, but the social and economic consequences of this, that increase a person's risk of future illness. For example, subsequent confiding relationships can mitigate the loss.

In the UK, African–Caribbean children are more likely to be taken into care than Whites (Maughan, 1989). New work, as yet unpublished, suggests that African–Caribbean women with psychosis are much more likely to have their children taken away than matched samples of Whites. Thus, children already suffering a personal loss may have added high environmental risk.

How do social and environmental factors lead to psychosis?

A number of hypotheses try to explain how social forces cause illness. The fundamental cause hypothesis links differences in health between groups to money, power, prestige and social connections, which strongly influence people's ability to avoid risks and to minimise the consequences of any disease that emerges (Link, 1996). Institutional racism and differential access to services are organisational expressions of the fundamental social cause hypothesis (King, 1996). The increased exposure of African–Caribbeans to poor quality housing, pollution and infectious agents may all increase their rates of illness. Income inequality may lead to poor health in a number of ways, for example, through individual frustration or underinvestment in human or in social capital (Kawachi *et al*, 1997). Political marginalisation allows disparities to persist, as the will and the impetus to produce effective remedial measures may be lacking (Meneffee, 1996). The myriad effects of racism have already been discussed.

Stress

Despite the multitude of mechanisms at an ecological or group level through which social factors might influence health, most research has concentrated on 'stress'. The physiology of stress is complex. Severe or recurrent stress may lead to long-term changes in neuro-endocrine modulation systems, which may make the body more sensitive to stress and make other neuro-endocrine pathways more sensitive in general. Prolonged stress leads to a number of physiological changes that produce ill health. There are documented effects on the immune system, cardiovascular system, renal system and the brain (Walker & Diforio, 1997).

The individual's perception of the threat and their level of control over it are important in the production of stress. Both are influenced by personality, history, culture, social buffers, the media, the place of the individual in the social strata and the type of threat (Freeman, 1985; Kleinman, 1991).

Control may be exerted by action to remove the stressor or by adaptation. Adaptive responses may decrease stress in the short term, but may lead to harm in the long term.

However, not all the associations can or should be explained at an individual, or even family, level and there are pitfalls in doing so. Offering mechanisms based on the individual to explain group effects is an ecological fallacy (Diez-Roux, 1988). For instance, whether an individual gets an infection depends not only on his or her susceptibility, but also on 'herd' immunity – the level of susceptibility in the general community. There are links between the two, but they do not explain each other. They have different mechanisms of action and work at different levels.

Stress can produce a number of adverse behavioural changes, including substance misuse, which may have effects on both the individual and society. Stress may also have positive effects, defining self-efficacy, self-worth and the ability of families and communities to act cohesively. Current biomedical reductionist theories rarely acknowledge that stress is more than an individual response with a physiological correlate. The community-level effects argue for hypotheses in which stress is conceptualised as an ecological variable.

Social disorganisation

Older models of the mechanism through which the environment could produce illness tried to link individual- and community-level hypotheses. The disorganisation model posits that if the ties joining individuals and their society are broken, there is stress, anxiety and social pathology (Freeman, 1985).

Change and adaptation can make a society vulnerable to crisis if existing cultural guidelines for coping do not work, forcing new types of behaviour to be tried. New behaviour clashes with old culture, undermining its stability, and the change defines the culture rather than the culture defining itself (Freeman, 1985). Because the society is in flux it is difficult to produce consensus and trust, which leads to further sociocultural flux and decreased social cohesion and efficacy.

However, adversity does not always lead to social disorder. There may well be disorganisation due to low socio-economic status in inner-city minority areas with little residential stability, but high levels of sub-cultural order may remain.

Some have argued that anomie may be the cause of high rates of physical illness and mental illness. Anomie and disorganisation may coexist and be part of a complex long-term process acting on different families over differing timescales with different results.

Complex modelling

There are links between macrosocial-, community- and individual-level variables (Diez-Roux, 1988). Culture and community can be a response to macrosocial pressures, as can the size of a family and the nature of family ties. Hence, social support, an important buffer to the effects of macrosocial forces such as planned levels of unemployment, will depend on the history of the effects of such forces on the culture and the community. The level of social support is likely to be low in an inner-city community in which restructuring of the labour market and other political decisions have led to urban decay and highly mobile populations. But the levels of resilience to outside pressures may be high in communities with a history of oppression.

When investigating links between illness and societal factors researchers have often taken a unidirectional approach and tried to elucidate causal mechanisms. However, it is likely that there are a multitude of links between factors which may not be causal; furthermore, if there is causality there is also reverse causality.

There are important caveats to bear in mind when considering this research. More often than not studies have been cross-sectional, even though most adult diseases have long courses of development. Most prevalent environmental hazards, such as tobacco smoke and atmospheric pollution, take decades to exert their effects (Bartley *et al*, 1997). This is important in that it makes social processes difficult to measure adequately and investigation of lifetime trajectories may be important (Bartley *et al*, 1997). For example, children from poor families are more likely to fail at school, find low-paid work, experience early unemployment and produce lower birth-weight babies. Low birth-weight babies are more likely to have problems during childhood and an increased risk of chronic disease in middle age. These trajectories are amplified by social strata and macropolitical forces, and in concert they help to shape the social and psychological environment in which people live. Such lifespan effects call for long-term research and solutions (Bartley *et al*, 1997).

A similar pathways theory could be set to link institutional racism in social service housing placements to the incidence of mental illness in African–Caribbeans. African–Caribbeans are more likely to be housed in poorer conditions (Littlewood & Lipsedge, 1997).

Such neighbourhoods are more likely to be rapidly changing, violent and to have higher rates of substance misuse. Material and social deprivation increase the incidence of adverse life events. This in turn increases the risk of mental ill health (Brown & Purdo, 1981). However, in deprived areas there are fewer health resources and finding help is more difficult. Poorer access due to ethnic minority status compounds this reduced health service provision and a history of inadequate provision may make African–Caribbeans less likely to visit or trust their general practitioner if they have mental health problems (Lloyd & St Louis, 1999). African–Caribbeans present later than Whites and with more severe symptoms, which may lead to more coercive treatment – the police are also more likely to be involved. More coercive treatment leads to poorer subsequent engagement with services, further coercion (including use of the Mental Health Act) and more police involvement (Cole *et al*, 1995; Davies *et al*, 1996; van Os *et al*, 1997). African–Caribbeans with mental health problems are more likely to be compulsorily hospitalised under the Mental Health Act, to have had contact with the police and to live in low socio-economic environments. For parents, all of these are potent predictors of having their children taken into care. This places an added environmental burden on the children, who are more likely to suffer subsequent mental illness. This is just one of a number of downward spirals that could be described.

Conclusions

Mental health is linked to social forces on a number of levels, from the cultural choices that lead us to decide what illness is and how it is expressed, through the political choices that are made to maintain socio-economic strata, to the levels of stress we, as communities and nations, accept and the physical and social environments we build.

The individual may encounter risk factors that increase the chance of developing an illness, but the the risk factors themselves are the result of a complex nexus of social forces. Myriad harmful and beneficial forces create a milieu in which disease is produced. Noxious agents at the level of the individual, community and society interact with vulnerabilities and strengths at each of these levels.

African–Caribbeans are more likely to experience most of the social forces that have been linked to poorer physical and mental health. The wide variety of social forces involved, their complex inter-relationships and the fact that they may exert effects over many years may explain why these important factors are not easy to research.

Implications for prevention strategies

To date, service development has focused on improving the detection of psychiatric illness and its outcome. Work claiming an excess of affective symptoms in psychosis in African–Caribbeans (McKenzie *et al*, 2000*b*) could lead to a trial of the use of prophylaxis for affective illness in this group.

The focus on improving services is understandable given the current state of our knowledge of the social aetiology of psychosis. Furthemore, reducing secondary social harm may cut the incidence of psychosis in subsequent generations, for example, by reducing the number of children of patients with psychosis that are placed in care.

However, the move from a proposed biological aetiology to an environmental aetiology and the discovery that the incidence of psychosis is higher in African–Caribbeans than in Whites opens new horizons for primary intervention.

It could be argued that the lack of hard aetiological evidence militates against primary prevention of specific illness. However, it could also be argued that the complex web of causation and the longitudinal effects of both identified and as yet unidentified social risk factors may make identification of specific risk factors or mechanisms very difficult. Moreover, the elucidation of the exact mechanism or mechanisms may not change the prevention strategy. The most likely strategies are a mixture of behavioural and social change, which many would class as the building blocks of a modern society. Furthermore, there is an ethical argument against a delay in implementing interventions that may be beneficial and that at least will be harmless.

The economic cost of interventions is important. But it is also important to note that primary prevention efforts, especially in a sociocultural context, have implications for a number of risk factors and a number of conditions – not just the specific illness targeted (World Health Organization, 1998). Interventions are based on broad conceptual models, rather than on magic bullets, and in general are inexpensive when their wider effects outside the targeted illness are taken into account (World Health Organization, 1998).

Better education, housing, sanitation and nutrition have been the most potent factors in improving the health of this nation (Acheson, 1990). The lack of scientific precision before the implementation of policy measures aimed at achieving these did not deter public health officials from proposing bold strategies. The public health movement has had more of an impact on the rates of illness and life expectancy than the setting up of the National Health Service (Acheson, 1990).

Wilkinson (1996) has argued that the level of income in equality in an OECD (Organization for Economic Co-operation and Development) country is the best predictor of mortality levels. Moreover, increasing inequality over time decreases overall life expectancy, while decreasing income inequality over time increases overall life expectancy. Others have argued that low social cohesion and efficacy are just as important (Kawachi *et al*; 1997, Amick *et al*, 1995). Relative wealth and perceptions of community are linked to health status, and the mechanisms through which these factors act are likely to be psychological. Though these mechanisms and pathways have not been elucidated, such theories have been instrumental deciding government policy (Secretary of State for Health, 1998).

In deciding which illnesses should be the subject of new primary preventive efforts, incidence, prevalence, severity, importance, controllability and cost are all important factors. On any measure, psychosis in the African–Caribbean community would score highly as a priority (World Health Organization, 1998).

In psychiatry, there has been more success in changing the family's micro-environment than its macro-environment, and it has been easier to look at proximal precipitants such as expressed emotion and stress than more distal predisposing factors such as education and the economy (Scott & Leff, 1994). But the importance of wider social forces in the incidence of psychosis in African–Caribbeans argues for the targeting by primary intervention of macro-environmental and distal factors.

There are a number of areas in which wider social policy reform could decrease disparities in the incidence rate of psychosis between African–Caribbeans and Whites. For example, the quality of housing and the quality of life in cities have been shown to be linked to mental ill health; therefore strategies to improve the built environment and the social environment could reduce differences in psychological well-being. Reducing pollution and improving access to transport and recreational opportunities could form part of such a strategy.

The development and maintenance of support systems independent of the mental health system and the active creation of new support systems for individuals and communities could offer social buffers against the effects of external stress, which could decrease incident cases. Wider measures such as fairer employment laws and effective monitoring of, and remedial action to counter, institutionalised racism and job discrimination could decrease disparities in employment and social service provision.

A fairer education system, with an emphasis on valuing diversity, more cross-cultural input to the National Curriculum and attention to opportunites for indivudual and personality development in inner-city neighbourhoods may well form the substrate for enhanced mental health.

More targeted schemes, such as increased support for Black families in crisis and less reliance on the removal of children into care, could be important and effective. However, their implementation will probably have to be in the context of the development of more cohesive communities through increased investment in education and social life.

Similarly, initiatives such as education about the effects of stress, the use of crisis services and medical practitioners in the early treatment of psychological distress, and education planning for and dealing with predictable life events and transitions may prevent distress from developing into chronic psychological problems. For all of this, the development of wider support networks is the long-term key.

Effective primary prevention often falls outside the normal remit of mental health services. This may be why primary prevention has not been high on the agenda. However, the WHO (1998) concluded that doctors interested in the field could develop their potential to act as advocates and advisers to professionals in other sectors. And, as Eisenberg (1981) stated,

> "what matters is not the mode of action of the agent, the venue in which it is applied, or the academic discipline of the practitioner, but the effectiveness of the measure in preventing diseases manifested by disturbances in mental function".

Aetiological research links the increased incidence of psychotic illness in African–Caribbeans to political marginalisation, racism, a noxious urban environment, lower social class, lower levels of social capital and poor education. A desired improvement in all these areas would not be contentious, but in order for this to happen the relative importance of each item in the crowded political agenda will have to increase. This will depend on the pressure brought to bear on politicians.

Scott & Leff (1994) concluded that doctors need to set up alliances with political and pressure groups to encourage the Government to pursue preventive strategies for the good of patients. Similarly, psychiatrists could support local groups that aim to improve the community. Psychiatrists would be right to be cautious in straying from their areas of speciality into the uncharted waters of politics. However, if a decrease in the incidence of schizophrenia in African–Caribbeans is the desired outcome, social policy research, health impact assessment and primary prevention are the logical conclusions of aetiological research which posits socio-environmental causes for the higher incidence recorded in this group.

The widespread and long-term nature of the problems and the solutions makes proper evaluation of specific initiatives very difficult. Furthermore, elucidation of mechanisms will not necessarily lead to a change in public policy recommendations, which tend to be broad and conceptual rather than focused. Improving mental health services alone is unlikely significantly to change the increased incidence of psychotic illness in African–Caribbeans that has been documented in the UK for decades. It is unclear how much more it is necessary to know before it is unethical not to support the development and pursuance of a holistic mental health and social health policy for UK African–Caribbeans. How long does the African–Caribbean community have to wait before primary prevention is at the top of the agenda?

Conclusions

I have attempted to show how important primary prevention could be to the mental health of minority ethnic communities. I have used the example of the high rates of psychosis in UK African–Caribbeans because psychosis is an area in which primary prevention is not high on health agendas. However, a review of the research shows that social factors are thought to be important in the increased incidence of psychosis and that there are possible avenues for primary prevention even at our current level of knowledge. I would argue that in a speciality where there are so few cures, primary prevention should have a higher priority.

References

ACHESON, E. D. (1990) Edwin Chadwick and the world we live in. *Lancet*, **336**, 1482–1485.

AMICK, B. C., LEVINE, S., TARLOV, A. R., *et al* (eds) (1995) *Society and Health*. New York: Oxford University Press.

ANDREASSON, S., ALLBECK, P. & RYDBERG, U. (1989) Schizophrenia in users and non-users of cannabis: a longitudinal study. *Acta Psychiatrica Scandinavica*, **79**, 505–510.

BAHL, V. (1999) Mental illness: a national perspective. In *Ethnicity: An Agenda for Mental Health* (eds D. Bhugra & V. Bahl), pp. 7–22. London: Gaskell.

BARTLEY, M., BLANE, D. & MONTGOMERY, S. (1997) Health and lifecourse: why safety nets matter. *British Medical Journal*, **314**, 1194–1196.

BELL, C. C. & JENKINS, E. J. (1993) Community violence and children on Chicago's Southside. *Psychiatry*, **56**, 46–54.

BHUGRA, D. & BAHL, V. (eds) (1999) *Ethnicity: An Agenda for Mental Health*. London: Gaskell.

——, HILWIG, M., HOSSIEN, B., *et al* (1996) First contact incidence rates of schizophrenia in Trinidad and one year follow-up. *British Journal of Psychiatry*, **169**, 587–592.

——, LEFF, J., MALLETT, R., *et al* (1997) Incidence and outcome of schizophrenia in whites, African Caribbeans and Asians in London. *Psychological Medicine*, **27**, 791–798).

BROWN, G. W. & HARRIS, T. (1975) *Social Origins of Depression*. New York: Free Press.

—— & PURDO, R (1981) Psychiatric disorder in a rural and urban population. 1: Aetiology of depression. *Psychological Medicine*, **11**, 581–599.

CALLAN, A.F. (1996) Schizophrenia in Afro-Caribbean immigrants. *Journal of the Royal Society of Medicine*, **89**, 253–256.

CANADIAN TASK FORCE ON MENTAL HEALTH ISSUES (1988) *After the Door has Opened*. Ottawa: Ministry of Supply Services.

CAPLAN, A. F. (1964) *Principles of Preventive Psychiatry*. New York: Basic Books.

CASTLE, D. J., WESSELY, S., VAN OS, J, *et al* (1998) *Psychosis in the Inner City. The Camberwell First Episode Study. Maudsley Monograph 40*. Hove: Psychology Press, p. 22.

COLE, E., LEAVEY, G., KING, M., *et al* (1995) Pathways to care for patients with a first episode of psychosis. A comparison of ethnic groups. *British Journal of Psychiatry*, **167**, 770–776.

DAVIES, S., THORNICROFT, G., LEESE, M., *et al* (1996) Ethnic differences in the risk of compulsory psychiatric admissions among representative cases of psychosis in London. *British Medical Journal*, **312**, 533–537.

DIEZ-ROUX, A. V. (1988) Bringing context back into epidemiology: variables and fallacies in multi-level analysis. *American Journal of Public Health*, **88**, 216–222.

DOHRENWEND, B. S. & DOHRENWEND, B. P. (1974) *Stressful Life Events: Their Nature and Effects*. New York: John Wiley & Sons.

EISENBERG, L. (1981) A research framework for evaluating the promotion of mental health and prevention of mental illness. *Public Health Reports*, **96**, 3–19.

FREEMAN, H. (1985) *Mental Health and the Environment*. London: Churchill Livingstone.

FRYER, P. (1984) *Staying Power: The History of Black People in Britain*. London: Pluto.

GOODMAN, R. & RICHARDS, H. (1995) Child and adolescent psychiatric presentations of second generation Afro-Caribbeans in Britain. *British Journal of Psychiatry*,**167**, 362–369.

HALPERN, D. (1993) Minorities and mental health. *Social Science and Medicine*, **36**, 597–607.

HARRISON, G., OWENS, D., HOLTON, A., *et al* (1988) A prospective study of severe mental disorder in Afro-Caribbean patients. *Psychological Medicine*, **18**, 643–657.

——, AMIN, S., SWARAN P. SINGH, *et al* (1999) Outcome of psychosis in people of African–Caribbean family origin. Population based first episode study. *British Journal of Psychiatry*, **175**, 43–49.

HICKLING, F. W. & RODGERS-JOHNSON, P. (1995) The incidence of first contact schizophrenia in Jamaica. *British Journal of Psychiatry*, **167**, 193–196.

HUTCHINSON, J., TAKEI, N., FAHY, T., *et al* (1996) Morbid risk of schizophrenia in first degree relatives of white and African–Caribbean patients with psychosis. *British Journal of Psychiatry*, **169**, 776–780.

——, BHUGRA, D., *et al* (1997) Increased rate of psychosis among African–Caribbeans in Britain is not due to an excess of pregnancy and birth complications. *British Journal of Psychiatry*, **171**, 145–147.

HUTTUMEN, M. O. (1989) Maternal stress during pregnancy and the behavior of offspring. In *Early Influences Shaping the Individual* (ed. S. Doxiadis), pp. 175–182. New York: Plenum Press.

JENKINS, E. J. & BELL, C. C. (1997) Exposure and response to community violence among children and adolescents. In *Children in a Violent Society* (ed. J. D. Osofsky), pp. 9–31. New York: Guilford Press.

——, KENNEDY, P., LOCKNER, K., *et al* (1997) Social capital, income inequality and mortality. *American Journal of Public Health*, **87**, 1491–1498.

KING, G. (1996) Institutional racism and the medical health complex: a conceptual analysis. *Ethnicity and Disease*, **6**, 30–46.

KING, M., COKER, E., LEAVEY, G., *et al* (1994) Incidence of psychotic illness in London: a comparison of ethnic groups. *British Medical Journal*, **309**, 1115–1119.

KLEINMAN, A. (1991) Do social relations and cultural meanings contribute to the onset and course of mental illness? In *Rethinking Psychiatry* (ed. A. Kleinman), pp. 53–76. New York: Free Press.

LAVIEST, T. (1993) *Poverty, Empowerment, Health Consequences for African–Americans.* Milbank Memorial Fund 1.1.

LEWIS, D., DAVID. A., ANDREASON, S., *et al* (1992) Schizophrenia and city life. *Lancet*, **340**, 137–140.

LILLIE-BLANTON, M., ANTHONY, J. & SCHUSTER, C. (1993) Probing the meaning of racial/ethnic differences in crack cocaine. *JAMA*, **269**, 993.

—— & LAVIEST, T. (1996) Race, ethnicity, the social environment and health. *Social Science and Medicine*, **43**, 83–91.

LITTLEWOOD, R. & LIPSEDGE, M. (1997) *Aliens and Alienists.* London: Routledge.

LLOYD, K. & ST LOUIS, L. (1999) Common mental disorders among African–Caribbean general practice attenders in Brixton, London. In *Ethnicity: An Agenda for Mental Health* (eds D. Bughra & V. Bahl), pp. 60–69. London: Gaskell.

MARCELIS, M., TAKEI, N. & VAN OS, J. (1999) Urbanization and risk for schizophrenia: does the effect operate before or around the time of illness onset? *Psychological Medicine*, **29**, 1197–1203.

MARMOT, M. G., SMITH, G. D., STANSFELD, S., *et al* (1991) Health inequalities among British civil servants: the Whitehall II study. *Lancet*, **337**, 1387–1393.

MAUGHAN, B. (1989) Growing up in the inner city. *Paediatric and Perinatal Epidemiology*, **3**, 195–215.

McKENZIE, K. & MURRAY, R. M. (1999) Risk factors for mental illness in African–Caribbeans. In *Ethnicity: An Agenda for Mental Health* (eds D. Bhugra & V. Bahl). London: Gaskell.

——, VAN OS, J., FAHY, T., *et al* (1995) Psychosis of good prognosis in Afro-Caribbean people now living in the United Kingdom. *British Medical Journal*, **311**, 1325–1328.

McKENZIE, K., JONES, P., LEWIS, S., *et al* (2000*a*) Lower prevalence of pre-morbid neurological illness in African–Caribbean than White psychotic patients in the UK. *Psychological Medicine* (in press).

——, SAMELE, C., VAN HORN, E., *et al*, ON BEHALF OF UK700 GROUP (2000*b*) A comparison of psychosis and its treatment in patients of Caribbean origin and British Whites. *Social Psychiatry and Psychiatric Epidemiology* (in press).

MENEFFEE, L., (1996) Are black Americans entitled to equal health care? A new research paradigm. *Ethnicity and Disease*, **6**, 56–68.

MURRAY, R. M. & O'CALLAGHAN, E. (1991) Neurodevelopmental schizophrenia. *Schizophrenia Monitor*, **1**, 1–3.

NIGAONKAR, V., WESSELY, S. & MURRAY, R. M. (1988) Prevalence of familiarity, obstetric complications and structural brain damage in schizophrenia patients. *British Journal of Psychiatry*, **153**, 191–197.

PAYKEL, E. S. & JENKINS, R. (eds) (1994) *Prevention in Psychiatry.* London: Gaskell.

PERRY, M. J. (1996) The relationship between social class and mental disorder. *Journal of Primary Prevention*, **17**, 1–7.

QUINTON, D. (1988) Urbanism and child mental health. *Journal of Child Psychology and Psychiatry*, **29**, 11–20.

RICE, D. C. (1996) Behavioral effects of lead: commonalities between experimental and epidemiological data. *Environmental Health Perspectives*, **104**, 337–351.

SARTORIUS, N., JABLENSKY, A., KORTEN, A., *et al* (1986) Early manifestations and first contact incidence of schizophrenia in different cultures. *Psychological Medicine* ,**16**, 909–928.

SCOTT, J. & LEFF, J. (1994) Social factors , social interventions and prevention. In *Prevention in Psychiatry* (eds E. S. Paykel & R. Jenkins), pp. 25–31. London: Gaskell.

SECRETARY OF STATE FOR HEALTH (1998) *Our Healthier Nation: A Contract for Health.* London: HMSO.

SELTEN, J.-P., SLAETS, J. P. J. & KAHN, R. S. (1997) Schizophrenia in Surinamese and Dutch Antillean immigrants to The Netherlands: evidence of an increased incidence. *Psychological Medicine,* **27**, 807–811.

SUGARMAN, P. A. & CRAUFURD, D. (1994) Schizophrenia in the Afro-Caribbean community. *British Journal of Psychiatry,* **164**, 474–480.

TASK FORCE ON ADOLESCENT ASSAULT VICTIM NEEDS (1996) Adolescent assault victim needs: a review of issues and a model protocol. *Pediatrics,* **98**, 991–1001.

TIMMS, D. W. G. (1996) Social mobility and mental health in a Swedish cohort. *Social Psychiatry and Psychiatric Epidemiology,* **31**, 38–48.

US DEPARTMENT OF HEALTH AND HUMAN SERVICES (1990) *National Household Survey on Drug Abuse.* ADM 90-1692. Washington DC: National Institute of Drugs Abuse, US Department of Health and Human Services Publications.

VAILLANT, G. E. (1964) Prospective prediction of schizophrenic remission. *Archives of General Psychiatry,* **11**, 509–518.

VAN OS, J., MCKENZIE, K. & JONES, P. (1997) Cultural differences in pathways to care, service use and treated outcomes. *Current Opinion in Psychiatry,* **10**, 178–182.

——, JONES, P., SHAM, P., *et al* (1998) Risk factors for onset and persistence of psychosis. *Social Psychiatry and Psychiatric Epidemiology,* **33**, 596–605.

—— & SELTEN, J. P. (1998) Prenatal exposure to maternal stress and subsequent schizophrenia. The May, 1940 invasion of The Netherlands. *British Journal of Psychiatry,* **172**, 324–326.

VOGEL, H. (1997) Cocaine wreaks subtle damage on developing brains. *Science,* **278**, 38–39.

WALKER, E. F. & DIFORIO, D. (1997) Schizophrenia: a neural diathesis-stress model. *Psychological Review,* **104**, 667–685.

WARNER, R. (1985) *Recovery from Schizophrenia: Psychiatry and the Political Economy.* New York: Routledge & Kegan Paul.

WEICH, S. & LEWIS, G. (1998) Poverty, unemployment and common mental disorders: population based cohort study. *British Medical Journal,* **317**, 115–119.

WESSELY, S., CASTLE, D., DER, G., *et al* (1991) Schizophrenia and Afro-Caribbeans: a case control study. *British Journal of Psychiatry,* **159**, 795–801.

WILLIAMS, D. (1996) Racism and health: a research agenda. *Ethnicity and Disease,* **6**, 1–6.

WINNEKE, G. & KRAMER, U. (1997) Neurobehavioral aspects of lead neurotoxicity in children. *Central European Journal of Public Health,* **5**, 65–69.

WORLD HEALTH ORGANIZATION (1998) *Primary Prevention of Mental Neurological and Psychosocial Disorders.* Geneva: WHO.

17 Services for ethnic minorities: conceptual issues

DINESH BHUGRA

Editors' introduction

The keystone of therapist–patient interaction is the health care system within which it takes place. When developing services for Black and other ethnic minority groups it is essential that certain key principles are followed. The debate about whether there should be separate services for these groups modelled on women-only services continues unresolved. Both types of service have advantages and disadvantages.

Bhugra highlights the need for identifying the explanatory models used by the local communities and determining how these can match those of service providers. The assessment will allow a theme of commonality to emerge. The development of psychiatric services should be a bottom-up rather than a top-down process, and emphasis may need to shift from psychiatric diagnosis alone to the multiple and complex needs of patients and their carers. Theoretical models should include both epidemiological and cultural needs, and clear priorities should be set in consultation with local communities. Various models for different psychiatric sub-specialities suggest that innovation is often necessary.

Models suggest that successful services are those in which the community has a stake and that the patients and their families find acceptable and appropriate. Such services will increase the workload of team members, but there will be a corresponding increase in patient and carer satisfaction. This must impinge on prognosis if patients seek help at an early stage and are more likely to agree with and accept the treatment being offered.

The involvement of the community (represented by religious leaders, teachers, the local media and individuals such as councillors and general practitioners) makes it more likely that the community's influence will hold sway over a longer period and that the services will be successful.

A number of key issues must be taken into account when services are being planned for ethnic minority groups in the UK. There is considerable evidence (referred to elsewhere in this volume) that the incidence and prevalence of certain mental illnesses is higher in some ethnic groups and yet their take-up of statutory services is rather poor. Although two large groups – African–Caribbean and South Asian – migrated to the UK for broadly similar economic reasons at around the same time (more Africans were subsequently expelled from East Africa), it is apparent that the cultural patterns and patterns of settling in have been different and it has been argued that some of these factors may play a role in the genesis of mental illnesses (see also Chapter 4, this volume). The differing mental health needs of primary migrants and their progeny need to be acknowledged, as do their models of illness and the pathways they choose to gain access to mental health care.

There remain unresolved issues in the planning and delivery of services for ethnic minorities (Bhugra, 1997). These include whether separate services should be offered in order to increase the take-up rate. This remains an attractive option with several advantages, such as the development of specialist services on the model of diabetic and asthma clinics, where skills in cultural competences can be acquired and retained, allowing cultural and ethnic matching of patients and therapists. Such a move might also help reduce the stigma of psychiatric services, thereby increasing the take-up rate. Disadvantages of this approach include the possibility of resentment and alienation in the majority community, who may see pampering and special treatment for minority groups. Ethnic matching of therapists and patients might not be feasible or successful. An additional problem is that such a service is likely to become 'ghettoised', producing a sense of isolation and alienation in the members of ethnic minorities who are providing services. At a political level such an option may be attractive in the short term. Then pulling the drawbridge may leave service providers even more frustrated and isolated (Bhui *et al*, 1999).

The optimal way of developing services for local communities has to be a bottom-up approach. If the services are already in place, it is vital that regular consultations with the community continue and that services are modified accordingly. A mixture of public and private service provision will contribute different facets to the actual delivery of psychiatric services.

For services to succeed and be acceptable to the community, explanatory models of illness must be studied. Such an investigation will rely on simple, easy-to-use questionnaires to gather information on possible causes and management (Lloyd *et al*, 1998). This approach also allows the clinician to identify the disease and illness models that are important to the patients and their carers (see below). In addition, generalisation of epidemiological data from other studies and local data collection will allow providers to identify the needs of the local population and modify service delivery. Within the collection of local epidemiological data, the population and ethnicity breakdown will form an important baseline.

Another point that planners must take into account is the distinction between demand and need, which often do not match. Methods of needs assessment have already been described (Chapter 15, this volume). A clear distinction between need, demand and supply will determine the success of services. The demand for a certain service depends on a number of factors, for example, vocalisation of demands and media exposure. Thus, vocal demands may be funded while unvoiced needs will remain unmet.

Explanatory models and epidemiology

Bhui (Chapter 3, this volume) has already discussed the implications of epidemiological factors in ethnic minority groups and their role in the development of services. Here I will focus on the relationship between epidemiology and the explanatory models that determine the pathways to care. In older immigrants, help-seeking may be limited due to language barriers, poor experience of services, inadequate knowledge of available resources, as well as to the poor response of statutory services. In addition, the multiplicity of physical and psychological symptoms may well influence patterns of help-seeking. For example, some patients may go to general practitioners only with their physical symptoms.

Families (Fandetti & Gelfand, 1978) and other personal contacts (Kleinman, 1980) account for 70–80% of healing activities. Thus, mental health services and resources may not be perceived as entirely appropriate for dealing with problems even if the family and personal sectors are not able to provide expert advice. An additional factor in seeking help is the interaction between the therapist and the patient. Various background factors are associated with such an interaction. For example, the therapist's ethnic background, culture, past experience, education, social class and professional expertise may well clash with those of the patient, so that the interaction between therapist and patient is endangered by the power embedded in the therapist.

A key factor in the interaction is that the therapist is often interested in *what* is wrong, whereas the patient may well be interested in *why* something is wrong. Anthropologists have taken the lead in considering this dichotomy. For example, Littlewood (1990;

Chapter 2, this volume) argues that the classificatory (particularly lexical) categories of ordinary people (patients) may not 'fit' with those used by psychiatrists. Kleinman (1980) suggests that the construction of the illness experience is a key function of the health care system and is a personally and socially adaptive response. He suggests that 'disease' refers to a malfunctioning biological and/or psychological process, while 'illness' refers to both psychosocial experiences and the perceived disease. These latter will include attention to symptoms, perception, affective responses, cognition and valuation of the disease and its manifestation. Such a distinction between illness and disease is useful in developing services. For example, planners and service providers may well be intrigued by the rate of disease, whereas the patients' take-up of services will be determined by their psychosocial experiences embedded in the illness models. The service providers need to be aware of this distinction – the professionals are interested in the disease, whereas the carers and patients may be interested in the illness. In chronic conditions, such as chronic schizophrenia or bipolar affective disorder, the distinction between disease and illness may well become blurred and labelling of each symptom may provide a different concept and will be linked with early help-seeking.

Littlewood (1990) suggests that psychiatry is entangled in its own roots, as its area of interest encompasses not only the experiential and behavioural correlates of abnormal cerebral processes, but also the individuals' responses to their life history, social environment and family circle. Thus, schizophrenia can be viewed in a variety of ways depending, for example, on one's frame of reference, personal identification and sympathies, as well as the urgency of the situation.

Hahn and Kleinman (1983) point out that within the hierarchy of medical specialism, status and power are related to the therapeutic techniques employed and the parts of the body treated, thereby granting a cultural symbolism to each part of the body within each speciality. This is bound to affect the delivery of services. In addition, cultural systems form the theoretical framework of both the patient and the therapist, and this raises the issue of the impact of culture on sickness and healing (Kleinman, 1978). Thus, the universality of diagnostic systems and their acceptance must be questioned.

While psychiatrists argue that disease categories must be analysed in terms of the indigenous culture's values and the roles and conflicts these seem to generate, anthropologists study behaviours of aliens in various settings (Skultans, 1993). Reiss (1993) describes the coming together of anthropology and psychiatry in psychoanalytically informed observations of child development. A number of anthropologists have advocated classification of medical systems for cross-cultural comparisons in personal and naturalistic settings, with internalisation and externalisation as two extremes (e.g. Koss, 1987). Koss emphasises that the crux of differences between anthropological (ethnoscientific studies of ethnomedical categories of illness) and psychiatric (mainly epidemiological studies) approaches lies in the description and understanding of their ultimate goal: the latter is subordinated to concerns with diagnosis and treatment.

As mentioned above, the explanatory model approach provides a more patient-centred view of clinical encounters and tasks (Kleinman, 1978). Kleinman proposes that in each sector of the health care system, explanatory models can be elicited from practitioners, patients, family and community members for particular conditions, as well as particular sickness episodes. These should contain explanations of aetiology, onset of symptoms, pathophysiology, course of sickness (severity as well as type of sick role) and treatment. It is worth emphasising that explanatory models are not static: not only do they vary from episode to episode, but they are also likely to vary within the same episode. Although these are very important factors in developing services and identifying needs, it is important to note that reliance on explanatory models alone may well produce an imbalance. Explanatory models may well be influenced by need. Rogler (1993) highlights the role of culture in helping the therapist to reach a diagnosis, and proposes that culture and cultural factors be used in the assessment of mental health as an essential part of programmatic research focusing on general issues of validity in psychiatric diagnosis. Using focus groups to collect qualitative data (Rogler *et al*, 1994; Bhugra *et al*, 1997), psychiatrically relevant symptoms can be assessed and symptoms can be configured into disorders, so that subsequent diagnostic interviews can be arranged.

The other aim of such a strategy has to include epidemiological methods of data collection. There have been suggestions that people from African–Caribbean and Asian communities are less likely to be diagnosed as having depression, manic depression and neurotic disorders (London, 1986). Brewin (1980) reported that Asians visited their GPs as frequently as their White counterparts, but that the admission rates of the former for psychiatric disorders were lower than expected. In several studies, Cochrane and Stopes-Roe (1977, 1980, 1981) showed that the rates of psychiatric morbidity varied dramatically across different ethnic groups, with socio-economic deprivation and discrimination playing an important role in variations in levels of psychopathology. Social class, gender, unemployment and so on have been suggested as key factors in explaining these discrepancies (Cochrane and Stopes-Roe, 1980). The rates of neurotic disorder in ethnic minority groups are variable (Jacob *et al*, 1998; Nazroo, 1997). Jacob *et al* (1998) observed that rates of common mental disorders were as high among Asian females as their White counterparts, but that GPs even from similar cultural and linguistic backgrounds were less likely to recognise them. Their Western training may be one explanation of this anomaly.

This brief overview illustrates that we still have a long way to go in order to identify common mental disorders and manage them properly in Black and other ethnic minority patients.

Some issues in management

Management of mental distress in various ethnic groups in the professional (or statutory) sector is based on Western models of illness, whereas in the personal and social sectors the approach is likely to be a pluralist mixture of alternative and complementary health practices. Sufficient clinical and research evidence exists to suggest that drop-out rates, poor compliance with medication and antipathy to treatment are common among ethnic minority groups. The perceived and real discrimination in treatment in these groups is not likely to endear statutory services to patients and their carers. In addition, culturally insensitive and inappropriate services are likely to lead to further alienation of patients and carers. It must be emphasised that not all members of ethnic minority groups will see services through a cultural glass, and therapists and practitioners should not believe that all members of these groups have the same views on service delivery.

Although Katon & Kleinman (1981) suggest a structured strategy of negotiation between patients and practitioners, beginning with an understanding of explanatory models, Koss (1987) urges a note of caution. He points out that such an approach has to overcome two key problems. First, the understanding of meanings of illness remains a daunting task, for both the patient and the practitioner, especially when both participants in the therapeutic interaction are not familiar with each other's cultural beliefs. Second, the strength of the clinician's belief may be so great that there is little permission for competing treatment approaches. For biopathological processes such as rheumatoid arthritis or cervical cancer, there are no great difficulties in making diagnoses across cultures, whereas for psychopathological processes cultural differences can cause major dilemmas (Westermeyer, 1985).

Diagnostic and management strategies for different conditions have been previously discussed (Bhugra, 1993; Bhui *et al*, 1995; Bhugra & Bhui, 1998*a*). The notion and reliability of psychiatric diagnoses become important at aetiological and prevention levels. The setting up of services may be planned at national level, but they are implemented at local level. Thus, models for a rural town may not be entirely appropriate for the inner city.

One possible move forward could include reliance on multi-axial needs assessment (Thornicroft *et al*, 1992, 1999; Chapter 15, in this volume). This would mean moving the focus from psychiatric diagnosis to a broader understanding of biopsychosocial models. It would be helpful to identify a set of outcomes, in discussion with the patients and their carers. Since quality assurance includes notions of optimal, social and personal functioning and assessment of impairments (which must be minimised and which are sensitive to therapeutic intervention), there appears to be a gradual and subtle shift towards setting of services according to these needs.

World Health Organization models

Meads (1983) describes the World Health Organization (WHO) Reason for Encounter Classification (RFE–C), which classifies the reasons for seeking health care from the perspective of the patient. Such an approach is, by definition, patient oriented, rather than disease oriented or even provider oriented. Meads suggests that most classifications are designed to classify the health care provider's interpretation of the patient's illness, disease or injury, and that it makes sense to move away from this and focus on the patient's perspective. In the RFE–C approach the reasons for the encounter are those given by the patients before the therapist or health practitioner has made any judgement on their validity or accuracy.

Once the stated reasons for contact have been established, the clinician defines the problem and take appropriate action. The emphasis is on understanding and not on diagnosis, and such a classification has three guiding principles:

(a) the reasons for the encounter must be understood and agreed upon by the patient and health care provider, who must recognise them as an acceptable description;

(b) the physician's written record of the patient's reasons must be as close as possible to the patient's own words;

(c) the reasons for the encounter must represent the starting point for action (or the decision not to act) by the health care provider.

Such a classification system is designed along the axes of 'chapters' and 'components'. Some chapters cover body systems, and others remain non-anatomical and are entitled 'general', 'psychological' and 'social'. Unlike the categories described in the International Classification of Diseases (ICD; World Health Organization, 1992) of neoplasms, trauma, injuries and congenital disorder, the basic representation is of disease. Each chapter is subdivided into seven components: symptoms and complaints, screening and preventative procedures, treatment, procedures and medication, test results, administration, and other diseases and diagnoses.

The construction of the RFE–C was influenced by existing major classifications, and a seven-country feasibility test was carried out (Meads, 1983). Allowing the patient to lead the identification of needs not only has clinical implications; it also has value as a research instrument, since it can provide an improved description of the natural history of ill health that enables individuals, families and communities to recognise ill health and disease early and to be involved in management. It will also allow individuals and their families to identify reasons for crossing the threshold from self-care to being patients.

This information may make it possible to develop mechanisms to reduce inappropriate referrals to higher levels of the health service, identify high-risk groups of patients and otherwise improve the cost-effectiveness of primary health care (Meads, 1983). The emphasis here is on self-report and identification of symptoms, which lead to the patient becoming adept at self-care and working with other partners in health care provision.

Goldberg (1992) recommends that in general medical settings those in psychological distress are identified in three ways: first, from high scores on screening tests; second, as 'cases' seen by the doctor; and third, from a standardised research diagnosis. The classification is based on the patient's need for intervention and distinguishes between those who have a formal mental disorder and those who do not. Not only does it take into account the process of labelling and compliance, but also it is linked to primary health care workers. The use of such a system has the advantage of combining the caring concepts of the general practitioner and specialist with the perception of the patient. Goldberg (1992) argues that classifications of mental disorders proposed by psychiatrists are of no great assistance to primary care physicians. In countries and health care systems in which psychiatric services are difficult to contact or are very limited and in which most psychiatric care is provided by the primary care services, such a model is very attractive. Each of the three groups needs a different kind of service and intervention. The first group, which is probably the largest, will include those whose emotional distress may benefit from recognition and discussion, but who will get better without medical treatment. These people will not benefit from being told that they have a mental illness. The second group includes those with long-standing neurotic symptoms associated with intractable social or interpersonal problems. This group will benefit from social interventions and counselling. The third group will have 'mental illness' and is likely to benefit from active treatment. At one level this model, with treatability as an option, is attractive and it appears to be culturally sensitive, because culture can determine who enters each group. However, there is every likelihood that not everyone will fall into these three categories and the use of screening tests that are not culturally sensitive will create problems of its own.

Characteristics of psychiatric services

According to the Royal College of Psychiatrists (Bhugra *et al*, 1995), services must be acceptable, accessible and accountable. Access is often restricted for geographical, physical, cognitive, attitudinal and bureaucratic reasons. Accountability has to be shown to several stakeholders, including patients and their families, communities, employers, professional bodies and colleagues. Any successful service also has to provide continuity within which the patient's individuality and sovereignty are respected (see Bhugra *et al*, 1995, for a detailed discussion). Wooff (1992) recommends the following guidelines for setting up services:

(a) establish the extent and nature of needs
(b) outline principles, aims and objectives
(c) set priorities
(d) set strategies
(e) monitor outcomes and modify strategies accordingly.

As Bhugra *et al* (1995) point out, such a model depends on: a definition of mental illness; properly resourced, bottom-up information systems, with agreement on the purpose(s) of each component within the network or shared system, for priority of resources; the involvement of service users, carers and their advocates in the decision-making process; consensus on the relationships between managerial and clinical responsibilities, and on the responsibilities of different professional groups; clearly documented, individually negotiated care plans; clearly documented operational policies for each service component; systems for resource management; monitoring and management control systems. Chiu (1994) reported that the sociocultural background of patients from the lower east side of Manhattan influenced their behavioural expression of underlying psychiatric disorders. In his sample, the Chinese more readily accepted a treatment approach that began and ended at home: they saw hospital as the 'end of the road'. Jewish patients, however, accepted hospitalisation more readily, viewing home treatments as painful, prolonged and uncertain.

Practical problems: a UK perspective

As stated above, the first step in setting up services for ethnic minorities has usually been a thorough assessment of the ethnic distribution of the local population and of their needs. In the future it might be better to move the emphasis away from diagnoses and diagnosis-based perceived needs and towards RFE–C classification, which gives a clearer picture of why people need help and of their expectations of such help.

Ethnic monitoring of patients coming into contact with services will go some way towards establishing their numbers, allowing assessment of epidemiological data on various illnesses and helping in the recruitment of staff who are familiar with different cultures, religions and languages. An awareness of cultural norms (such as rites of passage, religious taboos and dietary restrictions) is essential for staff caring for patients from ethnic minorities. Untrained people or family members should not be used as interpreters.

Psychiatric specialities

The roles of various psychiatric specialities beneath the broader umbrella of psychiatric services vary.

General psychiatry services

General psychiatry currently uses the short or episodic illness model, and it therefore provides a reactive, short-term formula for care. Psychiatric crises can be very varied and services must be appropriate and flexible to provide adequate emergency care. The reliable identification of a patient's need at the point of first contact is crucial in providing any kind of emergency care. Clinical and research evidence suggests that most Black patients enter the psychiatric system through emergency services, presenting with life-threatening or non-life-threatening problems.

Support services interfere least in individuals' normal social roles, aiming to help people to cope with problems themselves using their own resources. Joint work with non-statutory organisations may provide non-threatening, culturally appropriate and culture-sensitive services. Supplementary services provide additional aids or resources necessary to enable people to live a normal life. Substitute care emphasises the provision of services that allow individuals to withdraw from the pressures of their normal social roles in order to gain stability and establish a new equilibrium, so that they can return to their environment. Additional responses might include helplines, walk-in services, crisis beds and emergency peripatetic services.

Long-term (rehabilitative) services

Bridges *et al* (1994) defined rehabilitation as a process that aims to minimise the negative effects of the dynamic relationships between biological, psychological, functional and environmental factors associated with mental disorder and to maximise the individual's latent abilities and strengths. Broad aims include prevention of impairments, restoration of potential abilities and slowing down of deterioration to enable optimal levels of self-determination to be reached, execution of personal responsibilities and independence. Furthermore, the aims must include a reduction in burden on the carers and improvement in the individual's overall sense of well-being. These can be achieved by a combination of behavioural and psychological interventions. Not all of these interventions are culturally appropriate: as McCarthy (1987) points out, issues of control and manipulation, with overtones of master–slave relationships, are laden with meaning for some populations. Similarly, the use of social skills programmes can be fraught with problems in cultures in which, for example, assertiveness within the family or social 'dating' may be unacceptable. Patients who develop chronic long-term mental illness and have enduring illnesses and disabilities will have complex biological, psychological, social and material needs. The Care Programme Approach is useful in moving away from acute or intermittent models of care.

People with chronic and disabling illnesses may have enduring psychiatric disorder, which may be continuous or fluctuate in intensity and severity. Associated disabilities in social functioning, which also tend to vary, complicate the picture. Social expectations are likely to vary across cultures, and identification of needs in terms of psychological and social as well as environmental factors is crucial in the provision of appropriate services. Specialist rehabilitation services may be required, and standard rehabilitation may not be appropriate, useful or sensitive to the needs of ethnic minority patients. For example, some communities may see behavioural therapies as demeaning or punitive. If accommodation is provided, it should offer access to ethnically and generally appropriate services. Different communities will place different emphasis on work and social support. Furthermore, perceived racism and high rates of unemployment may make retraining or the search for work seem pointless to patients and carers. As Bridges *et al* (1994) cautioned, rehabilitation services must provide long-term plans and appropriate asylum and must remember that social care and health care are not different.

Forensic psychiatry

As Cope illustrates in Chapter 13 (this volume), special hospitals and prisons contain many African–Caribbean men with a history of violence and aggression. Maden (1993) warns that the link between crime and ethnic origin is historical and that wide-ranging (and ill-formed) conclusions about 'human nature' and its 'biological' variation between races can be problematic. He suggests that emphasis should shift to the study of crime in relation to culture or society rather than to race. Social attitudes and stereotypes must be challenged, and court diversion schemes and rapid response to crisis must be introduced for mentally disordered offenders. Black patients are over-represented among the severely mentally disordered in prison. Maden (1992) reports that rates of psychosis in sentenced prisoners in England and Wales are 2.5 times higher among Blacks than Whites and suggests that there are considerable unmet needs for psychiatric treatment among Black prisoners. He recommends that clinical audit must include ethnicity and referrals as well as admissions. There is a complex interrelationship between ethnicity, mental illness and crime, and management must take into account broad socio-political changes as well as local needs and individual attitudes.

Liaison psychiatry services

Members of some ethnic minorities may present more with physical symptoms than with either psychological symptoms or a combination of the two. It is crucial that members of the liaison team are familiar with models of presentation. Here too, greater emphasis on presentation for care needs, rather than on diagnostic medical models would be useful.

In ethnic minorities the clinician often perceives the presentation as physical. Questions on psychological health are not included at all, or if they are, the patient's responses may be ignored. The whole perspective of somatisation is fraught with difficulties. Individual clinicians have been known to state that the use of somatic symptoms by ethnic minorities may reflect difficulties in language or expression of distress. But as Krause (1989) has demonstrated, the communication of distress in somatic ways is an accepted idiom. When faced with patients with atypical or unusual symptoms, it is important for the clinician to be aware of underlying psychological distress and symptoms. Whether these cases are dealt with by separate services or within a consultation liaison system is determined by local service planners. It is vital that clinicans have access, if needed, to the advice of individuals with knowledge of local communities.

Substance misuse

Rates of substance misuse vary across ethnic communities (see Chapter 12, this volume). Cochrane and Bal (1989) report that rates of hospital admission owing to alcohol misuse were much higher in Indian men and much lower in Pakistani men; men born in the Caribbean had conspicuously low rates. Others, such as McKeigue and Karmi (1993; see Cochrane, 1999) also report that African–Caribbeans consume less alcohol. Cochrane and Bal (1990), in a community survey using retrospective drinking diaries, observed that Sikhs were drinking more than other groups, which contributed to family problems. Although some cultures prohibit alcohol or drug use, this does not mean that individuals do not also use them. The provision of culturally sensitive services means that models of management can be developed in close liaison with local communities.

Psychotherapy

Psychoanalytic psychotherapies result from nineteenth-century European values and culture. Although, for example, Bose developed his psychoanalytic theories independent of Freud, his work was influential only in a small part of eastern India (Lloyd & Bhugra, 1993). If one sees psychotherapies as involving a healing agent, a sufferer who needs this healing and a healing relationship (Frank & Frank, 1991), one still has to place these components in a cultural and historical context. Issues surrounding ethnic matching of patient with therapist remain complex and contentious, and the evidence from the literature is mixed (for a review see Lloyd & Bhugra, 1993; Bhugra & Bhui, 1998b). Culturally sensitive models of therapy have been demonstrated by Nafsiyat (Kareem & Littlewood, 1992). Bhatti and Varghese (1995) give an overview of family therapy in India and suggest that family involvement reduced the duration of hospitalisation, increased the family's acceptance of the patient and enhanced family coping. A novel experiment of multiple family group interaction as an adjunct to family therapy has been described (Bhatti *et al*, 1985). In southern India, 2-year follow-up of families who had received brief integrative in-patient family therapy combined with group and individual therapies showed that 43% had good outcome and symptom relief and 23% had moderate recovery; in the remaining 34% the therapy was seen as a complete failure (Prabhu *et al*, 1988). Family therapy plays an important role in the treatment of several psychiatric conditions, for example: alcoholism (Bhatti, 1983); neurotic disorders (Bhatti & Channabasavana, 1986); and learning disability (Girimaji, 1994). In India indigenous treatments have been introduced to replace tools developed in the West (Neki, 1975; Bhatti *et al*, 1985). The process of family therapy includes the use of a co-therapist and assessment of family structure, leadership patterns, roles, communication and cohesiveness. These are the factors often used in marital and family therapy in the West. In the cultural context, the definition of the self and the family vary and it is important for clinicians to have a clear picture of normative data. Traditional Eastern approaches to mental health have important contributions to make to the future of Western psychotherapy. The Eastern emphasis on the importance of links between physical and psychological health has possibilities for resolving the mind–body dichotomy perceived in the Western tradition. Eastern cultures also strive to awaken human awareness and develop genuine human feeling as a necessary step towards reducing human suffering. Psychotherapy across cultures can and will flourish provided that the concepts of self in different cultures are understood and assimilated in any therapeutic work (Ikemi, 1979). Family work raises notions of 'missionary racism', where the therapist sees his or her goal as saving the sufferers from their plight. Some studies (e.g. Warren *et al*, 1973) have reported that Black parents saw family therapy as less helpful, thought that their therapists were alienating and felt that they were being poorly understood. Cognitive and humanistic therapies may be more likely to work with ethnic communities than behavioural or psychoanalytical models (in their pure sense). Appropriate cultural modifications may help (see Neki's 1975 work in India). Given the inevitability of differences between clients and therapists, almost all psychotherapy can be thought of as cross-cultural (Comas-Diaz, 1992), so training and assessment must be culturally appropriate.

Child and adolescent services

Child psychiatry services are affected by a range of social factors (see Chapter 10, this volume), some of which may be more relevant to ethnic minorities: unemployment and racial discrimination are just two of these. Although Asian children are said to be less likely to be seen in child psychiatric services, the evidence is based on clinical impressions rather than research. A significant number of ethnic minority children suffer the impact of culture change or feel trapped in their minority culture, rather than feeling at home in the majority culture. Psychiatric services must offer culturally appropriate services. The socio-economic deprivation associated with some ethnic minorities, together with feelings of alienation, may lead to children's needs being ignored. Furthermore, many ethnic communities live in deprived inner-city areas where schooling may be inadequate and may not cater for their cultural or religious needs. A combination of poor social environment and racism may contribute to a feeling of isolation and lack of support in children and adolescents, which may in turn exert stress on their parents and on statutory services. Unsupported social networks and social, economic and educational deprivation may contribute to poor development, both physically and emotionally. A thorough assessment of psychosocial and cultural factors may encourage both parents and children to seek help at an earlier stage and to attend services.

Old age services

With the number of ethnic minority elderly people likely to rise over the next few decades, it is important that purchasers and providers start planning for services. Cultural factors, such as reliance on self-help and ignorance of racism and inequalities, are likely to affect access to services. Family structures may be changing and are quite likely to affect help-seeking. A discussion of ethnic minority identities (especially the elderly) is likely to achieve precision, familiarity and acceptability of services (Manthorpe & Hettiaratchy, 1993; Chapter 8, this volume).

In ethnic minorities, feelings of alienation, changing roles within the family and changing expectations of each other from both children and the elderly are likely to add to feelings of bewilderment. This is not necessarily exclusive to the ethnic minority elderly. As Venkoba Rao (1993) states, a culture's views of ageing and dying will determine its mechanisms for coping with them. He observes that in India, economic and sociocultural changes have led to a fissuring of the family system and a decline in the support the elderly get from their families and the community. The individual may still wish for the traditional attitudes, and may feel disappointed and alienated when they are no longer offered. The stereotype of the constantly caring and involved family is a myth. The clinician must be aware that living within a family does not automatically ensure healthy integration. The absence of such integration may be more marked in those with psychological illness, and it also has a causal effect (Venkoba Rao, 1993). Ageing is a major life change and the elderly are vulnerable both physically and psychologically. Services must take into account traditional taboos and rites of passage along with socio-demographic profiles and the psychological morbidity of the population to be served.

Learning disability

The general factors of behavioural modification are even more relevant in children from ethnic minority backgrounds who a have learning disability. Family work must be handled sensitively, as different cultures have differing explanations for and ways of dealing with learning disabilities. Genetic counselling (Chapter 11, this volume) requires very careful consideration.

The model for providing services for ethnic minorities remains, rightly, in flux. Services must use the feedback from the patients, their carers and the community to resolve continuing dilemmas. The aim must be to provide services that are user-friendly, acceptable and accessible: services which the providers themselves would not be ashamed to use.

These descriptions are very much geared to the UK model of local health care.

Conclusions

The development of psychiatric services for different age groups and diagnostic problems is not always possible or even essential in some settings. The model described here is Western, and modifications to meet the needs of the local area and its ethnic minorities can and must be made if services are to succeed. However, the burden of mental illness and disability from mental health problems will vary.

No single model can account for the social, environmental and biological factors that produce mental illness. There is ample research evidence to suggest that many mental disorders are psychosocial, and regardless of the physiological processes involved, the quality of the individual's social environment influences both the vulnerability to and the course of the illness. People in emotional distress present themselves to the local health care system. Therefore any effort to provide mental health or clinical services must start from a local understanding of distress and illness, its signs and the meanings used to interpret it (Desjarlais *et al*, 1995). The influence of local medical knowledge on the experience and expression of mental illness is recursive: how illness is understood and responded to shapes the illness itself, organising symptoms, interpretations and care-seeking activities in behavioural pathways that differ across societies and ethnic groups (Carr & Vitaliano, 1985). Families, folk-healers and physicians are faced not with schizophrenia, depression or anxiety, but with *nervios*, soul-possession or other cultural beliefs (Desjarlais *et al*, 1995). The diversity of health care systems and the utilisation of such services determine their acceptance. As discussed above, all societies recognise mental distress: folk-healers deal with it and families manage a great burden of the illness. The cross-cultural diversity in the nature and efficacy of treatment all contribute towards the model of help-seeking.

Western psychiatric theory and clinical practice have permeated many cultures and societies. However, Western models may not have all the answers. Furthermore, if they do not work together with traditional or folk-healers they may alienate patients and their carers. A lack of financial resources, varying socio-politico-economic systems and inadequate studies of different treatment modalities have all contributed to a difficult situation in which services are poorly accepted. As Desjarlais *et al* (1995) recommend, although national plans are valuable, both national and regional commitments of resources are required. They suggest that the old asylum type of treatment must be replaced with placements that provide treatment, ensure basic human rights and protect both those with mental illnesss and the community. Small, purpose-built units are one option for crisis intervention, brief respite and short admissions. The increasing optimism about the role and development of community psychiatry, with its emphasis on developing services within the primary care system, offers the best opportunity for providing services that will be used and accepted by sufferers and carers, that will reduce stigma and that will eventually cut costs.

The models proposed by the World Health Organization (Meads, 1983) and Goldberg (1992), which focus attention on symptoms (reasons for encounters) rather than diagnostic categories and classificatory systems, are a step in the right direction. They may allow us to move away from the difficulties identified above in attempting to focus too narrowly on explanatory models. Another useful strategy would be for psychiatrists to function on a public health model, as teachers and supervisors. This might encourage community involvement at a local and personal level in identifying distress and ways of dealing with it. Extending the same model to schools and families might increase the stakeholding within the community, thereby encouraging the community to take on the responsibility and also reducing the sigma of mental illness.

As Bhui *et al* (1995) have suggested, Black people in the UK suffer multiple disadvantages and one way forward is to provide flexible care packages. This approach might likewise benefit ethnic minorties and those with mental ilnees in other cultures and societies. Training across the board must be improved. Chiu (1994) argues that in order to provide effective treatments in multicultural settings each group's identity, idiosyncrasies and background must be studied.

Acknowledgements

An earlier version of this chapter was published in the *International Journal of Social Psychiatry*, 1997, **43**, 16–28. I am grateful to Dr Frank Holloway and the publishers for their premission to use parts of it.

References

BHATTI, R. S. (1983) Family therapy in alcoholism. In *Christian Response to Alcohol and Drug Problems* (eds M. J. Lawton, J. Gangadason & K. Mathew), pp. 72–99. Kotayam: CMS Press.

— & CHANNABASAVANA, S. M. (1986) A study of neurosis: family interaction patterns and social variables. *Indian Journal of Psychiatry*, **28**, 133–139.

— & VARGHESE, M. (1995) Family therapy in India. *Indian Journal of Social Psychiatry*, **11**, 30–34.

—, Channabasavana, S. M., Prabhu, L., *et al* (1985) *A Manual on Family Typology Scale.* Bangalore: Eastern Press.

BHUGRA, D. (1993) Influence of culture on presentation and management of patients. In *Principles of Social Psychiatry* (eds D. Bhugra & J. Leff). Oxford. Blackwell Science.

— (1997) Setting up psychiatric services. *International Journal of Social Psychiatry*, **43**, 16–28.

— & BHUI, K. (1998*a*) Cross-cultural psychiatric assessments. *Advances in Psychiatric Treatment*, **3**, 103–110.

— & BHUI, K. (1998*b*) Cross-cultural aspects of psychotherapy. *British Journal of Psychotherapy*, **14**, 310–326.

—, BRIDGES, K. & THOMPSON, C. (1995) *Caring for a Community.* Council Report CR36. London: Royal College of Psychiatrists.

—, BALDWIN, D. & DESAI, M. (1997) Focus groups: implications for primary care and cross-cultural psychiatry. *Primary Care Psychiatry*, **3**, 45–50.

BHUI, K. S., CHRISTIE, Y. & BHUGRA, D. (1995) Essential elements of culturally sensitive psychiatric services. *International Journal of Social Psychiatry*, **41**, 242–256.

—, BHUGRA, D. & MCKENZIE, K. (1999) *Services for Black and Ethnic Minority Patients: Separated or Integrated.* Maudsley Discussion Document. London: Institute of Psychiatry.

BREWIN, C. (1980) Explaining the lower rates of psychiatric treatment among Asian immigrants to the United Kingdom. *Social Psychiatry*, **15**, 17–19.

BRIDGES, K., HUXLEY, P. & OLIVER, J. (1994) Psychiatric rehabilitation: redefined for the 1990s. *International Journal of Social Psychiatry*, **40**, 1–16.

CARR, J. & VITALIANO, P. (1985) The theoretical implications of conveying research on depression and culture-bound syndromes. In *Culture and Depression* (eds. A. Kleinman & B. Good), pp. 244–266. Berkeley: University of California Press.

CHIU, T. L. (1994) The unique challenges faced by psychiatrists and other mental health professionals working in a multicultural setting. *International Journal of Social Psychiatry*, **40**, 61–74.

COCHRANE, R. (1999) Ethnicity, drinking patterns and alcohol-related problems in England. In *Ethnicity: An Agenda for Mental Health* (eds D. Bhugra & V. Bahl), pp. 70–84. London: Gaskell.

— & BAL, S. (1989) Mental hospital admission rates of immigrants to England: a comparison of 1971 and 1981. *Social Psychiatry and Psychiatric Epidemiology*, **24**, 2–12.

— & — (1990) The drinking habits of Sikh, Hindu, Muslim and white men in the West Midlands: a community survey. *British Journal of Addiction*, **85**, 759–769.

— & STOPES-ROE, M. (1977) Mental illness in immigrants to England and Wales: an analysis of mental hospital admissions (1971). *Social Psychiatry*, **12**, 25–35.

— & — (1980) Factors affecting the distribution of psychological symptoms in urban areas of England. *Acta Psychiatrica Scandinavica*, **61**, 445–460.

— & — (1981) Social class and psychological disorders in natives and immigrants to the United Kingdom. *International Journal of Social Psychiatry*, **27**, 173–183.

COMAS-DIAZ, L. (1992) The future of psychotherapy with ethnic minorities. *Psychotherapy*, **29**, 88–94.

DESJARLAIS, R., EISENBERG, L., GOOD, B., *et al* (1995) *World Mental Health.* New York: Oxford University Press.

348   Bhugra

FANDETTI, D. V. & GELFAND, D. A. (1978) Attitudes towards symptoms and services in the ethnic family and neighbourhood. *American Journal of Orthopsychiatry*, **48**, 477–486.

FRANK, J. & FRANK, J. (1991) *Persuasion and Healing*, pp. 1–50. Baltimore: Johns Hopkins University Press.

GIRIMAJI, S. C. (1994) *A study of the evaluation of the effectiveness of brief inpatient family intervention versus outpatient intervention for MR children.* Report. New Delhi: Indian Council for Medical Research.

GOLDBERG, D. (1992) A classification of psychological distress for use in primary care settings. *Social Science Medicine*, **35**, 189–193.

HAHN, R. & KLEINMAN, A. (1983) Biomedical practice and anthropological theory: frameworks and directions. *American Review of Anthropology*, **12**, 305–333.

IKEMI, Y. (1979) Eastern and Western approaches to self regulation: similarities and differences. *Canadian Journal of Psychiatry*, **24**, 471–480.

JACOB, K. S., BHUGRA, D., LLOYD, K., *et al* (1998) Common mental disorders, explanatory models and consultation behaviours among Indian women living in the UK. *Journal of the Royal Society of Medicine*, **91**, 66–71.

KAREEM J. & LITTLEWOOD, R. (1992) *Intercultural Therapy: Themes, Interpretations and Practice.* Oxford: Blackwell Science.

KATON, W. & KLEINMAN, A. (1981) Doctor–patient negotiation and other social strategies in patient care. In *The Relevance of Social Science for Medicine* (eds L. Eisenberg & A. Kleinman). Dordrecht: D. Reidel.

KLEINMAN, A. (1978) Concept and a model for the comparison of medical systems as cultural systems. *Social Science and Medicine*, **12**, 85–93.

—— (1980) *Patients and Healers in the Context of Culture.* Berkeley, CA: University of California Press.

KOSS, J. (1987) *Ethnomedical Categories in the Diagnosis and Treatment of Hispanic Patients: A Review of the Studies and Implications for Research*, pp. 187–206. Simon Bolivar Research Monograph. Chicago, IL: Univeristy of Illinois Press.

KRAUSE, I. B. (1989) The sinking heart: a Punjabi communication of distress. *Social Science and Medicine*, **29**, 563–575.

LITTLEWOOD, R. (1990) From categories to contexts: a decade of the new cross-cultural psychiatry. *British Journal of Psychiatry*, **156**, 696–702.

LLOYD, K. & BHUGRA, D. (1993) Cross-cultural aspects of psychotherapy. *International Review of Psychiatry*, **5**, 291–304.

——, JACOB, K. S., PATEL, V., *et al* (1998) The development of the Short Explanatory Model Interview (SEMI). *Psychological Medicine*, **28**, 1231–1237.

LONDON, M. (1986) Mental illness among immigrant minorities in the United Kingdom. *British Journal of Psychiatry*, **149**, 265–275.

McCARTHY, B. (1987) Clinical work with ethnic minorities. In *New Developments in Clinical Psychology* (ed. F. Watts). Chichester: John Wiley & Sons.

McKEIGUE, P. & KARMI, G. (1993) Alcohol consumption and alcohol-related problems in Afro-Caribbean and South Asians in the United Kingdom. *Alcohol and Alcoholism*, **28**, 1–10.

MADEN, A. (1992) Psychiatric disorder in women serving a prison sentence. Unpublished MD thesis. University of London

—— (1993) Crime, culture and ethnicity. *International Review of Psychiatry*, **5**, 281–289.

MANTHORPE, J. & HETTIARATCHY, P. (1993) Ethnic minority elders in the UK. *International Review of Psychiatry*, **5**, 171–178.

MEADS, S. (1983) Improving the health of Black Americans: lessons from community mental health movement. *Millbank Quarterly*, **65**, 348–380.

NAZROO, J. (1997) *Ethnicity and Health.* London: Policy Studies Institute.

NEKI, J. S. (1975) Psychotherapy in India: past, present and future. *American Journal of Psychotherapy*, **29**, 92–100.

Prabhu, L., Desai, N., Ragurarm, A., *et al* (1988) Outcome of family therapy: a two year follow up. *International Journal of Social Psychiatry*, **34**, 112–117.

Reiss, P. (1993) Culture in psychiatric diagnosis: an issue of scientific accuracy. *Psychiatry*, **56**, 321–323.

Rogler, L. H. (1993) Culture in psychiatric diagnosis: an issue of scientific accuracy. *Psychiatry*, **56**, 324–327.

——, Corkes, D. E. & Malgady, R. G. (1994) The mental health relevance of idioms of distress: anger and perceptions of injustice among New York Puerto Ricans. *Journal of Nervous and Mental Disease*, **182**, 327–330.

Skultans, V. (1993) The case of cross-cultural psychiatry: squaring the circle. *International Review of Psychiatry*, **5**, 125–128.

Thornicroft, G., Brewin, C. R. & Wing, J. (1992) *Measuring Mental Health Needs*. London: Gaskell.

——, Parkman, S. & Ruiggeri, M. (1999) Satisfaction with mental health services. In *Ethnicity: An Agenda for Mental Health*, pp. 158–165 London: Gaskell.

Venkoba Rao, A. (1993) Psychiatry of old age in India. *International Review of Psychiatry*, **5**, 165–170.

Warren, R., Jackson, A., Nugaris, J., *et al* (1973) Differential attitudes of black and white patients towards treatment in a child guidance clinic. *American Journal of Orthopsychiatry*, **43**, 384–395.

Westermeyer, J. (1985). Psychiatric diagnosis across cultural boundaries. *American Journal of Psychiatry*, **142**, 798–805.

Wooff, K. (1992) Service organisation and planning. In *Innovations in the Psychological Management of Schizophrenia* (eds M. Birchwood & N. Tarvier), pp. 277–304. Chichester: John Wiley & Sons.

World Health Organization (1992) *The Tenth Revision of the International Classification of Diseases and Related Health Problems* (ICD–10). Geneva: WHO.

Index

n after a page number refers to a footnote

abuse
    child abuse 206
    and learning disability 217
    racial abuse 79, 84–85
access to services, elderly people 188
accidents, as cause of learning disability
    217
accountability, legal, and psychiatric
    illnesses 21, 22
acculturation 9, 10, 129–133
    contact and conflict in 124
    definitions 11, 114–116
    generational difference 130, 132
    at group level 114
    at individual level 115
    language in 115
    levels of 9, 113, 114, 124
    measurement of 123–125
    models of 12–13
    process of 113–114
    psychological 12, 114
    qualitative methods of gaining
        information 133, 134
    research variables 123
    and social class 131
    types of 124–125
acculturation illnesses 34
acculturative stress 123, 125, 131
adaptation 113, 117, 124, 130
adherence *see* compliance
adjectival racism 78
adolescent psychiatric services 343–
    344
adolescents 198, 202, 205
adoption 206–207

advocacy services 280
advocates 227
    general practitioners as 325
affirmative action *see* positive
    discrimination
Africa, colonial, depression in 32
African–Caribbean people
    alcohol 142–143, 248, 342
    cannabis 245, 247, 312
    crime rates 268–269
    environmental risk factors 313
    forensic psychiatry services 264–265,
        270, 276–278
    in high security hospitals 277–
        278
    mentally disordered offenders
        270–275
    migrants 9
    migrants, second generation 13
    neurological illness 312
    over-representation of, in criminal
        justice system 264–265, 266–267,
        271, 272
    psychiatric morbidity 148
    psychosis in 311
    risk factors, biological 311–313
    schizophrenia 13, 139–142, 277,
        311–312
    substance misuse 245, 246, 247–248,
        312
    see also Black people; Caribbean-
        born people
African communities, substance misuse
    in 247–248
aggression sanctions 297

alcohol consumption/problems
    African and African–Caribbean
        communities 142–143, 248, 342
    Asian communities 139, 145, 250, 342
    and violence 318
alienation, definition 11
alienists 22
alternative health practitioners 147
Alzheimer's disease, Care Needs of
    Ethnic Older Persons with Alzheimer's
    (CNEOPSA) 180, 182, 186–187, 189
Alzheimer's Disease Society, audio
    tapes 169
American Association of Mental
    Retardation 231
amok 25, 29, 30, 33, 39
Anglo-conformity 126
anomie 11, 320–321
anorexia nervosa 200–201
anoxia, as cause of learning disability 217
anthropology 113, 333–334
    social anthropology 40
anti-discriminatory policy training 287
anxiety 92, 107, 155
arctic hysteria (*piblokto*) 29, 31
Asian people
    alcohol 139, 145, 250, 342
    cannabis 249
    crime rates 268–269
    migrants, second generation 13
    psychiatric morbidity 148
    service admission rates 139, 143
    somatisation symptoms 147
    substance misuse 248–250, 342
    from Uganda 7
    women, minor psychological
        morbidity 144
    women, self-harm and suicide 145–146
    see also Indian subcontinent
asphyxia, as cause of learning disability
    217
assimilation 12, 113–114, 114, 125, 127
    bilingualism in 115, 126
    definition 12, 114
    impact on non-dominant groups 127
    types of 114
asylum-seekers 93
attacks, racial 60, 79, 94, 95, 97
audit, psychogeriatric services 170
audit tools, cultural sensitivity 288
autism 218, 222

autonomic arousal 107
autosomal recessive disorders 215–218

betel preparations, Asian communities 249
*Between Services for the Mentally
    Handicapped* (White Paper) 224
bias *see* Eurocentric bias; *and under*
    research
bilingualism
    in assimilation 115, 126
    in psychogeriatric services health
        workers 163
    in researchers 62–63
birth injury/infection, as cause of
    learning disability 217
black box epidemiology 57
Black Drug Workers Forum 260
Black identity 87–88
Black people
    Black identity 87–88
    discriminatory attitudes towards? 179
    independent separate mental health
        services 290–291
    and voluntary sector 232–233, 235
    see also African–Caribbean people;
        African communities
blame *see* self-blame
body language 297
brain abscess, as cause of learning
    disability 217
brain-fag syndrome 34
British Crime Surveys 95, 96, 249,
    270, 271–272
Broadmoor Hospital 277–278
Buddhism, guidance on substance misuse
    244
bulimia 147, 200
burglary, race-related 97

cannabis
    African and African–Caribbean
        communities 245, 247, 312
    Asian communities 249
    cannabis psychosis, overdiagnosis of 245
    Cypriot communities 250
    mentally disordered prisoners' use of
        271
    no specific misuse service 253
    psychological/psychosocial treatment
        251
    as risk factor in psychosis 312

cannibal-compulsion syndrome
(*windigo*) 29–30, 35–36, 43
carbon monoxide levels 316
Care Needs of Ethnic Older Persons
with Alzheimer's (CNEOPSA) 180,
182, 186–187, 189
care pathways, in mental health
services 88
care professionals, need for non-
discriminatory attitude 178–179
Care Programme Approach 340
Caribbean-born people
depression 148
service admission rates 139
see also African–Caribbean people
case–control studies 67
category fallacy 303
censuses 53, 94, 246
cerebral palsy, as cause of learning
disability 216
challenging behaviour
criteria 219
distinguishing from emotional
disorders 222
learning disabilities and 218–220
reducing 219–220
child abuse 206
child psychiatry 191–210
cross-cultural working 203–207
cultural diversity in staff teams 203
culture and 193
information gathering 204–205
interpreters 204–205, 206
for a multicultural community 201–
203
outreach or clinic-based? 203
research 192, 207
services 343–344
tiered approach 201, 202
childrearing 40–41, 115
children
authoritarian style with 196–197
conduct problems 192, 195–196
and crime 316
cross-cultural similarities in disorders
191–192
ethnic identity 81–83
gender expectations 200
identity confusion 200
influence of school on behaviour and
development 199

institutional racism, impact of 196, 199
limit setting 195
parental control 195–196
parental perceptions of disorder 201
and parenting style 195–197
self-esteem 82, 199
separation 197
substance misuse 316–317
taken into care 319, 325
in urban areas 316–317
Chinese people, in Britain 144
Christianity, guidance on substance
misuse 244
civilised oppression 51
Climate for Racism Scale 102
clinical supervision 294–295
clothing 80
Clunis, Christopher 285
CNEOPSA (Care Needs of Ethnic Older
Persons with Alzheimer's) 180, 182,
186–187, 189
cocaine
Asian communities 249
and foetal development 316–317
cognitive–development theories of
personality 117–118
cohort studies 67
colonies 25
French *v.* English 43
see also imperialism; imperial
psychiatry
communication
in learning difficulty services 238
non-verbal 14
in psychogeriatric services 163–164,
169
refugees and 10–11
in social services 185, 188
community care 224–230
and learning disabilities 226–228
National Health Service and Community
Care Act 1990 184–185, 186, 224
philosophy and principles underlying
planning 225–226
community liaison role, multi-disciplinary
team members 291–292
community services, elderly people's
awareness of and satisfaction with
157–158
complaints procedures, interpreters for
288–289

compliance (adherence) 90, 335
compulsions 144
conduct problems, in children 192,
   195–196
conferences, on mental health needs 284
confidentiality, fears about, as barrier
to use of substance misuse services 251,
   254–255
conflict
   culture conflict 13, 124
   with mental health services 89
   in needs assessment 303
conscience 116
contact, in acculturation 124
control groups, in research 63–64
coping behaviour 61
court diversion schemes 272
crack 247, 249
crime
   British Crime Surveys 95, 96, 249,
      270, 271–272
   children living in cities 316
   racially motivated? 95–96
   victims of 269–270
   see also offenders; police; prison
      population; race-related crime
crime rates, Asian and African–
   Caribbean people 268–269
crime statistics, by ethnic origin 78–79
criminal justice process 265–267
   disparity between ethnic groups 266–
      267
   sentencing, racial differences in 267
   stages in 266
criminal justice system 265–270
   discrimination in 268
   over-representation of African–
      Caribbean people 264–265, 266–
      267, 271, 272
cross-cultural competency instrument 295
cross-cultural mental health services
   child health services 203–207
   cross-cultural competency instrument
      295
   guidelines for staff 256–257
   history of 289–291
   holistic service 293
   improving care for ethnic minorities
      287–291
   independent sector, separate services
      for Black people 290–291

models of service delivery 291–293
non-pharmacological treatments 293
policy, organisational and government
   287–288
professional–patient relationship
   285–286, 294
research 290–291
service design and utilisation, USA
   experience 287–288
statutory sector 289–291, 291–292,
   292–293
supervision in 291, 293, 294–295
training 285–286, 291, 293
voluntary sector *see* voluntary sector
cross-cultural work, guidelines for
   256–257
cultural awareness training 287
cultural beliefs, and mental disorder
   200–201
cultural bias, in research 2
cultural heritage 76
cultural identity 11–17, 124, 125–129
Cultural Mistrust Inventory 102
cultural psychiatry 33, 35, 39–44
cultural qualities, in acculturation 128–
   129
cultural relativism 14
cultural sensitivity
   audit tools 288
   people with learning disabilities 237–
      239
   psychogeriatric services 165, 166,
      168–169
   residential homes 186
   social services 184
   therapy models 342
cultural syndromes 43
culture 20
   childhood experiences 40–41
   and child psychiatry 193
   compromise between conflicting
      interests 36
   conflict and resistance 34–39
   covert/overt levels of 113
   definition 76
   ethnicity relating to 56
   high culture 35
   locus of 112
   national 29–31
   v. nature 20–21, 40n7
   not inborn 76

culture (contd)
  pathologisation of 37
  role in development of individual 112
  stress perception 137
culture-bound (culture-specific)
  illnesses/syndromes 32–34, 39, 41,
  43, 44
culture-change 34
culture conflict 13, 124
culture shock 132
Cypriot communities, substance misuse
  250
cytomegalovirus, as cause of learning
  disability 216

danger events 92
day centres, psychogeriatric services 167
day hospitals, psychogeriatric services
  164–165
deculturation 115, 129
Defeat Depression campaign, Royal
  College of Psychiatrists 170
delirium tremens 26n3
delusions 24
dementia, in elderly people 154–155,
  156, 160
  CNEOPSA study 180, 182, 186–187,
  189
depersonalisation 122
depression 31–32, 92, 92–93, 105–
  106, 144
  aetiology 92, 159–160
  in elderly people 155, 159–160
  parental 194
  and social class 315
  and social isolation 317–318
  somatic symptoms 159
depressogenic events 93, 100
deprivation 55, 321–322
  as cause of learning disability 217
descriptive epidemiology 53
determinants 57
diabetes, as cause of learning disability 216
diagnosis, psychiatric 14–17, 88
  misdiagnosis 15, 140–141
diagnostic assessment, in patient's first
  language 288
diagnostic overshadowing, learning
  disabilities and 222
Difference Indicators Scale 102
difficulties 93, 100

discrimination
  anti-discriminatory policy training 287
  disguised discrimination 77
  people with learning difficulties 229
  positive discrimination 80
  racial 79, 94, 101
  disease, *v.* illness 333
disguised discrimination 77
disorganisation *see* social disorganisation
distress
  local idioms of 14–15
  in refugees 131–132
divorce 193, 198, 206
double jeopardy 160
Down's syndrome, as cause of learning
  disability 216
drapetomania 42n8
drop-out rates 335
drugs
  as cause of learning disability 216
  importation of 265
  in prison population 271
  and violence 318
  see also substance misuse; substance
  misuse services
Durkheim, Emile 11

eating disorders 34–35, 146–147,
  200–201
economic appraisals, study design 305
Ecstasy (3,4-methylenedioxymeth-
  amphetamine/MDMA), Asian
  communities 249
education
  and illness prevention strategies 325
  in psychogeriatric services 170
  and social class 315
  supervision in 294–295
  see also training
efficiency evaluation 305
effort evaluation 305
ego 116
elderly people 151–176
  access to services 188
  ageing profile 180–181
  care development overview 182–187
  care from extended families 153–
  154, 183
  Care Needs of Ethnic Older Persons
  with Alzheimer's (CNEOPSA) 180,
  182, 186–187, 189

carers' profile 168
context, content and conduct 179–180
definition 152
dementia 154–155, 156
demography 153–154
depression in 155, 159–160
diagnostic issues 158–160
gender ratio 153
Government report on social services
    185–186
GP examinations for patients over
    75 years of age 166
household patterns 153
illness severity and resultant
    disability 155–156
inadequacy of health and social
    services 182, 187–188
increasing proportion of 153
long-term needs, PRIAE report 187–
    188
long-term unemployment, effects of
    182
marital status 153
mental illness, difficulties in
    diagnosing 158–160
multiple jeopardy 160
prevalence of mental illness 154–155
psychiatrists' approach to 178–179
reluctance to leave home 165, 166
services, awareness and use of 156–
    158, 182, 183–184, 344
suicide 154
see also psychogeriatric services
EMIC (Explanatory Model Interview
    Catalogue) 69–70
emotional disorders, and learning
    disabilities 220–221, 222
employment 11, 132
see also unemployment; work
encephalitis, as cause of learning
    disability 217
English, as additional language 62, 66, 94
environment
    and psychosis 319–322
    as risk factor in schizophrenia 313, 317
    urban 316–317
epidemiology 51
    black box epidemiology 57
    data analysis 70
    definition 52–53
    descriptive 53

explanatory models of illness 332–
    335
life events in 60–61
equal opportunities policies 235, 238,
    278, 279, 287
ethnic categories 53–54, 55
ethnic groups
    by age 181
    definitions 53–54
    relative status 84
ethnic identity 81–85, 87
    Black identity 87–88
    others' perception of 84
    research studies 85–88
ethnicity
    as a process 55
    relating to culture 56
    as research variable 54–56
    and self-awareness 83–84
    statistical flaws 138
ethnic minority, definition 152
ethnic minority groups/populations
    93–94
    ageing profile 180–181
    amalgamation *v.* subgroups 153
    in Britain 3, 16, 50, 94
    demographic trends 180–181
    'early ageing' 182
    geographical distribution 94, 246
    in-patient admissions 142–143
    mental health concerns 6
    second generation 94
    socio-economic position 181–182
ethnic monitoring 288
ethnic psychoses 36
ethnic unconscious 36
ethnography 69–71
ethnopsychiatry 43
Eurocentric bias
    in psychiatry 2, 14, 15
    in psychology 14
    in psychotherapy and counselling 15
    in research 2
European Union, mobility in 93
European Year against Racism 178
evaluation *see* service evaluation
evaluative research 304–305
Explanatory Model Interview Catalogue
    (EMIC) 69–70
explanatory models *see under* illness
extended families 153–154, 183, 194

Fair Access 188
faith 125
faith healers 167–168
families
    extended 153–154, 183, 194
    healing activities 332
    and mental illness 318
    size of, and mortality rates 194
    structure 194
family therapy 205–206, 342–343
fatigue 144
'feeling low' 159
financial worries 315
focus groups 69, 334
foetal alcohol syndrome, as cause of
    learning disability 216
food 127
food scarcity 200
forensic psychiatry services 264–283, 341
    African–Caribbean people 276–278
        over-representation of 264–265, 270
    ethnic differences in contact with
        272–273
    inter-agency working 280
    for mentally disordered offenders 275
    services offered 264–265
form/content dichotomy 21–28, 23–
    25, 35
fostering 206–207
fragile X syndrome, as cause of learning
    disability 216
Freud, Sigmund 116–117

Gastarbeiter 7, 8, 9
gastroenteritis, as cause of learning
    disability 217
gender, differences in rates of mental
    disorder in children 200
gender expectations, children 200
gender ratio, elderly people 153
general practitioners (GPs)
    as advocates and advisers 325
    disclosure of racial incidents to 98
    examinations for patients over 75 years
        of age 166
    psychogeriatric services 157, 166
generational differences, in immigrants
    13–14
genetic factors
    in child disorders 192
    in learning disabilities 214, 216, 218

Geriatric Mental State Examination 155
ghetto cultures 245
Gilles de la Tourette's syndrome 26n3
GPs *see* general practitioners

hallucinations 24
harassment, racial 94, 95, 97
hate crimes, USA 96
Headstart 199
health
    determinants of 57–60
    racism and 103–105
    see also ill health
health services
    health service research (HSR) 51
    inadequacy of, for elderly people
        182, 187–188
    v. social services provision 186
heritage, cultural 76
heroin
    African and African–Caribbean
        communities 247
    Asian communities 249
high security hospitals 275, 277–278
    African–Caribbean people in 277–278
    Broadmoor Hospital 277–278
    see also secure units
Hinduism, guidance on substance misuse
    244
HIV prevention initiatives 259
Home Office Drugs Prevention
    Initiative 259
Hong Kong
    migrants from, service admission
        rates 139
    see also Asian people
hospitals *see* high security hospitals;
    secure units
household patterns, elderly people 153
housing 88, 316, 321–322, 324
hyperuricaemia, as cause of learning
    disability 216
hypochondriasis, misdiagnosis as 15
hypothyroidism, as cause of learning
    disability 216
hypoxia, as cause of learning disability
    217
hysteria 19, 31

ICD (International Classification of
    Diseases) (WHO) 213, 336–337

id 116
identity
    cultural identity 11–17, 124, 125–129
    identity confusion in children 200
    Social Psychological Theories of
        Identity 230
ill health
    determinants of 57–60
    religion as risk factor 58–60
    risk factors 57–60
    see also illness
illness
    causal mechanisms 321
    culture-bound (culture-specific) 32–
        34, 39, 41, 43, 44
    v. disease 333
    explanatory models of 331–332
        and epidemiology 332–335
        for particular conditions 334
    as transformation state 40
    variation in presentation of 31
    see also ill health; mental disorders/
        illness; psychiatric disorders/illnesses
immigrants *see* migrants
immigration *see* migration
Immigration Acts 79
immunity from infection 320
imperialism
    relevance of psychiatry to 41–42
    see also colonies
imperial psychiatry 28–34, 41–43
income inequality 319, 324
independent sector
    integration with statutory sector?
        292–293
    separate services for Black people
        290–291
Indian subcontinent, migrants from 7, 9
    food purity 127
    service admission rates 139
    see also Asian people; Punjabi people
infection, as cause of learning disability
    216, 217
information
    about access to learning disability
        services 227
    information gathering, child psychiatry
        204–205
    provision of, in social services 185, 188
    see also communication
information bias, in research 66–67

injury, as cause of learning disability
    216, 217
in-patient admissions, ethnic minority
    groups 142–143
in-patient care, psychogeriatric services
    165–166
institutional racism 97–99, 314
    definition 97–99
    fears of, as barrier to use of substance
        misuse services 251, 255–257
    in housing placements 321–322
    impact on children 196, 199
    in mental health services 89
integration 114, 125
intellectual impairment, definition 213
intelligence tests 230–231
inter-agency working, in forensic
    psychiatry services 280
Inter-Departmental Group on Ageing 188
International Classification of Diseases
    (ICD) (WHO) 213, 336–337
International Pilot Study of Schizophrenia
    (IPSS) 26–27n3, 68
interpersonal phobia (*taijin kyofusho*) 38
interpersonal relationships 119
interpreters
    in child psychiatry 204–205, 206
    for complaints procedures 288–289
    in learning disability services 238
    in psychogeriatric services 163–164
intoxication *see* alcohol consumption/
    problems
intra-uterine growth retardation, as
    cause of learning disability 217
intraventricular haemorrhage, as cause
    of learning disability 217
Inuit 30
IPSS (International Pilot Study of
    Schizophrenia) 26–27n3, 68
IQ tests 230–231
Irish people
    migrants in Britain 3, 7, 16
    self-harm and suicide 146
irradiation, as cause of learning disability
    216
irritability 144
Islam, guidance on substance misuse
    244
isolation, social isolation 10–11, 132,
    317–318
izzat (respectability; honour) 248–249

Jews, migration from eastern Europe
  and Russia 7
job applications 77
jokes, racist 78, 79
judges (in courts of law) 79

kayak angst 31
Khat 247–248
kifafa 34
Klinefelter syndrome, as cause of
  learning disability 216
kuru 34

labelling process 220
labels, diagnosis as 70
language 126–127
  in acculturation 115
  body language 297
  English as additional language 62, 66, 94
  among ethnic minority populations 94
  first language 288
  language barriers 1, 14–15
  local idioms 1, 14–15
  racist 95
  refugees and 10–11
  and self-awareness 82
  see also bilingualism; cultural
    sensitivity; information; interpreters
latah 30, 33, 39
Lawrence, Stephen 103, 187
lead poisoning 317
learned behaviour 118
learning difficulty, definition 213
learning disabilities 211–242, 344–345
  assessment 230–232
  assessment forms 227–228
  causes 214–215, 216–217
  and challenging behaviour 218–220
  classification 213–214
  community care issues 226–228
  culture sensitivity 237–239
  definition 211–212, 213
  diagnostic overshadowing 222
  double disadvantage 226–228
  dual diagnosis 220–224
  and emotional disorders 220–221, 222
  forward planning agenda 232–239
  genetic origin 214, 216, 218
  incidence 215, 216–217
  instruments for detecting mental
    illness 222

needs-led services 236–237
offenders with 222–223
prevalence 214, 215, 221
race equality in 235–236
research and policy 234–235
risk factors 218
victim blaming 218
legal accountability, and psychiatric
  illnesses 21, 22
legal powers
  mental health 2–3, 15–16
  see also Mental Health Act 1983
leisure 127–128
Lesch–Nyhan disease, as cause of
  learning disability 216
liaison psychiatry services 167–168, 341
life events 92–93, 318
  danger 92
  definition 93
  in epidemiology 60–61
  loss 92, 318
  and psychiatric morbidity 91–92, 93
  racial 98–101
    definition 100
    impact of 108
    measuring perceptions of 101–103
    Racial Life Events Scale (RALES)
      102, 102–103
  see also depression; stress
locus of control 105
long-term care, Royal Commission
  report 187
long-term (rehabilitative) psychiatry
  services 340
loss events 92, 318
LSD (lysergic acid diethylamide) 249
lysergic acid diethylamide (LSD) 249

Macpherson Report 97–99, 187, 188–189
malkadi 34
malnutrition, as cause of learning
  disability 216
marital conflict and separation 193,
  198, 206
marital status, elderly people 153
marriage, between first cousins, as cause
  of learning disabilities 215–218
master–slave relationship 340
MDMA (3,4-methylenedioxymeth-
  amphetamine/Ecstasy), Asian
  communities 249

mediating factors in health outcome 105
medical specialism, status and power 333
medical training, health and culture in 287
medication 296
medicine, Western 18–19
  dealing with 'culture' 18, 35
  relief of distress 41
medium secure units 276
  reasons for, and sources of, admission 275
melancholia 19
meningitis, as cause of learning disability 217
mental deficiency, definition 212
mental disorders/illness 129–133, 137–150
  carers' role in identifying problems 223
  classification 336–338
  common disorders 144–145
  and cultural beliefs 200–201
  description 300–301
  discrimination in treatment? 223–224
  illness patterns 137–143
  morbidity levels 144
  non-psychotic 144
  over-diagnosis 245
  psychiatry's part in managing 303
  service usage 137–143
  see also psychiatric disorders/illnesses;
    psychosis; schizophrenia
mental distress, management of 335–336
mental handicap, definition 212
Mental Health Act 1983 2, 224, 274
  detainees under 270
mental health professionals, professional culture and training 289
mental health services
  adherence 90
  bottom-up development approach 331
  conflict with 90
  diagnosis 89
  key issues in planning 331
  liaison between children's and adult services 203
  parental perceptions and use of 195, 202
  pathways to care 89
  racism in 88–90

satisfaction with 90
separate services? 331
staff assignment 89
treatment 89
under-use of? 6–7
utilisation of 89
see also cross-cultural mental health services; psychiatric services
mental illness *see* mental disorders/ illness
mental impairment, definition 212
mentally disordered offenders
  African–Caribbean people 270–275
  future provision for 278–280
  psychiatric services for 275
mental retardation, definition 213
mental subnormality, definition 212
Mental Test Score 155
metabolism, inborn errors of, as cause of learning disability 216
3,4-methylenedioxymethamphetamine (MDMA/Ecstasy), Asian communities 249
migrants
  common mental disorders 129–133
  definition 7
  generational differences 13–14
  migrant workers 8
  social class distribution 3–4, 16
  stress in 123
  survival strategies 269
  see also refugees
migration 3–4, 314
  changes associated with 10–11
  health risks 131–132
  history of 7–8, 93
  stages in 12
  types of 8–10
mind–body dichotomy, in psychiatry and psychology 14
Mini Mental State Examination (MMSE) 155
minority ethnic groups/population *see* ethnic minority groups/populations
'missionary racism' 343
modal personality 35
monitoring, ethnic monitoring 288
moral retardation 19
morbidity, national psychiatric morbidity surveys 61–62
morbus anglicus 19

mortality rates, influencing family size
194
moth madness 34
multi-disciplinary teams
community liaison roles for individual
members 291–292
as focus for training 295–296
supervision in 297
multiple jeopardy 160

National Health Service and Community
Care Act 1990 184–185, 186, 224
national psychiatric morbidity surveys
61–62
National Service Framework on Older
People 188
nature, *v.* culture 20–21, 40*n*7
needs
definition 301–302
v. demand and supply 332
v. demands and wants 301
see also needs assessment; needs
measurement
needs assessment 301–302, 336
bottom-up approach 303
category fallacy 303
conflicts in 303
focus of 306–307
key factors in 302
key themes 306
process of 302
purpose 301
qualitative/quantitative approaches
303–307
see also needs measurement; service
evaluation
needs measurement
approaches 302
problems in 302–303
see also needs assessment
Negromachy 87
nervous specialists 22
neural tube defects, as cause of learning
disability 216
neurasthenia 19, 22
neurofibromatosis, as cause of learning
disability 216
neurological illnesses 312, 313
neurotoxins, as cause of learning
disability 217
new (symbolic) racism 79–81

normalisation of pathology 31
Normalisation Social Role Valorisation
225–226, 228–230
nostalgia, in refugees 132

observer bias, in research 66–67
Oedipus complex 38
offences *see* crime; race-related crime
offenders with learning disabilities 222–
223
see also mentally disordered offenders
Ojibwa 30, 35
opiates 250, 251, 253
outcome evaluation 305
out-groups 100–101
out-patient clinics, psychogeriatric
services 164
outreach or clinic-based?, child
psychiatry 203
outreach work, substance misuse
services 257–258
overcrowding 317
overstimulation 317

parents
depression 194
loss of 318
parental control of children 195–196
parental perceptions and use of
mental health services 195, 202
parenting styles 195–197
participant observation 69
PAS–ADD (Psychiatric Assessment
Schedule for Adults with Development
Disabilities) 222
Patient's Charter 288–289
Perceived Racism Scale 102
Perceptions of Racism Scale 102
Personal Construct Theory 230
Personal Discrimination Scale 102
personal identity 122
personality
cognitive–development theories
117–118
concepts of 116–122
phenomenological approaches 119
psychoanalytic theories 116–117
social learning theory 118–119
see also self
personality types 115–116
personhood 124

phenomenological approaches to personality 119
phenylketonuria, as cause of learning disability 216
piblokto (arctic hysteria) 29, 31
placental insufficiency, as cause of learning disability 216
police
    contact with people with mental disorder 273–275
    as gatekeepers 274
    offences reported to 265–266
    records 95
    see also crime; offenders; race-related crime
Policy Research Institute on Ageing and Ethnicity (PRIAE) report 187–188
population distribution, by age and ethnicity 180–181
positive discrimination 80
positivism 26n2
post-traumatic stress disorder (PTSD) 107
poverty 60, 88, 198–199
Prader–Willi syndrome, as cause of learning disability 216
prayer, as form of coping 61
prejudice 4, 16–17, 75–76, 76–81
    definition 75
    disciplinary offences in workplace 79
    forms of 77–81
    see also racism
prematurity, as cause of learning disability 217
Present State Examination (PSE) 68
prevalence rates, interpretation of 3
prevention 310–311
    primary prevention 310–311, 323–326
    types of 310
prevention strategies, implications for 323–326
PRIAE (Policy Research Institute on Ageing and Ethnicity) report 187–188
primary care 147
primary prevention 310–311, 323–326
    cost 323
Prins Report 277–278
prison population 79, 265
    drug importation 265
    drug use by prisoners with mental disorder 271

ethnicity of mentally disordered prisoners 271–272
    over-representation of African–Caribbean people 265, 267, 271, 272
    psychosis in Black prisoners 271
    race relations problems 268
    transfers to psychiatric hospitals 272
    UK residents compared 271–272
probation officers, reports 268
process evaluation 305
professional–patient relationship, cross-cultural 285–286, 294
protective factors 61
Psychiatric Assessment Schedule for Adults with Development Disabilities (PAS–ADD) 222
psychiatric disorders/illnesses 105–108
    classification 27
    form/content dichotomy 21–28, 23–25, 35
    and legal accountability 21, 22
    measurement of 67–69
    models of 25–26
    see also diagnosis; mental disorders/illness
psychiatric illnesses *see* psychiatric disorders/illnesses
psychiatric morbidity
    life events and 91–92, 93, 99–100
    national surveys 61–62
    racism and 105
    variations between communities 334–335
psychiatric services
    characteristics 338
    child and adolescent services 343–344
    forensic psychiatry *see* forensic psychiatry services
    general services 339–340
    guidelines for 338
    learning disability *see* learning disabilities
    liaison psychiatry services 341
    long-term (rehabilitative) services 340
    practical problems 339
    psychotherapy 15, 342–343
    services for elderly people *see* elderly people; psychogeriatric services
    specialities 339–345
    substance abuse *see* substance misuse
psychiatric specialities *see* psychiatric services

psychiatry
  background 1–3
  cultural psychiatry 33, 35, 39–44
  ethnopsychiatry 43
  historical development of 14, 19–20
  imperial psychiatry 28–34, 41–43
  practice not seen as benign 15–16
  in socio-politial context 1, 7, 67
  transcultural 159
psychic energy 21
psychoanalytic psychotherapies 342–343
psychoanalytic theories of personality
  116–117
psychogeriatric services 151–176
  age cut-off 152
  assessment, initial 162–163, 166
  audio tapes 169
  audit and quality assurance 170
  bilingual health workers 163
  communication 163–164, 169
  cultural sensitivity 165, 166, 168–169
  current services and utilisation 156–158
  data requirements for planning 152–
    158
  day centres 167
  day hospitals 164–165
  education, for staff and patients 170
  epidemiology 154–156
  equipment 169
  evening/weekend services 161
  faith healers 167–168
  follow-up site 164
  future directions 171
  GPs' role 157, 166
  home visits 162, 164, 166
  in-patient care 165–166
  integrated *v.* segregated services
    160–161
  interpreters/translators 163–164
  liaison services 167–168
  literature/talking books 169
  location of 168
  multiple jeopardy 160
  out-patient clinics 164
  planning 160–170
  referral sources and modes 161
  residential homes 167, 186
  secondary care services 157
  sexual segregation 168–169
  staffing levels and mix 169–170
  transportation 165

voluntary agencies 158, 167
  see also elderly people
psychological acculturation 19, 114
psychological morbidity, racism and 105
psychological problems, cultural
  differences in presentation 1–2
psychology, historical development 14
Psychopathology Instrument for
  Mentally Retarded Adults 222
psychosis 107–108
  in African–Caribbean people 311
  Black prisoners 271, 272, 274
  cannabis as risk factor in 312
  environmental factors leading to
    319–322
  neurodevelopmental hypothesis 312
  risk factors, biological 311–313
  social factors and 313, 313–319,
    319–322
  see also schizophrenia
psychosocial factors, in child disorders
  192
psychotherapy 15, 342–343
psychotic illness 92
PTSD (post-traumatic stress disorder) 107
public health measures 309, 323–324
  see also prevention
Punjabi people 55–56, 64–66
purity mania (*suchi-bar*) 38
purity syndromes 38

Qat 247–248
quality assurance 170, 336

race-related crime 94–99
  difficulty in obtaining data 94–95
  ethnic differences 96
  ethnicity of victims 97
  geographical differences 96
  hate crimes, USA 96
  highly publicised incidents 103
  offence types 97
  racist language 95
  unreported incidents 96–97
  USA *v.* UK 96
Race Relations Act 1976 152, 179, 268
race thinking 76
racial abuse 79, 84–85
racial attacks/harassment 60, 79, 94,
  95, 97
  behavioural responses to 98

Racial Climate Scale 102
racial disadvantage 79
racial discrimination *see* discrimination
racial incidents, disclosure pathways 98, 99
racial life events *see under* life events
Racial Life Events Scale (RALES) 102, 102–103
racial prejudice *see* prejudice
Racial Reactions Scales 102
racial stereotyping 268, 273, 280
racism 4, 16, 75–81, 140, 314
  adjectival 78
  affecting mental and physical health 101
  definition 75, 101
  European Year against Racism 178
  and health 103–105
  individual 89
  inevitability of? 285
  institutional *see* institutional racism
  measuring perceptions of 101–103
  and mental health services 88–90
  'missionary racism' 343
  new (symbolic) racism 79–81
  and psychological and psychiatric morbidity 105
  and research 50
  types of 89, 102
  see also prejudice
racist jokes 78, 79
racist language 95
RALES (Racial Life Events Scale) 102, 102–103
Reason for Encounter Classification (RFE–C) (WHO) 336, 337, 339
Reed Report 278
reflection *see* self-reflection
refugees 9–10, 93
  distress in 131–132
  employment issues 11
  language and communication issues 10–11
  nostalgia in 132
  post-war, from Eastern Europe 7
  risk factors for psychological morbidity 10
regional secure units 276
  admissions to 285
rehabilitation, definition 340
rehabilitative (long-term) psychiatry services 340

rejection 114–115
relativism, cultural 14
religion 125–126
  response bias and misclassifications 58–60
  as risk factor of ill health 58–60
  and substance misuse 244
research 49–51
  bilingual researchers 62–63
  case–control studies 67
  cohort studies 67
  control groups and bias 63–64
  cross-cultural mental health services 290–291
  cultural bias 2
  cultural variations, potential for flawed interpretations 56, 61, 68
  data collection 61, 67
  design 61, 67
  differing attitudes to research and researcher 65–66
  ethnic categories in 53–54
  ethnicity as research variable 54–56
  ethnographic field work 69–71
  Eurocentric bias 2
  evaluative 304–305
  information bias 66–67
  national psychiatric morbidity surveys 61–62
  observer bias 66–67
  participant observation 69
  piloting stage 67
  planning stage 61
  practical problems 64–66
  racism and 50
  recruitment 61–66
  researcher bias 103
  research paradigm 52
  research variables 52–56
  response bias and misclassifications 58–60, 67
  selection bias 61–66
  taped interviews 67
residential homes, psychogeriatric services 167, 186
respectability (*izzat*) 248–249
response bias, in research 58–60, 67
RFE–C (Reason for Encounter Classification) (WHO) 336, 337, 339
rhesus incompatibility, as cause of learning disability 217

risk assessment systems, in forensic psychiatry services 280
risk factors 57–60, 61
    African–Caribbean people 311–313
    for psychological morbidity in refugees 10
    substance misuse 318
risk management 296–297
Ritchie Report 285
rites of passage 126
Royal College of Psychiatrists, Defeat Depression campaign 170
Royal Commission on Long Term Care, report 187
rubella virus, as cause of learning disability 215, 216

satisfaction *see* user satisfaction
schizophrenia
    in African–Caribbean mentally disordered offenders 270–271, 272
    African–Caribbean people 13, 139–142, 277, 311–312
    Asian people 139, 143
    and brain damage 312
    Caribbean-born people 139, 140
    diagnosis 68, 71
    differing perspectives of 333
    environmental factors 313, 317
    increased risk of arrest and conviction 273–274
    International Pilot Study of Schizophrenia (IPSS) 26–27n3, 68
    migration, effect of 314
    misdiagnosis of 140–141
    prevalence 221–222
    prognosis 68, 69, 70
    and social class 315
    symptoms 25
    and unemployment 314–315
    in urban environment 316, 317
    see also psychosis
school 80
    influence on children's behaviour and development 199
    inter-ethnic interaction 84–85
    teachers' attitudes 199
secondary care services, for elderly people 157
secondary prevention 310

secure units
    medium/regional 275, 276, 285
    see also high security hospitals
segregation, as result of rejection 114–115
selection bias, in research 61–66
self
    concepts of 115, 116–122, 133–134
    elements of 119–121
    in individual context 119–122
    individuals' perception of 122
    in social contexts 121–122
    see also personality
self-awareness (self-consciousness) 81–82, 83–84
self-blame 31
    v. system blame 105
self-categorisation 122
self-consciousness *see* self-awareness
self-enhancement 121, 122
self-esteem 85–87, 93, 122
    children 82, 199
self-harm 133, 145–146
self-help
    children's and adolescents' groups 202
    voluntary sector organisations 184
selfhood 124
self-identity 117, 122
self-image 117, 122
self-improvement 121
self-knowledge 121
self-reflection 117
Seligman error 29
separation 197
    marital 193, 198, 206
Service Accomplishments 225–226, 230
service evaluation
    defining goals 305
    health economics 304–306
    process *v.* individual 305
    quality of care 306
    types of 304–305
    see also needs assessment
service user satisfaction *see* user satisfaction
settlers 8–9
shamanism 29, 36
shen kuei 38
sickle cell anaemia 25
'significant alter' 121

Signposts for Success (DoH publication) 225, 232
Sikh headwear 80
Sikhism, guidance on substance misuse 244
Simpson, O. J. 103
'sinking heart' 159
smoking, as cause of learning disability 216
social anthropology 40
social class 315, 316–317
    and acculturation 131
    migrants 3–4, 16
social disorganisation 320–321
social displacement syndrome 10
social factors, and psychosis 313, 313–319, 319–322
social identity 122
social interaction 82–83, 119
social isolation 10–11, 132, 317–318
social learning theory of personality 118–119
Social Psychological Theories of Identity 230
social qualities, in acculturation 128–129
social role changes 132
social role valorisation *see* Normalisation Social Role Valorisation
social services
    for Black elderly people 182–184
    communication 185, 188
    cultural sensitivity 184
    elderly people's awareness and use of 158, 183–184
    Government report on 185–186
    v. health services provision 186
    inadequacy of, for elderly people 182, 187–188
    information provision 185, 188
social status
    effect on racial distress 101
    status inconsistency 100–101
social support 321
societies
    differing modes of thought 41
    as transformation states 40
    unicultural 123
socio-economic class
    urban environment 316–317
    and work 315

socio-political context of psychiatry 1, 7, 67
somatic symptoms 159
somatisation disorders/symptoms 147, 201
South Asian people *see* Asian people
specialisms *see* medical specialism; psychiatric services
spleen 19
staff assignment, mental health services 89
status epilepticus, as cause of learning disability 217
statutory sector 289–291, 291–292
    integration of independent and voluntary sectors with? 292–293
stereotyping *see* racial stereotyping
steroid misuse, Asian communities 249
stimulants 250, 251
stress 319–320
    acculturative 123, 125, 131
    adaptive responses 320
    factors contributing to 100
    maternal 318
    mechanisms 100
    in migrants 123
    out-group–in-group model 100–101
    positive effects of 320
    post-traumatic stress disorder (PTSD) 107
    race-related, measurement of 103
    and social class 315
    social stress models 92
stressors, race-related, defences against 101
Sturge–Weber syndrome, as cause of learning disability 217
stylised expressive traditional behaviours 39
substance misuse 243–263, 342
    African and African–Caribbean communities 245, 246, 247–248, 312
    Asian communities 248–250
    in children 316–317
    Cypriot communities 250
    desire for race-specific services 252–253
    epidemiology 245–250
    and mental health 245
    related to social status and environment 316

substance misuse (contd)
  religious guidance 244
  research 260–261
  risk factors 198, 318
  and social inequalities/exclusion 247
  see also drugs
substance misuse services
  barriers to uptake of 250–252
    overcoming barriers 252–260
  feedback 255–257
  outreach work 257–258
  perceptions of
    fears about confidentiality 251,
      254–255
    institutional racism 251, 255–257
    for opiate users only 253
    run for and by White people 252–
      253
    Western medical model 254
  prevention work 258–260
  staff training and guidelines 255–257
  support/supervision for workers 260
  under-representation of Black and
    ethnic minority service users 250–
    251
  young people 258
suchi-bai (purity mania) 38
suicide 145–146, 154, 194
superego 116
supervision
  of children in urban areas 316
  clinical 294–295
  in cross-cultural mental health services
    291, 293, 294–295
  educational 294–295
  in multi-disciplinary teams 297
  for substance-misuse service workers
    260
support, for substance-misuse service
  workers 260
support systems 324
symbolic interactionism 117
symbolic (new) racism 79–81
symptoms 22–23, 25
syphilis, as cause of learning disability
  216
system blame, *v.* self-blame 105

taijin kyofusho (interpersonal phobia) 38
terminology, variations in definitions
  of ethnic groups 53–54

tertiary prevention 310
tests, intelligence tests 231
Thatcher, Margaret 80–81
therapist–patient relationship 332–333
They Look After Their Own, Don't They?
  (Government report) 185
threats, race related 97
threshold of tolerance 229
tolerance 78–79
  threshold of 229
toxaemia, as cause of learning disability
  216
toxoplasmosis, as cause of learning
  disability 216
traditional healers 292–293, 345–346
traditional values 81
training
  anti-discriminatory policy 287
  anti-racist 238
  in cross-cultural mental health
    services 285–286, 291, 293
  cultural awareness 287
  ethnic and cultural issues 280
  medical, health and culture in 287
  mental health professionals 289
  multi-disciplinary teams as focus for
    295–296
  for work with people with learning
    disabilities 221
  see also education
transcultural psychiatry 159
translators *see* interpreters
transportation, psychogeriatric services
  165
treatment, in mental health services 89
triple jeopardy 160
tuberous sclerosis, as cause of learning
  disability 216
Turner's syndrome, as cause of learning
  disability 216
typhoid, as cause of learning disability
  217

Uganda, exodus of Asian people from 7
unemployment 88, 132, 148, 314–315
  Black groups 60, 79
unicultural societies 123
United States of America, internal
  colonisation 42n8
urban environment 316–317, 324
user satisfaction 90, 305

values, traditional 81
vandalism, race-related 97
victim blaming, learning disabilities 218
violence 97, 318
voluntary sector 291
  and Black communities 232–233, 235
  integration with statutory sector?
    292–293
  psychogeriatric services 158, 167
  self-help organisations 184
voodoo death 43
vulnerability factors 61

West Indian migrants in Britain 7
White population, normative behavioural
  patterns? 2

WHO *see* World Health Organization
'Who Are You' test 83–84
windigo (cannibal-compulsion syndrome)
  29–30, 35–36, 43
work 315
  see also employment; unemployment
World Health Organization (WHO)
  classification of impairments,
    disabilities and handicaps 213–214
  International Classification of
    Diseases (ICD) 213, 336–337
  International Pilot Study of
    Schizophrenia (IPSS) 26–27n3, 68
  models 336–338, 346
  Reason for Encounter Classification
    (RFE–C) 336, 337, 339